2013 | THE LITTLE DATA BOOK

THE WORLD BANK

The Little Data Book 2013 is a product of the Development Data Group of the Development
Economics Vice Presidency of the World Bank.

Design by Communications Development Incorporated, Washington, DC.
Cover photo by Arne Hoel/World Bank.

Contents

Acknowledgments

The *Little Data Book 2013* was prepared by a team led by Soong Sup Lee under the management of Neil Fantom and comprising Liu Cui, Vanessa Moreira da Silva, Federico Escaler, Mahyar Eshragh-Tabary, Juan Feng, Masako Hiraga, Wendy Huang, Bala Bhaskar Naidu Kalimili, Buyant Erdene Khaltarkhuu, Elysee Kiti, Ibrahim Levent, Hiroko Maeda, Johan Mistiaen, Maurice Nsabimana, William Prince, Evis Rucaj, Rubena Sukaj, Emi Suzuki, Maryna Taran, Jomo Tariku, and Olga Vybornaia working closely with other teams in the Development Data Group of the Development Economics Vice Presidency. The work was carried out under the management of Shaida Badiee. Azita Amjadi and Alison Kwong coordinated all stages of production; Barton Matheson Willse & Worthington typeset the book. Staff from The World Bank's Office of the Publisher oversaw publication and dissemination of the book.

Foreword

The *Little Data Book 2013* is a pocket edition of *World Development Indicators 2013*. It is intended as a quick reference for users of the *World Development Indicators* database, book, and mobile app. The database, which covers more than 1,200 indicators and spans more than 50 years, is available at data.worldbank.org.

The 214 country tables in *The Little Data Book* present the latest available data for World Bank member countries and other economies with populations of more than 30,000. The 14 summary tables cover regional and income group aggregates.

For more information about these data or other World Bank data publications, visit our data Web site at data.worldbank.org, e-mail us at data@worldbank .org, call our data hotline 800 590 1906 or 202 473 7824, or fax us at 202 522 1498.

To order *World Development Indicators 2013*, visit the publications Web site at www.worldbank.org/publications, call 800 645 7247 or 703 661 1580, or fax 703 661 1501.

Data notes

The data in this book are for 1990, 2000, and 2011 or the most recent year unless otherwise noted in the table or the *Glossary*.

- Growth rates are proportional changes from the previous year unless otherwise noted.

- Regional aggregates include data for low- and middle-income economies only.

- Figures in italics indicate data for years or periods other than those specified.

Symbols used:

..	indicates that data are not available or that aggregates cannot be calculated because of missing data.
0 or 0.0	indicates zero or small enough that the number would round to zero at the displayed number of decimal places.
$	indicates current U.S. dollars.

Lettered notes on some country tables can be found in the *Notes* on page 232.

Data are shown for economies with populations greater than 30,000 or for smaller economies if they are members of the World Bank. The term *country* (used interchangeably with *economy*) does not imply political independence or official recognition by the World Bank but refers to any economy for which the authorities report separate social or economic statistics.

The selection of indicators in these pages includes some of those being used to monitor progress toward the Millennium Development Goals. For more information about the eight goals—halving poverty and increasing well-being by 2015—please see the other books in the *World Development Indicators 2013* family of products.

Regional tables

The country composition of regions is based on the World Bank's analytical regions and may differ from common geographic usage.

East Asia and Pacific

American Samoa, Cambodia, China, Fiji, Indonesia, Kiribati, Democratic People's Republic of Korea, Lao People's Democratic Republic, Malaysia, Marshall Islands, Federated States of Micronesia, Mongolia, Myanmar, Palau, Papua New Guinea, Philippines, Samoa, Solomon Islands, Thailand, Timor-Leste, Tonga, Tuvalu, Vanuatu, Vietnam.

Europe and Central Asia

Albania, Armenia, Azerbaijan, Belarus, Bosnia and Herzegovina, Bulgaria, Georgia, Kazakhstan, Kosovo, Kyrgyz Republic, Latvia, Lithuania, Former Yugoslav Republic of Macedonia, Moldova, Montenegro, Romania, Russian Federation, Serbia, Tajikistan, Turkey, Turkmenistan, Ukraine, Uzbekistan.

Latin America and the Caribbean

Antigua and Barbuda, Argentina, Belize, Bolivia, Brazil, Chile, Colombia, Costa Rica, Cuba, Dominica, Dominican Republic, Ecuador, El Salvador, Grenada, Guatemala, Guyana, Haiti, Honduras, Jamaica, Mexico, Nicaragua, Panama, Paraguay, Peru, St. Lucia, St. Vincent and the Grenadines, Suriname, Uruguay, República Bolivariana de Venezuela.

Middle East and North Africa

Algeria, Djibouti, Arab Republic of Egypt, Islamic Republic of Iran, Iraq, Jordan, Lebanon, Libya, Morocco, Syrian Arab Republic, Tunisia, West Bank and Gaza, Republic of Yemen.

South Asia

Afghanistan, Bangladesh, Bhutan, India, Maldives, Nepal, Pakistan, Sri Lanka.

Sub-Saharan Africa

Angola, Benin, Botswana, Burkina Faso, Burundi, Cameroon, Cape Verde, Central African Republic, Chad, Comoros, Democratic Republic of the Congo, Republic of Congo, Côte d'Ivoire, Eritrea, Ethiopia, Gabon, The Gambia, Ghana, Guinea, Guinea-Bissau, Kenya, Lesotho, Liberia, Madagascar, Malawi, Mali, Mauritania, Mauritius, Mozambique, Namibia, Niger, Nigeria, Rwanda, São Tomé and Príncipe, Senegal, Seychelles, Sierra Leone, Somalia, South Africa, South Sudan, Sudan, Swaziland, Tanzania, Togo, Uganda, Zambia, Zimbabwe.

World

Population (millions)	6,974.2	Population growth (%)	1.2
Surface area (1,000 sq. km)	134,269	Population living below $1.25 a day (%)	..
GNI, Atlas ($ billions)	66,354.3	GNI per capita, Atlas ($)	9,514
GNI, PPP ($ billions)	80,624.2	GNI per capita, PPP ($)	11,560

	1990	2000	2011
People			
Share of poorest 20% in nat'l consumption/income (%)	..	..	..
Life expectancy at birth (years)	65	67	70
Total fertility rate (births per woman)	3.2	2.7	2.4
Adolescent fertility rate (births per 1,000 women 15–19)	..	63	53
Contraceptive prevalence (% of married women 15–49)	58	61	..
Births attended by skilled health staff (% of total)	..	60	66
Under-five mortality rate (per 1,000 live births)	87	73	51
Child malnutrition, underweight (% of under age 5)	25.1	20.3	15.7
Child immunization, measles (% of ages 12–23 mos.)	73	72	85
Primary completion rate, total (% of relevant age group)	80	82	90
Gross secondary enrollment, total (% of relevant age group)	50	60	70
Ratio of girls to boys in primary & secondary school (%)	86	92	97
HIV prevalence rate (% population of ages 15–49)	0.3	0.8	0.8
Environment			
Forests (1,000 sq. km)	41,608	40,761	39,633
Deforestation (avg. annual %, 1990–2000 and 2000–2010)		0.2	0.1
Freshwater use (% of internal resources)	..	8.4	9.2
Access to improved water source (% total pop.)	76	83	88
Access to improved sanitation facilities (% total pop.)	47	56	63
Energy use per capita (kilograms of oil equivalent)	1,663	1,650	1,851
Carbon dioxide emissions per capita (metric tons)	4.2	4.1	4.7
Electricity use per capita (kilowatt-hours)	2,117	2,381	2,975
Economy			
GDP ($ billions)	21,985	32,334	70,020
GDP growth (annual %)	3.0	4.2	2.7
GDP implicit price deflator (annual % growth)	7.6	4.6	5.5
Value added in agriculture (% of GDP)	5	4	3
Value added in industry (% of GDP)	33	29	26
Value added in services (% of GDP)	62	68	71
Exports of goods and services (% of GDP)	19	25	29
Imports of goods and services (% of GDP)	20	25	30
Gross capital formation (% of GDP)	23	22	20
Central government revenue (% of GDP)	..	25.7	23.0
Central government cash surplus/deficit (% of GDP)	..	-0.2	-5.9
States and markets			
Starting a business (days)	..	51	30
Stock market capitalization (% of GDP)	47.3	101.3	68.7
Military expenditures (% of GDP)	3.7	2.3	2.5
Mobile cellular subscriptions (per 100 people)	0.2	12.1	85.5
Individuals using the Internet (% of population)	0.0	6.7	32.7
Paved roads (% of total)	..	49.4	55.2
High-technology exports (% of manufactured exports)	18	24	18
Global links			
Merchandise trade (% of GDP)	32	41	52
Net barter terms of trade index (2000 = 100)	..	..	..
Total external debt stocks ($ millions)	..	..	..
Total debt service (% of exports)	..	..	..
Net migration (thousands)	..	..	..
Remittances received ($ billions)	68	136	479
Foreign direct investment, net inflows ($ billions)	196	1,319	1,654
Net official development assistance received ($ billions)	58	50	135

East Asia & Pacific

Population (millions)	1,974.2	Population growth (%)	0.7
Surface area (1,000 sq. km)	16,302	Population living below $1.25 a day (%)	12.5
GNI, Atlas ($ billions)	8,387.3	GNI per capita, Atlas ($)	4,248
GNI, PPP ($ billions)	14,344.6	GNI per capita, PPP ($)	7,266

	1990	2000	2011
People			
Share of poorest 20% in nat'l consumption/income (%)	..	..	..
Life expectancy at birth (years)	68	70	72
Total fertility rate (births per woman)	2.6	2.0	1.8
Adolescent fertility rate (births per 1,000 women 15–19)	..	20	19
Contraceptive prevalence (% of married women 15–49)	75	78	..
Births attended by skilled health staff (% of total)	84	85	91
Under-five mortality rate (per 1,000 live births)	56	40	21
Child malnutrition, underweight (% of under age 5)	20.1	11.1	5.5
Child immunization, measles (% of ages 12–23 mos.)	89	82	95
Primary completion rate, total (% of relevant age group)	100	97	97
Gross secondary enrollment, total (% of relevant age group)	39	60	79
Ratio of girls to boys in primary & secondary school (%)	88	98	103
HIV prevalence rate (% population of ages 15–49)	0.1	0.2	0.2
Environment			
Forests (1,000 sq. km)	4,602	4,524	4,712
Deforestation (avg. annual %, 1990–2000 and 2000–2010)		0.1	−0.4
Freshwater use (% of internal resources)	..	9.5	10.9
Access to improved water source (% total pop.)	68	80	90
Access to improved sanitation facilities (% total pop.)	30	48	66
Energy use per capita (kilograms of oil equivalent)	712	869	1,520
Carbon dioxide emissions per capita (metric tons)	1.8	2.3	4.6
Electricity use per capita (kilowatt-hours)	460	876	2,337
Economy			
GDP ($ billions)	671	1,727	9,313
GDP growth (annual %)	5.5	7.5	8.3
GDP implicit price deflator (annual % growth)	6.7	3.0	4.4
Value added in agriculture (% of GDP)	25	15	11
Value added in industry (% of GDP)	40	44	45
Value added in services (% of GDP)	35	41	44
Exports of goods and services (% of GDP)	22	35	39
Imports of goods and services (% of GDP)	21	31	35
Gross capital formation (% of GDP)	35	31	42
Central government revenue (% of GDP)	7.1	8.2	13.1
Central government cash surplus/deficit (% of GDP)	..	−2.6	..
States and markets			
Starting a business (days)	..	53	37
Stock market capitalization (% of GDP)	16.4	46.9	50.6
Military expenditures (% of GDP)	2.3	1.8	1.8
Mobile cellular subscriptions (per 100 people)	0.0	5.8	80.9
Individuals using the Internet (% of population)	0.0	1.9	33.5
Paved roads (% of total)	..	14.4	50.6
High-technology exports (% of manufactured exports)	17	32	26
Global links			
Merchandise trade (% of GDP)	47	59	57
Net barter terms of trade index (2000 = 100)	..	..	..
Total external debt stocks ($ billions)	234	497	1,243
Total debt service (% of exports)	17.7	11.4	4.7
Net migration (millions)	−0.2	−1.8	−5.2
Remittances received ($ billions)	3.1	16.7	85.9
Foreign direct investment, net inflows ($ billions)	10	45	275
Net official development assistance received ($ billions)	7.7	8.6	7.6

Europe & Central Asia

Population (millions)	408.1	Population growth (%)	0.5
Surface area (1,000 sq. km)	23,614	Population living below $1.25 a day (%)	0.7
GNI, Atlas ($ billions)	3,156.6	GNI per capita, Atlas ($)	7,734
GNI, PPP ($ billions)	5,845.7	GNI per capita, PPP ($)	14,323

	1990	2000	2011
People			
Share of poorest 20% in nat'l consumption/income (%)	..	..	..
Life expectancy at birth (years)	68	68	71
Total fertility rate (births per woman)	2.3	1.6	1.8
Adolescent fertility rate (births per 1,000 women 15–19)	..	35	26
Contraceptive prevalence (% of married women 15–49)	..	..	74
Births attended by skilled health staff (% of total)	99	92	98
Under-five mortality rate (per 1,000 live births)	48	35	21
Child malnutrition, underweight (% of under age 5)	10.7	4.2	1.5
Child immunization, measles (% of ages 12-23 mos.)	82	93	94
Primary completion rate, total (% of relevant age group)	95	93	98
Gross secondary enrollment, total (% of relevant age group)	89	87	89
Ratio of girls to boys in primary & secondary school (%)	97	96	98
HIV prevalence rate (% population of ages 15–49)	0.1	0.3	0.6
Environment			
Forests (1,000 sq. km)	8,735	8,754	8,788
Deforestation (avg. annual %, 1990–2000 and 2000–2010)		0.0	0.0
Freshwater use (% of internal resources)	..	6.3	6.3
Access to improved water source (% total pop.)	90	93	96
Access to improved sanitation facilities (% total pop.)	80	83	84
Energy use per capita (kilograms of oil equivalent)	4,063	2,683	3,015
Carbon dioxide emissions per capita (metric tons)	9.6	6.8	7.1
Electricity use per capita (kilowatt-hours)	4,515	3,332	4,059
Economy			
GDP ($ billions)	952	710	3,635
GDP growth (annual %)	-1.0	7.5	5.9
GDP implicit price deflator (annual % growth)	13.6	23.1	8.9
Value added in agriculture (% of GDP)	19	11	8
Value added in industry (% of GDP)	42	35	35
Value added in services (% of GDP)	39	55	57
Exports of goods and services (% of GDP)	20	37	35
Imports of goods and services (% of GDP)	23	31	35
Gross capital formation (% of GDP)	28	20	25
Central government revenue (% of GDP)	..	..	28.4
Central government cash surplus/deficit (% of GDP)	..	..	0.6
States and markets			
Starting a business (days)	..	41	15
Stock market capitalization (% of GDP)	2.4	17.4	32.9
Military expenditures (% of GDP)	14.6	3.4	3.0
Mobile cellular subscriptions (per 100 people)	0.0	6.6	132.5
Individuals using the Internet (% of population)	0.0	2.0	42.1
Paved roads (% of total)	..	83.7	69.1
High-technology exports (% of manufactured exports)	..	10	6
Global links			
Merchandise trade (% of GDP)	..	52	57
Net barter terms of trade index (2000 = 100)	..	..	..
Total external debt stocks ($ billions)	138	360	1,484
Total debt service (% of exports)	..	18.3	17.8
Net migration (millions)	-1.2	-2.3	-0.6
Remittances received ($ billions)	3.2	9.3	43.0
Foreign direct investment, net inflows ($ billions)	1	10	119
Net official development assistance received ($ billions)	1.4	4.5	7.1

Latin America & Caribbean

Population (millions)	589.0	Population growth (%)	1.1
Surface area (1,000 sq. km)	20,394	Population living below $1.25 a day (%)	5.5
GNI, Atlas ($ billions)	5,050.3	GNI per capita, Atlas ($)	8,574
GNI, PPP ($ billions)	6,822.0	GNI per capita, PPP ($)	11,582

	1990	2000	2011
People			
Share of poorest 20% in nat'l consumption/income (%)	..	..	..
Life expectancy at birth (years)	68	72	74
Total fertility rate (births per woman)	3.2	2.6	2.2
Adolescent fertility rate (births per 1,000 women 15-19)	..	83	71
Contraceptive prevalence (% of married women 15-49)	58	..	..
Births attended by skilled health staff (% of total)	75	86	..
Under-five mortality rate (per 1,000 live births)	53	34	19
Child malnutrition, underweight (% of under age 5)	7.2	4.8	3.1
Child immunization, measles (% of ages 12-23 mos.)	76	93	93
Primary completion rate, total (% of relevant age group)	83	97	102
Gross secondary enrollment, total (% of relevant age group)	61	83	90
Ratio of girls to boys in primary & secondary school (%)	101	101	102
HIV prevalence rate (% population of ages 15-49)	0.3	0.4	0.4
Environment			
Forests (1,000 sq. km)	10,389	9,899	9,420
Deforestation (avg. annual %, 1990-2000 and 2000-2010)		0.5	0.4
Freshwater use (% of internal resources)	..	2.0	2.0
Access to improved water source (% total pop.)	86	90	94
Access to improved sanitation facilities (% total pop.)	68	75	79
Energy use per capita (kilograms of oil equivalent)	1,046	1,134	1,312
Carbon dioxide emissions per capita (metric tons)	2.2	2.5	2.7
Electricity use per capita (kilowatt-hours)	1,170	1,581	1,973
Economy			
GDP ($ billions)	1,116	2,059	5,646
GDP growth (annual %)	0.3	4.0	4.7
GDP implicit price deflator (annual % growth)	23.8	7.0	5.8
Value added in agriculture (% of GDP)	9	6	6
Value added in industry (% of GDP)	36	29	32
Value added in services (% of GDP)	56	65	62
Exports of goods and services (% of GDP)	17	20	23
Imports of goods and services (% of GDP)	15	21	24
Gross capital formation (% of GDP)	19	20	22
Central government revenue (% of GDP)	19.4	18.0	..
Central government cash surplus/deficit (% of GDP)	-2.6	-1.5	..
States and markets			
Starting a business (days)	..	76	58
Stock market capitalization (% of GDP)	7.6	31.7	42.0
Military expenditures (% of GDP)	3.6	1.4	1.3
Mobile cellular subscriptions (per 100 people)	0.0	12.1	107.2
Individuals using the Internet (% of population)	0.0	3.8	39.2
Paved roads (% of total)	..	26.3	23.3
High-technology exports (% of manufactured exports)	6	16	11
Global links			
Merchandise trade (% of GDP)	23	36	38
Net barter terms of trade index (2000 = 100)	..	..	..
Total external debt stocks ($ billions)	443	760	1,233
Total debt service (% of exports)	24.6	38.6	13.4
Net migration (millions)	-3.2	-3.9	-5.1
Remittances received ($ billions)	5.7	20.2	59.5
Foreign direct investment, net inflows ($ billions)	8	79	162
Net official development assistance received ($ billions)	5.1	4.8	11.6

Middle East & North Africa

Population (millions)	336.5	Population growth (%)	1.7
Surface area (1,000 sq. km)	8,775	Population living below $1.25 a day (%)	2.4
GNI, Atlas ($ billions)	1,279.5	GNI per capita, Atlas ($)	3,866
GNI, PPP ($ billions)	2,619.2	GNI per capita, PPP ($)	8,052

	1990	2000	2011
People			
Share of poorest 20% in nat'l consumption/income (%)	..	..	..
Life expectancy at birth (years)	64	69	72
Total fertility rate (births per woman)	4.9	3.2	2.7
Adolescent fertility rate (births per 1,000 women 15–19)	..	43	37
Contraceptive prevalence (% of married women 15–49)	43	61	..
Births attended by skilled health staff (% of total)	..	78	..
Under-five mortality rate (per 1,000 live births)	70	48	32
Child malnutrition, underweight (% of under age 5)	11.9	8.9	6.3
Child immunization, measles (% of ages 12–23 mos.)	83	90	89
Primary completion rate, total (% of relevant age group)	76	83	90
Gross secondary enrollment, total (% of relevant age group)	56	68	74
Ratio of girls to boys in primary & secondary school (%)	80	89	93
HIV prevalence rate (% population of ages 15–49)	0.1	0.1	..
Environment			
Forests (1,000 sq. km)	207	208	211
Deforestation (avg. annual %, 1990–2000 and 2000–2010)		-0.1	-0.1
Freshwater use (% of internal resources)	..	120.3	122.1
Access to improved water source (% total pop.)	86	87	89
Access to improved sanitation facilities (% total pop.)	73	81	88
Energy use per capita (kilograms of oil equivalent)	829	1,034	1,372
Carbon dioxide emissions per capita (metric tons)	2.5	3.1	4.1
Electricity use per capita (kilowatt-hours)	733	1,063	1,658
Economy			
GDP ($ billions)	266	434	1,202
GDP growth (annual %)	7.4	3.4	4.2
GDP implicit price deflator (annual % growth)	17.0	4.9	8.8
Value added in agriculture (% of GDP)	18	13	..
Value added in industry (% of GDP)	32	43	..
Value added in services (% of GDP)	50	44	..
Exports of goods and services (% of GDP)	23	27	..
Imports of goods and services (% of GDP)	34	25	..
Gross capital formation (% of GDP)	29	24	..
Central government revenue (% of GDP)	..	..	30.5
Central government cash surplus/deficit (% of GDP)	..	..	-3.1
States and markets			
Starting a business (days)	..	48	25
Stock market capitalization (% of GDP)	..	17.7	..
Military expenditures (% of GDP)	2.9	3.5	3.5
Mobile cellular subscriptions (per 100 people)	0.0	2.2	88.9
Individuals using the Internet (% of population)	0.0	0.9	26.9
Paved roads (% of total)	..	73.5	85.5
High-technology exports (% of manufactured exports)	..	3	3
Global links			
Merchandise trade (% of GDP)	42	48	67
Net barter terms of trade index (2000 = 100)	..	..	..
Total external debt stocks ($ billions)	137	144	166
Total debt service (% of exports)	24.3	14.4	5.1
Net migration (millions)	-0.6	-1.3	-1.6
Remittances received ($ billions)	9.6	11.5	41.3
Foreign direct investment, net inflows ($ billions)	0.7	3.9	16.3
Net official development assistance received ($ billions)	11.7	4.6	15.1

South Asia

Population (millions)	1,656.5	Population growth (%)	1.4
Surface area (1,000 sq. km)	5,131	Population living below $1.25 a day (%)	31.0
GNI, Atlas ($ billions)	2,174.5	GNI per capita, Atlas ($)	1,313
GNI, PPP ($ billions)	5,523.5	GNI per capita, PPP ($)	3,334

	1990	2000	2011
People			
Share of poorest 20% in nat'l consumption/income (%)	..	..	..
Life expectancy at birth (years)	59	62	66
Total fertility rate (births per woman)	4.2	3.3	2.7
Adolescent fertility rate (births per 1,000 women 15–19)	..	101	71
Contraceptive prevalence (% of married women 15–49)	41	45	51
Births attended by skilled health staff (% of total)	..	36	48
Under-five mortality rate (per 1,000 live births)	119	89	62
Child malnutrition, underweight (% of under age 5)	51.9	42.7	33.2
Child immunization, measles (% of ages 12–23 mos.)	56	57	77
Primary completion rate, total (% of relevant age group)	62	67	88
Gross secondary enrollment, total (% of relevant age group)	35	44	58
Ratio of girls to boys in primary & secondary school (%)	68	80	95
HIV prevalence rate (% population of ages 15–49)	0.1	0.4	0.3
Environment			
Forests (1,000 sq. km)	795	794	818
Deforestation (avg. annual %, 1990–2000 and 2000–2010)		0.0	-0.3
Freshwater use (% of internal resources)	42.8	45.9	51.6
Access to improved water source (% total pop.)	71	81	90
Access to improved sanitation facilities (% total pop.)	22	29	38
Energy use per capita (kilograms of oil equivalent)	340	405	519
Carbon dioxide emissions per capita (metric tons)	0.7	1.0	1.4
Electricity use per capita (kilowatt-hours)	242	350	555
Economy			
GDP ($ billions)	412	623	2,296
GDP growth (annual %)	5.4	4.2	6.1
GDP implicit price deflator (annual % growth)	8.6	3.7	8.1
Value added in agriculture (% of GDP)	29	24	18
Value added in industry (% of GDP)	26	26	27
Value added in services (% of GDP)	45	51	55
Exports of goods and services (% of GDP)	9	14	23
Imports of goods and services (% of GDP)	11	16	30
Gross capital formation (% of GDP)	23	23	32
Central government revenue (% of GDP)	13.3	12.0	12.0
Central government cash surplus/deficit (% of GDP)	-3.3	-3.9	-3.8
States and markets			
Starting a business (days)	..	47	19
Stock market capitalization (% of GDP)	10.5	25.5	48.2
Military expenditures (% of GDP)	3.3	3.0	2.5
Mobile cellular subscriptions (per 100 people)	0.0	0.3	68.8
Individuals using the Internet (% of population)	0.0	0.5	9.4
Paved roads (% of total)	..	57.0	40.4
High-technology exports (% of manufactured exports)	3	5	6
Global links			
Merchandise trade (% of GDP)	16	23	41
Net barter terms of trade index (2000 = 100)	..	..	..
Total external debt stocks ($ billions)	126	162	454
Total debt service (% of exports)	31.6	17.5	6.7
Net migration (millions)	-1.9	-2.5	-8.6
Remittances received ($ billions)	5.6	17.2	97.5
Foreign direct investment, net inflows ($ billions)	0.5	4.4	35.7
Net official development assistance received ($ billions)	6.0	4.1	16.7

Sub-Saharan Africa

Population (millions)	874.8	Population growth (%)		2.5
Surface area (1,000 sq. km)	24,242	Population living below $1.25 a day (%)		48.5
GNI, Atlas ($ billions)	1,100.8	GNI per capita, Atlas ($)		1,258
GNI, PPP ($ billions)	1,946.2	GNI per capita, PPP ($)		2,225

	1990	2000	2011
People			
Share of poorest 20% in nat'l consumption/income (%)	..	..	..
Life expectancy at birth (years)	50	50	55
Total fertility rate (births per woman)	6.3	5.6	4.9
Adolescent fertility rate (births per 1,000 women 15-19)	..	131	106
Contraceptive prevalence (% of married women 15-49)	16	22	25
Births attended by skilled health staff (% of total)	..	42	48
Under-five mortality rate (per 1,000 live births)	178	154	109
Child malnutrition, underweight (% of under age 5)	29.2	25.3	21.4
Child immunization, measles (% of ages 12-23 mos.)	57	53	74
Primary completion rate, total (% of relevant age group)	52	53	70
Gross secondary enrollment, total (% of relevant age group)	23	25	40
Ratio of girls to boys in primary & secondary school (%)	81	84	90
HIV prevalence rate (% population of ages 15-49)	2.5	5.9	4.9
Environment			
Forests (1,000 sq. km)	7,406	6,983	6,056
Deforestation (avg. annual %, 1990-2000 and 2000-2010)		0.6	0.5
Freshwater use (% of internal resources)	..	3.2	3.2
Access to improved water source (% total pop.)	48	55	61
Access to improved sanitation facilities (% total pop.)	26	28	31
Energy use per capita (kilograms of oil equivalent)	680	655	683
Carbon dioxide emissions per capita (metric tons)	0.9	0.8	0.9
Electricity use per capita (kilowatt-hours)	531	521	553
Economy			
GDP ($ billions)	300	336	1,266
GDP growth (annual %)	1.2	3.6	4.7
GDP implicit price deflator (annual % growth)	9.1	5.8	7.9
Value added in agriculture (% of GDP)	19	16	12
Value added in industry (% of GDP)	32	29	30
Value added in services (% of GDP)	49	54	58
Exports of goods and services (% of GDP)	26	32	33
Imports of goods and services (% of GDP)	25	31	37
Gross capital formation (% of GDP)	18	17	21
Central government revenue (% of GDP)	..	..	24.5
Central government cash surplus/deficit (% of GDP)	..	..	-1.3
States and markets			
Starting a business (days)	..	62	32
Stock market capitalization (% of GDP)	..	89.7	..
Military expenditures (% of GDP)	3.0	1.9	1.5
Mobile cellular subscriptions (per 100 people)	0.0	1.7	53.3
Individuals using the Internet (% of population)	0.0	0.5	12.7
Paved roads (% of total)	..	18.1	16.3
High-technology exports (% of manufactured exports)	..	4	3
Global links			
Merchandise trade (% of GDP)	42	52	63
Net barter terms of trade index (2000 = 100)	..	..	..
Total external debt stocks ($ billions)	176	213	296
Total debt service (% of exports)	..	11.9	3.4
Net migration (millions)	-1.3	-1.3	-2.0
Remittances received ($ billions)	1.8	4.8	31.1
Foreign direct investment, net inflows ($ billions)	1.2	6.6	40.3
Net official development assistance received ($ billions)	17.8	13.0	46.3

Income group tables

For operational and analytical purposes the World Bank's main criterion for classifying economies is gross national income (GNI) per capita. Each economy in *The Little Data Book* is classified as low income, middle income, or high income. Low- and middle-income economies are sometimes referred to as developing economies. The use of the term is convenient; it is not intended to imply that all economies in the group are experiencing similar development or that other economies have reached a preferred or final stage of development. Classification by income does not necessarily reflect development status. Note: Classifications are fixed during the World Bank's fiscal year (ending on June 30), thus countries remain in the categories in which they are classified irrespective of any revisions to their per capita income data.

Low-income economies are those with a GNI per capita of $1,025 or less in 2011.

Middle-income economies are those with a GNI per capita of more than $1,025 but less than $12,476. Lower-middle-income and upper-middle-income economies are separated at a GNI per capita of $4,036.

High-income economies are those with a GNI per capita of $12,496 or more.

Euro area includes the member states of the Economic and Monetary Union of the European Union that have adopted the euro as their currency: Austria, Belgium, Cyprus, Estonia, Finland, France, Germany, Greece, Ireland, Italy, Luxembourg, Malta, Netherlands, Portugal, Slovak Republic, Slovenia, and Spain.

Low income

Population (millions)	816.8	Population growth (%)		2.1
Surface area (1,000 sq. km)	16,582	Population living below $1.25 a day (%)		*48.0*
GNI, Atlas ($ billions)	466.0	GNI per capita, Atlas ($)		571
GNI, PPP ($ billions)	1,125.4	GNI per capita, PPP ($)		1,378

	1990	2000	2011
People			
Share of poorest 20% in nat'l consumption/income (%)	..	..	..
Life expectancy at birth (years)	53	55	59
Total fertility rate (births per woman)	5.7	4.8	4.0
Adolescent fertility rate (births per 1,000 women 15–19)	..	120	92
Contraceptive prevalence (% of married women 15–49)	23	32	37
Births attended by skilled health staff (% of total)	..	33	47
Under-five mortality rate (per 1,000 live births)	164	133	95
Child malnutrition, underweight (% of under age 5)	40.1	31.0	22.6
Child immunization, measles (% of ages 12–23 mos.)	57	59	77
Primary completion rate, total (% of relevant age group)	46	51	68
Gross secondary enrollment, total (% of relevant age group)	21	30	42
Ratio of girls to boys in primary & secondary school (%)	78	87	92
HIV prevalence rate (% population of ages 15–49)	2.0	3.3	2.4
Environment			
Forests (1,000 sq. km)	4,741	4,427	4,131
Deforestation (avg. annual %, 1990–2000 and 2000–2010)		0.6	0.6
Freshwater use (% of internal resources)	..	3.6	4.5
Access to improved water source (% total pop.)	54	58	65
Access to improved sanitation facilities (% total pop.)	21	30	37
Energy use per capita (kilograms of oil equivalent)	385	320	363
Carbon dioxide emissions per capita (metric tons)	..	0.3	0.3
Electricity use per capita (kilowatt-hours)	224	174	242
Economy			
GDP ($ billions)	145	167	476
GDP growth (annual %)	2.9	3.5	6.0
GDP implicit price deflator (annual % growth)	8.0	5.4	9.2
Value added in agriculture (% of GDP)	38	34	25
Value added in industry (% of GDP)	20	21	25
Value added in services (% of GDP)	43	45	50
Exports of goods and services (% of GDP)	12	18	27
Imports of goods and services (% of GDP)	21	25	42
Gross capital formation (% of GDP)	18	19	25
Central government revenue (% of GDP)	..	10.7	..
Central government cash surplus/deficit (% of GDP)	..	..	..
States and markets			
Starting a business (days)	..	62	30
Stock market capitalization (% of GDP)	..	..	..
Military expenditures (% of GDP)	2.8	2.2	1.6
Mobile cellular subscriptions (per 100 people)	0.0	0.3	41.7
Individuals using the Internet (% of population)	0.0	0.1	6.0
Paved roads (% of total)	..	14.4	18.5
High-technology exports (% of manufactured exports)	..	3	..
Global links			
Merchandise trade (% of GDP)	29	39	58
Net barter terms of trade index (2000 = 100)	..	..	..
Total external debt stocks ($ billions)	92	112	133
Total debt service (% of exports)	26.0	11.2	4.6
Net migration (millions)	–3.0	–2.9	–6.8
Remittances received ($ billions)	1.4	4.1	27.6
Foreign direct investment, net inflows ($ billions)	0.6	2.4	18.3
Net official development assistance received ($ billions)	14.5	10.6	42.6

Middle income

Population (millions)	5,022.4	Population growth (%)	1.1
Surface area (1,000 sq. km)	81,876	Population living below $1.25 a day (%)	17.4
GNI, Atlas ($ billions)	20,835.4	GNI per capita, Atlas ($)	4,148
GNI, PPP ($ billions)	36,311.9	GNI per capita, PPP ($)	7,230

	1990	2000	2011
People			
Share of poorest 20% in nat'l consumption/income (%)	..	..	..
Life expectancy at birth (years)	64	67	69
Total fertility rate (births per woman)	3.3	2.6	2.3
Adolescent fertility rate (births per 1,000 women 15–19)	..	60	50
Contraceptive prevalence (% of married women 15–49)	60	63	..
Births attended by skilled health staff (% of total)	..	66	70
Under-five mortality rate (per 1,000 live births)	82	67	46
Child malnutrition, underweight (% of under age 5)	25.9	20.7	16.0
Child immunization, measles (% of ages 12–23 mos.)	74	73	85
Primary completion rate, total (% of relevant age group)	83	86	94
Gross secondary enrollment, total (% of relevant age group)	46	59	71
Ratio of girls to boys in primary & secondary school (%)	84	92	98
HIV prevalence rate (% population of ages 15–49)	0.2	0.6	0.7
Environment			
Forests (1,000 sq. km)	27,393	26,737	25,874
Deforestation (avg. annual %, 1990–2000 and 2000–2010)		0.2	0.1
Freshwater use (% of internal resources)	..	8.5	9.5
Access to improved water source (% total pop.)	73	82	90
Access to improved sanitation facilities (% total pop.)	39	50	59
Energy use per capita (kilograms of oil equivalent)	1,020	965	1,310
Carbon dioxide emissions per capita (metric tons)	2.4	2.4	3.5
Electricity use per capita (kilowatt-hours)	940	1,063	1,823
Economy			
GDP ($ billions)	3,562	5,719	23,041
GDP growth (annual %)	1.9	5.4	6.3
GDP implicit price deflator (annual % growth)	12.6	7.0	6.4
Value added in agriculture (% of GDP)	18	11	9
Value added in industry (% of GDP)	37	35	36
Value added in services (% of GDP)	46	53	55
Exports of goods and services (% of GDP)	19	27	30
Imports of goods and services (% of GDP)	19	25	30
Gross capital formation (% of GDP)	26	24	30
Central government revenue (% of GDP)	..	17.0	19.2
Central government cash surplus/deficit (% of GDP)	..	-2.3	..
States and markets			
Starting a business (days)	..	56	35
Stock market capitalization (% of GDP)	18.9	36.3	47.7
Military expenditures (% of GDP)	5.7	2.1	2.0
Mobile cellular subscriptions (per 100 people)	0.0	4.8	86.2
Individuals using the Internet (% of population)	0.0	1.7	27.1
Paved roads (% of total)	..	37.6	50.5
High-technology exports (% of manufactured exports)	..	19	17
Global links			
Merchandise trade (% of GDP)	32	45	51
Net barter terms of trade index (2000 = 100)	..	..	..
Total external debt stocks ($ billions)	1,163	2,025	4,743
Total debt service (% of exports)	21.7	20.5	8.9
Net migration (millions)	-5.4	-10.3	-16.4
Remittances received ($ billions)	28	76	331
Foreign direct investment, net inflows ($ billions)	21	146	630
Net official development assistance received ($ billions)	32.9	26.9	50.6

Lower middle income

Population (millions)	2,532.7	Population growth (%)		1.6
Surface area (1,000 sq. km)	20,842	Population living below $1.25 a day (%)		26.7
GNI, Atlas ($ billions)	4,488.5	GNI per capita, Atlas ($)		1,772
GNI, PPP ($ billions)	9,719.0	GNI per capita, PPP ($)		3,837

	1990	2000	2011
People			
Share of poorest 20% in nat'l consumption/income (%)	..	..	..
Life expectancy at birth (years)	60	62	66
Total fertility rate (births per woman)	4.2	3.4	2.9
Adolescent fertility rate (births per 1,000 women 15–19)	..	85	66
Contraceptive prevalence (% of married women 15–49)	40	46	51
Births attended by skilled health staff (% of total)	..	48	57
Under-five mortality rate (per 1,000 live births)	110	88	62
Child malnutrition, underweight (% of under age 5)	38.1	31.1	24.3
Child immunization, measles (% of ages 12–23 mos.)	61	62	78
Primary completion rate, total (% of relevant age group)	70	74	90
Gross secondary enrollment, total (% of relevant age group)	41	47	61
Ratio of girls to boys in primary & secondary school (%)	77	84	95
HIV prevalence rate (% population of ages 15–49)	0.2	0.7	0.7
Environment			
Forests (1,000 sq. km)	6,356	5,943	5,168
Deforestation (avg. annual %, 1990–2000 and 2000–2010)		0.6	0.3
Freshwater use (% of internal resources)	..	18.4	20.2
Access to improved water source (% total pop.)	70	80	87
Access to improved sanitation facilities (% total pop.)	29	39	47
Energy use per capita (kilograms of oil equivalent)	595	573	667
Carbon dioxide emissions per capita (metric tons)	1.1	1.2	1.6
Electricity use per capita (kilowatt-hours)	449	474	698
Economy			
GDP ($ billions)	868	1,264	4,793
GDP growth (annual %)	3.8	4.0	5.5
GDP implicit price deflator (annual % growth)	11.5	5.2	7.5
Value added in agriculture (% of GDP)	26	20	17
Value added in industry (% of GDP)	30	33	32
Value added in services (% of GDP)	44	47	51
Exports of goods and services (% of GDP)	18	26	29
Imports of goods and services (% of GDP)	21	27	35
Gross capital formation (% of GDP)	24	22	29
Central government revenue (% of GDP)	16.2	13.6	15.6
Central government cash surplus/deficit (% of GDP)	-1.5	-3.9	-3.9
States and markets			
Starting a business (days)	..	56	31
Stock market capitalization (% of GDP)	9.5	23.9	43.2
Military expenditures (% of GDP)	3.0	2.8	2.0
Mobile cellular subscriptions (per 100 people)	0.0	1.2	80.1
Individuals using the Internet (% of population)	0.0	0.6	16.2
Paved roads (% of total)	..	30.0	43.7
High-technology exports (% of manufactured exports)	..	16	9
Global links			
Merchandise trade (% of GDP)	30	45	53
Net barter terms of trade index (2000 = 100)	..	..	..
Total external debt stocks ($ billions)	444	592	1,171
Total debt service (% of exports)	25.0	16.7	9.5
Net migration (millions)	-4.7	-8.7	-12.7
Remittances received ($ billions)	16	40	202
Foreign direct investment, net inflows ($ billions)	4	11	109
Net official development assistance received ($ billions)	23.0	17.2	37.3

Upper middle income

Population (millions)	2,489.7	Population growth (%)	0.7
Surface area (1,000 sq. km)	61,034	Population living below $1.25 a day (%)	8.1
GNI, Atlas ($ billions)	16,340.5	GNI per capita, Atlas ($)	6,563
GNI, PPP ($ billions)	26,646.2	GNI per capita, PPP ($)	10,703

	1990	2000	2011
People			
Share of poorest 20% in nat'l consumption/income (%)	..	..	..
Life expectancy at birth (years)	69	70	73
Total fertility rate (births per woman)	2.6	2.0	1.8
Adolescent fertility rate (births per 1,000 women 15–19)	..	34	30
Contraceptive prevalence (% of married women 15–49)	76	80	..
Births attended by skilled health staff (% of total)	90	93	97
Under-five mortality rate (per 1,000 live births)	51	37	20
Child malnutrition, underweight (% of under age 5)	12.3	6.3	2.9
Child immunization, measles (% of ages 12–23 mos.)	90	87	96
Primary completion rate, total (% of relevant age group)	97	98	98
Gross secondary enrollment, total (% of relevant age group)	51	72	85
Ratio of girls to boys in primary & secondary school (%)	91	99	102
HIV prevalence rate (% population of ages 15–49)	0.1	0.5	0.7
Environment			
Forests (1,000 sq. km)	21,037	20,794	20,705
Deforestation (avg. annual %, 1990–2000 and 2000–2010)		0.1	0.0
Freshwater use (% of internal resources)	..	5.2	5.6
Access to improved water source (% total pop.)	76	85	93
Access to improved sanitation facilities (% total pop.)	46	60	73
Energy use per capita (kilograms of oil equivalent)	1,381	1,324	1,948
Carbon dioxide emissions per capita (metric tons)	3.5	3.6	5.5
Electricity use per capita (kilowatt-hours)	1,359	1,603	2,942
Economy			
GDP ($ billions)	2,693	4,455	18,246
GDP growth (annual %)	1.4	5.8	6.6
GDP implicit price deflator (annual % growth)	15.4	9.6	5.8
Value added in agriculture (% of GDP)	15	9	7
Value added in industry (% of GDP)	38	36	37
Value added in services (% of GDP)	46	55	55
Exports of goods and services (% of GDP)	19	27	31
Imports of goods and services (% of GDP)	18	25	29
Gross capital formation (% of GDP)	27	24	30
Central government revenue (% of GDP)	..	14.8	20.1
Central government cash surplus/deficit (% of GDP)	..	–1.8	..
States and markets			
Starting a business (days)	..	56	40
Stock market capitalization (% of GDP)	20.3	39.4	48.8
Military expenditures (% of GDP)	6.4	2.0	2.0
Mobile cellular subscriptions (per 100 people)	0.0	8.2	92.4
Individuals using the Internet (% of population)	0.0	2.6	38.2
Paved roads (% of total)	..	50.4	57.1
High-technology exports (% of manufactured exports)	..	20	19
Global links			
Merchandise trade (% of GDP)	32	45	51
Net barter terms of trade index (2000 = 100)	..	..	..
Total external debt stocks ($ billions)	720	1,434	3,572
Total debt service (% of exports)	20.6	21.6	8.8
Net migration (millions)	-0.7	-1.6	-3.7
Remittances received ($ billions)	11	35	128
Foreign direct investment, net inflows ($ billions)	17	135	521
Net official development assistance received ($ billions)	9.7	9.0	11.9

Low and middle income

Population (millions)	5,839.2	Population growth (%)	1.3
Surface area (1,000 sq. km)	98,458	Population living below $1.25 a day (%)	20.6
GNI, Atlas ($ billions)	21,324.4	GNI per capita, Atlas ($)	3,652
GNI, PPP ($ billions)	37,436.4	GNI per capita, PPP ($)	6,411

	1990	2000	2011
People			
Share of poorest 20% in nat'l consumption/income (%)	..	..	..
Life expectancy at birth (years)	63	65	68
Total fertility rate (births per woman)	3.6	2.9	2.5
Adolescent fertility rate (births per 1,000 women 15–19)	..	69	57
Contraceptive prevalence (% of married women 15–49)	56	59	..
Births attended by skilled health staff (% of total)	..	59	65
Under-five mortality rate (per 1,000 live births)	95	79	56
Child malnutrition, underweight (% of under age 5)	28.0	22.6	17.4
Child immunization, measles (% of ages 12–23 mos.)	72	70	84
Primary completion rate, total (% of relevant age group)	78	80	89
Gross secondary enrollment, total (% of relevant age group)	43	55	66
Ratio of girls to boys in primary & secondary school (%)	84	91	97
HIV prevalence rate (% population of ages 15–49)	0.4	0.9	0.9
Environment			
Forests (1,000 sq. km)	32,134	31,164	30,005
Deforestation (avg. annual %, 1990–2000 and 2000–2010)		0.3	0.2
Freshwater use (% of internal resources)	..	7.9	8.9
Access to improved water source (% total pop.)	71	79	86
Access to improved sanitation facilities (% total pop.)	37	47	56
Energy use per capita (kilograms of oil equivalent)	963	901	1,210
Carbon dioxide emissions per capita (metric tons)	2.1	2.2	3.1
Electricity use per capita (kilowatt-hours)	878	975	1,661
Economy			
GDP ($ billions)	3,703	5,888	23,543
GDP growth (annual %)	2.0	5.4	6.3
GDP implicit price deflator (annual % growth)	10.8	6.6	6.9
Value added in agriculture (% of GDP)	18	12	10
Value added in industry (% of GDP)	36	35	36
Value added in services (% of GDP)	46	53	54
Exports of goods and services (% of GDP)	19	27	30
Imports of goods and services (% of GDP)	19	25	31
Gross capital formation (% of GDP)	26	24	30
Central government revenue (% of GDP)	..	16.8	19.0
Central government cash surplus/deficit (% of GDP)	..	-2.3	..
States and markets			
Starting a business (days)	..	57	34
Stock market capitalization (% of GDP)	18.6	35.8	47.4
Military expenditures (% of GDP)	5.6	2.1	2.0
Mobile cellular subscriptions (per 100 people)	0.0	4.2	80.0
Individuals using the Internet (% of population)	0.0	1.5	24.3
Paved roads (% of total)	..	30.1	38.4
High-technology exports (% of manufactured exports)	..	19	17
Global links			
Merchandise trade (% of GDP)	32	45	52
Net barter terms of trade index (2000 = 100)	..	..	..
Total external debt stocks ($ billions)	1,255	2,137	4,876
Total debt service (% of exports)	21.8	20.4	8.8
Net migration (millions)	-8.4	-13.1	-23.2
Remittances received ($ billions)	29	80	358
Foreign direct investment, net inflows ($ billions)	22	149	648
Net official development assistance received ($ billions)	56	49	135

High income

Population (millions)	1,135.0	Population growth (%)	0.6
Surface area (1,000 sq. km)	35,812	Population living below $1.25 a day (%)	..
GNI, Atlas ($ billions)	45,242.5	GNI per capita, Atlas ($)	39,860
GNI, PPP ($ billions)	43,724.5	GNI per capita, PPP ($)	38,523

	1990	2000	2011
People			
Share of poorest 20% in nat'l consumption/income (%)	..	..	..
Life expectancy at birth (years)	75	78	80
Total fertility rate (births per woman)	1.8	1.7	1.7
Adolescent fertility rate (births per 1,000 women 15–19)	..	23	17
Contraceptive prevalence (% of married women 15–49)	70	70	..
Births attended by skilled health staff (% of total)	..	..	..
Under-five mortality rate (per 1,000 live births)	12	8	6
Child malnutrition, underweight (% of under age 5)	1.3	1.5	1.7
Child immunization, measles (% of ages 12–23 mos.)	84	91	93
Primary completion rate, total (% of relevant age group)	97	98	100
Gross secondary enrollment, total (% of relevant age group)	92	99	102
Ratio of girls to boys in primary & secondary school (%)	100	100	99
HIV prevalence rate (% population of ages 15–49)	0.3	0.3	0.4
Environment			
Forests (1,000 sq. km)	9,475	9,597	9,629
Deforestation (avg. annual %, 1990–2000 and 2000–2010)		–0.1	0.0
Freshwater use (% of internal resources)	..	10.4	10.3
Access to improved water source (% total pop.)	99	99	100
Access to improved sanitation facilities (% total pop.)	100	99	100
Energy use per capita (kilograms of oil equivalent)	4,649	5,146	4,782
Carbon dioxide emissions per capita (metric tons)	11.8	12.5	11.4
Electricity use per capita (kilowatt-hours)	7,394	8,946	9,415
Economy			
GDP ($ billions)	18,282	26,448	46,606
GDP growth (annual %)	3.2	3.9	1.5
GDP implicit price deflator (annual % growth)	5.4	3.3	2.1
Value added in agriculture (% of GDP)	3	2	1
Value added in industry (% of GDP)	32	27	24
Value added in services (% of GDP)	65	71	74
Exports of goods and services (% of GDP)	19	24	29
Imports of goods and services (% of GDP)	20	25	30
Gross capital formation (% of GDP)	23	22	18
Central government revenue (% of GDP)	..	27.4	23.1
Central government cash surplus/deficit (% of GDP)	..	0.1	–6.4
States and markets			
Starting a business (days)	..	33	18
Stock market capitalization (% of GDP)	50.9	114.8	78.6
Military expenditures (% of GDP)	3.4	2.3	2.8
Mobile cellular subscriptions (per 100 people)	1.1	50.1	114.1
Individuals using the Internet (% of population)	0.3	31.0	75.8
Paved roads (% of total)	..	87.5	84.6
High-technology exports (% of manufactured exports)	19	26	18
Global links			
Merchandise trade (% of GDP)	32	40	53
Net barter terms of trade index (2000 = 100)	..	..	..
Total external debt stocks ($ millions)	..	..	..
Total debt service (% of exports)	..	..	..
Net migration (millions)	8.5	13.3	22.9
Remittances received ($ billions)	39	56	121
Foreign direct investment, net inflows ($ billions)	175	1,171	1,006
Net official development assistance received ($ millions)	2,656	344	41

Euro area

Population (millions)	332.9	Population growth (%)		0.3
Surface area (1,000 sq. km)	2,629	Population living below $1.25 a day (%)		..
GNI, Atlas ($ billions)	12,871.5	GNI per capita, Atlas ($)		38,661
GNI, PPP ($ billions)	11,735.7	GNI per capita, PPP ($)		35,250

	1990	2000	2011
People			
Share of poorest 20% in nat'l consumption/income (%)	..	..	..
Life expectancy at birth (years)	76	78	81
Total fertility rate (births per woman)	1.5	1.5	1.6
Adolescent fertility rate (births per 1,000 women 15-19)	..	11	8
Contraceptive prevalence (% of married women 15-49)	..	..	..
Births attended by skilled health staff (% of total)	..	..	..
Under-five mortality rate (per 1,000 live births)	10	6	4
Child malnutrition, underweight (% of under age 5)	..	..	..
Child immunization, measles (% of ages 12-23 mos.)	74	87	93
Primary completion rate, total (% of relevant age group)	98	99	99
Gross secondary enrollment, total (% of relevant age group)	93	103	108
Ratio of girls to boys in primary & secondary school (%)	101	100	99
HIV prevalence rate (% population of ages 15-49)	0.2	0.3	0.3
Environment			
Forests (1,000 sq. km)	859	924	955
Deforestation (avg. annual %, 1990-2000 and 2000-2010)		-0.8	-0.3
Freshwater use (% of internal resources)	..	20.7	19.1
Access to improved water source (% total pop.)	100	100	100
Access to improved sanitation facilities (% total pop.)	100	100	100
Energy use per capita (kilograms of oil equivalent)	3,508	3,728	3,461
Carbon dioxide emissions per capita (metric tons)	8.7	8.3	7.4
Electricity use per capita (kilowatt-hours)	5,337	6,320	6,847
Economy			
GDP ($ billions)	5,691	6,256	13,080
GDP growth (annual %)	3.5	3.8	1.5
GDP implicit price deflator (annual % growth)	3.4	3.4	1.3
Value added in agriculture (% of GDP)	3	2	2
Value added in industry (% of GDP)	33	28	26
Value added in services (% of GDP)	64	70	72
Exports of goods and services (% of GDP)	27	37	44
Imports of goods and services (% of GDP)	27	36	42
Gross capital formation (% of GDP)	23	22	20
Central government revenue (% of GDP)	..	36.3	35.1
Central government cash surplus/deficit (% of GDP)	..	0.0	-3.1
States and markets			
Starting a business (days)	..	51	13
Stock market capitalization (% of GDP)	21.1	86.9	41.9
Military expenditures (% of GDP)	2.5	1.8	1.5
Mobile cellular subscriptions (per 100 people)	0.5	60.2	125.1
Individuals using the Internet (% of population)	0.1	22.8	73.4
Paved roads (% of total)	..	91.8	87.3
High-technology exports (% of manufactured exports)	13	20	15
Global links			
Merchandise trade (% of GDP)	44	61	71
Net barter terms of trade index (2000 = 100)	..	..	..
Total external debt stocks ($ millions)	..	..	..
Total debt service (% of exports)	..	..	..
Net migration (millions)	2.1	3.0	6.3
Remittances received ($ billions)	27.9	33.3	75.7
Foreign direct investment, net inflows ($ billions)	53	423	320
Net official development assistance received ($ millions)	43.7	82.1	..

Country tables

China

Unless otherwise noted, data for China do not include data for Hong Kong SAR, China; Macao SAR, China; or Taiwan, China.

Cyprus

GNI and GDP data and data calculated using GNI and GDP refer to the area controlled by the government of the Republic of Cyprus.

France

Data for Mayotte, to which a reference appeared in previous editions, are included in data for France.

Georgia

GNI, GDP and population data and data calculated using GNI, GDP and population exclude Abkhazia and South Ossetia.

Kosovo, Montenegro, and Serbia

Data for each country are shown separately where available. However, some indicators for Serbia prior to 2006 include data for Montenegro; these data are noted in the tables. Moreover, data for most indicators for Serbia from 1999 onward exclude data for Kosovo, which in 1999 became a territory under international administration pursuant to UN Security Council Resolution 1244 (1999). Kosovo became a member of the World Bank on June 29, 2009, and its data are shown where available.

Moldova

GNI, GDP and population data and data calculated using GNI, GDP and population exclude Transnistria.

Morocco

GNI and GDP data and data calculated using GNI and GDP include Former Spanish Sahara.

South Sudan and Sudan

South Sudan declared its independence on July 9, 2011. Data are shown separately for South Sudan where available. However, data reported for Sudan include South Sudan unless otherwise noted.

Tanzania

GNI and GDP data and data calculated using GNI and GDP refer to mainland Tanzania only.

For more information, see *World Development Indicators 2013* or data .worldbank.org.

Afghanistan

South Asia		Low income

Population (millions)	35.3	Population growth (%)	2.7
Surface area (1,000 sq. km)	652	Population living below $1.25 a day (%)	..
GNI, Atlas ($ billions)	16.6	GNI per capita, Atlas ($)	470
GNI, PPP ($ billions)	40.3	GNI per capita, PPP ($)	1,140

	1990	2000	2011
People			
Share of poorest 20% in nat'l consumption/income (%)	..	..	9.4
Life expectancy at birth (years)	42	45	49
Total fertility rate (births per woman)	8.0	7.7	6.2
Adolescent fertility rate (births per 1,000 women 15-19)	..	182	103
Contraceptive prevalence (% of married women 15-49)	..	5	21
Births attended by skilled health staff (% of total)	..	12	39
Under-five mortality rate (per 1,000 live births)	192	136	101
Child malnutrition, underweight (% of under age 5)	..	32.9	..
Child immunization, measles (% of ages 12-23 mos.)	20	27	62
Primary completion rate, total (% of relevant age group)	27	..	..
Gross secondary enrollment, total (% of relevant age group)	11	11	49
Ratio of girls to boys in primary & secondary school (%)	54	0	66
HIV prevalence rate (% population of ages 15-49)	0.1	0.1	0.1
Environment			
Forests (1,000 sq. km)	14	14	14
Deforestation (avg. annual %, 1990-2000 and 2000-2010)		0.0	0.0
Freshwater use (% of internal resources)	..	43.0	43.0
Access to improved water source (% total pop.)	2	22	50
Access to improved sanitation facilities (% total pop.)	29	32	37
Energy use per capita (kilograms of oil equivalent)	..	..	..
Carbon dioxide emissions per capita (metric tons)	0.14	0.03	0.19
Electricity use per capita (kilowatt-hours)	..	..	..
Economy			
GDP ($ billions)	..	2.5	19.2
GDP growth (annual %)	..	8.4	5.7
GDP implicit price deflator (annual % growth)	..	11.7	12.9
Value added in agriculture (% of GDP)	..	38	21
Value added in industry (% of GDP)	..	24	23
Value added in services (% of GDP)	..	38	57
Exports of goods and services (% of GDP)	..	32	18
Imports of goods and services (% of GDP)	..	65	63
Gross capital formation (% of GDP)	..	34	25
Central government revenue (% of GDP)	..	..	11.2
Central government cash surplus/deficit (% of GDP)	..	..	-0.6
States and markets			
Starting a business (days)	..	..	7
Stock market capitalization (% of GDP)	..	..	..
Military expenditures (% of GDP)	..	2.1	4.7
Mobile cellular subscriptions (per 100 people)	0.0	0.0	54.3
Individuals using the Internet (% of population)	0.0	0.0	5.0
Paved roads (% of total)	..	23.7	29.3
High-technology exports (% of manufactured exports)	..	..	..
Global links			
Merchandise trade (% of GDP)	..	72	35
Net barter terms of trade index (2000 = 100)	..	100	146
Total external debt stocks ($ millions)	286	..	2,623
Total debt service (% of exports)	..	..	..
Net migration (thousands)	-1,484	-376	-381
Remittances received ($ millions)	..	..	..
Foreign direct investment, net inflows ($ millions)	-0.3	0.2	83.4
Net official development assistance received ($ millions)	122	136	6,711

Albania

Population (millions)	3.2	Population growth (%)	0.4
Surface area (1,000 sq. km)	29	Population living below $1.25 a day (%)	<2
GNI, Atlas ($ billions)	12.8	GNI per capita, Atlas ($)	3,980
GNI, PPP ($ billions)	28.4	GNI per capita, PPP ($)	8,820

	1990	2000	2011
People			
Share of poorest 20% in nat'l consumption/income (%)	..	9.1	8.1
Life expectancy at birth (years)	72	74	77
Total fertility rate (births per woman)	3.2	2.2	1.5
Adolescent fertility rate (births per 1,000 women 15–19)	..	15	16
Contraceptive prevalence (% of married women 15–49)	..	58	69
Births attended by skilled health staff (% of total)	93	99	99
Under-five mortality rate (per 1,000 live births)	41	26	14
Child malnutrition, underweight (% of under age 5)	..	17.0	6.3
Child immunization, measles (% of ages 12–23 mos.)	88	95	99
Primary completion rate, total (% of relevant age group)	..	102	..
Gross secondary enrollment, total (% of relevant age group)	89	72	..
Ratio of girls to boys in primary & secondary school (%)	95	96	..
HIV prevalence rate (% population of ages 15–49)	..	..	..
Environment			
Forests (1,000 sq. km)	7.9	7.7	7.8
Deforestation (avg. annual %, 1990–2000 and 2000–2010)		0.3	-0.1
Freshwater use (% of internal resources)	4.5	6.8	6.8
Access to improved water source (% total pop.)	97	98	95
Access to improved sanitation facilities (% total pop.)	76	84	94
Energy use per capita (kilograms of oil equivalent)	813	580	648
Carbon dioxide emissions per capita (metric tons)	2.3	1.0	0.9
Electricity use per capita (kilowatt-hours)	522	1,445	1,770
Economy			
GDP ($ billions)	2.1	3.7	13.0
GDP growth (annual %)	-9.6	7.3	3.0
GDP implicit price deflator (annual % growth)	-0.5	4.3	3.0
Value added in agriculture (% of GDP)	36	29	19
Value added in industry (% of GDP)	48	19	16
Value added in services (% of GDP)	16	52	66
Exports of goods and services (% of GDP)	15	19	34
Imports of goods and services (% of GDP)	23	37	56
Gross capital formation (% of GDP)	29	25	25
Central government revenue (% of GDP)	..	23.4	..
Central government cash surplus/deficit (% of GDP)	..	-6.7	..
States and markets			
Starting a business (days)	..	41	4
Stock market capitalization (% of GDP)	..	..	..
Military expenditures (% of GDP)	5.9	1.2	1.5
Mobile cellular subscriptions (per 100 people)	0.0	1.0	96.4
Individuals using the Internet (% of population)	0.0	0.1	49.0
Paved roads (% of total)	..	39.0	..
High-technology exports (% of manufactured exports)	..	1	1
Global links			
Merchandise trade (% of GDP)	29	37	57
Net barter terms of trade index (2000 = 100)	..	100	94
Total external debt stocks ($ billions)	0.3	1.1	5.9
Total debt service (% of exports)	4.3	3.7	9.3
Net migration (thousands)	23	-270	-48
Remittances received ($ millions)	152	598	1,162
Foreign direct investment, net inflows ($ millions)	20	143	1,370
Net official development assistance received ($ millions)	11	318	307

Algeria

Middle East & North Africa		Upper middle income
Population (millions)	36.0	Population growth (%)	1.4
Surface area (1,000 sq. km)	2,382	Population living below $1.25 a day (%)	..
GNI, Atlas ($ billions)	160.8	GNI per capita, Atlas ($)	4,470
GNI, PPP ($ billions)	299.0	GNI per capita, PPP ($)	8,310

	1990	2000	2011
People			
Share of poorest 20% in nat'l consumption/income (%)	6.5	..	..
Life expectancy at birth (years)	67	70	73
Total fertility rate (births per woman)	4.7	2.6	2.2
Adolescent fertility rate (births per 1,000 women 15-19)	..	10	6
Contraceptive prevalence (% of married women 15-49)	51	64	61
Births attended by skilled health staff (% of total)	77	93	95
Under-five mortality rate (per 1,000 live births)	66	46	30
Child malnutrition, underweight (% of under age 5)	9.2	5.4	..
Child immunization, measles (% of ages 12-23 mos.)	83	80	95
Primary completion rate, total (% of relevant age group)	81	82	94
Gross secondary enrollment, total (% of relevant age group)	62	75	95
Ratio of girls to boys in primary & secondary school (%)	82	98	98
HIV prevalence rate (% population of ages 15-49)	..	..	..
Environment			
Forests (1,000 sq. km)	17	16	15
Deforestation (avg. annual %, 1990-2000 and 2000-2010)		0.5	0.6
Freshwater use (% of internal resources)	40.0	54.8	54.8
Access to improved water source (% total pop.)	94	89	83
Access to improved sanitation facilities (% total pop.)	88	92	95
Energy use per capita (kilograms of oil equivalent)	877	885	1,138
Carbon dioxide emissions per capita (metric tons)	3.1	2.9	3.5
Electricity use per capita (kilowatt-hours)	541	695	1,026
Economy			
GDP ($ billions)	62.0	54.8	188.7
GDP growth (annual %)	0.8	2.2	2.5
GDP implicit price deflator (annual % growth)	30.3	24.6	11.4
Value added in agriculture (% of GDP)	11	9	7
Value added in industry (% of GDP)	48	59	62
Value added in services (% of GDP)	40	33	31
Exports of goods and services (% of GDP)	23	41	31
Imports of goods and services (% of GDP)	25	21	21
Gross capital formation (% of GDP)	29	25	41
Central government revenue (% of GDP)	..	..	42.9
Central government cash surplus/deficit (% of GDP)	..	..	-0.3
States and markets			
Starting a business (days)	..	25	25
Stock market capitalization (% of GDP)	..	..	..
Military expenditures (% of GDP)	1.5	3.4	4.6
Mobile cellular subscriptions (per 100 people)	0.0	0.3	99.0
Individuals using the Internet (% of population)	0.0	0.5	14.0
Paved roads (% of total)	67.0	68.9	77.1
High-technology exports (% of manufactured exports)	1	4	0
Global links			
Merchandise trade (% of GDP)	37	57	64
Net barter terms of trade index (2000 = 100)	74	100	199
Total external debt stocks ($ billions)	28.2	25.4	6.1
Total debt service (% of exports)	65.1	..	0.8
Net migration (thousands)	-70	-140	-140
Remittances received ($ millions)	352	790	203
Foreign direct investment, net inflows ($ millions)	0	280	2,721
Net official development assistance received ($ millions)	332	200	208

American Samoa

Population (thousands)	70	Population growth (%)		1.6
Surface area (sq. km)	200	Population living below $1.25 a day (%)		..
GNI, Atlas ($ millions)	..	GNI per capita, Atlas ($)		..
GNI, PPP ($ millions)	..	GNI per capita, PPP ($)		..

	1990	2000	2011
People			
Share of poorest 20% in nat'l consumption/income (%)	..	..	..
Life expectancy at birth (years)	..	..	..
Total fertility rate (births per woman)	..	..	..
Adolescent fertility rate (births per 1,000 women 15–19)	..	..	..
Contraceptive prevalence (% of married women 15–49)	..	..	..
Births attended by skilled health staff (% of total)	..	100	..
Under-five mortality rate (per 1,000 live births)	..	..	..
Child malnutrition, underweight (% of under age 5)	..	..	..
Child immunization, measles (% of ages 12–23 mos.)	..	..	..
Primary completion rate, total (% of relevant age group)	..	..	..
Gross secondary enrollment, total (% of relevant age group)	93	..	..
Ratio of girls to boys in primary & secondary school (%)	103	..	..
HIV prevalence rate (% population of ages 15–49)	..	..	..
Environment			
Forests (sq. km)	184	181	177
Deforestation (avg. annual %, 1990–2000 and 2000–2010)		0.2	0.2
Freshwater use (% of internal resources)	..	..	..
Access to improved water source (% total pop.)	..	..	..
Access to improved sanitation facilities (% total pop.)	..	..	..
Energy use per capita (kilograms of oil equivalent)	..	..	..
Carbon dioxide emissions per capita (metric tons)	..	..	..
Electricity use per capita (kilowatt-hours)	..	..	..
Economy			
GDP ($ millions)	..	..	..
GDP growth (annual %)	..	..	..
GDP implicit price deflator (annual % growth)	..	..	..
Value added in agriculture (% of GDP)	..	..	..
Value added in industry (% of GDP)	..	..	..
Value added in services (% of GDP)	..	..	..
Exports of goods and services (% of GDP)	..	..	..
Imports of goods and services (% of GDP)	..	..	..
Gross capital formation (% of GDP)	..	..	..
Central government revenue (% of GDP)	..	..	..
Central government cash surplus/deficit (% of GDP)	..	..	..
States and markets			
Starting a business (days)	..	..	..
Stock market capitalization (% of GDP)	..	..	..
Military expenditures (% of GDP)	..	..	..
Mobile cellular subscriptions (per 100 people)	0.0	3.5	..
Individuals using the Internet (% of population)	0.0	..	..
Paved roads (% of total)	..	..	..
High-technology exports (% of manufactured exports)	..	..	..
Global links			
Merchandise trade (% of GDP)	..	..	..
Net barter terms of trade index (2000 = 100)	..	100	129
Total external debt stocks ($ millions)	..	..	..
Total debt service (% of exports)	..	..	..
Net migration (thousands)	..	..	..
Remittances received ($ millions)	..	..	..
Foreign direct investment, net inflows ($ millions)	..	..	..
Net official development assistance received ($ millions)	..	..	..

Andorra

High income

Population (thousands)	86	Population growth (%)	1.5
Surface area (sq. km)	470	Population living below $1.25 a day (%)	..
GNI, Atlas ($ billions)	3.4	GNI per capita, Atlas ($)	41,750
GNI, PPP ($ millions)	..	GNI per capita, PPP ($)	..

	1990	2000	2011
People			
Share of poorest 20% in nat'l consumption/income (%)	..	..	..
Life expectancy at birth (years)	..	..	..
Total fertility rate (births per woman)	..	..	1.2
Adolescent fertility rate (births per 1,000 women 15–19)	..	..	..
Contraceptive prevalence (% of married women 15–49)	..	..	..
Births attended by skilled health staff (% of total)	..	..	..
Under-five mortality rate (per 1,000 live births)	8	5	3
Child malnutrition, underweight (% of under age 5)	..	..	..
Child immunization, measles (% of ages 12–23 mos.)	..	97	99
Primary completion rate, total (% of relevant age group)	..	102	63
Gross secondary enrollment, total (% of relevant age group)	..	79	87
Ratio of girls to boys in primary & secondary school (%)	..	101	102
HIV prevalence rate (% population of ages 15–49)	..	..	..
Environment			
Forests (sq. km)	160	160	160
Deforestation (avg. annual %, 1990–2000 and 2000–2010)		0.0	0.0
Freshwater use (% of internal resources)	..	..	..
Access to improved water source (% total pop.)	100	100	100
Access to improved sanitation facilities (% total pop.)	100	100	100
Energy use per capita (kilograms of oil equivalent)	..	..	..
Carbon dioxide emissions per capita (metric tons)	..	8.1	6.2
Electricity use per capita (kilowatt-hours)	..	..	..
Economy			
GDP ($ millions)	1,029	1,134	3,712
GDP growth (annual %)	3.8	1.2	3.6
GDP implicit price deflator (annual % growth)	7.3	4.5	3.2
Value added in agriculture (% of GDP)	..	..	..
Value added in industry (% of GDP)	..	..	..
Value added in services (% of GDP)	..	..	..
Exports of goods and services (% of GDP)	..	..	..
Imports of goods and services (% of GDP)	..	..	..
Gross capital formation (% of GDP)	..	..	..
Central government revenue (% of GDP)	..	..	..
Central government cash surplus/deficit (% of GDP)	..	..	..
States and markets			
Starting a business (days)	..	..	..
Stock market capitalization (% of GDP)	..	..	..
Military expenditures (% of GDP)	..	..	..
Mobile cellular subscriptions (per 100 people)	0.0	36.4	75.5
Individuals using the Internet (% of population)	0.0	10.5	81.0
Paved roads (% of total)	..	..	..
High-technology exports (% of manufactured exports)	..	11	..
Global links			
Merchandise trade (% of GDP)	..	..	..
Net barter terms of trade index (2000 = 100)	..	100	..
Total external debt stocks ($ millions)	..	..	..
Total debt service (% of exports)	..	..	..
Net migration (thousands)	..	..	..
Remittances received ($ millions)	..	..	..
Foreign direct investment, net inflows ($ millions)	..	..	..
Net official development assistance received ($ millions)	..	..	..

Angola

Sub-Saharan Africa   **Upper middle income**

Population (millions)	19.6	Population growth (%)	2.8
Surface area (1,000 sq. km)	1,247	Population living below $1.25 a day (%)	*54.3*
GNI, Atlas ($ billions)	75.2	GNI per capita, Atlas ($)	3,830
GNI, PPP ($ billions)	102.7	GNI per capita, PPP ($)	5,230

	1990	2000	2011
People			
Share of poorest 20% in nat'l consumption/income (%)	..	2.0	..
Life expectancy at birth (years)	41	45	51
Total fertility rate (births per woman)	7.2	6.8	5.3
Adolescent fertility rate (births per 1,000 women 15–19)	..	207	153
Contraceptive prevalence (% of married women 15–49)	..	6	..
Births attended by skilled health staff (% of total)	..	*45*	47
Under-five mortality rate (per 1,000 live births)	243	199	158
Child malnutrition, underweight (% of under age 5)	..	27.5	15.6
Child immunization, measles (% of ages 12–23 mos.)	38	41	88
Primary completion rate, total (% of relevant age group)	*34*	..	47
Gross secondary enrollment, total (% of relevant age group)	11	15	31
Ratio of girls to boys in primary & secondary school (%)	..	82	79
HIV prevalence rate (% population of ages 15–49)	0.6	1.6	2.1
Environment			
Forests (1,000 sq. km)	610	597	584
Deforestation (avg. annual %, 1990–2000 and 2000–2010)		0.2	0.2
Freshwater use (% of internal resources)	..	*0.4*	0.4
Access to improved water source (% total pop.)	42	46	51
Access to improved sanitation facilities (% total pop.)	29	42	58
Energy use per capita (kilograms of oil equivalent)	569	538	716
Carbon dioxide emissions per capita (metric tons)	0.4	0.7	1.4
Electricity use per capita (kilowatt-hours)	61	89	*248*
Economy			
GDP ($ billions)	10.3	4.2	104.3
GDP growth (annual %)	-0.3	3.0	3.9
GDP implicit price deflator (annual % growth)	10.9	418.2	24.2
Value added in agriculture (% of GDP)	18	6	9
Value added in industry (% of GDP)	41	72	62
Value added in services (% of GDP)	41	22	29
Exports of goods and services (% of GDP)	39	90	65
Imports of goods and services (% of GDP)	21	63	43
Gross capital formation (% of GDP)	12	13	11
Central government revenue (% of GDP)	..	..	..
Central government cash surplus/deficit (% of GDP)	..	..	..
States and markets			
Starting a business (days)	..	*119*	68
Stock market capitalization (% of GDP)	..	..	..
Military expenditures (% of GDP)	*7.1*	6.4	3.5
Mobile cellular subscriptions (per 100 people)	0.0	0.2	48.4
Individuals using the Internet (% of population)	0.0	0.1	14.8
Paved roads (% of total)	..	10.4	..
High-technology exports (% of manufactured exports)	..	..	..
Global links			
Merchandise trade (% of GDP)	53	264	84
Net barter terms of trade index (2000 = 100)	94	100	245
Total external debt stocks ($ billions)	8.6	9.8	21.1
Total debt service (% of exports)	8.1	20.9	4.2
Net migration (thousands)	-150	-126	82
Remittances received ($ millions)	..	..	0.2
Foreign direct investment, net inflows ($ millions)	-335	879	-3,024
Net official development assistance received ($ millions)	266	302	200

Antigua and Barbuda

Latin America & Caribbean		Upper middle income	
Population (thousands)	90	Population growth (%)	1.0
Surface area (sq. km)	440	Population living below $1.25 a day (%)	..
GNI, Atlas ($ billions)	1.1	GNI per capita, Atlas ($)	11,940
GNI, PPP ($ billions)	1.6	GNI per capita, PPP ($)	17,900

	1990	2000	2011
People			
Share of poorest 20% in nat'l consumption/income (%)	..	..	..
Life expectancy at birth (years)	74	75	..
Total fertility rate (births per woman)	1.7	1.7	..
Adolescent fertility rate (births per 1,000 women 15-19)	..	..	..
Contraceptive prevalence (% of married women 15-49)	53	53	..
Births attended by skilled health staff (% of total)	..	100	100
Under-five mortality rate (per 1,000 live births)	27	15	8
Child malnutrition, underweight (% of under age 5)	..	..	..
Child immunization, measles (% of ages 12-23 mos.)	89	95	99
Primary completion rate, total (% of relevant age group)	98	..	98
Gross secondary enrollment, total (% of relevant age group)	122	79	105
Ratio of girls to boys in primary & secondary school (%)	98	..	95
HIV prevalence rate (% population of ages 15-49)	..	..	..
Environment			
Forests (sq. km)	103	100	98
Deforestation (avg. annual %, 1990-2000 and 2000-2010)		0.3	0.2
Freshwater use (% of internal resources)	9.6	9.6	9.6
Access to improved water source (% total pop.)	91	91	..
Access to improved sanitation facilities (% total pop.)	95	95	..
Energy use per capita (kilograms of oil equivalent)	1,589	..	..
Carbon dioxide emissions per capita (metric tons)	4.8	4.4	5.3
Electricity use per capita (kilowatt-hours)	..	..	..
Economy			
GDP ($ millions)	392	788	1,118
GDP growth (annual %)	2.5	5.1	-5.0
GDP implicit price deflator (annual % growth)	2.3	15.0	2.1
Value added in agriculture (% of GDP)	4	2	2
Value added in industry (% of GDP)	20	16	18
Value added in services (% of GDP)	76	82	79
Exports of goods and services (% of GDP)	89	63	48
Imports of goods and services (% of GDP)	87	64	58
Gross capital formation (% of GDP)	32	29	29
Central government revenue (% of GDP)	..	..	..
Central government cash surplus/deficit (% of GDP)	..	..	..
States and markets			
Starting a business (days)	..	..	21
Stock market capitalization (% of GDP)	..	..	..
Military expenditures (% of GDP)	..	..	..
Mobile cellular subscriptions (per 100 people)	0.0	28.3	196.4
Individuals using the Internet (% of population)	0.0	6.5	82.0
Paved roads (% of total)	..	33.0	..
High-technology exports (% of manufactured exports)	..	0	0
Global links			
Merchandise trade (% of GDP)	70	58	47
Net barter terms of trade index (2000 = 100)	..	100	75
Total external debt stocks ($ millions)	..	..	..
Total debt service (% of exports)	..	..	..
Net migration (thousands)	..	..	..
Remittances received ($ millions)	12.5	20.7	20.5
Foreign direct investment, net inflows ($ millions)	60.6	43.1	57.7
Net official development assistance received ($ millions)	4.6	9.8	15.3

Argentina

Latin America & Caribbean   **Upper middle income**

Population (millions)	40.8	Population growth (%)	0.9
Surface area (1,000 sq. km)	2,780	Population living below $1.25 a day (%)	<2
GNI, Atlas ($ billions)	..	GNI per capita, Atlas ($)	..
GNI, PPP ($ billions)	..	GNI per capita, PPP ($)	..

	1990	2000	2011
People			
Share of poorest 20% in nat'l consumption/income (%)	5.0	3.2	4.4
Life expectancy at birth (years)	71	74	76
Total fertility rate (births per woman)	3.0	2.5	2.2
Adolescent fertility rate (births per 1,000 women 15-19)	..	64	55
Contraceptive prevalence (% of married women 15-49)	..	65	..
Births attended by skilled health staff (% of total)	96	98	95
Under-five mortality rate (per 1,000 live births)	28	20	14
Child malnutrition, underweight (% of under age 5)	..	..	..
Child immunization, measles (% of ages 12-23 mos.)	93	91	93
Primary completion rate, total (% of relevant age group)	..	99	107
Gross secondary enrollment, total (% of relevant age group)	71	87	90
Ratio of girls to boys in primary & secondary school (%)	107	101	104
HIV prevalence rate (% population of ages 15-49)	0.2	0.3	0.4
Environment			
Forests (1,000 sq. km)	348	319	292
Deforestation (avg. annual %, 1990-2000 and 2000-2010)		0.9	0.8
Freshwater use (% of internal resources)	..	11.8	11.8
Access to improved water source (% total pop.)	94	96	..
Access to improved sanitation facilities (% total pop.)	90	91	..
Energy use per capita (kilograms of oil equivalent)	1,411	1,650	1,847
Carbon dioxide emissions per capita (metric tons)	3.4	3.8	4.4
Electricity use per capita (kilowatt-hours)	1,303	2,085	2,904
Economy			
GDP ($ billions)	141	284	..
GDP growth (annual %)	-2.4	-0.8	..
GDP implicit price deflator (annual % growth)	2,076.8	1.0	..
Value added in agriculture (% of GDP)	8	5	11
Value added in industry (% of GDP)	36	28	31
Value added in services (% of GDP)	56	67	59
Exports of goods and services (% of GDP)	10	11	22
Imports of goods and services (% of GDP)	5	12	20
Gross capital formation (% of GDP)	14	16	23
Central government revenue (% of GDP)	..	14.1	..
Central government cash surplus/deficit (% of GDP)	..	-5.7	..
States and markets			
Starting a business (days)	..	66	26
Stock market capitalization (% of GDP)	2.3	58.4	9.8
Military expenditures (% of GDP)	1.4	1.1	0.7
Mobile cellular subscriptions (per 100 people)	0.0	17.6	134.9
Individuals using the Internet (% of population)	0.0	7.0	47.7
Paved roads (% of total)	28.5	29.4	..
High-technology exports (% of manufactured exports)	8	9	8
Global links			
Merchandise trade (% of GDP)	12	18	35
Net barter terms of trade index (2000 = 100)	64	100	135
Total external debt stocks ($ billions)	63	147	115
Total debt service (% of exports)	37.1	64.0	15.3
Net migration (thousands)	120	-50	-200
Remittances received ($ millions)	23	86	686
Foreign direct investment, net inflows ($ billions)	1.8	10.4	8.7
Net official development assistance received ($ millions)	169	52	85

Armenia

Europe & Central Asia		Lower middle income	
Population (millions)	3.1	Population growth (%)	0.3
Surface area (1,000 sq. km)	30	Population living below $1.25 a day (%)	2.5
GNI, Atlas ($ billions)	10.4	GNI per capita, Atlas ($)	3,360
GNI, PPP ($ billions)	18.9	GNI per capita, PPP ($)	6,100

	1990	2000	2011
People			
Share of poorest 20% in nat'l consumption/income (%)	..	7.6	8.8
Life expectancy at birth (years)	68	71	74
Total fertility rate (births per woman)	2.5	1.7	1.7
Adolescent fertility rate (births per 1,000 women 15–19)	..	44	34
Contraceptive prevalence (% of married women 15–49)	56	61	55
Births attended by skilled health staff (% of total)	100	97	100
Under-five mortality rate (per 1,000 live births)	47	30	18
Child malnutrition, underweight (% of under age 5)	..	2.6	5.3
Child immunization, measles (% of ages 12–23 mos.)	93	92	97
Primary completion rate, total (% of relevant age group)	..	93	83
Gross secondary enrollment, total (% of relevant age group)	..	90	89
Ratio of girls to boys in primary & secondary school (%)	..	104	103
HIV prevalence rate (% population of ages 15–49)	0.1	0.2	0.2
Environment			
Forests (1,000 sq. km)	3.5	3.0	2.6
Deforestation (avg. annual %, 1990–2000 and 2000–2010)		1.3	1.5
Freshwater use (% of internal resources)	..	25.3	41.2
Access to improved water source (% total pop.)	90	92	98
Access to improved sanitation facilities (% total pop.)	88	89	90
Energy use per capita (kilograms of oil equivalent)	2,171	651	791
Carbon dioxide emissions per capita (metric tons)	1.2	1.1	1.5
Electricity use per capita (kilowatt-hours)	2,718	1,295	1,606
Economy			
GDP ($ billions)	2.3	1.9	10.2
GDP growth (annual %)	-11.7	5.9	4.6
GDP implicit price deflator (annual % growth)	79.4	-1.4	4.2
Value added in agriculture (% of GDP)	17	26	21
Value added in industry (% of GDP)	52	39	37
Value added in services (% of GDP)	31	35	42
Exports of goods and services (% of GDP)	35	23	23
Imports of goods and services (% of GDP)	46	51	48
Gross capital formation (% of GDP)	47	19	31
Central government revenue (% of GDP)	..	17.7	22.5
Central government cash surplus/deficit (% of GDP)	..	-0.7	-2.7
States and markets			
Starting a business (days)	..	18	8
Stock market capitalization (% of GDP)	..	0.1	0.4
Military expenditures (% of GDP)	2.1	3.6	4.0
Mobile cellular subscriptions (per 100 people)	0.0	0.6	103.6
Individuals using the Internet (% of population)	0.0	1.3	32.0
Paved roads (% of total)	99.2	91.3	93.6
High-technology exports (% of manufactured exports)	..	5	3
Global links			
Merchandise trade (% of GDP)	..	62	53
Net barter terms of trade index (2000 = 100)	..	100	129
Total external debt stocks ($ billions)	0.0	1.0	7.4
Total debt service (% of exports)	1.2	9.2	25.4
Net migration (thousands)	-68	-225	-75
Remittances received ($ millions)	..	87	1,994
Foreign direct investment, net inflows ($ millions)	2	104	663
Net official development assistance received ($ millions)	3	216	374

Aruba

Population (thousands)	108	Population growth (%)	0.6
Surface area (sq. km)	180	Population living below $1.25 a day (%)	..
GNI, Atlas ($ billions)	..	GNI per capita, Atlas ($)	..
GNI, PPP ($ millions)	..	GNI per capita, PPP ($)	..

	1990	2000	2011
People			
Share of poorest 20% in nat'l consumption/income (%)	..	..	..
Life expectancy at birth (years)	73	74	75
Total fertility rate (births per woman)	2.2	1.9	1.7
Adolescent fertility rate (births per 1,000 women 15-19)	..	44	28
Contraceptive prevalence (% of married women 15-49)	..	..	..
Births attended by skilled health staff (% of total)	..	96	..
Under-five mortality rate (per 1,000 live births)	..	..	..
Child malnutrition, underweight (% of under age 5)	..	..	..
Child immunization, measles (% of ages 12-23 mos.)	..	..	..
Primary completion rate, total (% of relevant age group)	..	98	91
Gross secondary enrollment, total (% of relevant age group)	..	97	91
Ratio of girls to boys in primary & secondary school (%)	..	99	98
HIV prevalence rate (% population of ages 15-49)	..	..	..
Environment			
Forests (sq. km)	4.0	4.0	4.2
Deforestation (avg. annual %, 1990-2000 and 2000-2010)		0.0	0.0
Freshwater use (% of internal resources)			
Access to improved water source (% total pop.)	100	100	100
Access to improved sanitation facilities (% total pop.)	..	..	..
Energy use per capita (kilograms of oil equivalent)	..	..	..
Carbon dioxide emissions per capita (metric tons)	29.6	24.7	21.5
Electricity use per capita (kilowatt-hours)	..	..	..
Economy			
GDP ($ millions)	872	1,859	..
GDP growth (annual %)	12.0	3.7	..
GDP implicit price deflator (annual % growth)	5.7	4.0	..
Value added in agriculture (% of GDP)	..	..	..
Value added in industry (% of GDP)	..	..	..
Value added in services (% of GDP)	..	..	..
Exports of goods and services (% of GDP)	101	70	..
Imports of goods and services (% of GDP)	161	91	..
Gross capital formation (% of GDP)	..	..	..
Central government revenue (% of GDP)	..	..	..
Central government cash surplus/deficit (% of GDP)	..	..	..
States and markets			
Starting a business (days)	..	..	..
Stock market capitalization (% of GDP)	..	..	..
Military expenditures (% of GDP)	..	..	..
Mobile cellular subscriptions (per 100 people)	0.0	16.6	122.6
Individuals using the Internet (% of population)	0.0	15.4	57.1
Paved roads (% of total)	..	..	..
High-technology exports (% of manufactured exports)	..	..	5
Global links			
Merchandise trade (% of GDP)	58	54	..
Net barter terms of trade index (2000 = 100)	..	100	119
Total external debt stocks ($ millions)	..	..	..
Total debt service (% of exports)	..	..	..
Net migration (thousands)	-5.2	6.3	4.0
Remittances received ($ millions)	2.6	7.9	5.3
Foreign direct investment, net inflows ($ millions)	131	-128	544
Net official development assistance received ($ millions)	30.0	-7.4	..

Australia

Population (millions)	22.3	Population growth (%)	1.2
Surface area (1,000 sq. km)	7,741	Population living below $1.25 a day (%)	..
GNI, Atlas ($ billions)	1,111.4	GNI per capita, Atlas ($)	49,790
GNI, PPP ($ billions)	862.0	GNI per capita, PPP ($)	38,610

	1990	2000	2011
People			
Share of poorest 20% in nat'l consumption/income (%)	..	..	..
Life expectancy at birth (years)	77	79	82
Total fertility rate (births per woman)	1.9	1.8	1.9
Adolescent fertility rate (births per 1,000 women 15–19)	..	18	13
Contraceptive prevalence (% of married women 15–49)	..	71	..
Births attended by skilled health staff (% of total)	100	100	..
Under-five mortality rate (per 1,000 live births)	9	6	5
Child malnutrition, underweight (% of under age 5)	..	..	..
Child immunization, measles (% of ages 12–23 mos.)	86	91	94
Primary completion rate, total (% of relevant age group)	..	..	..
Gross secondary enrollment, total (% of relevant age group)	134	162	131
Ratio of girls to boys in primary & secondary school (%)	100	100	97
HIV prevalence rate (% population of ages 15–49)	0.1	0.1	0.2
Environment			
Forests (1,000 sq. km)	1,545	1,549	1,484
Deforestation (avg. annual %, 1990–2000 and 2000–2010)		0.0	0.4
Freshwater use (% of internal resources)	..	4.6	4.6
Access to improved water source (% total pop.)	100	100	100
Access to improved sanitation facilities (% total pop.)	100	100	100
Energy use per capita (kilograms of oil equivalent)	5,053	5,645	5,366
Carbon dioxide emissions per capita (metric tons)	16.8	17.2	18.4
Electricity use per capita (kilowatt-hours)	8,527	10,194	10,286
Economy			
GDP ($ billions)	311	416	1,379
GDP growth (annual %)	3.6	3.8	1.9
GDP implicit price deflator (annual % growth)	6.1	2.6	6.1
Value added in agriculture (% of GDP)	5	4	2
Value added in industry (% of GDP)	31	27	20
Value added in services (% of GDP)	64	70	78
Exports of goods and services (% of GDP)	15	19	21
Imports of goods and services (% of GDP)	17	21	20
Gross capital formation (% of GDP)	29	26	27
Central government revenue (% of GDP)	..	25.9	23.0
Central government cash surplus/deficit (% of GDP)	..	2.0	-3.7
States and markets			
Starting a business (days)	..	2	2
Stock market capitalization (% of GDP)	35.0	89.7	86.9
Military expenditures (% of GDP)	2.1	1.9	1.9
Mobile cellular subscriptions (per 100 people)	1.1	44.7	108.3
Individuals using the Internet (% of population)	0.6	46.8	79.0
Paved roads (% of total)	35.0	41.6	43.5
High-technology exports (% of manufactured exports)	8	15	13
Global links			
Merchandise trade (% of GDP)	26	33	37
Net barter terms of trade index (2000 = 100)	..	100	201
Total external debt stocks ($ millions)	..	..	..
Total debt service (% of exports)	..	..	..
Net migration (thousands)	667	466	1,125
Remittances received ($ billions)	2.4	1.9	1.9
Foreign direct investment, net inflows ($ billions)	8.1	13.6	67.6
Net official development assistance received ($ millions)	..	..	..

Austria

Population (millions)	8.4	Population growth (%)	0.4
Surface area (1,000 sq. km)	84	Population living below $1.25 a day (%)	..
GNI, Atlas ($ billions)	405.7	GNI per capita, Atlas ($)	48,170
GNI, PPP ($ billions)	354.0	GNI per capita, PPP ($)	42,030

	1990	2000	2011
People			
Share of poorest 20% in nat'l consumption/income (%)	..	8.6	..
Life expectancy at birth (years)	76	78	81
Total fertility rate (births per woman)	1.5	1.4	1.4
Adolescent fertility rate (births per 1,000 women 15-19)	..	14	10
Contraceptive prevalence (% of married women 15-49)	..	..	..
Births attended by skilled health staff (% of total)	100	..	..
Under-five mortality rate (per 1,000 live births)	9	6	4
Child malnutrition, underweight (% of under age 5)	..	..	..
Child immunization, measles (% of ages 12-23 mos.)	60	75	76
Primary completion rate, total (% of relevant age group)	..	101	98
Gross secondary enrollment, total (% of relevant age group)	101	98	99
Ratio of girls to boys in primary & secondary school (%)	94	97	97
HIV prevalence rate (% population of ages 15-49)	0.1	0.1	0.4
Environment			
Forests (1,000 sq. km)	38	38	39
Deforestation (avg. annual %, 1990-2000 and 2000-2010)		-0.2	-0.1
Freshwater use (% of internal resources)	6.9	6.6	6.6
Access to improved water source (% total pop.)	100	100	100
Access to improved sanitation facilities (% total pop.)	100	100	100
Energy use per capita (kilograms of oil equivalent)	3,236	3,565	3,873
Carbon dioxide emissions per capita (metric tons)	7.9	8.0	7.4
Electricity use per capita (kilowatt-hours)	6,111	7,076	8,356
Economy			
GDP ($ billions)	165	192	418
GDP growth (annual %)	4.3	3.7	2.7
GDP implicit price deflator (annual % growth)	3.0	0.9	2.2
Value added in agriculture (% of GDP)	4	2	2
Value added in industry (% of GDP)	32	31	29
Value added in services (% of GDP)	64	67	69
Exports of goods and services (% of GDP)	37	46	57
Imports of goods and services (% of GDP)	37	44	54
Gross capital formation (% of GDP)	25	25	23
Central government revenue (% of GDP)	..	37.7	36.1
Central government cash surplus/deficit (% of GDP)	..	-2.0	-2.2
States and markets			
Starting a business (days)	..	25	25
Stock market capitalization (% of GDP)	7.0	15.6	19.7
Military expenditures (% of GDP)	1.2	1.0	0.9
Mobile cellular subscriptions (per 100 people)	1.0	76.4	154.8
Individuals using the Internet (% of population)	0.1	33.7	79.8
Paved roads (% of total)	100.0	100.0	100.0
High-technology exports (% of manufactured exports)	8	15	12
Global links			
Merchandise trade (% of GDP)	55	73	88
Net barter terms of trade index (2000 = 100)	..	100	89
Total external debt stocks ($ millions)	..	..	..
Total debt service (% of exports)	..	..	..
Net migration (thousands)	111	65	160
Remittances received ($ billions)	0.6	1.8	2.7
Foreign direct investment, net inflows ($ billions)	0.7	8.5	15.7
Net official development assistance received ($ millions)	..	..	..

Azerbaijan

Europe & Central Asia		Upper middle income	
Population (millions)	9.2	Population growth (%)	1.3
Surface area (1,000 sq. km)	87	Population living below $1.25 a day (%)	<2
GNI, Atlas ($ billions)	48.5	GNI per capita, Atlas ($)	5,290
GNI, PPP ($ billions)	82.1	GNI per capita, PPP ($)	8,950

	1990	2000	2011
People			
Share of poorest 20% in nat'l consumption/income (%)	..	7.5	8.0
Life expectancy at birth (years)	65	67	71
Total fertility rate (births per woman)	2.7	2.0	1.9
Adolescent fertility rate (births per 1,000 women 15–19)	..	37	32
Contraceptive prevalence (% of married women 15–49)	..	55	51
Births attended by skilled health staff (% of total)	97	84	88
Under-five mortality rate (per 1,000 live births)	95	69	45
Child malnutrition, underweight (% of under age 5)	..	14.0	8.4
Child immunization, measles (% of ages 12–23 mos.)	52	67	67
Primary completion rate, total (% of relevant age group)	96	90	93
Gross secondary enrollment, total (% of relevant age group)	89	76	100
Ratio of girls to boys in primary & secondary school (%)	100	99	98
HIV prevalence rate (% population of ages 15–49)	0.1	0.1	0.1
Environment			
Forests (1,000 sq. km)	9.4	9.4	9.4
Deforestation (avg. annual %, 1990–2000 and 2000–2010)		0.0	0.0
Freshwater use (% of internal resources)	..	124.1	150.5
Access to improved water source (% total pop.)	70	74	80
Access to improved sanitation facilities (% total pop.)	..	62	82
Energy use per capita (kilograms of oil equivalent)	3,653	1,420	1,307
Carbon dioxide emissions per capita (metric tons)	7.8	3.7	5.5
Electricity use per capita (kilowatt-hours)	2,584	2,040	1,603
Economy			
GDP ($ billions)	8.9	5.3	63.4
GDP growth (annual %)	-0.7	11.1	1.0
GDP implicit price deflator (annual % growth)	83.5	12.5	16.7
Value added in agriculture (% of GDP)	29	17	6
Value added in industry (% of GDP)	33	45	67
Value added in services (% of GDP)	38	38	27
Exports of goods and services (% of GDP)	44	39	63
Imports of goods and services (% of GDP)	39	38	24
Gross capital formation (% of GDP)	27	21	17
Central government revenue (% of GDP)	..	..	13.6
Central government cash surplus/deficit (% of GDP)	..	..	1.4
States and markets			
Starting a business (days)	..	105	8
Stock market capitalization (% of GDP)	..	0.1	..
Military expenditures (% of GDP)	2.1	2.3	4.9
Mobile cellular subscriptions (per 100 people)	0.0	5.2	108.7
Individuals using the Internet (% of population)	0.0	0.1	50.0
Paved roads (% of total)	..	49.4	50.6
High-technology exports (% of manufactured exports)	..	5	1
Global links			
Merchandise trade (% of GDP)	..	55	70
Net barter terms of trade index (2000 = 100)	..	100	188
Total external debt stocks ($ billions)	0.0	1.6	8.4
Total debt service (% of exports)	..	6.4	4.9
Net migration (thousands)	-151	-128	53
Remittances received ($ millions)	..	57	1,893
Foreign direct investment, net inflows ($ millions)	..	130	4,485
Net official development assistance received ($ millions)	0	139	293

Bahamas, The

High income

Population (thousands)	347	Population growth (%)		1.2
Surface area (1,000 sq. km)	14	Population living below $1.25 a day (%)		..
GNI, Atlas ($ billions)	7.5	GNI per capita, Atlas ($)		21,970
GNI, PPP ($ billions)	10.2	GNI per capita, PPP ($)		29,790

	1990	2000	2011
People			
Share of poorest 20% in nat'l consumption/income (%)	..	..	..
Life expectancy at birth (years)	69	72	75
Total fertility rate (births per woman)	2.6	2.1	1.9
Adolescent fertility rate (births per 1,000 women 15-19)	..	51	29
Contraceptive prevalence (% of married women 15-49)	62	45	..
Births attended by skilled health staff (% of total)	99	99	99
Under-five mortality rate (per 1,000 live births)	22	17	16
Child malnutrition, underweight (% of under age 5)	..	..	..
Child immunization, measles (% of ages 12–23 mos.)	86	93	90
Primary completion rate, total (% of relevant age group)	..	82	97
Gross secondary enrollment, total (% of relevant age group)	86	82	96
Ratio of girls to boys in primary & secondary school (%)	102	98	104
HIV prevalence rate (% population of ages 15–49)	3.9	3.6	2.8
Environment			
Forests (1,000 sq. km)	5.2	5.2	5.2
Deforestation (avg. annual %, 1990–2000 and 2000–2010)		0.0	0.0
Freshwater use (% of internal resources)	..	..	..
Access to improved water source (% total pop.)	96	96	..
Access to improved sanitation facilities (% total pop.)	100	100	100
Energy use per capita (kilograms of oil equivalent)	2,520	..	..
Carbon dioxide emissions per capita (metric tons)	7.6	6.0	7.6
Electricity use per capita (kilowatt-hours)	..	..	..
Economy			
GDP ($ billions)	3.2	6.3	7.8
GDP growth (annual %)	-1.6	4.1	1.6
GDP implicit price deflator (annual % growth)	5.1	0.9	-1.4
Value added in agriculture (% of GDP)	3	3	2
Value added in industry (% of GDP)	16	18	16
Value added in services (% of GDP)	81	80	82
Exports of goods and services (% of GDP)	54	44	43
Imports of goods and services (% of GDP)	56	62	57
Gross capital formation (% of GDP)	29	28	27
Central government revenue (% of GDP)	15.7	14.8	18.5
Central government cash surplus/deficit (% of GDP)	-1.9	0.3	-3.5
States and markets			
Starting a business (days)	..	..	31
Stock market capitalization (% of GDP)	..	..	..
Military expenditures (% of GDP)	..	..	..
Mobile cellular subscriptions (per 100 people)	0.8	10.6	86.1
Individuals using the Internet (% of population)	0.0	8.0	65.0
Paved roads (% of total)	52.0	57.4	..
High-technology exports (% of manufactured exports)	..	7	0
Global links			
Merchandise trade (% of GDP)	88	42	49
Net barter terms of trade index (2000 = 100)	..	100	109
Total external debt stocks ($ millions)	..	..	..
Total debt service (% of exports)	..	..	..
Net migration (thousands)	-0.9	-2.7	6.4
Remittances received ($ millions)	..	..	..
Foreign direct investment, net inflows ($ millions)	-17	250	595
Net official development assistance received ($ millions)	3.2	..	..

Bahrain

High income

Population (millions)	1.3	Population growth (%)	4.8
Surface area (sq. km)	760	Population living below $1.25 a day (%)	..
GNI, Atlas ($ billions)	20.1	GNI per capita, Atlas ($)	15,920
GNI, PPP ($ billions)	26.8	GNI per capita, PPP ($)	21,200

	1990	2000	2011
People			
Share of poorest 20% in nat'l consumption/income (%)	..	..	..
Life expectancy at birth (years)	72	74	75
Total fertility rate (births per woman)	3.7	2.7	2.5
Adolescent fertility rate (births per 1,000 women 15-19)	..	17	15
Contraceptive prevalence (% of married women 15-49)	54	..	..
Births attended by skilled health staff (% of total)	..	..	97
Under-five mortality rate (per 1,000 live births)	21	12	10
Child malnutrition, underweight (% of under age 5)	6.3	..	..
Child immunization, measles (% of ages 12-23 mos.)	87	98	99
Primary completion rate, total (% of relevant age group)	104	93	..
Gross secondary enrollment, total (% of relevant age group)	88	99	..
Ratio of girls to boys in primary & secondary school (%)	103	104	..
HIV prevalence rate (% population of ages 15-49)	..	..	..
Environment			
Forests (sq. km)	2.0	4.0	5.4
Deforestation (avg. annual %, 1990-2000 and 2000-2010)		-5.6	-3.6
Freshwater use (% of internal resources)	5,975.0	5,975.0	8,935.0
Access to improved water source (% total pop.)	..	..	..
Access to improved sanitation facilities (% total pop.)	..	..	..
Energy use per capita (kilograms of oil equivalent)	8,826	9,190	7,754
Carbon dioxide emissions per capita (metric tons)	24.1	29.2	20.7
Electricity use per capita (kilowatt-hours)	6,573	8,994	9,814
Economy			
GDP ($ billions)	4.2	8.0	22.9
GDP growth (annual %)	4.4	5.3	4.5
GDP implicit price deflator (annual % growth)	4.8	14.3	13.7
Value added in agriculture (% of GDP)	1	..	..
Value added in industry (% of GDP)	46	..	..
Value added in services (% of GDP)	53	..	..
Exports of goods and services (% of GDP)	116	89	81
Imports of goods and services (% of GDP)	95	64	59
Gross capital formation (% of GDP)	16	10	27
Central government revenue (% of GDP)	27.1	32.9	..
Central government cash surplus/deficit (% of GDP)	-2.3	8.5	..
States and markets			
Starting a business (days)	..	..	9
Stock market capitalization (% of GDP)	..	83.1	89.0
Military expenditures (% of GDP)	5.1	4.0	3.4
Mobile cellular subscriptions (per 100 people)	1.0	32.2	128.0
Individuals using the Internet (% of population)	0.0	6.2	77.0
Paved roads (% of total)	75.4	77.6	82.1
High-technology exports (% of manufactured exports)	..	0	0
Global links			
Merchandise trade (% of GDP)	177	136	119
Net barter terms of trade index (2000 = 100)	..	100	129
Total external debt stocks ($ millions)	..	..	..
Total debt service (% of exports)	..	..	..
Net migration (thousands)	13	19	448
Remittances received ($ millions)	..	..	..
Foreign direct investment, net inflows ($ millions)	-183	364	781
Net official development assistance received ($ millions)	138	60	..

Bangladesh

South Asia   **Low income**

Population (millions)	150.5	Population growth (%)	1.2
Surface area (1,000 sq. km)	144	Population living below $1.25 a day (%)	43.3
GNI, Atlas ($ billions)	117.8	GNI per capita, Atlas ($)	780
GNI, PPP ($ billions)	291.7	GNI per capita, PPP ($)	1,940

	1990	2000	2011
People			
Share of poorest 20% in nat'l consumption/income (%)	9.5	8.7	8.9
Life expectancy at birth (years)	59	65	69
Total fertility rate (births per woman)	4.5	3.1	2.2
Adolescent fertility rate (births per 1,000 women 15–19)	..	116	70
Contraceptive prevalence (% of married women 15–49)	40	54	61
Births attended by skilled health staff (% of total)	..	12	32
Under-five mortality rate (per 1,000 live births)	139	84	46
Child malnutrition, underweight (% of under age 5)	61.5	48.2	41.3
Child immunization, measles (% of ages 12–23 mos.)	65	72	96
Primary completion rate, total (% of relevant age group)	46	..	..
Gross secondary enrollment, total (% of relevant age group)	21	48	51
Ratio of girls to boys in primary & secondary school (%)	75	..	..
HIV prevalence rate (% population of ages 15–49)	0.1	0.1	0.1
Environment			
Forests (1,000 sq. km)	15	15	14
Deforestation (avg. annual %, 1990–2000 and 2000–2010)		0.2	0.2
Freshwater use (% of internal resources)	..	..	34.2
Access to improved water source (% total pop.)	77	79	81
Access to improved sanitation facilities (% total pop.)	39	47	56
Energy use per capita (kilograms of oil equivalent)	121	144	209
Carbon dioxide emissions per capita (metric tons)	0.1	0.2	0.3
Electricity use per capita (kilowatt-hours)	49	103	279
Economy			
GDP ($ billions)	30.1	47.1	111.9
GDP growth (annual %)	5.9	5.9	6.7
GDP implicit price deflator (annual % growth)	6.3	1.9	7.5
Value added in agriculture (% of GDP)	30	26	18
Value added in industry (% of GDP)	21	25	28
Value added in services (% of GDP)	48	49	54
Exports of goods and services (% of GDP)	6	14	23
Imports of goods and services (% of GDP)	14	19	32
Gross capital formation (% of GDP)	17	23	25
Central government revenue (% of GDP)	..	9.8	12.0
Central government cash surplus/deficit (% of GDP)	..	-0.7	-0.9
States and markets			
Starting a business (days)	..	50	19
Stock market capitalization (% of GDP)	1.1	2.5	21.0
Military expenditures (% of GDP)	1.1	1.4	1.3
Mobile cellular subscriptions (per 100 people)	0.0	0.2	56.1
Individuals using the Internet (% of population)	0.0	0.1	5.0
Paved roads (% of total)	7.2	9.5	9.5
High-technology exports (% of manufactured exports)	0	0	..
Global links			
Merchandise trade (% of GDP)	18	32	54
Net barter terms of trade index (2000 = 100)	117	100	55
Total external debt stocks ($ billions)	12.3	15.6	27.0
Total debt service (% of exports)	34.6	10.5	5.5
Net migration (thousands)	-289	-956	-2,908
Remittances received ($ billions)	0.8	2.0	12.1
Foreign direct investment, net inflows ($ millions)	3	280	798
Net official development assistance received ($ billions)	2.1	1.2	1.5

Barbados

High income

Population (thousands)	274	Population growth (%)	0.2
Surface area (sq. km)	430	Population living below $1.25 a day (%)	..
GNI, Atlas ($ billions)	3.5	GNI per capita, Atlas ($)	12,660
GNI, PPP ($ billions)	5.2	GNI per capita, PPP ($)	18,900

	1990	2000	2011
People			
Share of poorest 20% in nat'l consumption/income (%)	..	..	..
Life expectancy at birth (years)	74	75	77
Total fertility rate (births per woman)	1.7	1.6	1.6
Adolescent fertility rate (births per 1,000 women 15–19)	..	48	41
Contraceptive prevalence (% of married women 15–49)	55	55	..
Births attended by skilled health staff (% of total)	..	98	100
Under-five mortality rate (per 1,000 live births)	18	17	20
Child malnutrition, underweight (% of under age 5)	..	..	..
Child immunization, measles (% of ages 12–23 mos.)	87	94	93
Primary completion rate, total (% of relevant age group)	..	99	111
Gross secondary enrollment, total (% of relevant age group)	86	105	104
Ratio of girls to boys in primary & secondary school (%)	94	108	105
HIV prevalence rate (% population of ages 15–49)	0.4	0.8	0.9
Environment			
Forests (sq. km)	84	84	84
Deforestation (avg. annual %, 1990–2000 and 2000–2010)		0.0	0.0
Freshwater use (% of internal resources)	..	76.1	76.1
Access to improved water source (% total pop.)	100	100	100
Access to improved sanitation facilities (% total pop.)	100	100	100
Energy use per capita (kilograms of oil equivalent)	1,241	..	..
Carbon dioxide emissions per capita (metric tons)	4.1	4.4	5.8
Electricity use per capita (kilowatt-hours)	..	..	..
Economy			
GDP ($ billions)	1.7	2.6	3.7
GDP growth (annual %)	-4.8	2.3	-5.3
GDP implicit price deflator (annual % growth)	5.5	0.8	3.4
Value added in agriculture (% of GDP)	7	4	3
Value added in industry (% of GDP)	20	16	23
Value added in services (% of GDP)	73	79	74
Exports of goods and services (% of GDP)	49	50	47
Imports of goods and services (% of GDP)	52	57	52
Gross capital formation (% of GDP)	19	19	15
Central government revenue (% of GDP)	..	..	29.3
Central government cash surplus/deficit (% of GDP)	..	..	-8.6
States and markets			
Starting a business (days)	..	..	18
Stock market capitalization (% of GDP)	16.5	66.0	124.1
Military expenditures (% of GDP)	..	..	..
Mobile cellular subscriptions (per 100 people)	0.0	10.6	127.0
Individuals using the Internet (% of population)	0.0	4.0	71.8
Paved roads (% of total)	86.8	98.6	..
High-technology exports (% of manufactured exports)	20	23	14
Global links			
Merchandise trade (% of GDP)	54	56	62
Net barter terms of trade index (2000 = 100)	..	100	111
Total external debt stocks ($ millions)	..	..	..
Total debt service (% of exports)	..	..	..
Net migration (thousands)	-5.4	-1.9	0.0
Remittances received ($ millions)	38	115	82
Foreign direct investment, net inflows ($ millions)	11	19	334
Net official development assistance received ($ millions)	2.6	0.2	16.2

Belarus

Europe & Central Asia		Upper middle income	

Population (millions)	9.5	Population growth (%)	-0.2
Surface area (1,000 sq. km)	208	Population living below $1.25 a day (%)	<2
GNI, Atlas ($ billions)	55.2	GNI per capita, Atlas ($)	5,830
GNI, PPP ($ billions)	137.0	GNI per capita, PPP ($)	14,460

	1990	2000	2011
People			
Share of poorest 20% in nat'l consumption/income (%)	11.1	8.5	9.2
Life expectancy at birth (years)	71	69	71
Total fertility rate (births per woman)	1.9	1.3	1.5
Adolescent fertility rate (births per 1,000 women 15-19)	..	28	21
Contraceptive prevalence (% of married women 15-49)	..	..	..
Births attended by skilled health staff (% of total)	100	100	100
Under-five mortality rate (per 1,000 live births)	17	14	6
Child malnutrition, underweight (% of under age 5)	..	..	..
Child immunization, measles (% of ages 12-23 mos.)	94	98	99
Primary completion rate, total (% of relevant age group)	94	100	104
Gross secondary enrollment, total (% of relevant age group)	97	85	105
Ratio of girls to boys in primary & secondary school (%)	..	101	98
HIV prevalence rate (% population of ages 15-49)	0.1	0.1	0.4
Environment			
Forests (1,000 sq. km)	78	83	87
Deforestation (avg. annual %, 1990-2000 and 2000-2010)		-0.6	-0.4
Freshwater use (% of internal resources)	..	11.7	11.7
Access to improved water source (% total pop.)	100	100	100
Access to improved sanitation facilities (% total pop.)	93	93	93
Energy use per capita (kilograms of oil equivalent)	4,470	2,467	2,922
Carbon dioxide emissions per capita (metric tons)	8.6	5.3	6.3
Electricity use per capita (kilowatt-hours)	4,381	2,989	3,564
Economy			
GDP ($ billions)	17.4	12.7	55.1
GDP growth (annual %)	-1.2	5.8	5.3
GDP implicit price deflator (annual % growth)	103.6	185.3	58.4
Value added in agriculture (% of GDP)	24	14	10
Value added in industry (% of GDP)	47	39	44
Value added in services (% of GDP)	29	47	46
Exports of goods and services (% of GDP)	46	69	88
Imports of goods and services (% of GDP)	44	72	90
Gross capital formation (% of GDP)	27	25	36
Central government revenue (% of GDP)	31.5	28.7	31.4
Central government cash surplus/deficit (% of GDP)	-4.8	0.1	1.9
States and markets			
Starting a business (days)	..	79	5
Stock market capitalization (% of GDP)	..	..	..
Military expenditures (% of GDP)	..	1.3	1.1
Mobile cellular subscriptions (per 100 people)	0.0	0.5	111.9
Individuals using the Internet (% of population)	0.0	1.9	39.6
Paved roads (% of total)	95.8	86.4	86.4
High-technology exports (% of manufactured exports)	..	4	3
Global links			
Merchandise trade (% of GDP)	..	125	156
Net barter terms of trade index (2000 = 100)	..	100	104
Total external debt stocks ($ billions)	0.0	2.6	29.1
Total debt service (% of exports)	0.6	5.1	4.5
Net migration (thousands)	-32.5	0.0	-50.0
Remittances received ($ millions)	0	139	814
Foreign direct investment, net inflows ($ millions)	7	119	4,002
Net official development assistance received ($ millions)	..	..	128

Belgium

Population (millions)	11.0	Population growth (%)	1.1
Surface area (1,000 sq. km)	31	Population living below $1.25 a day (%)	..
GNI, Atlas ($ billions)	506.2	GNI per capita, Atlas ($)	45,930
GNI, PPP ($ billions)	431.4	GNI per capita, PPP ($)	39,150

	1990	2000	2011
People			
Share of poorest 20% in nat'l consumption/income (%)	..	8.5	..
Life expectancy at birth (years)	76	78	80
Total fertility rate (births per woman)	1.6	1.7	1.8
Adolescent fertility rate (births per 1,000 women 15-19)	..	19	12
Contraceptive prevalence (% of married women 15-49)	78	76	..
Births attended by skilled health staff (% of total)	..	99	..
Under-five mortality rate (per 1,000 live births)	10	6	4
Child malnutrition, underweight (% of under age 5)	..	..	..
Child immunization, measles (% of ages 12-23 mos.)	85	82	95
Primary completion rate, total (% of relevant age group)	78	..	91
Gross secondary enrollment, total (% of relevant age group)	99	145	111
Ratio of girls to boys in primary & secondary school (%)	101	105	98
HIV prevalence rate (% population of ages 15-49)	0.1	0.2	0.3
Environment			
Forests (1,000 sq. km)	6.8	6.7	6.8
Deforestation (avg. annual %, 1990-2000 and 2000-2010)		0.2	-0.2
Freshwater use (% of internal resources)	..	62.8	51.8
Access to improved water source (% total pop.)	100	100	100
Access to improved sanitation facilities (% total pop.)	100	100	100
Energy use per capita (kilograms of oil equivalent)	4,844	5,707	5,077
Carbon dioxide emissions per capita (metric tons)	10.9	11.3	9.6
Electricity use per capita (kilowatt-hours)	6,380	8,248	8,388
Economy			
GDP ($ billions)	203	233	514
GDP growth (annual %)	3.1	3.7	1.8
GDP implicit price deflator (annual % growth)	2.8	2.0	2.0
Value added in agriculture (% of GDP)	2	1	1
Value added in industry (% of GDP)	31	27	22
Value added in services (% of GDP)	67	72	78
Exports of goods and services (% of GDP)	67	78	84
Imports of goods and services (% of GDP)	65	75	83
Gross capital formation (% of GDP)	23	23	22
Central government revenue (% of GDP)	..	42.8	41.1
Central government cash surplus/deficit (% of GDP)	..	0.0	-3.6
States and markets			
Starting a business (days)	..	56	4
Stock market capitalization (% of GDP)	32.2	78.4	44.8
Military expenditures (% of GDP)	2.3	1.4	1.1
Mobile cellular subscriptions (per 100 people)	0.4	55.3	116.6
Individuals using the Internet (% of population)	0.0	29.4	78.0
Paved roads (% of total)	81.2	78.2	78.2
High-technology exports (% of manufactured exports)	..	10	10
Global links			
Merchandise trade (% of GDP)	117	157	183
Net barter terms of trade index (2000 = 100)	..	100	100
Total external debt stocks ($ millions)	..	..	..
Total debt service (% of exports)	..	..	..
Net migration (thousands)	52	61	200
Remittances received ($ billions)	3.6	4.0	10.9
Foreign direct investment, net inflows ($ billions)	..	18	102
Net official development assistance received ($ millions)	..	..	..

Belize

Latin America & Caribbean		Lower middle income	
Population (thousands)	357	Population growth (%)	3.4
Surface area (1,000 sq. km)	23	Population living below $1.25 a day (%)	..
GNI, Atlas ($ billions)	1.3	GNI per capita, Atlas ($)	3,710
GNI, PPP ($ billions)	2.2	GNI per capita, PPP ($)	6,090

	1990	2000	2011
People			
Share of poorest 20% in nat'l consumption/income (%)	3.0	3.3	..
Life expectancy at birth (years)	72	74	76
Total fertility rate (births per woman)	4.5	3.6	2.7
Adolescent fertility rate (births per 1,000 women 15–19)	..	97	72
Contraceptive prevalence (% of married women 15–49)	47	56	34
Births attended by skilled health staff (% of total)	77	100	94
Under-five mortality rate (per 1,000 live births)	44	26	17
Child malnutrition, underweight (% of under age 5)	5.4	..	4.9
Child immunization, measles (% of ages 12–23 mos.)	86	96	98
Primary completion rate, total (% of relevant age group)	92	94	110
Gross secondary enrollment, total (% of relevant age group)	62	65	76
Ratio of girls to boys in primary & secondary school (%)	94	95	93
HIV prevalence rate (% population of ages 15–49)	1.0	2.3	2.3
Environment			
Forests (1,000 sq. km)	16	15	14
Deforestation (avg. annual %, 1990–2000 and 2000–2010)		0.6	0.7
Freshwater use (% of internal resources)	..	0.9	0.9
Access to improved water source (% total pop.)	74	86	98
Access to improved sanitation facilities (% total pop.)	77	83	90
Energy use per capita (kilograms of oil equivalent)	562	..	..
Carbon dioxide emissions per capita (metric tons)	1.6	2.8	1.2
Electricity use per capita (kilowatt-hours)	..	..	..
Economy			
GDP ($ millions)	413	832	1,448
GDP growth (annual %)	10.6	13.0	1.9
GDP implicit price deflator (annual % growth)	2.8	0.4	1.5
Value added in agriculture (% of GDP)	20	17	12
Value added in industry (% of GDP)	22	21	23
Value added in services (% of GDP)	58	62	65
Exports of goods and services (% of GDP)	62	53	66
Imports of goods and services (% of GDP)	60	74	65
Gross capital formation (% of GDP)	26	32	27
Central government revenue (% of GDP)	25.4	20.4	25.3
Central government cash surplus/deficit (% of GDP)	-0.6	-5.7	-1.6
States and markets			
Starting a business (days)	..	..	44
Stock market capitalization (% of GDP)	..	..	..
Military expenditures (% of GDP)	1.1	0.9	1.1
Mobile cellular subscriptions (per 100 people)	0.0	6.7	70.0
Individuals using the Internet (% of population)	0.0	6.0	14.0
Paved roads (% of total)	..	17.0	..
High-technology exports (% of manufactured exports)	0	0	0
Global links			
Merchandise trade (% of GDP)	83	89	83
Net barter terms of trade index (2000 = 100)	..	100	104
Total external debt stocks ($ millions)	143	630	1,278
Total debt service (% of exports)	7.2	17.5	13.9
Net migration (thousands)	-4.7	-2.0	-1.0
Remittances received ($ millions)	18.5	26.4	75.7
Foreign direct investment, net inflows ($ millions)	17.2	23.3	95.3
Net official development assistance received ($ millions)	30.3	14.7	29.8

Benin

Sub-Saharan Africa

Low income

Population (millions)	9.1	Population growth (%)		2.8
Surface area (1,000 sq. km)	115	Population living below $1.25 a day (%)		47.3
GNI, Atlas ($ billions)	7.1	GNI per capita, Atlas ($)		780
GNI, PPP ($ billions)	14.6	GNI per capita, PPP ($)		1,610

	1990	2000	2011
People			
Share of poorest 20% in nat'l consumption/income (%)	..	7.0	..
Life expectancy at birth (years)	49	53	56
Total fertility rate (births per woman)	6.7	6.0	5.2
Adolescent fertility rate (births per 1,000 women 15–19)	..	120	100
Contraceptive prevalence (% of married women 15–49)	..	19	17
Births attended by skilled health staff (% of total)	..	66	74
Under-five mortality rate (per 1,000 live births)	177	140	106
Child malnutrition, underweight (% of under age 5)	..	21.5	20.2
Child immunization, measles (% of ages 12–23 mos.)	79	70	72
Primary completion rate, total (% of relevant age group)	19	40	75
Gross secondary enrollment, total (% of relevant age group)	..	23	51
Ratio of girls to boys in primary & secondary school (%)	..	61	79
HIV prevalence rate (% population of ages 15–49)	3.2	1.8	1.2
Environment			
Forests (1,000 sq. km)	58	51	45
Deforestation (avg. annual %, 1990–2000 and 2000–2010)		1.3	1.0
Freshwater use (% of internal resources)	..	1.3	1.3
Access to improved water source (% total pop.)	57	66	75
Access to improved sanitation facilities (% total pop.)	5	9	13
Energy use per capita (kilograms of oil equivalent)	348	304	413
Carbon dioxide emissions per capita (metric tons)	0.1	0.2	0.6
Electricity use per capita (kilowatt-hours)	..	61	90
Economy			
GDP ($ billions)	2.0	2.4	7.3
GDP growth (annual %)	9.0	4.9	3.5
GDP implicit price deflator (annual % growth)	2.2	4.5	2.4
Value added in agriculture (% of GDP)	35	35	32
Value added in industry (% of GDP)	12	13	13
Value added in services (% of GDP)	53	52	54
Exports of goods and services (% of GDP)	19	25	15
Imports of goods and services (% of GDP)	27	30	27
Gross capital formation (% of GDP)	14	19	18
Central government revenue (% of GDP)	..	15.6	17.2
Central government cash surplus/deficit (% of GDP)	..	0.6	-1.4
States and markets			
Starting a business (days)	..	32	26
Stock market capitalization (% of GDP)	..	..	..
Military expenditures (% of GDP)	1.7	0.6	1.0
Mobile cellular subscriptions (per 100 people)	0.0	0.9	85.3
Individuals using the Internet (% of population)	0.0	0.2	3.5
Paved roads (% of total)	20.0	9.5	..
High-technology exports (% of manufactured exports)	..	0	0
Global links			
Merchandise trade (% of GDP)	28	43	62
Net barter terms of trade index (2000 = 100)	107	100	125
Total external debt stocks ($ billions)	1.1	1.4	1.4
Total debt service (% of exports)	9.9	13.6	2.5
Net migration (thousands)	-8.7	-29.3	50.0
Remittances received ($ millions)	101	87	185
Foreign direct investment, net inflows ($ millions)	62	60	118
Net official development assistance received ($ millions)	267	243	677

Bermuda

High income

Population (thousands)	65	Population growth (%)		0.7
Surface area (sq. km)	50	Population living below $1.25 a day (%)		..
GNI, Atlas ($ billions)	..	GNI per capita, Atlas ($)		..
GNI, PPP ($ millions)	..	GNI per capita, PPP ($)		..

	1990	2000	2011
People			
Share of poorest 20% in nat'l consumption/income (%)	..	..	..
Life expectancy at birth (years)	74	78	79
Total fertility rate (births per woman)	..	1.7	1.8
Adolescent fertility rate (births per 1,000 women 15–19)	..	..	..
Contraceptive prevalence (% of married women 15–49)	..	..	..
Births attended by skilled health staff (% of total)	..	..	..
Under-five mortality rate (per 1,000 live births)	..	..	..
Child malnutrition, underweight (% of under age 5)	..	..	..
Child immunization, measles (% of ages 12–23 mos.)	..	..	..
Primary completion rate, total (% of relevant age group)	..	97	100
Gross secondary enrollment, total (% of relevant age group)	..	79	77
Ratio of girls to boys in primary & secondary school (%)	..	104	107
HIV prevalence rate (% population of ages 15–49)	..	..	..
Environment			
Forests (sq. km)	10.0	10.0	10.0
Deforestation (avg. annual %, 1990–2000 and 2000–2010)		0.0	0.0
Freshwater use (% of internal resources)	..	..	..
Access to improved water source (% total pop.)	..	..	..
Access to improved sanitation facilities (% total pop.)	..	..	..
Energy use per capita (kilograms of oil equivalent)	..	..	..
Carbon dioxide emissions per capita (metric tons)	9.9	8.0	7.2
Electricity use per capita (kilowatt-hours)	..	..	..
Economy			
GDP ($ billions)	1.6	3.5	5.8
GDP growth (annual %)	0.0	9.3	–1.9
GDP implicit price deflator (annual % growth)	6.0	–4.2	1.2
Value added in agriculture (% of GDP)	..	1	1
Value added in industry (% of GDP)	..	12	8
Value added in services (% of GDP)	..	88	91
Exports of goods and services (% of GDP)	..	..	26
Imports of goods and services (% of GDP)	..	..	36
Gross capital formation (% of GDP)	..	..	..
Central government revenue (% of GDP)	..	..	..
Central government cash surplus/deficit (% of GDP)	..	..	..
States and markets			
Starting a business (days)	..	..	..
Stock market capitalization (% of GDP)	..	61.7	26.6
Military expenditures (% of GDP)	..	..	..
Mobile cellular subscriptions (per 100 people)	1.9	20.7	135.8
Individuals using the Internet (% of population)	0.0	42.9	88.3
Paved roads (% of total)	..	..	..
High-technology exports (% of manufactured exports)	..	..	..
Global links			
Merchandise trade (% of GDP)	41	22	17
Net barter terms of trade index (2000 = 100)	..	100	72
Total external debt stocks ($ millions)	..	..	..
Total debt service (% of exports)	..	..	..
Net migration (thousands)	..	..	..
Remittances received ($ millions)	..	..	1,253
Foreign direct investment, net inflows ($ millions)	..	67	111
Net official development assistance received ($ millions)	42.2	..	..

Bhutan

South Asia		Lower middle income

Population (thousands)	738	Population growth (%)	1.7
Surface area (1,000 sq. km)	38	Population living below $1.25 a day (%)	10.2
GNI, Atlas ($ billions)	1.6	GNI per capita, Atlas ($)	2,130
GNI, PPP ($ billions)	4.1	GNI per capita, PPP ($)	5,570

	1990	2000	2011
People			
Share of poorest 20% in nat'l consumption/income (%)	..	5.4	6.6
Life expectancy at birth (years)	53	61	67
Total fertility rate (births per woman)	5.8	3.7	2.3
Adolescent fertility rate (births per 1,000 women 15–19)	..	65	46
Contraceptive prevalence (% of married women 15–49)	..	31	66
Births attended by skilled health staff (% of total)	..	24	65
Under-five mortality rate (per 1,000 live births)	138	89	54
Child malnutrition, underweight (% of under age 5)	34.0	14.1	12.7
Child immunization, measles (% of ages 12–23 mos.)	93	78	95
Primary completion rate, total (% of relevant age group)	24	51	103
Gross secondary enrollment, total (% of relevant age group)	..	41	75
Ratio of girls to boys in primary & secondary school (%)	..	86	103
HIV prevalence rate (% population of ages 15–49)	0.1	0.1	0.3
Environment			
Forests (1,000 sq. km)	30	31	33
Deforestation (avg. annual %, 1990–2000 and 2000–2010)		-0.3	-0.3
Freshwater use (% of internal resources)	..	..	0.4
Access to improved water source (% total pop.)	..	86	96
Access to improved sanitation facilities (% total pop.)	..	39	44
Energy use per capita (kilograms of oil equivalent)	100	..	..
Carbon dioxide emissions per capita (metric tons)	0.2	0.7	0.6
Electricity use per capita (kilowatt-hours)	..	..	..
Economy			
GDP ($ millions)	300	439	1,732
GDP growth (annual %)	10.9	6.9	5.6
GDP implicit price deflator (annual % growth)	5.7	2.3	5.7
Value added in agriculture (% of GDP)	35	27	16
Value added in industry (% of GDP)	25	36	44
Value added in services (% of GDP)	40	37	40
Exports of goods and services (% of GDP)	27	29	37
Imports of goods and services (% of GDP)	31	53	56
Gross capital formation (% of GDP)	30	48	59
Central government revenue (% of GDP)	17.0	22.9	22.9
Central government cash surplus/deficit (% of GDP)	-5.8	-2.4	0.5
States and markets			
Starting a business (days)	..	62	36
Stock market capitalization (% of GDP)	..	10.3	..
Military expenditures (% of GDP)	..	..	..
Mobile cellular subscriptions (per 100 people)	0.0	0.0	65.6
Individuals using the Internet (% of population)	0.0	0.4	21.0
Paved roads (% of total)	77.1	62.0	40.4
High-technology exports (% of manufactured exports)	..	0	0
Global links			
Merchandise trade (% of GDP)	50	63	92
Net barter terms of trade index (2000 = 100)	..	100	152
Total external debt stocks ($ millions)	84	212	1,035
Total debt service (% of exports)	..	..	11.1
Net migration (thousands)	1.6	0.1	16.8
Remittances received ($ millions)	..	..	10.4
Foreign direct investment, net inflows ($ millions)	..	2.5	16.4
Net official development assistance received ($ millions)	46	53	144

Bolivia

Latin America & Caribbean   **Lower middle income**

Population (millions)	10.1	Population growth (%)	1.6
Surface area (1,000 sq. km)	1,099	Population living below $1.25 a day (%)	15.6
GNI, Atlas ($ billions)	20.4	GNI per capita, Atlas ($)	2,020
GNI, PPP ($ billions)	49.3	GNI per capita, PPP ($)	4,890

	1990	2000	2011
People			
Share of poorest 20% in nat'l consumption/income (%)	5.6	0.8	2.1
Life expectancy at birth (years)	59	63	67
Total fertility rate (births per woman)	4.9	4.1	3.3
Adolescent fertility rate (births per 1,000 women 15–19)	..	85	75
Contraceptive prevalence (% of married women 15–49)	30	53	61
Births attended by skilled health staff (% of total)	43	69	71
Under-five mortality rate (per 1,000 live births)	120	81	51
Child malnutrition, underweight (% of under age 5)	9.7	5.9	4.5
Child immunization, measles (% of ages 12–23 mos.)	53	84	84
Primary completion rate, total (% of relevant age group)	71	99	95
Gross secondary enrollment, total (% of relevant age group)	..	80	81
Ratio of girls to boys in primary & secondary school (%)	..	97	99
HIV prevalence rate (% population of ages 15–49)	0.6	0.5	0.3
Environment			
Forests (1,000 sq. km)	628	601	569
Deforestation (avg. annual %, 1990–2000 and 2000–2010)		0.4	0.5
Freshwater use (% of internal resources)	..	0.7	0.7
Access to improved water source (% total pop.)	70	80	88
Access to improved sanitation facilities (% total pop.)	18	22	27
Energy use per capita (kilograms of oil equivalent)	392	450	737
Carbon dioxide emissions per capita (metric tons)	0.8	1.2	1.5
Electricity use per capita (kilowatt-hours)	274	421	616
Economy			
GDP ($ billions)	4.9	8.4	23.9
GDP growth (annual %)	4.6	2.5	5.2
GDP implicit price deflator (annual % growth)	16.3	5.2	14.6
Value added in agriculture (% of GDP)	17	15	13
Value added in industry (% of GDP)	35	30	39
Value added in services (% of GDP)	48	55	49
Exports of goods and services (% of GDP)	23	18	44
Imports of goods and services (% of GDP)	24	27	38
Gross capital formation (% of GDP)	13	18	20
Central government revenue (% of GDP)	..	18.4	..
Central government cash surplus/deficit (% of GDP)	..	-8.7	..
States and markets			
Starting a business (days)	..	60	50
Stock market capitalization (% of GDP)	..	20.7	17.2
Military expenditures (% of GDP)	2.8	2.1	1.5
Mobile cellular subscriptions (per 100 people)	0.0	7.0	82.8
Individuals using the Internet (% of population)	0.0	1.4	30.0
Paved roads (% of total)	4.3	6.6	8.5
High-technology exports (% of manufactured exports)	7	40	14
Global links			
Merchandise trade (% of GDP)	33	36	67
Net barter terms of trade index (2000 = 100)	102	100	175
Total external debt stocks ($ billions)	4.4	5.9	6.5
Total debt service (% of exports)	39.4	39.8	4.9
Net migration (thousands)	-100	-100	-165
Remittances received ($ millions)	5	127	1,043
Foreign direct investment, net inflows ($ millions)	27	736	859
Net official development assistance received ($ millions)	545	482	759

Bosnia and Herzegovina

Europe & Central Asia   **Upper middle income**

Population (millions)	3.8	Population growth (%)		–0.2
Surface area (1,000 sq. km)	51	Population living below $1.25 a day (%)		<2
GNI, Atlas ($ billions)	18.0	GNI per capita, Atlas ($)		4,780
GNI, PPP ($ billions)	34.5	GNI per capita, PPP ($)		9,190

	1990	2000	2011
People			
Share of poorest 20% in nat'l consumption/income (%)	..	9.1	6.7
Life expectancy at birth (years)	67	74	76
Total fertility rate (births per woman)	1.7	1.4	1.1
Adolescent fertility rate (births per 1,000 women 15–19)	..	22	14
Contraceptive prevalence (% of married women 15–49)	..	48	36
Births attended by skilled health staff (% of total)	97	100	100
Under-five mortality rate (per 1,000 live births)	19	10	8
Child malnutrition, underweight (% of under age 5)	..	4.2	1.6
Child immunization, measles (% of ages 12–23 mos.)	52	80	89
Primary completion rate, total (% of relevant age group)	..	..	76
Gross secondary enrollment, total (% of relevant age group)	..	..	89
Ratio of girls to boys in primary & secondary school (%)	..	..	102
HIV prevalence rate (% population of ages 15–49)	..	..	..
Environment			
Forests (1,000 sq. km)	22	22	22
Deforestation (avg. annual %, 1990–2000 and 2000–2010)		0.1	0.0
Freshwater use (% of internal resources)	..	..	1.0
Access to improved water source (% total pop.)	97	97	99
Access to improved sanitation facilities (% total pop.)	..	95	95
Energy use per capita (kilograms of oil equivalent)	1,629	1,177	1,703
Carbon dioxide emissions per capita (metric tons)	1.0	6.3	8.0
Electricity use per capita (kilowatt-hours)	3,044	2,062	3,110
Economy			
GDP ($ billions)	..	5.5	18.1
GDP growth (annual %)	..	5.5	1.7
GDP implicit price deflator (annual % growth)	..	28.8	1.8
Value added in agriculture (% of GDP)	..	11	9
Value added in industry (% of GDP)	..	23	26
Value added in services (% of GDP)	..	66	65
Exports of goods and services (% of GDP)	..	29	42
Imports of goods and services (% of GDP)	..	76	65
Gross capital formation (% of GDP)	..	21	21
Central government revenue (% of GDP)	..	37.1	40.0
Central government cash surplus/deficit (% of GDP)	..	0.7	–1.2
States and markets			
Starting a business (days)	..	68	37
Stock market capitalization (% of GDP)	..	..	..
Military expenditures (% of GDP)	..	3.6	1.4
Mobile cellular subscriptions (per 100 people)	0.0	2.5	84.5
Individuals using the Internet (% of population)	0.0	1.1	60.0
Paved roads (% of total)	54.0	52.3	92.1
High-technology exports (% of manufactured exports)	..	2	3
Global links			
Merchandise trade (% of GDP)	..	76	93
Net barter terms of trade index (2000 = 100)	..	100	101
Total external debt stocks ($ billions)	0.5	2.8	10.7
Total debt service (% of exports)	..	14.2	10.9
Net migration (thousands)	–24	282	–10
Remittances received ($ billions)	..	1.6	2.0
Foreign direct investment, net inflows ($ millions)	..	146	380
Net official development assistance received ($ millions)	0	738	425

Botswana

Sub-Saharan Africa		Upper middle income	
Population (millions)	2.0	Population growth (%)	1.2
Surface area (1,000 sq. km)	582	Population living below $1.25 a day (%)	..
GNI, Atlas ($ billions)	15.2	GNI per capita, Atlas ($)	7,470
GNI, PPP ($ billions)	29.5	GNI per capita, PPP ($)	14,550

	1990	2000	2011
People			
Share of poorest 20% in nat'l consumption/income (%)	..	..	..
Life expectancy at birth (years)	64	51	53
Total fertility rate (births per woman)	4.7	3.4	2.7
Adolescent fertility rate (births per 1,000 women 15–19)	..	66	45
Contraceptive prevalence (% of married women 15–49)	33	44	53
Births attended by skilled health staff (% of total)	78	94	95
Under-five mortality rate (per 1,000 live births)	53	81	26
Child malnutrition, underweight (% of under age 5)	..	10.7	11.2
Child immunization, measles (% of ages 12–23 mos.)	87	91	94
Primary completion rate, total (% of relevant age group)	89	89	97
Gross secondary enrollment, total (% of relevant age group)	40	75	82
Ratio of girls to boys in primary & secondary school (%)	108	102	100
HIV prevalence rate (% population of ages 15–49)	6.2	26.8	23.4
Environment			
Forests (1,000 sq. km)	137	125	112
Deforestation (avg. annual %, 1990–2000 and 2000–2010)		0.9	1.0
Freshwater use (% of internal resources)	4.7	8.1	8.1
Access to improved water source (% total pop.)	93	95	96
Access to improved sanitation facilities (% total pop.)	38	52	62
Energy use per capita (kilograms of oil equivalent)	912	1,045	1,128
Carbon dioxide emissions per capita (metric tons)	1.6	2.4	2.2
Electricity use per capita (kilowatt-hours)	716	906	1,586
Economy			
GDP ($ billions)	3.8	5.6	17.3
GDP growth (annual %)	6.8	5.9	5.7
GDP implicit price deflator (annual % growth)	6.3	0.0	10.7
Value added in agriculture (% of GDP)	5	3	3
Value added in industry (% of GDP)	61	53	46
Value added in services (% of GDP)	34	45	52
Exports of goods and services (% of GDP)	55	53	39
Imports of goods and services (% of GDP)	50	41	44
Gross capital formation (% of GDP)	37	32	31
Central government revenue (% of GDP)	50.8	..	31.5
Central government cash surplus/deficit (% of GDP)	19.1	..	-1.7
States and markets			
Starting a business (days)	..	108	61
Stock market capitalization (% of GDP)	6.6	17.4	23.7
Military expenditures (% of GDP)	4.1	3.3	2.1
Mobile cellular subscriptions (per 100 people)	0.0	12.6	142.8
Individuals using the Internet (% of population)	0.0	2.9	7.0
Paved roads (% of total)	32.0	35.3	..
High-technology exports (% of manufactured exports)	..	1	1
Global links			
Merchandise trade (% of GDP)	98	84	76
Net barter terms of trade index (2000 = 100)	98	100	82
Total external debt stocks ($ millions)	553	458	2,396
Total debt service (% of exports)	4.3	2.0	1.4
Net migration (thousands)	5.8	24.5	18.7
Remittances received ($ millions)	85.6	26.2	62.6
Foreign direct investment, net inflows ($ millions)	96	57	587
Net official development assistance received ($ millions)	145	31	126

Brazil

Latin America & Caribbean		Upper middle income	
Population (millions)	196.7	Population growth (%)	0.9
Surface area (1,000 sq. km)	8,515	Population living below $1.25 a day (%)	6.1
GNI, Atlas ($ billions)	2,107.7	GNI per capita, Atlas ($)	10,720
GNI, PPP ($ billions)	2,245.8	GNI per capita, PPP ($)	11,420

	1990	2000	2011
People			
Share of poorest 20% in nat'l consumption/income (%)	2.2	2.1	2.9
Life expectancy at birth (years)	66	70	73
Total fertility rate (births per woman)	2.8	2.4	1.8
Adolescent fertility rate (births per 1,000 women 15–19)	..	87	76
Contraceptive prevalence (% of married women 15–49)	59	..	81
Births attended by skilled health staff (% of total)	70	96	97
Under-five mortality rate (per 1,000 live births)	58	36	16
Child malnutrition, underweight (% of under age 5)	5.3	3.7	2.2
Child immunization, measles (% of ages 12–23 mos.)	78	99	97
Primary completion rate, total (% of relevant age group)	92	108	..
Gross secondary enrollment, total (% of relevant age group)	..	110	..
Ratio of girls to boys in primary & secondary school (%)	..	103	..
HIV prevalence rate (% population of ages 15–49)	0.2	0.4	0.3
Environment			
Forests (1,000 sq. km)	5,748	5,459	5,173
Deforestation (avg. annual %, 1990–2000 and 2000–2010)		0.5	0.5
Freshwater use (% of internal resources)	..	1.1	1.1
Access to improved water source (% total pop.)	89	94	98
Access to improved sanitation facilities (% total pop.)	68	74	79
Energy use per capita (kilograms of oil equivalent)	937	1,074	1,363
Carbon dioxide emissions per capita (metric tons)	1.4	1.9	1.9
Electricity use per capita (kilowatt-hours)	1,454	1,901	2,384
Economy			
GDP ($ billions)	462	645	2,477
GDP growth (annual %)	-4.3	4.3	2.7
GDP implicit price deflator (annual % growth)	2,735.5	6.2	7.0
Value added in agriculture (% of GDP)	8	6	5
Value added in industry (% of GDP)	39	28	28
Value added in services (% of GDP)	53	67	67
Exports of goods and services (% of GDP)	8	10	12
Imports of goods and services (% of GDP)	7	12	13
Gross capital formation (% of GDP)	20	18	20
Central government revenue (% of GDP)	22.8	19.9	25.0
Central government cash surplus/deficit (% of GDP)	-3.4	-1.8	-2.6
States and markets			
Starting a business (days)	..	152	119
Stock market capitalization (% of GDP)	3.6	35.1	49.6
Military expenditures (% of GDP)	6.3	1.8	1.4
Mobile cellular subscriptions (per 100 people)	0.0	13.3	124.3
Individuals using the Internet (% of population)	0.0	2.9	45.0
Paved roads (% of total)	9.7	5.5	13.5
High-technology exports (% of manufactured exports)	6	19	10
Global links			
Merchandise trade (% of GDP)	12	18	20
Net barter terms of trade index (2000 = 100)	66	100	136
Total external debt stocks ($ billions)	120	243	404
Total debt service (% of exports)	22.6	85.9	19.4
Net migration (thousands)	-92	-100	-500
Remittances received ($ billions)	0.6	1.6	2.8
Foreign direct investment, net inflows ($ billions)	1.0	32.8	71.5
Net official development assistance received ($ millions)	151	231	870

Brunei Darussalam

Population (thousands)	406	Population growth (%)	1.7
Surface area (1,000 sq. km)	5.8	Population living below $1.25 a day (%)	..
GNI, Atlas ($ billions)	12.5	GNI per capita, Atlas ($)	31,800
GNI, PPP ($ billions)	19.6	GNI per capita, PPP ($)	49,910

	1990	2000	2011
People			
Share of poorest 20% in nat'l consumption/income (%)	..	..	..
Life expectancy at birth (years)	74	76	78
Total fertility rate (births per woman)	3.5	2.4	2.0
Adolescent fertility rate (births per 1,000 women 15-19)	..	27	23
Contraceptive prevalence (% of married women 15-49)	..	..	..
Births attended by skilled health staff (% of total)	..	99	100
Under-five mortality rate (per 1,000 live births)	12	10	7
Child malnutrition, underweight (% of under age 5)	..	..	..
Child immunization, measles (% of ages 12-23 mos.)	99	99	91
Primary completion rate, total (% of relevant age group)	98	120	120
Gross secondary enrollment, total (% of relevant age group)	72	89	112
Ratio of girls to boys in primary & secondary school (%)	100	100	101
HIV prevalence rate (% population of ages 15-49)	..	..	..
Environment			
Forests (1,000 sq. km)	4.1	4.0	3.8
Deforestation (avg. annual %, 1990-2000 and 2000-2010)		0.4	0.4
Freshwater use (% of internal resources)	0.9	1.1	1.1
Access to improved water source (% total pop.)	..	..	..
Access to improved sanitation facilities (% total pop.)	..	..	..
Energy use per capita (kilograms of oil equivalent)	6,990	7,503	8,308
Carbon dioxide emissions per capita (metric tons)	25.5	20.0	23.7
Electricity use per capita (kilowatt-hours)	4,438	7,687	8,759
Economy			
GDP ($ billions)	3.5	6.0	16.4
GDP growth (annual %)	1.1	2.8	2.2
GDP implicit price deflator (annual % growth)	8.4	29.0	19.4
Value added in agriculture (% of GDP)	1	1	1
Value added in industry (% of GDP)	62	64	72
Value added in services (% of GDP)	37	35	28
Exports of goods and services (% of GDP)	62	67	81
Imports of goods and services (% of GDP)	37	36	29
Gross capital formation (% of GDP)	19	13	13
Central government revenue (% of GDP)	..	..	..
Central government cash surplus/deficit (% of GDP)	..	..	..
States and markets			
Starting a business (days)	..	..	101
Stock market capitalization (% of GDP)	..	..	..
Military expenditures (% of GDP)	6.6	4.1	2.5
Mobile cellular subscriptions (per 100 people)	0.7	29.0	109.2
Individuals using the Internet (% of population)	0.0	9.0	56.0
Paved roads (% of total)	31.4	34.7	81.1
High-technology exports (% of manufactured exports)	..	0	..
Global links			
Merchandise trade (% of GDP)	91	83	94
Net barter terms of trade index (2000 = 100)	..	100	201
Total external debt stocks ($ millions)	..	..	..
Total debt service (% of exports)	..	..	..
Net migration (thousands)	2.6	5.4	3.5
Remittances received ($ millions)	..	..	..
Foreign direct investment, net inflows ($ millions)	..	61	1,208
Net official development assistance received ($ millions)	3.9	..	..

Bulgaria

Europe & Central Asia		Upper middle income	
Population (millions)	7.3	Population growth (%)	-2.5
Surface area (1,000 sq. km)	111	Population living below $1.25 a day (%)	<2
GNI, Atlas ($ billions)	48.8	GNI per capita, Atlas ($)	6,640
GNI, PPP ($ billions)	105.8	GNI per capita, PPP ($)	14,400

	1990	2000	2011
People			
Share of poorest 20% in nat'l consumption/income (%)	10.5	6.5	8.5
Life expectancy at birth (years)	72	72	74
Total fertility rate (births per woman)	1.8	1.3	1.5
Adolescent fertility rate (births per 1,000 women 15-19)	..	47	38
Contraceptive prevalence (% of married women 15-49)	..	63	..
Births attended by skilled health staff (% of total)	99	100	100
Under-five mortality rate (per 1,000 live births)	22	21	12
Child malnutrition, underweight (% of under age 5)	..	1.6	..
Child immunization, measles (% of ages 12-23 mos.)	99	89	95
Primary completion rate, total (% of relevant age group)	100	97	106
Gross secondary enrollment, total (% of relevant age group)	99	93	89
Ratio of girls to boys in primary & secondary school (%)	99	98	97
HIV prevalence rate (% population of ages 15-49)	0.1	0.1	0.1
Environment			
Forests (1,000 sq. km)	33	34	40
Deforestation (avg. annual %, 1990-2000 and 2000-2010)		-0.1	-1.5
Freshwater use (% of internal resources)	35.7	29.2	29.1
Access to improved water source (% total pop.)	100	100	100
Access to improved sanitation facilities (% total pop.)	99	100	100
Energy use per capita (kilograms of oil equivalent)	3,276	2,286	2,370
Carbon dioxide emissions per capita (metric tons)	8.7	5.3	5.6
Electricity use per capita (kilowatt-hours)	4,759	3,674	4,476
Economy			
GDP ($ billions)	20.7	12.9	53.5
GDP growth (annual %)	-9.1	5.7	1.7
GDP implicit price deflator (annual % growth)	26.2	6.6	5.0
Value added in agriculture (% of GDP)	17	13	6
Value added in industry (% of GDP)	49	26	31
Value added in services (% of GDP)	34	61	63
Exports of goods and services (% of GDP)	33	50	67
Imports of goods and services (% of GDP)	37	56	66
Gross capital formation (% of GDP)	26	18	23
Central government revenue (% of GDP)	47.1	32.9	29.4
Central government cash surplus/deficit (% of GDP)	-5.0	-0.4	-2.0
States and markets			
Starting a business (days)	..	32	18
Stock market capitalization (% of GDP)	..	4.8	15.4
Military expenditures (% of GDP)	3.7	2.7	1.5
Mobile cellular subscriptions (per 100 people)	0.0	9.2	140.7
Individuals using the Internet (% of population)	0.0	5.4	51.0
Paved roads (% of total)	91.6	92.1	98.6
High-technology exports (% of manufactured exports)	..	3	7
Global links			
Merchandise trade (% of GDP)	49	88	113
Net barter terms of trade index (2000 = 100)	..	100	111
Total external debt stocks ($ billions)	10.9	12.0	39.9
Total debt service (% of exports)	19.4	18.2	12.2
Net migration (thousands)	-186	-108	-50
Remittances received ($ millions)	..	58	1,483
Foreign direct investment, net inflows ($ billions)	0.0	1.0	2.6
Net official development assistance received ($ millions)	..	..	..

Burkina Faso

Sub-Saharan Africa		Low income	
Population (millions)	17.0	Population growth (%)	3.0
Surface area (1,000 sq. km)	274	Population living below $1.25 a day (%)	44.6
GNI, Atlas ($ billions)	9.9	GNI per capita, Atlas ($)	580
GNI, PPP ($ billions)	22.5	GNI per capita, PPP ($)	1,330

	1990	2000	2011
People			
Share of poorest 20% in nat'l consumption/income (%)	..	7.0	6.7
Life expectancy at birth (years)	48	50	55
Total fertility rate (births per woman)	6.8	6.3	5.8
Adolescent fertility rate (births per 1,000 women 15-19)	..	133	119
Contraceptive prevalence (% of married women 15-49)	8	12	16
Births attended by skilled health staff (% of total)	42	31	66
Under-five mortality rate (per 1,000 live births)	208	182	146
Child malnutrition, underweight (% of under age 5)	29.6	33.7	26.0
Child immunization, measles (% of ages 12-23 mos.)	79	59	63
Primary completion rate, total (% of relevant age group)	18	24	45
Gross secondary enrollment, total (% of relevant age group)	6	10	23
Ratio of girls to boys in primary & secondary school (%)	..	70	89
HIV prevalence rate (% population of ages 15-49)	3.7	2.2	1.1
Environment			
Forests (1,000 sq. km)	68	62	56
Deforestation (avg. annual %, 1990-2000 and 2000-2010)		0.9	1.0
Freshwater use (% of internal resources)	3.0	7.9	7.9
Access to improved water source (% total pop.)	43	60	79
Access to improved sanitation facilities (% total pop.)	8	11	17
Energy use per capita (kilograms of oil equivalent)	..	..	..
Carbon dioxide emissions per capita (metric tons)	0.06	0.08	0.10
Electricity use per capita (kilowatt-hours)	..	..	..
Economy			
GDP ($ billions)	3.1	2.6	10.4
GDP growth (annual %)	-0.6	1.8	4.2
GDP implicit price deflator (annual % growth)	1.8	-1.7	3.2
Value added in agriculture (% of GDP)	29	29	34
Value added in industry (% of GDP)	21	25	24
Value added in services (% of GDP)	50	46	42
Exports of goods and services (% of GDP)	11	9	21
Imports of goods and services (% of GDP)	24	25	29
Gross capital formation (% of GDP)	19	17	24
Central government revenue (% of GDP)	..	11.7	16.2
Central government cash surplus/deficit (% of GDP)	..	-4.6	-2.4
States and markets			
Starting a business (days)	..	40	13
Stock market capitalization (% of GDP)	..	..	..
Military expenditures (% of GDP)	2.3	1.2	1.3
Mobile cellular subscriptions (per 100 people)	0.0	0.2	45.3
Individuals using the Internet (% of population)	0.0	0.1	3.0
Paved roads (% of total)	16.6	16.0	..
High-technology exports (% of manufactured exports)	..	3	6
Global links			
Merchandise trade (% of GDP)	22	31	44
Net barter terms of trade index (2000 = 100)	119	100	141
Total external debt stocks ($ billions)	0.8	1.4	2.4
Total debt service (% of exports)	9.4	18.8	2.5
Net migration (thousands)	-184	-137	-125
Remittances received ($ millions)	140	67	111
Foreign direct investment, net inflows ($ millions)	0.5	23.2	7.4
Net official development assistance received ($ millions)	327	180	990

Burundi

Sub-Saharan Africa		Low income
Population (millions)	8.6	Population growth (%)	2.3
Surface area (1,000 sq. km)	28	Population living below $1.25 a day (%)	81.3
GNI, Atlas ($ billions)	2.2	GNI per capita, Atlas ($)	250
GNI, PPP ($ billions)	5.2	GNI per capita, PPP ($)	610

	1990	2000	2011
People			
Share of poorest 20% in nat'l consumption/income (%)	7.9	5.1	9.0
Life expectancy at birth (years)	46	46	50
Total fertility rate (births per woman)	6.5	5.8	4.2
Adolescent fertility rate (births per 1,000 women 15–19)	..	33	20
Contraceptive prevalence (% of married women 15–49)	..	16	22
Births attended by skilled health staff (% of total)	..	25	60
Under-five mortality rate (per 1,000 live births)	183	165	139
Child malnutrition, underweight (% of under age 5)	..	38.9	..
Child immunization, measles (% of ages 12–23 mos.)	74	76	92
Primary completion rate, total (% of relevant age group)	41	26	62
Gross secondary enrollment, total (% of relevant age group)	5	11	28
Ratio of girls to boys in primary & secondary school (%)	79	80	95
HIV prevalence rate (% population of ages 15–49)	2.1	3.9	1.3
Environment			
Forests (1,000 sq. km)	2.9	2.0	1.7
Deforestation (avg. annual %, 1990–2000 and 2000–2010)		3.7	1.4
Freshwater use (% of internal resources)	..	2.9	2.9
Access to improved water source (% total pop.)	70	72	72
Access to improved sanitation facilities (% total pop.)	44	45	46
Energy use per capita (kilograms of oil equivalent)	..	..	..
Carbon dioxide emissions per capita (metric tons)	0.05	0.05	0.02
Electricity use per capita (kilowatt-hours)	..	..	..
Economy			
GDP ($ millions)	1,132	835	2,326
GDP growth (annual %)	3.5	-0.9	4.2
GDP implicit price deflator (annual % growth)	6.0	33.3	12.9
Value added in agriculture (% of GDP)	56	46	35
Value added in industry (% of GDP)	19	18	19
Value added in services (% of GDP)	25	36	46
Exports of goods and services (% of GDP)	8	7	5
Imports of goods and services (% of GDP)	28	17	34
Gross capital formation (% of GDP)	15	3	18
Central government revenue (% of GDP)	18.2	15.8	..
Central government cash surplus/deficit (% of GDP)	-2.3	-2.4	..
States and markets			
Starting a business (days)	..	13	8
Stock market capitalization (% of GDP)	..	..	..
Military expenditures (% of GDP)	3.5	5.1	2.7
Mobile cellular subscriptions (per 100 people)	0.0	0.3	22.3
Individuals using the Internet (% of population)	0.0	0.1	1.1
Paved roads (% of total)	..	7.1	..
High-technology exports (% of manufactured exports)	0	0	8
Global links			
Merchandise trade (% of GDP)	27	24	38
Net barter terms of trade index (2000 = 100)	128	100	173
Total external debt stocks ($ millions)	907	1,126	628
Total debt service (% of exports)	43.4	40.9	3.4
Net migration (thousands)	-3	-400	370
Remittances received ($ millions)	..	..	45.5
Foreign direct investment, net inflows ($ millions)	1.3	11.7	3.4
Net official development assistance received ($ millions)	263	93	579

Cambodia

Population (millions)	14.3	Population growth (%)	1.2
Surface area (1,000 sq. km)	181	Population living below $1.25 a day (%)	18.6
GNI, Atlas ($ billions)	11.7	GNI per capita, Atlas ($)	820
GNI, PPP ($ billions)	31.8	GNI per capita, PPP ($)	2,230

	1990	2000	2011
People			
Share of poorest 20% in nat'l consumption/income (%)	..	6.9	7.5
Life expectancy at birth (years)	55	57	63
Total fertility rate (births per woman)	5.7	3.8	2.5
Adolescent fertility rate (births per 1,000 women 15–19)	..	49	35
Contraceptive prevalence (% of married women 15–49)	..	24	51
Births attended by skilled health staff (% of total)	..	32	71
Under-five mortality rate (per 1,000 live births)	117	102	43
Child malnutrition, underweight (% of under age 5)	..	39.5	29.0
Child immunization, measles (% of ages 12–23 mos.)	34	65	93
Primary completion rate, total (% of relevant age group)	..	52	90
Gross secondary enrollment, total (% of relevant age group)	33	17	47
Ratio of girls to boys in primary & secondary school (%)	..	82	94
HIV prevalence rate (% population of ages 15–49)	0.5	1.2	0.6
Environment			
Forests (1,000 sq. km)	129	115	100
Deforestation (avg. annual %, 1990-2000 and 2000-2010)		1.1	1.3
Freshwater use (% of internal resources)	..	..	1.8
Access to improved water source (% total pop.)	31	44	64
Access to improved sanitation facilities (% total pop.)	9	17	31
Energy use per capita (kilograms of oil equivalent)	..	274	355
Carbon dioxide emissions per capita (metric tons)	0.05	0.18	0.33
Electricity use per capita (kilowatt-hours)	..	32	146
Economy			
GDP ($ billions)	2.5	3.7	12.8
GDP growth (annual %)	..	8.8	7.1
GDP implicit price deflator (annual % growth)	..	-3.2	3.4
Value added in agriculture (% of GDP)	47	38	37
Value added in industry (% of GDP)	13	23	24
Value added in services (% of GDP)	40	39	40
Exports of goods and services (% of GDP)	16	50	54
Imports of goods and services (% of GDP)	33	62	60
Gross capital formation (% of GDP)	12	18	17
Central government revenue (% of GDP)	..	10.3	12.0
Central government cash surplus/deficit (% of GDP)	..	-3.4	-4.2
States and markets			
Starting a business (days)	..	94	85
Stock market capitalization (% of GDP)	..	..	..
Military expenditures (% of GDP)	1.8	2.2	1.5
Mobile cellular subscriptions (per 100 people)	0.0	1.0	96.2
Individuals using the Internet (% of population)	0.0	0.0	3.1
Paved roads (% of total)	7.5	6.3	..
High-technology exports (% of manufactured exports)	..	0	0
Global links			
Merchandise trade (% of GDP)	30	91	127
Net barter terms of trade index (2000 = 100)	..	100	71
Total external debt stocks ($ billions)	1.8	2.6	4.3
Total debt service (% of exports)	4.1	1.7	1.0
Net migration (thousands)	150	94	-255
Remittances received ($ millions)	9	121	160
Foreign direct investment, net inflows ($ millions)	33	149	902
Net official development assistance received ($ millions)	41	396	792

Cameroon

Sub-Saharan Africa   **Lower middle income**

Population (millions)	20.0	Population growth (%)	2.2
Surface area (1,000 sq. km)	475	Population living below $1.25 a day (%)	9.6
GNI, Atlas ($ billions)	24.1	GNI per capita, Atlas ($)	1,210
GNI, PPP ($ billions)	46.7	GNI per capita, PPP ($)	2,330

	1990	2000	2011
People			
Share of poorest 20% in nat'l consumption/income (%)	..	6.5	6.7
Life expectancy at birth (years)	53	50	52
Total fertility rate (births per woman)	5.9	5.0	4.4
Adolescent fertility rate (births per 1,000 women 15–19)	..	139	118
Contraceptive prevalence (% of married women 15–49)	16	26	23
Births attended by skilled health staff (% of total)	64	60	64
Under-five mortality rate (per 1,000 live births)	145	140	127
Child malnutrition, underweight (% of under age 5)	10.0	15.1	16.6
Child immunization, measles (% of ages 12–23 mos.)	56	49	76
Primary completion rate, total (% of relevant age group)	54	51	78
Gross secondary enrollment, total (% of relevant age group)	25	28	51
Ratio of girls to boys in primary & secondary school (%)	82	85	86
HIV prevalence rate (% population of ages 15–49)	1.0	5.0	4.6
Environment			
Forests (1,000 sq. km)	243	221	197
Deforestation (avg. annual %, 1990–2000 and 2000–2010)		0.9	1.0
Freshwater use (% of internal resources)	0.1	0.4	0.4
Access to improved water source (% total pop.)	49	64	77
Access to improved sanitation facilities (% total pop.)	48	49	49
Energy use per capita (kilograms of oil equivalent)	409	402	363
Carbon dioxide emissions per capita (metric tons)	0.1	0.2	0.3
Electricity use per capita (kilowatt-hours)	193	173	271
Economy			
GDP ($ billions)	11.2	9.3	25.2
GDP growth (annual %)	-6.1	4.2	4.2
GDP implicit price deflator (annual % growth)	1.6	2.8	2.9
Value added in agriculture (% of GDP)	25	22	..
Value added in industry (% of GDP)	29	36	..
Value added in services (% of GDP)	46	42	..
Exports of goods and services (% of GDP)	20	29	31
Imports of goods and services (% of GDP)	17	25	35
Gross capital formation (% of GDP)	18	17	20
Central government revenue (% of GDP)	14.3	14.1	..
Central government cash surplus/deficit (% of GDP)	-5.6	0.1	..
States and markets			
Starting a business (days)	..	45	15
Stock market capitalization (% of GDP)	..	..	..
Military expenditures (% of GDP)	1.5	1.3	1.4
Mobile cellular subscriptions (per 100 people)	0.0	0.7	52.4
Individuals using the Internet (% of population)	0.0	0.3	5.0
Paved roads (% of total)	10.5	8.1	17.0
High-technology exports (% of manufactured exports)	3	1	5
Global links			
Merchandise trade (% of GDP)	31	36	44
Net barter terms of trade index (2000 = 100)	81	100	150
Total external debt stocks ($ billions)	6.6	10.6	3.1
Total debt service (% of exports)	20.5	20.8	3.5
Net migration (thousands)	24.8	-0.2	-19.0
Remittances received ($ millions)	23	30	115
Foreign direct investment, net inflows ($ millions)	-113	159	360
Net official development assistance received ($ millions)	444	377	623

Canada

Population (millions)	34.5	Population growth (%)	1.0
Surface area (1,000 sq. km)	9,985	Population living below $1.25 a day (%)	..
GNI, Atlas ($ billions)	1,570.9	GNI per capita, Atlas ($)	45,550
GNI, PPP ($ billions)	1,367.6	GNI per capita, PPP ($)	39,660

	1990	2000	2011
People			
Share of poorest 20% in nat'l consumption/income (%)	..	7.2	..
Life expectancy at birth (years)	77	79	81
Total fertility rate (births per woman)	1.8	1.5	1.6
Adolescent fertility rate (births per 1,000 women 15–19)	..	17	12
Contraceptive prevalence (% of married women 15–49)	..	74	..
Births attended by skilled health staff (% of total)	..	98	100
Under-five mortality rate (per 1,000 live births)	8	6	6
Child malnutrition, underweight (% of under age 5)	..	..	..
Child immunization, measles (% of ages 12–23 mos.)	89	96	98
Primary completion rate, total (% of relevant age group)	..	98	..
Gross secondary enrollment, total (% of relevant age group)	99	102	101
Ratio of girls to boys in primary & secondary school (%)	100	101	99
HIV prevalence rate (% population of ages 15–49)	0.2	0.3	0.3
Environment			
Forests (1,000 sq. km)	3,101	3,101	3,101
Deforestation (avg. annual %, 1990–2000 and 2000–2010)		0.0	0.0
Freshwater use (% of internal resources)	..	1.6	1.6
Access to improved water source (% total pop.)	100	100	100
Access to improved sanitation facilities (% total pop.)	100	100	100
Energy use per capita (kilograms of oil equivalent)	7,504	8,172	7,426
Carbon dioxide emissions per capita (metric tons)	16.2	17.4	15.2
Electricity use per capita (kilowatt-hours)	16,109	16,991	15,137
Economy			
GDP ($ billions)	583	725	1,736
GDP growth (annual %)	0.2	5.2	2.5
GDP implicit price deflator (annual % growth)	3.2	4.1	3.3
Value added in agriculture (% of GDP)	3	2	2
Value added in industry (% of GDP)	31	33	32
Value added in services (% of GDP)	66	65	66
Exports of goods and services (% of GDP)	26	46	31
Imports of goods and services (% of GDP)	26	40	32
Gross capital formation (% of GDP)	21	20	23
Central government revenue (% of GDP)	20.9	21.4	17.2
Central government cash surplus/deficit (% of GDP)	–5.1	2.3	–1.3
States and markets			
Starting a business (days)	..	3	5
Stock market capitalization (% of GDP)	41.5	116.1	109.8
Military expenditures (% of GDP)	2.0	1.1	1.4
Mobile cellular subscriptions (per 100 people)	2.1	28.5	79.7
Individuals using the Internet (% of population)	0.4	51.3	83.0
Paved roads (% of total)	35.0	39.9	..
High-technology exports (% of manufactured exports)	14	19	13
Global links			
Merchandise trade (% of GDP)	43	72	53
Net barter terms of trade index (2000 = 100)	..	100	122
Total external debt stocks ($ millions)	..	..	..
Total debt service (% of exports)	..	..	..
Net migration (thousands)	889	733	1,098
Remittances received ($ millions)	..	..	..
Foreign direct investment, net inflows ($ billions)	7.6	66.1	39.5
Net official development assistance received ($ millions)	..	..	..

Cape Verde

Population (thousands)	501	Population growth (%)	0.9
Surface area (1,000 sq. km)	4.0	Population living below $1.25 a day (%)	21.0
GNI, Atlas ($ billions)	1.8	GNI per capita, Atlas ($)	3,540
GNI, PPP ($ billions)	2.0	GNI per capita, PPP ($)	3,980

	1990	2000	2011
People			
Share of poorest 20% in nat'l consumption/income (%)	..	4.5	..
Life expectancy at birth (years)	65	69	74
Total fertility rate (births per woman)	5.3	3.7	2.3
Adolescent fertility rate (births per 1,000 women 15-19)	..	99	72
Contraceptive prevalence (% of married women 15-49)	24	53	..
Births attended by skilled health staff (% of total)	..	89	..
Under-five mortality rate (per 1,000 live births)	58	39	21
Child malnutrition, underweight (% of under age 5)	..	..	..
Child immunization, measles (% of ages 12-23 mos.)	79	86	96
Primary completion rate, total (% of relevant age group)	57	107	95
Gross secondary enrollment, total (% of relevant age group)	21	..	90
Ratio of girls to boys in primary & secondary school (%)	99	..	103
HIV prevalence rate (% population of ages 15-49)	0.8	1.0	1.0
Environment			
Forests (sq. km)	578	821	848
Deforestation (avg. annual %, 1990-2000 and 2000-2010)		-3.6	-0.4
Freshwater use (% of internal resources)	..	7.3	7.3
Access to improved water source (% total pop.)	80	83	88
Access to improved sanitation facilities (% total pop.)	35	44	61
Energy use per capita (kilograms of oil equivalent)	83	..	..
Carbon dioxide emissions per capita (metric tons)	0.3	0.4	0.6
Electricity use per capita (kilowatt-hours)	..	..	..
Economy			
GDP ($ millions)	307	539	1,901
GDP growth (annual %)	0.7	7.3	5.0
GDP implicit price deflator (annual % growth)	2.3	-1.9	3.9
Value added in agriculture (% of GDP)	14	13	10
Value added in industry (% of GDP)	21	15	18
Value added in services (% of GDP)	64	72	72
Exports of goods and services (% of GDP)	17	27	42
Imports of goods and services (% of GDP)	69	61	73
Gross capital formation (% of GDP)	44	31	37
Central government revenue (% of GDP)	..	..	27.7
Central government cash surplus/deficit (% of GDP)	..	..	-3.7
States and markets			
Starting a business (days)	..	..	11
Stock market capitalization (% of GDP)	..	..	..
Military expenditures (% of GDP)	1.0	1.3	0.5
Mobile cellular subscriptions (per 100 people)	0.0	4.5	79.2
Individuals using the Internet (% of population)	0.0	1.8	32.0
Paved roads (% of total)	78.0	69.0	..
High-technology exports (% of manufactured exports)	..	1	1
Global links			
Merchandise trade (% of GDP)	46	45	54
Net barter terms of trade index (2000 = 100)	100	100	106
Total external debt stocks ($ millions)	134	320	1,025
Total debt service (% of exports)	9.1	10.7	5.0
Net migration (thousands)	-34.0	-9.4	-17.3
Remittances received ($ millions)	59	87	177
Foreign direct investment, net inflows ($ millions)	0	33	105
Net official development assistance received ($ millions)	105	94	246

Cayman Islands

High income

Population (thousands)	57	Population growth (%)		0.9
Surface area (sq. km)	264	Population living below $1.25 a day (%)		..
GNI, Atlas ($ millions)	..	GNI per capita, Atlas ($)		..
GNI, PPP ($ millions)	..	GNI per capita, PPP ($)		..

	1990	2000	2011
People			
Share of poorest 20% in nat'l consumption/income (%)	..	..	..
Life expectancy at birth (years)	..	..	..
Total fertility rate (births per woman)	..	..	..
Adolescent fertility rate (births per 1,000 women 15–19)	..	..	..
Contraceptive prevalence (% of married women 15–49)	..	..	..
Births attended by skilled health staff (% of total)	..	..	..
Under-five mortality rate (per 1,000 live births)	..	..	..
Child malnutrition, underweight (% of under age 5)	..	..	..
Child immunization, measles (% of ages 12–23 mos.)	..	..	..
Primary completion rate, total (% of relevant age group)	..	107	..
Gross secondary enrollment, total (% of relevant age group)	..	99	..
Ratio of girls to boys in primary & secondary school (%)	..	94	..
HIV prevalence rate (% population of ages 15–49)	..	..	..
Environment			
Forests (sq. km)	124	124	127
Deforestation (avg. annual %, 1990–2000 and 2000–2010)		0.0	0.0
Freshwater use (% of internal resources)	..	..	..
Access to improved water source (% total pop.)	93	93	96
Access to improved sanitation facilities (% total pop.)	96	96	96
Energy use per capita (kilograms of oil equivalent)	..	..	..
Carbon dioxide emissions per capita (metric tons)	9.7	11.3	9.2
Electricity use per capita (kilowatt-hours)	..	..	..
Economy			
GDP ($ millions)	..	..	..
GDP growth (annual %)	..	..	..
GDP implicit price deflator (annual % growth)	..	..	..
Value added in agriculture (% of GDP)	..	..	..
Value added in industry (% of GDP)	..	..	..
Value added in services (% of GDP)	..	..	..
Exports of goods and services (% of GDP)	..	..	..
Imports of goods and services (% of GDP)	..	..	..
Gross capital formation (% of GDP)	..	..	..
Central government revenue (% of GDP)	..	..	..
Central government cash surplus/deficit (% of GDP)	..	..	..
States and markets			
Starting a business (days)	..	..	..
Stock market capitalization (% of GDP)	..	..	..
Military expenditures (% of GDP)		..	..
Mobile cellular subscriptions (per 100 people)	0.0	26.6	167.7
Individuals using the Internet (% of population)	0.0	..	69.5
Paved roads (% of total)	..	..	..
High-technology exports (% of manufactured exports)	..	..	..
Global links			
Merchandise trade (% of GDP)	..	..	..
Net barter terms of trade index (2000 = 100)	..	100	78
Total external debt stocks ($ millions)	..	..	..
Total debt service (% of exports)	..	..	..
Net migration (thousands)	..	..	..
Remittances received ($ millions)	..	..	..
Foreign direct investment, net inflows ($ billions)	0.0	7.6	7.4
Net official development assistance received ($ millions)	3.0	..	..

Central African Republic

Population (millions)	4.5	Population growth (%)	1.9
Surface area (1,000 sq. km)	623	Population living below $1.25 a day (%)	62.8
GNI, Atlas ($ billions)	2.1	GNI per capita, Atlas ($)	480
GNI, PPP ($ billions)	3.6	GNI per capita, PPP ($)	810

	1990	2000	2011
People			
Share of poorest 20% in nat'l consumption/income (%)	2.0	5.2	3.4
Life expectancy at birth (years)	49	44	48
Total fertility rate (births per woman)	5.8	5.4	4.5
Adolescent fertility rate (births per 1,000 women 15–19)	..	127	100
Contraceptive prevalence (% of married women 15–49)	..	28	15
Births attended by skilled health staff (% of total)	..	44	54
Under-five mortality rate (per 1,000 live births)	169	172	164
Child malnutrition, underweight (% of under age 5)	..	21.8	28.0
Child immunization, measles (% of ages 12–23 mos.)	82	36	62
Primary completion rate, total (% of relevant age group)	30	..	43
Gross secondary enrollment, total (% of relevant age group)	11	12	18
Ratio of girls to boys in primary & secondary school (%)	59	..	69
HIV prevalence rate (% population of ages 15–49)	8.6	8.5	4.6
Environment			
Forests (1,000 sq. km)	232	229	226
Deforestation (avg. annual %, 1990–2000 and 2000–2010)		0.1	0.1
Freshwater use (% of internal resources)	..	0.0	0.0
Access to improved water source (% total pop.)	58	63	67
Access to improved sanitation facilities (% total pop.)	11	22	34
Energy use per capita (kilograms of oil equivalent)	..	..	..
Carbon dioxide emissions per capita (metric tons)	0.07	0.07	0.05
Electricity use per capita (kilowatt-hours)	..	..	..
Economy			
GDP ($ millions)	1,488	914	2,195
GDP growth (annual %)	-2.1	-2.5	3.3
GDP implicit price deflator (annual % growth)	2.3	3.2	1.9
Value added in agriculture (% of GDP)	48	56	57
Value added in industry (% of GDP)	20	17	15
Value added in services (% of GDP)	33	27	28
Exports of goods and services (% of GDP)	15	21	12
Imports of goods and services (% of GDP)	28	25	23
Gross capital formation (% of GDP)	12	10	12
Central government revenue (% of GDP)	..	..	..
Central government cash surplus/deficit (% of GDP)	..	..	..
States and markets			
Starting a business (days)	..	22	22
Stock market capitalization (% of GDP)	..	..	..
Military expenditures (% of GDP)	1.5	1.1	2.6
Mobile cellular subscriptions (per 100 people)	0.0	0.1	40.6
Individuals using the Internet (% of population)	0.0	0.1	2.2
Paved roads (% of total)	..	2.7	6.8
High-technology exports (% of manufactured exports)	1	0	0
Global links			
Merchandise trade (% of GDP)	18	30	25
Net barter terms of trade index (2000 = 100)	238	100	82
Total external debt stocks ($ millions)	704	897	573
Total debt service (% of exports)	13.2	..	..
Net migration (thousands)	-41.0	11.3	5.0
Remittances received ($ millions)	0.1	..	..
Foreign direct investment, net inflows ($ millions)	1	1	109
Net official development assistance received ($ millions)	249	75	272

Chad

Sub-Saharan Africa		Low income	
Population (millions)	11.5	Population growth (%)	2.6
Surface area (1,000 sq. km)	1,284	Population living below $1.25 a day (%)	61.9
GNI, Atlas ($ billions)	8.3	GNI per capita, Atlas ($)	720
GNI, PPP ($ billions)	17.7	GNI per capita, PPP ($)	1,540

	1990	2000	2011
People			
Share of poorest 20% in nat'l consumption/income (%)	..	6.3	..
Life expectancy at birth (years)	51	48	50
Total fertility rate (births per woman)	6.7	6.6	5.9
Adolescent fertility rate (births per 1,000 women 15-19)	..	191	143
Contraceptive prevalence (% of married women 15-49)	..	8	5
Births attended by skilled health staff (% of total)	..	16	23
Under-five mortality rate (per 1,000 live births)	208	189	169
Child malnutrition, underweight (% of under age 5)	..	29.4	..
Child immunization, measles (% of ages 12-23 mos.)	32	28	28
Primary completion rate, total (% of relevant age group)	17	23	38
Gross secondary enrollment, total (% of relevant age group)	7	11	25
Ratio of girls to boys in primary & secondary school (%)	41	56	68
HIV prevalence rate (% population of ages 15-49)	2.3	3.7	3.1
Environment			
Forests (1,000 sq. km)	131	123	114
Deforestation (avg. annual %, 1990-2000 and 2000-2010)		0.6	0.7
Freshwater use (% of internal resources)	..	2.4	2.4
Access to improved water source (% total pop.)	39	45	51
Access to improved sanitation facilities (% total pop.)	8	10	13
Energy use per capita (kilograms of oil equivalent)	..	..	..
Carbon dioxide emissions per capita (metric tons)	0.02	0.02	0.04
Electricity use per capita (kilowatt-hours)	..	..	..
Economy			
GDP ($ billions)	1.7	1.4	10.6
GDP growth (annual %)	-4.2	-0.9	1.6
GDP implicit price deflator (annual % growth)	8.0	5.3	16.2
Value added in agriculture (% of GDP)	29	42	14
Value added in industry (% of GDP)	18	11	49
Value added in services (% of GDP)	53	46	38
Exports of goods and services (% of GDP)	13	17	41
Imports of goods and services (% of GDP)	28	35	25
Gross capital formation (% of GDP)	7	23	33
Central government revenue (% of GDP)	..	..	..
Central government cash surplus/deficit (% of GDP)	..	..	..
States and markets			
Starting a business (days)	..	64	62
Stock market capitalization (% of GDP)	..	..	..
Military expenditures (% of GDP)	3.3	1.9	2.3
Mobile cellular subscriptions (per 100 people)	0.0	0.1	31.8
Individuals using the Internet (% of population)	0.0	0.0	1.9
Paved roads (% of total)	0.8	0.8	..
High-technology exports (% of manufactured exports)	..	..	..
Global links			
Merchandise trade (% of GDP)	27	36	66
Net barter terms of trade index (2000 = 100)	112	100	209
Total external debt stocks ($ billions)	0.5	1.1	1.8
Total debt service (% of exports)	4.3	..	..
Net migration (thousands)	1.4	69.4	-75.0
Remittances received ($ millions)	0.8	..	..
Foreign direct investment, net inflows ($ millions)	9	115	1,855
Net official development assistance received ($ millions)	311	131	471

Channel Islands

Population (thousands)	154	Population growth (%)		0.3
Surface area (sq. km)	190	Population living below $1.25 a day (%)		..
GNI, Atlas ($ billions)	..	GNI per capita, Atlas ($)		..
GNI, PPP ($ millions)	..	GNI per capita, PPP ($)		..

	1990	2000	2011
People			
Share of poorest 20% in nat'l consumption/income (%)	..	..	..
Life expectancy at birth (years)	75	78	80
Total fertility rate (births per woman)	1.5	1.4	1.5
Adolescent fertility rate (births per 1,000 women 15–19)	..	13	9
Contraceptive prevalence (% of married women 15–49)	..	..	..
Births attended by skilled health staff (% of total)	..	..	..
Under-five mortality rate (per 1,000 live births)	..	..	..
Child malnutrition, underweight (% of under age 5)	..	..	..
Child immunization, measles (% of ages 12–23 mos.)	..	..	..
Primary completion rate, total (% of relevant age group)	..	..	..
Gross secondary enrollment, total (% of relevant age group)	..	..	..
Ratio of girls to boys in primary & secondary school (%)	..	..	..
HIV prevalence rate (% population of ages 15–49)	..	..	..
Environment			
Forests (sq. km)	8.0	8.0	8.0
Deforestation (avg. annual %, 1990–2000 and 2000–2010)		..	..
Freshwater use (% of internal resources)	..	..	..
Access to improved water source (% total pop.)	..	..	..
Access to improved sanitation facilities (% total pop.)	..	..	..
Energy use per capita (kilograms of oil equivalent)	..	..	..
Carbon dioxide emissions per capita (metric tons)	..	..	..
Electricity use per capita (kilowatt-hours)	..	..	..
Economy			
GDP ($ billions)	..	6.4	..
GDP growth (annual %)	..	5.8	..
GDP implicit price deflator (annual % growth)	..	3.9	..
Value added in agriculture (% of GDP)	..	..	..
Value added in industry (% of GDP)	..	..	..
Value added in services (% of GDP)	..	..	..
Exports of goods and services (% of GDP)	..	..	..
Imports of goods and services (% of GDP)	..	..	..
Gross capital formation (% of GDP)	..	..	..
Central government revenue (% of GDP)	..	..	..
Central government cash surplus/deficit (% of GDP)	..	..	..
States and markets			
Starting a business (days)	..	..	..
Stock market capitalization (% of GDP)	..	..	..
Military expenditures (% of GDP)	..	..	..
Mobile cellular subscriptions (per 100 people)	..	..	..
Individuals using the Internet (% of population)	..	..	..
Paved roads (% of total)	..	..	..
High-technology exports (% of manufactured exports)	..	..	..
Global links			
Merchandise trade (% of GDP)	..	..	..
Net barter terms of trade index (2000 = 100)	..	..	..
Total external debt stocks ($ millions)	..	..	..
Total debt service (% of exports)	..	..	..
Net migration (thousands)	6.1	2.8	4.5
Remittances received ($ millions)	..	..	..
Foreign direct investment, net inflows ($ millions)	..	..	..
Net official development assistance received ($ millions)	..	..	..

Chile

Latin America & Caribbean		Upper middle income	
Population (millions)	17.3	Population growth (%)	0.9
Surface area (1,000 sq. km)	756	Population living below $1.25 a day (%)	<2
GNI, Atlas ($ billions)	212.0	GNI per capita, Atlas ($)	12,280
GNI, PPP ($ billions)	282.1	GNI per capita, PPP ($)	16,330

	1990	2000	2011
People			
Share of poorest 20% in nat'l consumption/income (%)	3.6	3.7	4.3
Life expectancy at birth (years)	74	77	79
Total fertility rate (births per woman)	2.6	2.1	1.8
Adolescent fertility rate (births per 1,000 women 15-19)	..	64	56
Contraceptive prevalence (% of married women 15-49)	56	61	58
Births attended by skilled health staff (% of total)	99	100	100
Under-five mortality rate (per 1,000 live births)	19	11	9
Child malnutrition, underweight (% of under age 5)	..	0.7	0.5
Child immunization, measles (% of ages 12-23 mos.)	97	97	91
Primary completion rate, total (% of relevant age group)	..	98	99
Gross secondary enrollment, total (% of relevant age group)	78	83	89
Ratio of girls to boys in primary & secondary school (%)	101	100	100
HIV prevalence rate (% population of ages 15-49)	0.1	0.4	0.5
Environment			
Forests (1,000 sq. km)	153	158	163
Deforestation (avg. annual %, 1990-2000 and 2000-2010)		-0.4	-0.2
Freshwater use (% of internal resources)	2.3	1.3	1.3
Access to improved water source (% total pop.)	90	94	96
Access to improved sanitation facilities (% total pop.)	84	92	96
Energy use per capita (kilograms of oil equivalent)	1,062	1,633	1,877
Carbon dioxide emissions per capita (metric tons)	2.6	3.8	3.9
Electricity use per capita (kilowatt-hours)	1,246	2,487	3,297
Economy			
GDP ($ billions)	32	79	249
GDP growth (annual %)	3.7	4.5	6.0
GDP implicit price deflator (annual % growth)	22.5	10.3	2.8
Value added in agriculture (% of GDP)	9	6	3
Value added in industry (% of GDP)	41	32	39
Value added in services (% of GDP)	50	62	57
Exports of goods and services (% of GDP)	34	29	38
Imports of goods and services (% of GDP)	31	29	35
Gross capital formation (% of GDP)	25	23	25
Central government revenue (% of GDP)	..	20.5	22.9
Central government cash surplus/deficit (% of GDP)	..	-0.6	1.3
States and markets			
Starting a business (days)	..	27	8
Stock market capitalization (% of GDP)	43.1	76.1	108.7
Military expenditures (% of GDP)	4.2	3.6	3.2
Mobile cellular subscriptions (per 100 people)	0.1	22.1	129.7
Individuals using the Internet (% of population)	0.0	16.6	53.9
Paved roads (% of total)	13.8	18.4	23.3
High-technology exports (% of manufactured exports)	5	3	5
Global links			
Merchandise trade (% of GDP)	51	48	63
Net barter terms of trade index (2000 = 100)	114	100	213
Total external debt stocks ($ billions)	19.3	37.4	96.2
Total debt service (% of exports)	26.0	24.8	15.2
Net migration (thousands)	-40.0	60.0	30.0
Remittances received ($ millions)	0.4	13.3	4.1
Foreign direct investment, net inflows ($ billions)	0.7	4.9	17.3
Net official development assistance received ($ millions)	104	49	82

China

East Asia & Pacific		Upper middle income	
Population (millions)	1,344.1	Population growth (%)	0.5
Surface area (1,000 sq. km)	9,600	Population living below $1.25 a day (%)	*11.8*
GNI, Atlas ($ billions)	6,643.2	GNI per capita, Atlas ($)	4,940
GNI, PPP ($ billions)	11,270.8	GNI per capita, PPP ($)	8,390

	1990	2000	2011
People			
Share of poorest 20% in nat'l consumption/income (%)	8.0	*6.4*	..
Life expectancy at birth (years)[a]	69	71	73
Total fertility rate (births per woman)	2.3	1.7	1.6
Adolescent fertility rate (births per 1,000 women 15–19)	..	8	9
Contraceptive prevalence (% of married women 15–49)	85	84	85
Births attended by skilled health staff (% of total)	94	97	*100*
Under-five mortality rate (per 1,000 live births)	49	35	15
Child malnutrition, underweight (% of under age 5)	12.6	7.4	*3.4*
Child immunization, measles (% of ages 12–23 mos.)	98	84	99
Primary completion rate, total (% of relevant age group)	109	..	..
Gross secondary enrollment, total (% of relevant age group)	38	62	81
Ratio of girls to boys in primary & secondary school (%)	85	99	104
HIV prevalence rate (% population of ages 15–49)	..	..	0.1[b]
Environment			
Forests (1,000 sq. km)	1,571	1,770	2,096
Deforestation (avg. annual %, 1990–2000 and 2000–2010)		-1.2	-1.6
Freshwater use (% of internal resources)	*17.8*	18.7	19.7
Access to improved water source (% total pop.)	67	80	91
Access to improved sanitation facilities (% total pop.)	24	44	*64*
Energy use per capita (kilograms of oil equivalent)	768	937	*1,807*
Carbon dioxide emissions per capita (metric tons)	2.2	2.7	5.8
Electricity use per capita (kilowatt-hours)	511	993	*2,944*
Economy			
GDP ($ billions)	357	1,198	7,318
GDP growth (annual %)	3.8	8.4	9.3
GDP implicit price deflator (annual % growth)	5.8	2.1	7.8
Value added in agriculture (% of GDP)	27	15	10
Value added in industry (% of GDP)	41	46	47
Value added in services (% of GDP)	32	39	43
Exports of goods and services (% of GDP)	16	23	31
Imports of goods and services (% of GDP)	13	21	27
Gross capital formation (% of GDP)	36	35	48
Central government revenue (% of GDP)	6.3	7.1	*11.5*
Central government cash surplus/deficit (% of GDP)	..	-2.6	..
States and markets			
Starting a business (days)	..	48	33
Stock market capitalization (% of GDP)	*0.5*	48.5	46.3
Military expenditures (% of GDP)	2.6	1.9[c]	2.0[c]
Mobile cellular subscriptions (per 100 people)	0.0	6.7	73.2
Individuals using the Internet (% of population)	0.0	1.8	38.3
Paved roads (% of total)	..	..	53.5
High-technology exports (% of manufactured exports)	6	19	26
Global links			
Merchandise trade (% of GDP)	32	40	50
Net barter terms of trade index (2000 = 100)	102	100	73
Total external debt stocks ($ billions)	55	146	685
Total debt service (% of exports)	11.7	9.1	3.6
Net migration (thousands)	-236	-677	-1,884
Remittances received ($ billions)	0.2	4.8	40.5
Foreign direct investment, net inflows ($ billions)	3	38	220
Net official development assistance received ($ billions)	2.0	1.7	-0.8

Colombia

Latin America & Caribbean		Upper middle income	
Population (millions)	46.9	Population growth (%)	1.4
Surface area (1,000 sq. km)	1,142	Population living below $1.25 a day (%)	8.2
GNI, Atlas ($ billions)	284.9	GNI per capita, Atlas ($)	6,070
GNI, PPP ($ billions)	448.6	GNI per capita, PPP ($)	9,560

	1990	2000	2011
People			
Share of poorest 20% in nat'l consumption/income (%)	3.6	1.9	3.0
Life expectancy at birth (years)	68	71	74
Total fertility rate (births per woman)	3.1	2.6	2.1
Adolescent fertility rate (births per 1,000 women 15-19)	..	94	69
Contraceptive prevalence (% of married women 15-49)	66	77	79
Births attended by skilled health staff (% of total)	94	86	99
Under-five mortality rate (per 1,000 live births)	34	25	18
Child malnutrition, underweight (% of under age 5)	8.8	4.9	3.4
Child immunization, measles (% of ages 12-23 mos.)	82	80	88
Primary completion rate, total (% of relevant age group)	74	95	112
Gross secondary enrollment, total (% of relevant age group)	53	72	97
Ratio of girls to boys in primary & secondary school (%)	108	104	103
HIV prevalence rate (% population of ages 15-49)	0.3	0.5	0.5
Environment			
Forests (1,000 sq. km)	625	615	604
Deforestation (avg. annual %, 1990-2000 and 2000-2010)		0.2	0.2
Freshwater use (% of internal resources)	..	0.6	0.6
Access to improved water source (% total pop.)	89	91	92
Access to improved sanitation facilities (% total pop.)	67	73	77
Energy use per capita (kilograms of oil equivalent)	730	649	696
Carbon dioxide emissions per capita (metric tons)	1.7	1.5	1.6
Electricity use per capita (kilowatt-hours)	869	843	1,012
Economy			
GDP ($ billions)	40	100	333
GDP growth (annual %)	6.0	4.4	5.9
GDP implicit price deflator (annual % growth)	26.1	31.8	6.9
Value added in agriculture (% of GDP)	17	9	7
Value added in industry (% of GDP)	38	29	38
Value added in services (% of GDP)	45	62	55
Exports of goods and services (% of GDP)	21	16	19
Imports of goods and services (% of GDP)	15	17	20
Gross capital formation (% of GDP)	19	15	23
Central government revenue (% of GDP)	..	15.2	17.2
Central government cash surplus/deficit (% of GDP)	..	-5.8	0.3
States and markets			
Starting a business (days)	..	60	13
Stock market capitalization (% of GDP)	3.5	9.6	60.4
Military expenditures (% of GDP)	2.2	3.0	3.3
Mobile cellular subscriptions (per 100 people)	0.0	5.7	98.5
Individuals using the Internet (% of population)	0.0	2.2	40.4
Paved roads (% of total)	11.9	14.4	..
High-technology exports (% of manufactured exports)	5	8	4
Global links			
Merchandise trade (% of GDP)	31	25	33
Net barter terms of trade index (2000 = 100)	81	100	142
Total external debt stocks ($ billions)	17.4	33.2	76.9
Total debt service (% of exports)	43.3	29.8	15.6
Net migration (thousands)	-235	-150	-120
Remittances received ($ billions)	0.5	1.6	4.2
Foreign direct investment, net inflows ($ billions)	0.5	2.4	13.6
Net official development assistance received ($ millions)	89	186	1,130

Comoros

Population (thousands)	754	Population growth (%)		2.6
Surface area (1,000 sq. km)	1.9	Population living below $1.25 a day (%)		46.1
GNI, Atlas ($ millions)	581.0	GNI per capita, Atlas ($)		770
GNI, PPP ($ millions)	836.2	GNI per capita, PPP ($)		1,110

	1990	2000	2011
People			
Share of poorest 20% in nat'l consumption/income (%)	..	2.6	..
Life expectancy at birth (years)	56	58	61
Total fertility rate (births per woman)	5.6	5.3	4.9
Adolescent fertility rate (births per 1,000 women 15–19)	..	65	52
Contraceptive prevalence (% of married women 15–49)	..	26	..
Births attended by skilled health staff (% of total)	..	62	..
Under-five mortality rate (per 1,000 live births)	122	100	79
Child malnutrition, underweight (% of under age 5)	16.2	25.0	..
Child immunization, measles (% of ages 12–23 mos.)	87	70	72
Primary completion rate, total (% of relevant age group)	40	50	75
Gross secondary enrollment, total (% of relevant age group)	22	29	..
Ratio of girls to boys in primary & secondary school (%)	..	84	..
HIV prevalence rate (% population of ages 15–49)	0.1	0.1	0.1
Environment			
Forests (sq. km)	120	80	26
Deforestation (avg. annual %, 1990–2000 and 2000–2010)		4.0	9.3
Freshwater use (% of internal resources)	..	0.8	0.8
Access to improved water source (% total pop.)	87	92	95
Access to improved sanitation facilities (% total pop.)	17	28	36
Energy use per capita (kilograms of oil equivalent)	41	..	..
Carbon dioxide emissions per capita (metric tons)	0.2	0.1	0.2
Electricity use per capita (kilowatt-hours)	..	..	..
Economy			
GDP ($ millions)	250	202	610
GDP growth (annual %)	5.1	1.4	2.2
GDP implicit price deflator (annual % growth)	2.2	3.4	4.7
Value added in agriculture (% of GDP)	41	49	46
Value added in industry (% of GDP)	8	12	12
Value added in services (% of GDP)	50	40	42
Exports of goods and services (% of GDP)	14	17	15
Imports of goods and services (% of GDP)	37	33	52
Gross capital formation (% of GDP)	20	10	12
Central government revenue (% of GDP)	..	..	..
Central government cash surplus/deficit (% of GDP)	..	..	..
States and markets			
Starting a business (days)	..	..	20
Stock market capitalization (% of GDP)	..	..	..
Military expenditures (% of GDP)	..	..	..
Mobile cellular subscriptions (per 100 people)	0.0	0.0	28.7
Individuals using the Internet (% of population)	0.0	0.3	5.5
Paved roads (% of total)	69.3	76.5	..
High-technology exports (% of manufactured exports)	..	0	..
Global links			
Merchandise trade (% of GDP)	28	28	49
Net barter terms of trade index (2000 = 100)	86	100	76
Total external debt stocks ($ millions)	185	227	278
Total debt service (% of exports)	2.9	..	14.9
Net migration (thousands)	-4.5	-6.0	-10.0
Remittances received ($ millions)	9.9	..	..
Foreign direct investment, net inflows ($ millions)	0.4	0.1	6.8
Net official development assistance received ($ millions)	44.9	18.7	51.6

Congo, Dem. Rep.

Sub-Saharan Africa		Low income	
Population (millions)	67.8	Population growth (%)	2.7
Surface area (1,000 sq. km)	2,345	Population living below $1.25 a day (%)	87.7
GNI, Atlas ($ billions)	13.1	GNI per capita, Atlas ($)	190
GNI, PPP ($ billions)	23.2	GNI per capita, PPP ($)	340

	1990	2000	2011
People			
Share of poorest 20% in nat'l consumption/income (%)	..	..	5.5
Life expectancy at birth (years)	47	46	48
Total fertility rate (births per woman)	7.1	6.9	5.7
Adolescent fertility rate (births per 1,000 women 15-19)	..	235	177
Contraceptive prevalence (% of married women 15-49)	8	31	17
Births attended by skilled health staff (% of total)	..	61	80
Under-five mortality rate (per 1,000 live births)	181	181	168
Child malnutrition, underweight (% of under age 5)	..	33.6	28.2
Child immunization, measles (% of ages 12-23 mos.)	38	46	71
Primary completion rate, total (% of relevant age group)	49	32	59
Gross secondary enrollment, total (% of relevant age group)	22	..	40
Ratio of girls to boys in primary & secondary school (%)	70	..	79
HIV prevalence rate (% population of ages 15-49)	..	..	..
Environment			
Forests (1,000 sq. km)	1,604	1,572	1,538
Deforestation (avg. annual %, 1990-2000 and 2000-2010)		0.2	0.2
Freshwater use (% of internal resources)	..	0.1	0.1
Access to improved water source (% total pop.)	45	44	45
Access to improved sanitation facilities (% total pop.)	9	16	24
Energy use per capita (kilograms of oil equivalent)	324	336	360
Carbon dioxide emissions per capita (metric tons)	0.11	0.03	0.04
Electricity use per capita (kilowatt-hours)	124	92	95
Economy			
GDP ($ billions)	9.3	4.3	15.7
GDP growth (annual %)	-6.6	-6.9	6.9
GDP implicit price deflator (annual % growth)	109.0	515.8	13.4
Value added in agriculture (% of GDP)	31	50	46
Value added in industry (% of GDP)	29	20	22
Value added in services (% of GDP)	40	30	33
Exports of goods and services (% of GDP)	30	22	68
Imports of goods and services (% of GDP)	29	21	78
Gross capital formation (% of GDP)	9	3	21
Central government revenue (% of GDP)	10.1	3.7	23.5
Central government cash surplus/deficit (% of GDP)	-6.5	-4.2	3.8
States and markets			
Starting a business (days)	..	166	58
Stock market capitalization (% of GDP)	..	..	..
Military expenditures (% of GDP)	..	1.0	1.5
Mobile cellular subscriptions (per 100 people)	0.0	0.0	23.1
Individuals using the Internet (% of population)	0.0	0.0	1.2
Paved roads (% of total)	..	1.8	..
High-technology exports (% of manufactured exports)	..	..	..
Global links			
Merchandise trade (% of GDP)	43	35	77
Net barter terms of trade index (2000 = 100)	86	100	147
Total external debt stocks ($ billions)	10.3	11.8	5.4
Total debt service (% of exports)	..	..	2.4
Net migration (thousands)	75	-1,501	-24
Remittances received ($ millions)	..	..	115
Foreign direct investment, net inflows ($ millions)	-14	72	1,596
Net official development assistance received ($ millions)	896	177	5,522

Congo, Rep.

Sub-Saharan Africa   **Lower middle income**

Population (millions)	4.1	Population growth (%)	2.4
Surface area (1,000 sq. km)	342	Population living below $1.25 a day (%)	54.1
GNI, Atlas ($ billions)	9.3	GNI per capita, Atlas ($)	2,250
GNI, PPP ($ billions)	13.4	GNI per capita, PPP ($)	3,240

	1990	2000	2011
People			
Share of poorest 20% in nat'l consumption/income (%)	..	..	..
Life expectancy at birth (years)	56	54	57
Total fertility rate (births per woman)	5.4	4.9	4.5
Adolescent fertility rate (births per 1,000 women 15–19)	..	130	114
Contraceptive prevalence (% of married women 15–49)	..	..	..
Births attended by skilled health staff (% of total)	..	..	..
Under-five mortality rate (per 1,000 live births)	119	109	99
Child malnutrition, underweight (% of under age 5)	..	..	..
Child immunization, measles (% of ages 12–23 mos.)	75	34	90
Primary completion rate, total (% of relevant age group)	60	57	71
Gross secondary enrollment, total (% of relevant age group)	49	36	..
Ratio of girls to boys in primary & secondary school (%)	89	86	..
HIV prevalence rate (% population of ages 15–49)	5.1	3.9	3.3
Environment			
Forests (1,000 sq. km)	227	226	224
Deforestation (avg. annual %, 1990–2000 and 2000–2010)		0.1	0.1
Freshwater use (% of internal resources)	..	0.0	0.0
Access to improved water source (% total pop.)	..	70	71
Access to improved sanitation facilities (% total pop.)	..	20	18
Energy use per capita (kilograms of oil equivalent)	325	260	363
Carbon dioxide emissions per capita (metric tons)	0.5	0.3	0.5
Electricity use per capita (kilowatt-hours)	172	95	145
Economy			
GDP ($ billions)	2.8	3.2	14.4
GDP growth (annual %)	1.0	7.6	3.4
GDP implicit price deflator (annual % growth)	-1.0	47.0	10.7
Value added in agriculture (% of GDP)	13	5	3
Value added in industry (% of GDP)	41	72	77
Value added in services (% of GDP)	46	23	20
Exports of goods and services (% of GDP)	54	80	87
Imports of goods and services (% of GDP)	-17	44	35
Gross capital formation (% of GDP)	16	23	25
Central government revenue (% of GDP)	22.5	28.6	..
Central government cash surplus/deficit (% of GDP)	-13.1	1.9	..
States and markets			
Starting a business (days)	..	37	161
Stock market capitalization (% of GDP)	..	..	..
Military expenditures (% of GDP)	..	1.4	1.1
Mobile cellular subscriptions (per 100 people)	0.0	2.2	93.8
Individuals using the Internet (% of population)	0.0	0.0	5.6
Paved roads (% of total)	9.7	9.7	7.1
High-technology exports (% of manufactured exports)	5	..	4
Global links			
Merchandise trade (% of GDP)	57	92	110
Net barter terms of trade index (2000 = 100)	63	100	215
Total external debt stocks ($ billions)	4.9	4.9	2.5
Total debt service (% of exports)	34.6	1.7	..
Net migration (thousands)	1.1	35.3	49.9
Remittances received ($ millions)	4.4	10.4	..
Foreign direct investment, net inflows ($ millions)	23	166	2,931
Net official development assistance received ($ millions)	217	32	254

Costa Rica

Population (millions)	4.7	Population growth (%)	1.4
Surface area (1,000 sq. km)	51	Population living below $1.25 a day (%)	3.1
GNI, Atlas ($ billions)	36.1	GNI per capita, Atlas ($)	7,640
GNI, PPP ($ billions)	56.1	GNI per capita, PPP ($)	11,860

	1990	2000	2011
People			
Share of poorest 20% in nat'l consumption/income (%)	3.8	4.0	3.9
Life expectancy at birth (years)	76	78	79
Total fertility rate (births per woman)	3.2	2.4	1.8
Adolescent fertility rate (births per 1,000 women 15-19)	..	81	63
Contraceptive prevalence (% of married women 15-49)	75	80	82
Births attended by skilled health staff (% of total)	98	98	99
Under-five mortality rate (per 1,000 live births)	17	13	10
Child malnutrition, underweight (% of under age 5)	2.5	..	1.1
Child immunization, measles (% of ages 12-23 mos.)	90	82	83
Primary completion rate, total (% of relevant age group)	75	87	99
Gross secondary enrollment, total (% of relevant age group)	43	61	101
Ratio of girls to boys in primary & secondary school (%)	100	101	102
HIV prevalence rate (% population of ages 15-49)	0.1	0.2	0.3
Environment			
Forests (1,000 sq. km)	26	24	26
Deforestation (avg. annual %, 1990-2000 and 2000-2010)		0.8	-0.9
Freshwater use (% of internal resources)	..	2.4	2.4
Access to improved water source (% total pop.)	93	95	97
Access to improved sanitation facilities (% total pop.)	93	95	95
Energy use per capita (kilograms of oil equivalent)	660	755	998
Carbon dioxide emissions per capita (metric tons)	1.0	1.4	1.8
Electricity use per capita (kilowatt-hours)	1,089	1,524	1,855
Economy			
GDP ($ billions)	7.4	15.9	40.9
GDP growth (annual %)	3.9	1.8	4.2
GDP implicit price deflator (annual % growth)	17.1	7.0	4.1
Value added in agriculture (% of GDP)	12	9	6
Value added in industry (% of GDP)	30	32	26
Value added in services (% of GDP)	58	58	68
Exports of goods and services (% of GDP)	30	49	37
Imports of goods and services (% of GDP)	36	46	42
Gross capital formation (% of GDP)	18	17	21
Central government revenue (% of GDP)	..	..	24.4
Central government cash surplus/deficit (% of GDP)	..	..	-3.5
States and markets			
Starting a business (days)	..	77	60
Stock market capitalization (% of GDP)	5.5	18.3	3.5
Military expenditures (% of GDP)	..		
Mobile cellular subscriptions (per 100 people)	0.0	5.4	92.2
Individuals using the Internet (% of population)	0.0	5.8	42.1
Paved roads (% of total)	15.3	22.0	26.0
High-technology exports (% of manufactured exports)	..	52	41
Global links			
Merchandise trade (% of GDP)	46	77	65
Net barter terms of trade index (2000 = 100)	75	100	78
Total external debt stocks ($ billions)	3.8	4.7	10.3
Total debt service (% of exports)	24.5	8.2	13.5
Net migration (thousands)	25	128	76
Remittances received ($ millions)	12	136	520
Foreign direct investment, net inflows ($ millions)	163	409	2,157
Net official development assistance received ($ millions)	227	10	38

Côte d'Ivoire

Sub-Saharan Africa		Lower middle income	
Population (millions)	20.2	Population growth (%)	2.1
Surface area (1,000 sq. km)	322	Population living below $1.25 a day (%)	23.8
GNI, Atlas ($ billions)	22.1	GNI per capita, Atlas ($)	1,090
GNI, PPP ($ billions)	34.5	GNI per capita, PPP ($)	1,710

	1990	2000	2011
People			
Share of poorest 20% in nat'l consumption/income (%)	7.1	5.0	5.6
Life expectancy at birth (years)	53	50	55
Total fertility rate (births per woman)	6.3	5.2	4.3
Adolescent fertility rate (births per 1,000 women 15-19)	..	135	110
Contraceptive prevalence (% of married women 15-49)	..	15	13
Births attended by skilled health staff (% of total)	..	63	57
Under-five mortality rate (per 1,000 live births)	151	139	115
Child malnutrition, underweight (% of under age 5)	..	18.2	29.4
Child immunization, measles (% of ages 12-23 mos.)	56	68	49
Primary completion rate, total (% of relevant age group)	40	43	59
Gross secondary enrollment, total (% of relevant age group)	..	24	..
Ratio of girls to boys in primary & secondary school (%)	..	69	..
HIV prevalence rate (% population of ages 15-49)	5.8	6.6	3.0
Environment			
Forests (1,000 sq. km)	102	103	104
Deforestation (avg. annual %, 1990-2000 and 2000-2010)		-0.1	-0.2
Freshwater use (% of internal resources)	1.4	1.8	1.8
Access to improved water source (% total pop.)	76	77	80
Access to improved sanitation facilities (% total pop.)	20	22	24
Energy use per capita (kilograms of oil equivalent)	429	406	485
Carbon dioxide emissions per capita (metric tons)	0.5	0.4	0.3
Electricity use per capita (kilowatt-hours)	153	173	210
Economy			
GDP ($ billions)	10.8	10.4	24.1
GDP growth (annual %)	-1.1	-3.7	-4.7
GDP implicit price deflator (annual % growth)	-4.5	-0.4	5.0
Value added in agriculture (% of GDP)	32	24	24
Value added in industry (% of GDP)	23	25	30
Value added in services (% of GDP)	44	51	55
Exports of goods and services (% of GDP)	32	40	44
Imports of goods and services (% of GDP)	27	33	41
Gross capital formation (% of GDP)	7	11	16
Central government revenue (% of GDP)	..	..	..
Central government cash surplus/deficit (% of GDP)	..	..	..
States and markets			
Starting a business (days)	..	62	32
Stock market capitalization (% of GDP)	5.1	11.4	26.1
Military expenditures (% of GDP)	1.3	1.6	1.5
Mobile cellular subscriptions (per 100 people)	0.0	2.9	86.1
Individuals using the Internet (% of population)	0.0	0.2	2.2
Paved roads (% of total)	8.7	9.7	7.9
High-technology exports (% of manufactured exports)	..	3	15
Global links			
Merchandise trade (% of GDP)	48	61	74
Net barter terms of trade index (2000 = 100)	143	100	159
Total external debt stocks ($ billions)	17.3	12.2	12.0
Total debt service (% of exports)	35.4	22.7	4.7
Net migration (thousands)	325	90	-360
Remittances received ($ millions)	44	119	373
Foreign direct investment, net inflows ($ millions)	48	235	344
Net official development assistance received ($ millions)	686	351	1,437

Croatia

High income

Population (millions)	4.4	Population growth (%)		-0.3
Surface area (1,000 sq. km)	57	Population living below $1.25 a day (%)		<2
GNI, Atlas ($ billions)	59.6	GNI per capita, Atlas ($)		13,540
GNI, PPP ($ billions)	82.7	GNI per capita, PPP ($)		18,780

	1990	2000	2011
People			
Share of poorest 20% in nat'l consumption/income (%)	10.3	8.3	8.1
Life expectancy at birth (years)	72	73	77
Total fertility rate (births per woman)	1.6	1.4	1.5
Adolescent fertility rate (births per 1,000 women 15–19)	..	16	13
Contraceptive prevalence (% of married women 15–49)	..	69	..
Births attended by skilled health staff (% of total)	100	100	100
Under-five mortality rate (per 1,000 live births)	13	8	5
Child malnutrition, underweight (% of under age 5)	0.4	..	..
Child immunization, measles (% of ages 12–23 mos.)	90	93	96
Primary completion rate, total (% of relevant age group)	..	93	93
Gross secondary enrollment, total (% of relevant age group)	83	85	96
Ratio of girls to boys in primary & secondary school (%)	102	101	105
HIV prevalence rate (% population of ages 15–49)	0.1	0.1	0.1
Environment			
Forests (1,000 sq. km)	19	19	19
Deforestation (avg. annual %, 1990–2000 and 2000–2010)		-0.2	-0.2
Freshwater use (% of internal resources)	..	..	1.7
Access to improved water source (% total pop.)	99	99	99
Access to improved sanitation facilities (% total pop.)	99	99	99
Energy use per capita (kilograms of oil equivalent)	1,882	1,756	1,932
Carbon dioxide emissions per capita (metric tons)	3.7	4.4	4.9
Electricity use per capita (kilowatt-hours)	2,991	2,840	3,813
Economy			
GDP ($ billions)	24.8	21.5	62.5
GDP growth (annual %)	..	3.8	0.0
GDP implicit price deflator (annual % growth)	..	4.6	2.1
Value added in agriculture (% of GDP)	11	6	5
Value added in industry (% of GDP)	36	29	26
Value added in services (% of GDP)	53	65	68
Exports of goods and services (% of GDP)	78	42	42
Imports of goods and services (% of GDP)	86	45	42
Gross capital formation (% of GDP)	12	19	21
Central government revenue (% of GDP)	33.0	35.7	32.8
Central government cash surplus/deficit (% of GDP)	-4.6	-5.3	-4.6
States and markets			
Starting a business (days)	..	29	9
Stock market capitalization (% of GDP)	..	12.7	34.9
Military expenditures (% of GDP)	7.6	3.1	1.7
Mobile cellular subscriptions (per 100 people)	0.0	22.9	116.4
Individuals using the Internet (% of population)	0.0	6.6	70.7
Paved roads (% of total)	..	85.4	90.7
High-technology exports (% of manufactured exports)	6	9	8
Global links			
Merchandise trade (% of GDP)	88	57	58
Net barter terms of trade index (2000 = 100)	..	100	99
Total external debt stocks ($ millions)	..	..	..
Total debt service (% of exports)	..	..	..
Net migration (thousands)	7	-160	10
Remittances received ($ millions)	230	641	1,378
Foreign direct investment, net inflows ($ billions)	0.0	1.1	1.3
Net official development assistance received ($ millions)	0	66	151

Cuba

Latin America & Caribbean		Upper middle income	
Population (millions)	11.3	Population growth (%)	0.0
Surface area (1,000 sq. km)	110	Population living below $1.25 a day (%)	..
GNI, Atlas ($ billions)	61.5	GNI per capita, Atlas ($)	5,460
GNI, PPP ($ millions)	..	GNI per capita, PPP ($)	..

	1990	2000	2011
People			
Share of poorest 20% in nat'l consumption/income (%)	..	..	..
Life expectancy at birth (years)	74	76	79
Total fertility rate (births per woman)	1.8	1.6	1.5
Adolescent fertility rate (births per 1,000 women 15–19)	..	57	44
Contraceptive prevalence (% of married women 15–49)	..	73	74
Births attended by skilled health staff (% of total)	100	100	100
Under-five mortality rate (per 1,000 live births)	13	9	6
Child malnutrition, underweight (% of under age 5)	..	3.4	..
Child immunization, measles (% of ages 12–23 mos.)	94	94	99
Primary completion rate, total (% of relevant age group)	94	96	99
Gross secondary enrollment, total (% of relevant age group)	89	83	90
Ratio of girls to boys in primary & secondary school (%)	105	100	98
HIV prevalence rate (% population of ages 15–49)	0.1	0.1	0.2
Environment			
Forests (1,000 sq. km)	21	24	29
Deforestation (avg. annual %, 1990–2000 and 2000–2010)		-1.7	-1.7
Freshwater use (% of internal resources)	..	19.8	19.8
Access to improved water source (% total pop.)	82	90	94
Access to improved sanitation facilities (% total pop.)	80	86	91
Energy use per capita (kilograms of oil equivalent)	1,673	1,158	975
Carbon dioxide emissions per capita (metric tons)	3.2	2.3	2.8
Electricity use per capita (kilowatt-hours)	1,215	1,140	1,299
Economy			
GDP ($ billions)	28.6	30.6	60.8
GDP growth (annual %)	-2.9	5.9	2.1
GDP implicit price deflator (annual % growth)	5.3	1.7	1.0
Value added in agriculture (% of GDP)	14	8	5
Value added in industry (% of GDP)	19	28	21
Value added in services (% of GDP)	67	64	74
Exports of goods and services (% of GDP)	30	14	20
Imports of goods and services (% of GDP)	41	17	19
Gross capital formation (% of GDP)	25	13	12
Central government revenue (% of GDP)	..	..	..
Central government cash surplus/deficit (% of GDP)	..	..	..
States and markets			
Starting a business (days)	..	..	..
Stock market capitalization (% of GDP)	..	..	..
Military expenditures (% of GDP)	6.4	3.5	3.3
Mobile cellular subscriptions (per 100 people)	0.0	0.1	11.7
Individuals using the Internet (% of population)	0.0	0.5	23.2
Paved roads (% of total)	50.5	49.0	..
High-technology exports (% of manufactured exports)	..	21	..
Global links			
Merchandise trade (% of GDP)	34	21	32
Net barter terms of trade index (2000 = 100)	..	100	166
Total external debt stocks ($ millions)	..	..	..
Total debt service (% of exports)	..	..	..
Net migration (thousands)	-67	-156	-190
Remittances received ($ millions)	..	..	..
Foreign direct investment, net inflows ($ millions)	1	-10	110
Net official development assistance received ($ millions)	51.8	44.0	83.7

Curaçao

High income

Population (thousands)	146	Population growth (%)	1.3
Surface area (sq. km)	..	Population living below $1.25 a day (%)	..
GNI, Atlas ($ millions)	..	GNI per capita, Atlas ($)	..
GNI, PPP ($ millions)	..	GNI per capita, PPP ($)	..

	1990	2000	2011
People			
Share of poorest 20% in nat'l consumption/income (%)	..	..	..
Life expectancy at birth (years)	..	..	76
Total fertility rate (births per woman)	..	..	2.2
Adolescent fertility rate (births per 1,000 women 15–19)	..	..	..
Contraceptive prevalence (% of married women 15–49)	..	..	..
Births attended by skilled health staff (% of total)	..	..	..
Under-five mortality rate (per 1,000 live births)	..	..	..
Child malnutrition, underweight (% of under age 5)	..	..	..
Child immunization, measles (% of ages 12–23 mos.)	..	..	..
Primary completion rate, total (% of relevant age group)	..	..	..
Gross secondary enrollment, total (% of relevant age group)	..	..	..
Ratio of girls to boys in primary & secondary school (%)	..	..	..
HIV prevalence rate (% population of ages 15–49)	..	..	
Environment			
Forests (sq. km)	..		..
Deforestation (avg. annual %, 1990–2000 and 2000–2010)		..	..
Freshwater use (% of internal resources)	..		..
Access to improved water source (% total pop.)	..	..	..
Access to improved sanitation facilities (% total pop.)	..	..	..
Energy use per capita (kilograms of oil equivalent)	..	..	..
Carbon dioxide emissions per capita (metric tons)	..	..	..
Electricity use per capita (kilowatt-hours)	..	..	..
Economy			
GDP ($ millions)	..	..	..
GDP growth (annual %)	..	..	..
GDP implicit price deflator (annual % growth)	..	..	..
Value added in agriculture (% of GDP)	..	..	..
Value added in industry (% of GDP)	..	..	..
Value added in services (% of GDP)	..	..	..
Exports of goods and services (% of GDP)	..	..	..
Imports of goods and services (% of GDP)	..	..	..
Gross capital formation (% of GDP)	..	..	..
Central government revenue (% of GDP)	..	..	..
Central government cash surplus/deficit (% of GDP)	..	..	..
States and markets			
Starting a business (days)	..	..	..
Stock market capitalization (% of GDP)	..	..	..
Military expenditures (% of GDP)	..	..	..
Mobile cellular subscriptions (per 100 people)	..	..	..
Individuals using the Internet (% of population)	..	..	..
Paved roads (% of total)	..	..	..
High-technology exports (% of manufactured exports)	..	..	..
Global links			
Merchandise trade (% of GDP)	..	..	..
Net barter terms of trade index (2000 = 100)	..	..	100
Total external debt stocks ($ millions)	..	..	..
Total debt service (% of exports)	..	..	..
Net migration (thousands)	..	..	..
Remittances received ($ millions)	..	..	34.0
Foreign direct investment, net inflows ($ millions)	..	..	70.4
Net official development assistance received ($ millions)	..	..	..

Cyprus

Population (millions)	1.1	Population growth (%)	1.2
Surface area (1,000 sq. km)	9.3	Population living below $1.25 a day (%)	..
GNI, Atlas ($ billions)	23.7	GNI per capita, Atlas ($)	29,450
GNI, PPP ($ billions)	24.9	GNI per capita, PPP ($)	30,970

	1990	2000	2011
People			
Share of poorest 20% in nat'l consumption/income (%)	..	..	..
Life expectancy at birth (years)	77	78	80
Total fertility rate (births per woman)	2.4	1.7	1.5
Adolescent fertility rate (births per 1,000 women 15–19)	..	10	6
Contraceptive prevalence (% of married women 15–49)	..	..	..
Births attended by skilled health staff (% of total)	..	99	..
Under-five mortality rate (per 1,000 live births)	11	7	3
Child malnutrition, underweight (% of under age 5)	..	..	..
Child immunization, measles (% of ages 12–23 mos.)	77	86	87
Primary completion rate, total (% of relevant age group)	101	98	99
Gross secondary enrollment, total (% of relevant age group)	93	93	91
Ratio of girls to boys in primary & secondary school (%)	101	101	101
HIV prevalence rate (% population of ages 15–49)	..	..	..
Environment			
Forests (1,000 sq. km)	1.6	1.7	1.7
Deforestation (avg. annual %, 1990–2000 and 2000–2010)		-0.6	-0.1
Freshwater use (% of internal resources)	29.0	24.9	23.6
Access to improved water source (% total pop.)	100	100	100
Access to improved sanitation facilities (% total pop.)	100	100	100
Energy use per capita (kilograms of oil equivalent)	1,775	2,265	2,215
Carbon dioxide emissions per capita (metric tons)	6.1	7.3	7.5
Electricity use per capita (kilowatt-hours)	2,430	3,373	4,675
Economy			
GDP ($ billions)	5.6	9.3	24.7
GDP growth (annual %)	7.4	5.0	0.5
GDP implicit price deflator (annual % growth)	5.4	3.8	1.2
Value added in agriculture (% of GDP)	7	4	2
Value added in industry (% of GDP)	26	19	20
Value added in services (% of GDP)	67	77	78
Exports of goods and services (% of GDP)	52	55	40
Imports of goods and services (% of GDP)	57	55	47
Gross capital formation (% of GDP)	27	18	18
Central government revenue (% of GDP)	..	..	39.4
Central government cash surplus/deficit (% of GDP)	..	..	-6.3
States and markets			
Starting a business (days)	..	..	8
Stock market capitalization (% of GDP)	22.4	46.7	11.6
Military expenditures (% of GDP)	7.4	3.0	2.2
Mobile cellular subscriptions (per 100 people)	0.4	23.1	97.7
Individuals using the Internet (% of population)	0.0	15.3	57.7
Paved roads (% of total)	59.6	60.6	65.4
High-technology exports (% of manufactured exports)	4	2	27
Global links			
Merchandise trade (% of GDP)	63	51	42
Net barter terms of trade index (2000 = 100)	..	100	103
Total external debt stocks ($ millions)	..	..	..
Total debt service (% of exports)	..	..	..
Net migration (thousands)	17.2	53.3	44.2
Remittances received ($ millions)	79	64	127
Foreign direct investment, net inflows ($ millions)	127	855	1,080
Net official development assistance received ($ millions)	38.4	..	..

Czech Republic

High income

Population (millions)	10.5	Population growth (%)	-0.2
Surface area (1,000 sq. km)	79	Population living below $1.25 a day (%)	..
GNI, Atlas ($ billions)	196.3	GNI per capita, Atlas ($)	18,700
GNI, PPP ($ billions)	257.0	GNI per capita, PPP ($)	24,490

	1990	2000	2011
People			
Share of poorest 20% in nat'l consumption/income (%)	10.4	..	..
Life expectancy at birth (years)	71	75	78
Total fertility rate (births per woman)	1.9	1.1	1.4
Adolescent fertility rate (births per 1,000 women 15–19)	..	13	10
Contraceptive prevalence (% of married women 15–49)	78	..	..
Births attended by skilled health staff (% of total)	100	100	100
Under-five mortality rate (per 1,000 live births)	14	7	4
Child malnutrition, underweight (% of under age 5)	0.9	2.1	..
Child immunization, measles (% of ages 12–23 mos.)	98	98	98
Primary completion rate, total (% of relevant age group)	95	99	105
Gross secondary enrollment, total (% of relevant age group)	93	87	90
Ratio of girls to boys in primary & secondary school (%)	94	101	100
HIV prevalence rate (% population of ages 15–49)	0.1	0.1	0.1
Environment			
Forests (1,000 sq. km)	26	26	27
Deforestation (avg. annual %, 1990–2000 and 2000–2010)		0.0	-0.1
Freshwater use (% of internal resources)	..	13.3	12.9
Access to improved water source (% total pop.)	100	100	100
Access to improved sanitation facilities (% total pop.)	100	98	98
Energy use per capita (kilograms of oil equivalent)	4,797	3,991	4,087
Carbon dioxide emissions per capita (metric tons)	13.5	12.1	10.3
Electricity use per capita (kilowatt-hours)	5,600	5,694	6,321
Economy			
GDP ($ billions)	39	59	217
GDP growth (annual %)	-11.6	4.2	1.9
GDP implicit price deflator (annual % growth)	36.2	1.4	-0.8
Value added in agriculture (% of GDP)	8	4	2
Value added in industry (% of GDP)	40	37	36
Value added in services (% of GDP)	52	60	62
Exports of goods and services (% of GDP)	39	61	73
Imports of goods and services (% of GDP)	37	63	69
Gross capital formation (% of GDP)	23	30	25
Central government revenue (% of GDP)	33.6	29.4	29.1
Central government cash surplus/deficit (% of GDP)	0.1	-3.5	-4.4
States and markets			
Starting a business (days)	..	40	20
Stock market capitalization (% of GDP)	..	18.7	17.7
Military expenditures (% of GDP)	2.1	2.0	1.1
Mobile cellular subscriptions (per 100 people)	0.0	42.4	123.4
Individuals using the Internet (% of population)	0.0	9.8	73.0
Paved roads (% of total)	100.0	100.0	0.6
High-technology exports (% of manufactured exports)	4	8	16
Global links			
Merchandise trade (% of GDP)	75	104	145
Net barter terms of trade index (2000 = 100)	..	100	104
Total external debt stocks ($ millions)	..	..	..
Total debt service (% of exports)	..	..	..
Net migration (thousands)	-22	36	240
Remittances received ($ millions)	138	297	1,815
Foreign direct investment, net inflows ($ billions)	0.7	5.0	5.4
Net official development assistance received ($ millions)	..	..	..

Denmark

Population (millions)	5.6	Population growth (%)	0.4
Surface area (1,000 sq. km)	43	Population living below $1.25 a day (%)	..
GNI, Atlas ($ billions)	335.1	GNI per capita, Atlas ($)	60,160
GNI, PPP ($ billions)	233.5	GNI per capita, PPP ($)	41,920

	1990	2000	2011
People			
Share of poorest 20% in nat'l consumption/income (%)	..	..	..
Life expectancy at birth (years)	75	77	80
Total fertility rate (births per woman)	1.7	1.8	1.8
Adolescent fertility rate (births per 1,000 women 15–19)	..	7	5
Contraceptive prevalence (% of married women 15–49)	78		
Births attended by skilled health staff (% of total)	..	..	..
Under-five mortality rate (per 1,000 live births)	9	6	4
Child malnutrition, underweight (% of under age 5)	..	..	..
Child immunization, measles (% of ages 12–23 mos.)	84	99	87
Primary completion rate, total (% of relevant age group)	95	100	98
Gross secondary enrollment, total (% of relevant age group)	109	127	119
Ratio of girls to boys in primary & secondary school (%)	101	102	101
HIV prevalence rate (% population of ages 15–49)	0.1	0.1	0.2
Environment			
Forests (1,000 sq. km)	4.5	4.9	5.5
Deforestation (avg. annual %, 1990–2000 and 2000–2010)		-0.9	-1.1
Freshwater use (% of internal resources)	18.9	11.4	11.0
Access to improved water source (% total pop.)	100	100	100
Access to improved sanitation facilities (% total pop.)	100	100	100
Energy use per capita (kilograms of oil equivalent)	3,377	3,490	3,144
Carbon dioxide emissions per capita (metric tons)	9.7	8.9	8.3
Electricity use per capita (kilowatt-hours)	5,945	6,482	6,327
Economy			
GDP ($ billions)	136	160	334
GDP growth (annual %)	1.6	3.5	1.1
GDP implicit price deflator (annual % growth)	2.8	3.0	0.6
Value added in agriculture (% of GDP)	4	3	1
Value added in industry (% of GDP)	26	27	22
Value added in services (% of GDP)	70	71	77
Exports of goods and services (% of GDP)	37	47	53
Imports of goods and services (% of GDP)	33	40	48
Gross capital formation (% of GDP)	20	21	18
Central government revenue (% of GDP)	..	35.3	40.5
Central government cash surplus/deficit (% of GDP)	..	1.6	-2.0
States and markets			
Starting a business (days)	..	7	6
Stock market capitalization (% of GDP)	28.8	67.3	53.8
Military expenditures (% of GDP)	2.0	1.5	1.5
Mobile cellular subscriptions (per 100 people)	2.9	63.0	128.5
Individuals using the Internet (% of population)	0.1	39.2	90.0
Paved roads (% of total)	100.0	100.0	100.0
High-technology exports (% of manufactured exports)	16	21	14
Global links			
Merchandise trade (% of GDP)	52	60	63
Net barter terms of trade index (2000 = 100)	..	100	106
Total external debt stocks ($ millions)	..	..	..
Total debt service (% of exports)	..	..	..
Net migration (thousands)	32.8	74.6	90.3
Remittances received ($ millions)	464	667	1,273
Foreign direct investment, net inflows ($ billions)	1.1	36.0	13.1
Net official development assistance received ($ millions)	..	..	..

Djibouti

Middle East & North Africa		Lower middle income

Population (thousands)	906	Population growth (%)	1.9
Surface area (1,000 sq. km)	23	Population living below $1.25 a day (%)	18.8
GNI, Atlas ($ billions)	1.1	GNI per capita, Atlas ($)	1,270
GNI, PPP ($ billions)	2.1	GNI per capita, PPP ($)	2,450

	1990	2000	2011
People			
Share of poorest 20% in nat'l consumption/income (%)	..	6.0	..
Life expectancy at birth (years)	51	54	58
Total fertility rate (births per woman)	6.2	4.8	3.7
Adolescent fertility rate (births per 1,000 women 15-19)	..	30	20
Contraceptive prevalence (% of married women 15-49)	..	9	23
Births attended by skilled health staff (% of total)	..	61	93
Under-five mortality rate (per 1,000 live births)	122	106	90
Child malnutrition, underweight (% of under age 5)	20.2	25.4	29.6
Child immunization, measles (% of ages 12-23 mos.)	85	50	84
Primary completion rate, total (% of relevant age group)	32	28	57
Gross secondary enrollment, total (% of relevant age group)	11	14	39
Ratio of girls to boys in primary & secondary school (%)	72	71	83
HIV prevalence rate (% population of ages 15-49)	0.6	2.8	1.4
Environment			
Forests (sq. km)	56	56	56
Deforestation (avg. annual %, 1990-2000 and 2000-2010)		0.0	0.0
Freshwater use (% of internal resources)	..	6.3	6.3
Access to improved water source (% total pop.)	78	82	88
Access to improved sanitation facilities (% total pop.)	66	60	50
Energy use per capita (kilograms of oil equivalent)	231	..	..
Carbon dioxide emissions per capita (metric tons)	0.7	0.6	0.6
Electricity use per capita (kilowatt-hours)	..	..	..
Economy			
GDP ($ millions)	452	551	1,049
GDP growth (annual %)	-4.3	0.4	5.0
GDP implicit price deflator (annual % growth)	6.8	2.4	1.7
Value added in agriculture (% of GDP)	3	4	..
Value added in industry (% of GDP)	22	15	..
Value added in services (% of GDP)	75	81	..
Exports of goods and services (% of GDP)	54	35	..
Imports of goods and services (% of GDP)	78	50	..
Gross capital formation (% of GDP)	14	9	..
Central government revenue (% of GDP)	..	..	..
Central government cash surplus/deficit (% of GDP)	..	..	..
States and markets			
Starting a business (days)	..	..	37
Stock market capitalization (% of GDP)	..	..	..
Military expenditures (% of GDP)	6.9	4.7	3.7
Mobile cellular subscriptions (per 100 people)	0.0	0.0	21.3
Individuals using the Internet (% of population)	0.0	0.2	7.0
Paved roads (% of total)	..	45.0	..
High-technology exports (% of manufactured exports)	..	..	0
Global links			
Merchandise trade (% of GDP)	53	43	50
Net barter terms of trade index (2000 = 100)	..	100	78
Total external debt stocks ($ millions)	155	299	767
Total debt service (% of exports)	4.0	6.9	8.1
Net migration (thousands)	90.0	30.0	0.0
Remittances received ($ millions)	13.1	12.3	32.4
Foreign direct investment, net inflows ($ millions)	2.3	3.3	79.0
Net official development assistance received ($ millions)	207	72	142

Dominica

Latin America & Caribbean		Upper middle income	
Population (thousands)	68	Population growth (%)	-0.1
Surface area (sq. km)	750	Population living below $1.25 a day (%)	..
GNI, Atlas ($ millions)	475.5	GNI per capita, Atlas ($)	7,030
GNI, PPP ($ millions)	880.0	GNI per capita, PPP ($)	13,000

	1990	2000	2011
People			
Share of poorest 20% in nat'l consumption/income (%)	..	..	..
Life expectancy at birth (years)	74	77	..
Total fertility rate (births per woman)	2.5	1.9	..
Adolescent fertility rate (births per 1,000 women 15–19)	..	..	..
Contraceptive prevalence (% of married women 15–49)	..	50	..
Births attended by skilled health staff (% of total)	..	100	100
Under-five mortality rate (per 1,000 live births)	17	15	12
Child malnutrition, underweight (% of under age 5)	..	..	..
Child immunization, measles (% of ages 12–23 mos.)	88	99	99
Primary completion rate, total (% of relevant age group)	101	119	94
Gross secondary enrollment, total (% of relevant age group)	70	105	98
Ratio of girls to boys in primary & secondary school (%)	102	106	103
HIV prevalence rate (% population of ages 15–49)	..	..	..
Environment			
Forests (sq. km)	500	473	444
Deforestation (avg. annual %, 1990–2000 and 2000–2010)		0.6	0.6
Freshwater use (% of internal resources)	..	..	..
Access to improved water source (% total pop.)	..	95	..
Access to improved sanitation facilities (% total pop.)	..	81	..
Energy use per capita (kilograms of oil equivalent)	299	..	..
Carbon dioxide emissions per capita (metric tons)	0.8	1.5	1.9
Electricity use per capita (kilowatt-hours)	..	..	..
Economy			
GDP ($ millions)	166	324	484
GDP growth (annual %)	5.3	-1.0	-0.3
GDP implicit price deflator (annual % growth)	3.0	22.4	2.9
Value added in agriculture (% of GDP)	25	14	14
Value added in industry (% of GDP)	19	19	15
Value added in services (% of GDP)	56	67	71
Exports of goods and services (% of GDP)	55	45	34
Imports of goods and services (% of GDP)	81	56	54
Gross capital formation (% of GDP)	41	21	22
Central government revenue (% of GDP)	..	..	..
Central government cash surplus/deficit (% of GDP)	..	..	..
States and markets			
Starting a business (days)	..	..	13
Stock market capitalization (% of GDP)	..	..	..
Military expenditures (% of GDP)	..	..	..
Mobile cellular subscriptions (per 100 people)	0.0	1.7	164.0
Individuals using the Internet (% of population)	0.0	8.8	51.3
Paved roads (% of total)	45.6	50.4	50.4
High-technology exports (% of manufactured exports)	2	7	0
Global links			
Merchandise trade (% of GDP)	104	62	52
Net barter terms of trade index (2000 = 100)	..	100	104
Total external debt stocks ($ millions)	91	183	284
Total debt service (% of exports)	6.6	7.4	9.8
Net migration (thousands)	..	..	..
Remittances received ($ millions)	13.9	16.3	23.2
Foreign direct investment, net inflows ($ millions)	12.9	17.6	34.3
Net official development assistance received ($ millions)	19.6	15.2	24.8

Dominican Republic

Latin America & Caribbean		Upper middle income	
Population (millions)	10.1	Population growth (%)	1.3
Surface area (1,000 sq. km)	49	Population living below $1.25 a day (%)	2.2
GNI, Atlas ($ billions)	52.6	GNI per capita, Atlas ($)	5,240
GNI, PPP ($ billions)	94.7	GNI per capita, PPP ($)	9,420

	1990	2000	2011
People			
Share of poorest 20% in nat'l consumption/income (%)	4.2	3.7	4.7
Life expectancy at birth (years)	68	71	73
Total fertility rate (births per woman)	3.5	2.9	2.5
Adolescent fertility rate (births per 1,000 women 15-19)	..	110	105
Contraceptive prevalence (% of married women 15-49)	56	65	73
Births attended by skilled health staff (% of total)	92	98	98
Under-five mortality rate (per 1,000 live births)	58	39	25
Child malnutrition, underweight (% of under age 5)	8.4	3.5	3.4
Child immunization, measles (% of ages 12-23 mos.)	70	84	79
Primary completion rate, total (% of relevant age group)	..	78	92
Gross secondary enrollment, total (% of relevant age group)	..	59	76
Ratio of girls to boys in primary & secondary school (%)	..	104	99
HIV prevalence rate (% population of ages 15-49)	0.4	1.0	0.7
Environment			
Forests (1,000 sq. km)	20	20	20
Deforestation (avg. annual %, 1990-2000 and 2000-2010)		0.0	0.0
Freshwater use (% of internal resources)	..	16.6	16.6
Access to improved water source (% total pop.)	88	87	86
Access to improved sanitation facilities (% total pop.)	73	78	83
Energy use per capita (kilograms of oil equivalent)	570	909	840
Carbon dioxide emissions per capita (metric tons)	1.3	2.3	2.1
Electricity use per capita (kilowatt-hours)	388	728	1,442
Economy			
GDP ($ billions)	7.1	24.0	55.6
GDP growth (annual %)	-5.5	5.7	4.5
GDP implicit price deflator (annual % growth)	50.5	6.9	6.6
Value added in agriculture (% of GDP)	15	7	6
Value added in industry (% of GDP)	34	36	33
Value added in services (% of GDP)	60	57	61
Exports of goods and services (% of GDP)	34	37	25
Imports of goods and services (% of GDP)	44	46	35
Gross capital formation (% of GDP)	25	23	16
Central government revenue (% of GDP)	..	..	14.4
Central government cash surplus/deficit (% of GDP)	..	..	-2.9
States and markets			
Starting a business (days)	..	77	19
Stock market capitalization (% of GDP)	..	..	..
Military expenditures (% of GDP)	0.7	1.0	0.6
Mobile cellular subscriptions (per 100 people)	0.0	8.2	87.2
Individuals using the Internet (% of population)	0.0	3.7	35.5
Paved roads (% of total)	44.7	49.4	..
High-technology exports (% of manufactured exports)	..	1	2
Global links			
Merchandise trade (% of GDP)	73	63	47
Net barter terms of trade index (2000 = 100)	96	100	92
Total external debt stocks ($ billions)	4.4	4.6	15.4
Total debt service (% of exports)	12.4	5.7	10.4
Net migration (thousands)	-117	-139	-140
Remittances received ($ billions)	0.3	1.8	3.7
Foreign direct investment, net inflows ($ millions)	133	953	2,295
Net official development assistance received ($ millions)	102	56	234

Ecuador

Latin America & Caribbean		Upper middle income	
Population (millions)	14.7	Population growth (%)	1.4
Surface area (1,000 sq. km)	256	Population living below $1.25 a day (%)	4.6
GNI, Atlas ($ billions)	61.7	GNI per capita, Atlas ($)	4,200
GNI, PPP ($ billions)	124.7	GNI per capita, PPP ($)	8,510

	1990	2000	2011
People			
Share of poorest 20% in nat'l consumption/income (%)	..	3.0	4.3
Life expectancy at birth (years)	69	73	76
Total fertility rate (births per woman)	3.7	3.0	2.4
Adolescent fertility rate (births per 1,000 women 15–19)	..	85	81
Contraceptive prevalence (% of married women 15–49)	53	66	..
Births attended by skilled health staff (% of total)	..	99	..
Under-five mortality rate (per 1,000 live births)	52	34	23
Child malnutrition, underweight (% of under age 5)	..	6.2	..
Child immunization, measles (% of ages 12–23 mos.)	60	99	98
Primary completion rate, total (% of relevant age group)	92	99	112
Gross secondary enrollment, total (% of relevant age group)	57	57	88
Ratio of girls to boys in primary & secondary school (%)	100	100	101
HIV prevalence rate (% population of ages 15–49)	0.2	0.4	0.4
Environment			
Forests (1,000 sq. km)	138	118	97
Deforestation (avg. annual %, 1990–2000 and 2000–2010)		1.5	1.8
Freshwater use (% of internal resources)	..	3.5	3.5
Access to improved water source (% total pop.)	72	86	94
Access to improved sanitation facilities (% total pop.)	69	83	92
Energy use per capita (kilograms of oil equivalent)	587	651	836
Carbon dioxide emissions per capita (metric tons)	1.6	1.7	2.1
Electricity use per capita (kilowatt-hours)	479	652	1,055
Economy			
GDP ($ billions)	10.4	15.9	65.9
GDP growth (annual %)	2.7	2.8	7.8
GDP implicit price deflator (annual % growth)	5.9	-7.0	5.5
Value added in agriculture (% of GDP)	..	9	7
Value added in industry (% of GDP)	..	32	38
Value added in services (% of GDP)	..	59	55
Exports of goods and services (% of GDP)	33	37	33
Imports of goods and services (% of GDP)	32	31	39
Gross capital formation (% of GDP)	21	20	26
Central government revenue (% of GDP)	14.4	..	..
Central government cash surplus/deficit (% of GDP)	2.9	..	..
States and markets			
Starting a business (days)	..	92	56
Stock market capitalization (% of GDP)	0.6	4.4	8.8
Military expenditures (% of GDP)	2.0	1.7	3.5
Mobile cellular subscriptions (per 100 people)	0.0	3.9	104.5
Individuals using the Internet (% of population)	0.0	1.5	31.4
Paved roads (% of total)	13.4	18.9	14.8
High-technology exports (% of manufactured exports)	0	6	3
Global links			
Merchandise trade (% of GDP)	44	54	71
Net barter terms of trade index (2000 = 100)	114	100	130
Total external debt stocks ($ billions)	12.2	13.3	16.5
Total debt service (% of exports)	33.2	30.6	9.7
Net migration (thousands)	0	-250	-120
Remittances received ($ billions)	0.1	1.3	2.7
Foreign direct investment, net inflows ($ millions)	126	-23	568
Net official development assistance received ($ millions)	159	146	171

Egypt, Arab Rep.

Middle East & North Africa		Lower middle income

Population (millions)	82.5	Population growth (%)	1.7
Surface area (1,000 sq. km)	1,001	Population living below $1.25 a day (%)	<2
GNI, Atlas ($ billions)	214.7	GNI per capita, Atlas ($)	2,600
GNI, PPP ($ billions)	504.8	GNI per capita, PPP ($)	6,120

	1990	2000	2011
People			
Share of poorest 20% in nat'l consumption/income (%)	8.7	9.0	9.2
Life expectancy at birth (years)	62	69	73
Total fertility rate (births per woman)	4.4	3.3	2.7
Adolescent fertility rate (births per 1,000 women 15–19)	..	55	42
Contraceptive prevalence (% of married women 15–49)	48	56	60
Births attended by skilled health staff (% of total)	37	61	79
Under-five mortality rate (per 1,000 live births)	86	44	21
Child malnutrition, underweight (% of under age 5)	10.5	4.3	6.8
Child immunization, measles (% of ages 12–23 mos.)	86	98	96
Primary completion rate, total (% of relevant age group)	..	94	101
Gross secondary enrollment, total (% of relevant age group)	68	83	72
Ratio of girls to boys in primary & secondary school (%)	80	92	96
HIV prevalence rate (% population of ages 15–49)	0.1	0.1	0.1
Environment			
Forests (sq. km)	440	590	706
Deforestation (avg. annual %, 1990–2000 and 2000–2010)		-3.0	-1.7
Freshwater use (% of internal resources)	..	3,794.4	3,794.4
Access to improved water source (% total pop.)	93	96	99
Access to improved sanitation facilities (% total pop.)	72	86	95
Energy use per capita (kilograms of oil equivalent)	569	601	903
Carbon dioxide emissions per capita (metric tons)	1.3	2.1	2.7
Electricity use per capita (kilowatt-hours)	669	994	1,608
Economy			
GDP ($ billions)	43	100	230
GDP growth (annual %)	5.7	5.4	1.8
GDP implicit price deflator (annual % growth)	18.4	4.9	11.2
Value added in agriculture (% of GDP)	19	17	14
Value added in industry (% of GDP)	29	33	37
Value added in services (% of GDP)	52	50	49
Exports of goods and services (% of GDP)	20	16	23
Imports of goods and services (% of GDP)	33	23	30
Gross capital formation (% of GDP)	29	20	20
Central government revenue (% of GDP)	23.0	24.3	22.0
Central government cash surplus/deficit (% of GDP)	-2.0	-6.7	-10.1
States and markets			
Starting a business (days)	..	37	7
Stock market capitalization (% of GDP)	4.1	28.8	21.2
Military expenditures (% of GDP)	4.7	3.2	1.9
Mobile cellular subscriptions (per 100 people)	0.0	2.0	101.1
Individuals using the Internet (% of population)	0.0	0.6	38.7
Paved roads (% of total)	72.0	78.1	92.2
High-technology exports (% of manufactured exports)	..	0	1
Global links			
Merchandise trade (% of GDP)	37	20	39
Net barter terms of trade index (2000 = 100)	101	100	159
Total external debt stocks ($ billions)	33.0	29.2	35.0
Total debt service (% of exports)	28.6	9.8	7.4
Net migration (thousands)	-652	-946	-347
Remittances received ($ billions)	4.3	2.9	14.3
Foreign direct investment, net inflows ($ millions)	734	1,235	-483
Net official development assistance received ($ billions)	6.1	1.4	0.4

El Salvador

Latin America & Caribbean		Lower middle income	
Population (millions)	6.2	Population growth (%)	0.6
Surface area (1,000 sq. km)	21	Population living below $1.25 a day (%)	9.0
GNI, Atlas ($ billions)	21.7	GNI per capita, Atlas ($)	3,480
GNI, PPP ($ billions)	41.4	GNI per capita, PPP ($)	6,640

	1990	2000	2011
People			
Share of poorest 20% in nat'l consumption/income (%)	2.6	2.3	3.7
Life expectancy at birth (years)	66	70	72
Total fertility rate (births per woman)	4.0	2.9	2.2
Adolescent fertility rate (births per 1,000 women 15–19)	..	100	77
Contraceptive prevalence (% of married women 15–49)	53	67	73
Births attended by skilled health staff (% of total)	87	92	96
Under-five mortality rate (per 1,000 live births)	60	34	15
Child malnutrition, underweight (% of under age 5)	7.2	6.1	6.6
Child immunization, measles (% of ages 12–23 mos.)	98	97	89
Primary completion rate, total (% of relevant age group)	64	83	101
Gross secondary enrollment, total (% of relevant age group)	38	54	68
Ratio of girls to boys in primary & secondary school (%)	101	97	97
HIV prevalence rate (% population of ages 15–49)	0.1	0.4	0.6
Environment			
Forests (1,000 sq. km)	3.8	3.3	2.8
Deforestation (avg. annual %, 1990–2000 and 2000–2010)		1.3	1.5
Freshwater use (% of internal resources)	4.1	7.8	7.8
Access to improved water source (% total pop.)	74	82	88
Access to improved sanitation facilities (% total pop.)	75	83	87
Energy use per capita (kilograms of oil equivalent)	463	668	677
Carbon dioxide emissions per capita (metric tons)	0.5	1.0	1.0
Electricity use per capita (kilowatt-hours)	348	610	855
Economy			
GDP ($ billions)	4.8	13.1	23.1
GDP growth (annual %)	4.8	2.2	1.5
GDP implicit price deflator (annual % growth)	4.7	3.2	6.0
Value added in agriculture (% of GDP)	17	10	13
Value added in industry (% of GDP)	27	32	27
Value added in services (% of GDP)	55	58	60
Exports of goods and services (% of GDP)	19	27	28
Imports of goods and services (% of GDP)	31	42	47
Gross capital formation (% of GDP)	14	17	14
Central government revenue (% of GDP)	..	16.0	20.4
Central government cash surplus/deficit (% of GDP)	..	-4.7	-2.2
States and markets			
Starting a business (days)	..	115	17
Stock market capitalization (% of GDP)	..	15.5	23.7
Military expenditures (% of GDP)	4.2	1.2	1.0
Mobile cellular subscriptions (per 100 people)	0.0	12.5	133.5
Individuals using the Internet (% of population)	0.0	1.2	17.7
Paved roads (% of total)	14.4	19.8	46.9
High-technology exports (% of manufactured exports)	..	3	6
Global links			
Merchandise trade (% of GDP)	38	60	67
Net barter terms of trade index (2000 = 100)	84	100	90
Total external debt stocks ($ billions)	2.2	4.5	12.0
Total debt service (% of exports)	21.7	9.9	21.7
Net migration (thousands)	-291	-402	-292
Remittances received ($ billions)	0.4	1.8	3.7
Foreign direct investment, net inflows ($ millions)	2	173	247
Net official development assistance received ($ millions)	347	180	281

Equatorial Guinea

High income

Population (thousands)	720	Population growth (%)	2.8
Surface area (1,000 sq. km)	28	Population living below $1.25 a day (%)	..
GNI, Atlas ($ billions)	11.3	GNI per capita, Atlas ($)	15,670
GNI, PPP ($ billions)	18.4	GNI per capita, PPP ($)	25,620

	1990	2000	2011
People			
Share of poorest 20% in nat'l consumption/income (%)	..	..	..
Life expectancy at birth (years)	47	49	51
Total fertility rate (births per woman)	5.9	5.8	5.1
Adolescent fertility rate (births per 1,000 women 15-19)	..	131	116
Contraceptive prevalence (% of married women 15-49)	..	10	..
Births attended by skilled health staff (% of total)	..	65	..
Under-five mortality rate (per 1,000 live births)	190	152	118
Child malnutrition, underweight (% of under age 5)	..	15.7	..
Child immunization, measles (% of ages 12-23 mos.)	88	51	51
Primary completion rate, total (% of relevant age group)	..	55	52
Gross secondary enrollment, total (% of relevant age group)	43	31	..
Ratio of girls to boys in primary & secondary school (%)	82	81	..
HIV prevalence rate (% population of ages 15-49)	0.9	2.3	4.7
Environment			
Forests (1,000 sq. km)	19	17	16
Deforestation (avg. annual %, 1990-2000 and 2000-2010)		0.7	0.7
Freshwater use (% of internal resources)	..	0.1	0.1
Access to improved water source (% total pop.)	..	51	..
Access to improved sanitation facilities (% total pop.)	..	89	..
Energy use per capita (kilograms of oil equivalent)	..	..	..
Carbon dioxide emissions per capita (metric tons)	0.3	0.9	7.1
Electricity use per capita (kilowatt-hours)	..	..	..
Economy			
GDP ($ billions)	0.1	1.2	19.8
GDP growth (annual %)	3.3	12.5	7.8
GDP implicit price deflator (annual % growth)	-2.5	46.6	20.6
Value added in agriculture (% of GDP)	62	10	2
Value added in industry (% of GDP)	11	87	96
Value added in services (% of GDP)	28	3	2
Exports of goods and services (% of GDP)	32	99	71
Imports of goods and services (% of GDP)	70	86	47
Gross capital formation (% of GDP)	17	72	35
Central government revenue (% of GDP)	..	..	..
Central government cash surplus/deficit (% of GDP)	..	..	..
States and markets			
Starting a business (days)	..	..	135
Stock market capitalization (% of GDP)	..	..	..
Military expenditures (% of GDP)	..	..	..
Mobile cellular subscriptions (per 100 people)	0.0	1.0	59.1
Individuals using the Internet (% of population)	0.0	0.1	6.0
Paved roads (% of total)	..	..	..
High-technology exports (% of manufactured exports)	..	..	..
Global links			
Merchandise trade (% of GDP)	95	125	98
Net barter terms of trade index (2000 = 100)	38	100	226
Total external debt stocks ($ millions)	..	..	..
Total debt service (% of exports)	..	..	..
Net migration (thousands)	15.0	20.0	20.0
Remittances received ($ millions)	1.3	..	..
Foreign direct investment, net inflows ($ millions)	11	154	737
Net official development assistance received ($ millions)	60.2	21.3	24.2

Eritrea

Sub-Saharan Africa   **Low income**

Population (millions)	5.4	Population growth (%)	3.0
Surface area (1,000 sq. km)	118	Population living below $1.25 a day (%)	..
GNI, Atlas ($ billions)	2.3	GNI per capita, Atlas ($)	430
GNI, PPP ($ billions)	3.1	GNI per capita, PPP ($)	580

	1990	2000	2011
People			
Share of poorest 20% in nat'l consumption/income (%)	..	..	..
Life expectancy at birth (years)	48	56	61
Total fertility rate (births per woman)	6.2	5.4	4.4
Adolescent fertility rate (births per 1,000 women 15-19)	..	89	56
Contraceptive prevalence (% of married women 15-49)	..	8	..
Births attended by skilled health staff (% of total)	..	28	..
Under-five mortality rate (per 1,000 live births)	138	98	68
Child malnutrition, underweight (% of under age 5)	36.9	34.5	..
Child immunization, measles (% of ages 12-23 mos.)	18	76	99
Primary completion rate, total (% of relevant age group)	..	36	40
Gross secondary enrollment, total (% of relevant age group)	11	25	33
Ratio of girls to boys in primary & secondary school (%)	82	77	80
HIV prevalence rate (% population of ages 15-49)	0.2	1.1	0.6
Environment			
Forests (1,000 sq. km)	16	16	15
Deforestation (avg. annual %, 1990-2000 and 2000-2010)		0.3	0.3
Freshwater use (% of internal resources)	..	14.8	20.8
Access to improved water source (% total pop.)	43	54	61
Access to improved sanitation facilities (% total pop.)	9	11	14
Energy use per capita (kilograms of oil equivalent)	276	193	142
Carbon dioxide emissions per capita (metric tons)	..	0.2	0.1
Electricity use per capita (kilowatt-hours)	39	47	52
Economy			
GDP ($ millions)	477	634	2,609
GDP growth (annual %)	13.5	-13.1	8.7
GDP implicit price deflator (annual % growth)	-1.4	25.0	13.3
Value added in agriculture (% of GDP)	31	15	15
Value added in industry (% of GDP)	12	23	22
Value added in services (% of GDP)	57	62	63
Exports of goods and services (% of GDP)	11	15	5
Imports of goods and services (% of GDP)	45	82	20
Gross capital formation (% of GDP)	8	24	..
Central government revenue (% of GDP)	..	..	..
Central government cash surplus/deficit (% of GDP)	..	..	..
States and markets			
Starting a business (days)	..	91	84
Stock market capitalization (% of GDP)	..	..	..
Military expenditures (% of GDP)	22.0	36.4	..
Mobile cellular subscriptions (per 100 people)	0.0	0.0	4.5
Individuals using the Internet (% of population)	0.0	0.1	6.2
Paved roads (% of total)	19.4	21.8	..
High-technology exports (% of manufactured exports)	..	0	..
Global links			
Merchandise trade (% of GDP)	77	80	50
Net barter terms of trade index (2000 = 100)	99	100	82
Total external debt stocks ($ millions)	0	330	1,055
Total debt service (% of exports)	..	4.3	..
Net migration (thousands)	-3.8	-8.9	55.0
Remittances received ($ millions)	..	3.3	..
Foreign direct investment, net inflows ($ millions)	..	27.9	18.5
Net official development assistance received ($ millions)	5	177	163

Estonia

Population (millions)	1.3	Population growth (%)	0.0
Surface area (1,000 sq. km)	45	Population living below $1.25 a day (%)	<2
GNI, Atlas ($ billions)	20.4	GNI per capita, Atlas ($)	15,260
GNI, PPP ($ billions)	27.9	GNI per capita, PPP ($)	20,850

	1990	2000	2011
People			
Share of poorest 20% in nat'l consumption/income (%)	6.4	6.6	..
Life expectancy at birth (years)	69	70	76
Total fertility rate (births per woman)	2.0	1.4	1.5
Adolescent fertility rate (births per 1,000 women 15-19)	..	26	18
Contraceptive prevalence (% of married women 15-49)	..	..	..
Births attended by skilled health staff (% of total)	99	100	100
Under-five mortality rate (per 1,000 live births)	20	11	4
Child malnutrition, underweight (% of under age 5)	..	..	..
Child immunization, measles (% of ages 12-23 mos.)	74	93	94
Primary completion rate, total (% of relevant age group)	..	92	96
Gross secondary enrollment, total (% of relevant age group)	103	94	107
Ratio of girls to boys in primary & secondary school (%)	103	100	99
HIV prevalence rate (% population of ages 15-49)	0.1	0.5	1.3
Environment			
Forests (1,000 sq. km)	21	22	22
Deforestation (avg. annual %, 1990-2000 and 2000-2010)		-0.7	0.1
Freshwater use (% of internal resources)	..	11.5	14.1
Access to improved water source (% total pop.)	98	98	98
Access to improved sanitation facilities (% total pop.)	95	95	95
Energy use per capita (kilograms of oil equivalent)	6,316	3,443	4,140
Carbon dioxide emissions per capita (metric tons)	15.0	11.4	11.9
Electricity use per capita (kilowatt-hours)	5,890	4,629	6,464
Economy			
GDP ($ billions)	..	5.7	22.2
GDP growth (annual %)	..	9.7	8.3
GDP implicit price deflator (annual % growth)	..	4.8	2.9
Value added in agriculture (% of GDP)	..	5	4
Value added in industry (% of GDP)	..	28	29
Value added in services (% of GDP)	..	68	68
Exports of goods and services (% of GDP)	..	85	92
Imports of goods and services (% of GDP)	..	88	88
Gross capital formation (% of GDP)	..	28	25
Central government revenue (% of GDP)	..	29.4	33.4
Central government cash surplus/deficit (% of GDP)	..	0.2	1.0
States and markets			
Starting a business (days)	..	72	7
Stock market capitalization (% of GDP)	..	32.5	7.3
Military expenditures (% of GDP)	..	1.4	1.7
Mobile cellular subscriptions (per 100 people)	0.0	40.6	139.0
Individuals using the Internet (% of population)	0.0	28.6	76.5
Paved roads (% of total)	51.8	20.1	17.9
High-technology exports (% of manufactured exports)	..	30	13
Global links			
Merchandise trade (% of GDP)	..	157	155
Net barter terms of trade index (2000 = 100)	..	100	142
Total external debt stocks ($ millions)	..	..	..
Total debt service (% of exports)	..	..	..
Net migration (thousands)	15.0	-36.6	0.0
Remittances received ($ millions)	..	4	407
Foreign direct investment, net inflows ($ millions)	82	387	436
Net official development assistance received ($ millions)	..	..	..

Ethiopia

Sub-Saharan Africa			Low income
Population (millions)	84.7	Population growth (%)	2.1
Surface area (1,000 sq. km)	1,104	Population living below $1.25 a day (%)	30.7
GNI, Atlas ($ billions)	31.0	GNI per capita, Atlas ($)	370
GNI, PPP ($ billions)	93.8	GNI per capita, PPP ($)	1,110

	1990	2000	2011
People			
Share of poorest 20% in nat'l consumption/income (%)	..	9.2	..
Life expectancy at birth (years)	47	52	59
Total fertility rate (births per woman)	7.1	6.1	4.0
Adolescent fertility rate (births per 1,000 women 15–19)	..	103	53
Contraceptive prevalence (% of married women 15–49)	5	8	29
Births attended by skilled health staff (% of total)	..	6	10
Under-five mortality rate (per 1,000 live births)	198	139	77
Child malnutrition, underweight (% of under age 5)	..	42.0	29.2
Child immunization, measles (% of ages 12–23 mos.)	38	33	57
Primary completion rate, total (% of relevant age group)	23	23	58
Gross secondary enrollment, total (% of relevant age group)	14	14	38
Ratio of girls to boys in primary & secondary school (%)	68	65	90
HIV prevalence rate (% population of ages 15–49)	1.3	3.7	1.4
Environment			
Forests (1,000 sq. km)	167	137	122
Deforestation (avg. annual %, 1990–2000 and 2000–2010)		1.0	1.1
Freshwater use (% of internal resources)	..	4.6	4.6
Access to improved water source (% total pop.)	14	29	44
Access to improved sanitation facilities (% total pop.)	3	9	21
Energy use per capita (kilograms of oil equivalent)	308	284	400
Carbon dioxide emissions per capita (metric tons)	0.06	0.09	0.10
Electricity use per capita (kilowatt-hours)	22	23	54
Economy			
GDP ($ billions)	12.1	8.1	30.2
GDP growth (annual %)	2.7	6.1	7.3
GDP implicit price deflator (annual % growth)	3.3	6.9	24.4
Value added in agriculture (% of GDP)	54	50	46
Value added in industry (% of GDP)	11	12	11
Value added in services (% of GDP)	35	38	43
Exports of goods and services (% of GDP)	6	12	17
Imports of goods and services (% of GDP)	9	24	32
Gross capital formation (% of GDP)	13	20	26
Central government revenue (% of GDP)	12.4	11.9	11.0
Central government cash surplus/deficit (% of GDP)	-6.6	-4.2	-1.4
States and markets			
Starting a business (days)	..	46	15
Stock market capitalization (% of GDP)	..	..	..
Military expenditures (% of GDP)	6.5	7.6	1.1
Mobile cellular subscriptions (per 100 people)	0.0	0.0	16.7
Individuals using the Internet (% of population)	0.0	0.0	1.1
Paved roads (% of total)	15.0	12.0	13.7
High-technology exports (% of manufactured exports)	..	0	2
Global links			
Merchandise trade (% of GDP)	11	22	38
Net barter terms of trade index (2000 = 100)	125	100	136
Total external debt stocks ($ billions)	8.6	5.5	8.6
Total debt service (% of exports)	39.0	13.7	6.1
Net migration (thousands)	780	-277	-300
Remittances received ($ millions)	5	53	513
Foreign direct investment, net inflows ($ millions)	0	135	627
Net official development assistance received ($ billions)	1.0	0.7	3.6

Faeroe Islands

Population (thousands)	49	Population growth (%)		0.3
Surface area (1,000 sq. km)	1.4	Population living below $1.25 a day (%)		..
GNI, Atlas ($ millions)	..	GNI per capita, Atlas ($)		..
GNI, PPP ($ millions)	..	GNI per capita, PPP ($)		..

	1990	2000	2011
People			
Share of poorest 20% in nat'l consumption/income (%)	..	..	..
Life expectancy at birth (years)	77	79	82
Total fertility rate (births per woman)	..	..	..
Adolescent fertility rate (births per 1,000 women 15–19)	..	..	..
Contraceptive prevalence (% of married women 15–49)	..	..	..
Births attended by skilled health staff (% of total)	..	..	..
Under-five mortality rate (per 1,000 live births)	..	..	..
Child malnutrition, underweight (% of under age 5)	..	..	..
Child immunization, measles (% of ages 12–23 mos.)	..	..	..
Primary completion rate, total (% of relevant age group)	..	..	..
Gross secondary enrollment, total (% of relevant age group)	..	..	..
Ratio of girls to boys in primary & secondary school (%)	..	..	..
HIV prevalence rate (% population of ages 15–49)	..	..	..
Environment			
Forests (sq. km)	1.0	1.0	1.0
Deforestation (avg. annual %, 1990–2000 and 2000–2010)		0.0	0.0
Freshwater use (% of internal resources)	..	..	..
Access to improved water source (% total pop.)	..	..	..
Access to improved sanitation facilities (% total pop.)	..	..	..
Energy use per capita (kilograms of oil equivalent)	..	..	..
Carbon dioxide emissions per capita (metric tons)	13.1	14.3	14.6
Electricity use per capita (kilowatt-hours)	..	..	..
Economy			
GDP ($ millions)	..	1,062	2,198
GDP growth (annual %)	..	..	..
GDP implicit price deflator (annual % growth)	..	..	..
Value added in agriculture (% of GDP)	..	..	..
Value added in industry (% of GDP)	..	..	..
Value added in services (% of GDP)	..	..	..
Exports of goods and services (% of GDP)	..	..	..
Imports of goods and services (% of GDP)	..	..	..
Gross capital formation (% of GDP)	..	..	..
Central government revenue (% of GDP)	..	..	..
Central government cash surplus/deficit (% of GDP)	..	..	..
States and markets			
Starting a business (days)	..	..	..
Stock market capitalization (% of GDP)	..	..	..
Military expenditures (% of GDP)		..	
Mobile cellular subscriptions (per 100 people)	0.0	37.1	122.0
Individuals using the Internet (% of population)	0.0	32.9	80.7
Paved roads (% of total)	..	..	..
High-technology exports (% of manufactured exports)	0	0	1
Global links			
Merchandise trade (% of GDP)	..	95	70
Net barter terms of trade index (2000 = 100)	..	100	103
Total external debt stocks ($ millions)	..	..	..
Total debt service (% of exports)	..	..	..
Net migration (thousands)	..	..	..
Remittances received ($ millions)	..	43	146
Foreign direct investment, net inflows ($ millions)	..	..	..
Net official development assistance received ($ millions)	..	..	..

Fiji

East Asia & Pacific		**Lower middle income**	
Population (thousands)	868	Population growth (%)	0.9
Surface area (1,000 sq. km)	18	Population living below $1.25 a day (%)	5.9
GNI, Atlas ($ billions)	3.2	GNI per capita, Atlas ($)	3,720
GNI, PPP ($ billions)	4.0	GNI per capita, PPP ($)	4,610

	1990	2000	2011
People			
Share of poorest 20% in nat'l consumption/income (%)	..	4.1	6.2
Life expectancy at birth (years)	66	68	69
Total fertility rate (births per woman)	3.4	3.1	2.6
Adolescent fertility rate (births per 1,000 women 15-19)	..	43	43
Contraceptive prevalence (% of married women 15-49)	..	44	32
Births attended by skilled health staff (% of total)	..	99	100
Under-five mortality rate (per 1,000 live births)	30	22	16
Child malnutrition, underweight (% of under age 5)	6.9	..	..
Child immunization, measles (% of ages 12-23 mos.)	84	81	94
Primary completion rate, total (% of relevant age group)	..	95	103
Gross secondary enrollment, total (% of relevant age group)	77	78	90
Ratio of girls to boys in primary & secondary school (%)	98	103	104
HIV prevalence rate (% population of ages 15-49)	0.1	0.1	0.1
Environment			
Forests (1,000 sq. km)	10	10	10
Deforestation (avg. annual %, 1990-2000 and 2000-2010)		-0.3	-0.3
Freshwater use (% of internal resources)	..	0.3	0.3
Access to improved water source (% total pop.)	84	93	98
Access to improved sanitation facilities (% total pop.)	61	75	83
Energy use per capita (kilograms of oil equivalent)	392	..	..
Carbon dioxide emissions per capita (metric tons)	1.1	1.1	1.0
Electricity use per capita (kilowatt-hours)	..	..	..
Economy			
GDP ($ millions)	1,337	1,684	3,818
GDP growth (annual %)	5.8	-1.7	2.0
GDP implicit price deflator (annual % growth)	6.7	-4.7	10.2
Value added in agriculture (% of GDP)	20	17	13
Value added in industry (% of GDP)	24	22	19
Value added in services (% of GDP)	56	61	68
Exports of goods and services (% of GDP)	62	65	48
Imports of goods and services (% of GDP)	67	70	58
Gross capital formation (% of GDP)	14	17	24
Central government revenue (% of GDP)	26.8	..	..
Central government cash surplus/deficit (% of GDP)	0.9	..	..
States and markets			
Starting a business (days)	..	45	58
Stock market capitalization (% of GDP)	..	14.5	35.9
Military expenditures (% of GDP)	2.3	1.9	1.6
Mobile cellular subscriptions (per 100 people)	0.0	6.8	83.7
Individuals using the Internet (% of population)	0.0	1.5	28.0
Paved roads (% of total)	44.5	49.2	..
High-technology exports (% of manufactured exports)	12	0	4
Global links			
Merchandise trade (% of GDP)	94	84	83
Net barter terms of trade index (2000 = 100)	142	100	108
Total external debt stocks ($ millions)	308	182	861
Total debt service (% of exports)	9.1	2.4	1.3
Net migration (thousands)	-66.9	-42.3	-28.8
Remittances received ($ millions)	22	44	158
Foreign direct investment, net inflows ($ millions)	92	1	204
Net official development assistance received ($ millions)	49.6	29.1	75.2

Finland

High income

Population (millions)	5.4	Population growth (%)	0.5
Surface area (1,000 sq. km)	338	Population living below $1.25 a day (%)	..
GNI, Atlas ($ billions)	257.3	GNI per capita, Atlas ($)	47,760
GNI, PPP ($ billions)	202.9	GNI per capita, PPP ($)	37,760

	1990	2000	2011
People			
Share of poorest 20% in nat'l consumption/income (%)	..	9.6	..
Life expectancy at birth (years)	75	77	80
Total fertility rate (births per woman)	1.8	1.7	1.8
Adolescent fertility rate (births per 1,000 women 15-19)	..	12	9
Contraceptive prevalence (% of married women 15-49)	77	..	..
Births attended by skilled health staff (% of total)	100	100	..
Under-five mortality rate (per 1,000 live births)	7	4	3
Child malnutrition, underweight (% of under age 5)	..	..	..
Child immunization, measles (% of ages 12-23 mos.)	97	96	97
Primary completion rate, total (% of relevant age group)	102	96	98
Gross secondary enrollment, total (% of relevant age group)	115	125	108
Ratio of girls to boys in primary & secondary school (%)	109	105	102
HIV prevalence rate (% population of ages 15-49)	0.1	0.1	0.1
Environment			
Forests (1,000 sq. km)	219	225	222
Deforestation (avg. annual %, 1990-2000 and 2000-2010)		-0.3	0.1
Freshwater use (% of internal resources)	2.2	2.1	1.5
Access to improved water source (% total pop.)	100	100	100
Access to improved sanitation facilities (% total pop.)	100	100	100
Energy use per capita (kilograms of oil equivalent)	5,692	6,226	6,357
Carbon dioxide emissions per capita (metric tons)	10.4	10.1	10.0
Electricity use per capita (kilowatt-hours)	12,486	15,304	16,483
Economy			
GDP ($ billions)	139	122	263
GDP growth (annual %)	0.5	5.3	2.7
GDP implicit price deflator (annual % growth)	5.4	2.6	3.1
Value added in agriculture (% of GDP)	6	3	3
Value added in industry (% of GDP)	34	35	29
Value added in services (% of GDP)	60	62	68
Exports of goods and services (% of GDP)	23	44	41
Imports of goods and services (% of GDP)	24	34	41
Gross capital formation (% of GDP)	28	21	21
Central government revenue (% of GDP)	..	41.1	38.2
Central government cash surplus/deficit (% of GDP)	..	6.8	-0.5
States and markets			
Starting a business (days)	..	31	14
Stock market capitalization (% of GDP)	16.3	241.1	54.4
Military expenditures (% of GDP)	1.5	1.3	1.5
Mobile cellular subscriptions (per 100 people)	5.2	72.1	166.0
Individuals using the Internet (% of population)	0.4	37.2	89.4
Paved roads (% of total)	61.0	62.0	65.3
High-technology exports (% of manufactured exports)	8	27	9
Global links			
Merchandise trade (% of GDP)	39	66	62
Net barter terms of trade index (2000 = 100)	..	100	75
Total external debt stocks ($ millions)	..	..	..
Total debt service (% of exports)	..	..	..
Net migration (thousands)	15.5	19.6	72.6
Remittances received ($ millions)	63	473	751
Foreign direct investment, net inflows ($ billions)	0.8	9.1	-5.8
Net official development assistance received ($ millions)	..	..	..

France

High income

Population (millions)	65.4	Population growth (%)	0.5
Surface area (1,000 sq. km)	549	Population living below $1.25 a day (%)	..
GNI, Atlas ($ billions)	2,775.7	GNI per capita, Atlas ($)	42,420
GNI, PPP ($ billions)	2,349.8	GNI per capita, PPP ($)	35,910

	1990	2000	2011
People			
Share of poorest 20% in nat'l consumption/income (%)	..	..	..
Life expectancy at birth (years)	77	79	82
Total fertility rate (births per woman)	1.8	1.9	2.0
Adolescent fertility rate (births per 1,000 women 15-19)	..	8	6
Contraceptive prevalence (% of married women 15-49)	81	82	..
Births attended by skilled health staff (% of total)	99	..	..
Under-five mortality rate (per 1,000 live births)	9	5	4
Child malnutrition, underweight (% of under age 5)	..	..	..
Child immunization, measles (% of ages 12-23 mos.)	71	84	89
Primary completion rate, total (% of relevant age group)	103	97	..
Gross secondary enrollment, total (% of relevant age group)	95	108	113
Ratio of girls to boys in primary & secondary school (%)	103	100	100
HIV prevalence rate (% population of ages 15-49)	0.3	0.3	0.4
Environment			
Forests (1,000 sq. km)	145	154	160
Deforestation (avg. annual %, 1990-2000 and 2000-2010)		-0.6	-0.4
Freshwater use (% of internal resources)	18.8	16.4	15.8
Access to improved water source (% total pop.)	100	100	100
Access to improved sanitation facilities (% total pop.)	100	100	100
Energy use per capita (kilograms of oil equivalent)	3,842	4,135	3,843
Carbon dioxide emissions per capita (metric tons)	6.8	6.0	5.6
Electricity use per capita (kilowatt-hours)	5,965	7,238	7,729
Economy			
GDP ($ billions)	1,244	1,326	2,773
GDP growth (annual %)	2.6	3.7	1.7
GDP implicit price deflator (annual % growth)	2.8	1.6	1.3
Value added in agriculture (% of GDP)	4	3	2
Value added in industry (% of GDP)	27	23	19
Value added in services (% of GDP)	69	74	79
Exports of goods and services (% of GDP)	21	29	27
Imports of goods and services (% of GDP)	22	28	30
Gross capital formation (% of GDP)	22	20	21
Central government revenue (% of GDP)	..	43.2	42.8
Central government cash surplus/deficit (% of GDP)	..	-1.6	-5.2
States and markets			
Starting a business (days)	..	41	7
Stock market capitalization (% of GDP)	25.2	109.1	56.6
Military expenditures (% of GDP)	3.4	2.5	2.2
Mobile cellular subscriptions (per 100 people)	0.5	49.2	94.8
Individuals using the Internet (% of population)	0.1	14.3	79.6
Paved roads (% of total)	..	100.0	100.0
High-technology exports (% of manufactured exports)	17	25	24
Global links			
Merchandise trade (% of GDP)	36	50	47
Net barter terms of trade index (2000 = 100)	..	100	96
Total external debt stocks ($ millions)	..	..	..
Total debt service (% of exports)	..	..	..
Net migration (thousands)	278	188	500
Remittances received ($ billions)	4.0	8.6	19.3
Foreign direct investment, net inflows ($ billions)	13.2	42.4	45.2
Net official development assistance received ($ millions)	..	..	..

French Polynesia

Population (thousands)	274	Population growth (%)	1.1
Surface area (1,000 sq. km)	4.0	Population living below $1.25 a day (%)	..
GNI, Atlas ($ billions)	..	GNI per capita, Atlas ($)	..
GNI, PPP ($ millions)	..	GNI per capita, PPP ($)	..

	1990	2000	2011
People			
Share of poorest 20% in nat'l consumption/income (%)	..	..	..
Life expectancy at birth (years)	69	72	75
Total fertility rate (births per woman)	3.3	2.5	2.1
Adolescent fertility rate (births per 1,000 women 15–19)	..	58	49
Contraceptive prevalence (% of married women 15–49)	..	..	..
Births attended by skilled health staff (% of total)	..	99	..
Under-five mortality rate (per 1,000 live births)	..	..	..
Child malnutrition, underweight (% of under age 5)	..	..	..
Child immunization, measles (% of ages 12–23 mos.)	..	..	..
Primary completion rate, total (% of relevant age group)	..	..	..
Gross secondary enrollment, total (% of relevant age group)	67	..	..
Ratio of girls to boys in primary & secondary school (%)	111	..	..
HIV prevalence rate (% population of ages 15–49)	..	..	..
Environment			
Forests (1,000 sq. km)	0.6	1.1	1.6
Deforestation (avg. annual %, 1990–2000 and 2000–2010)		-6.7	-4.0
Freshwater use (% of internal resources)	..	..	..
Access to improved water source (% total pop.)	100	100	100
Access to improved sanitation facilities (% total pop.)	98	98	98
Energy use per capita (kilograms of oil equivalent)	..	..	..
Carbon dioxide emissions per capita (metric tons)	3.2	2.7	3.3
Electricity use per capita (kilowatt-hours)	..	..	..
Economy			
GDP ($ billions)	3.2	3.4	..
GDP growth (annual %)	2.2	4.0	..
GDP implicit price deflator (annual % growth)	0.8	1.0	..
Value added in agriculture (% of GDP)	1	5	..
Value added in industry (% of GDP)	..	..	..
Value added in services (% of GDP)	..	..	..
Exports of goods and services (% of GDP)	1	5	..
Imports of goods and services (% of GDP)	28	24	..
Gross capital formation (% of GDP)	..	..	..
Central government revenue (% of GDP)	..	..	..
Central government cash surplus/deficit (% of GDP)	..	..	..
States and markets			
Starting a business (days)	..	..	..
Stock market capitalization (% of GDP)	..	..	..
Military expenditures (% of GDP)	..	..	..
Mobile cellular subscriptions (per 100 people)	0.0	16.8	81.4
Individuals using the Internet (% of population)	0.0	6.4	49.0
Paved roads (% of total)	..	..	..
High-technology exports (% of manufactured exports)	..	8	16
Global links			
Merchandise trade (% of GDP)	33	35	..
Net barter terms of trade index (2000 = 100)	..	100	83
Total external debt stocks ($ millions)	..	..	..
Total debt service (% of exports)	..	..	..
Net migration (thousands)	-1.1	3.2	-0.4
Remittances received ($ millions)	..	408	700
Foreign direct investment, net inflows ($ millions)	..	10.9	39.9
Net official development assistance received ($ millions)	260	352	..

Gabon

Sub-Saharan Africa		Upper middle income	
Population (millions)	1.5	Population growth (%)	1.9
Surface area (1,000 sq. km)	268	Population living below $1.25 a day (%)	4.8
GNI, Atlas ($ billions)	12.4	GNI per capita, Atlas ($)	8,080
GNI, PPP ($ billions)	21.1	GNI per capita, PPP ($)	13,740

	1990	2000	2011
People			
Share of poorest 20% in nat'l consumption/income (%)	..	..	..
Life expectancy at birth (years)	61	60	63
Total fertility rate (births per woman)	5.2	4.1	3.2
Adolescent fertility rate (births per 1,000 women 15-19)	..	116	83
Contraceptive prevalence (% of married women 15-49)	..	33	..
Births attended by skilled health staff (% of total)	..	86	..
Under-five mortality rate (per 1,000 live births)	94	82	66
Child malnutrition, underweight (% of under age 5)	..	8.8	..
Child immunization, measles (% of ages 12-23 mos.)	76	55	55
Primary completion rate, total (% of relevant age group)	69	72	..
Gross secondary enrollment, total (% of relevant age group)	40	52	..
Ratio of girls to boys in primary & secondary school (%)	96	96	..
HIV prevalence rate (% population of ages 15-49)	1.2	5.0	5.0
Environment			
Forests (1,000 sq. km)	220	220	220
Deforestation (avg. annual %, 1990-2000 and 2000-2010)		0.0	0.0
Freshwater use (% of internal resources)	..	0.1	0.1
Access to improved water source (% total pop.)	..	85	87
Access to improved sanitation facilities (% total pop.)	..	36	33
Energy use per capita (kilograms of oil equivalent)	1,272	1,184	1,418
Carbon dioxide emissions per capita (metric tons)	5.2	0.9	1.1
Electricity use per capita (kilowatt-hours)	940	875	1,004
Economy			
GDP ($ billions)	6.0	5.1	17.1
GDP growth (annual %)	5.2	-1.9	4.8
GDP implicit price deflator (annual % growth)	15.4	28.1	17.4
Value added in agriculture (% of GDP)	7	6	4
Value added in industry (% of GDP)	43	56	64
Value added in services (% of GDP)	50	38	32
Exports of goods and services (% of GDP)	46	69	65
Imports of goods and services (% of GDP)	31	33	36
Gross capital formation (% of GDP)	22	22	27
Central government revenue (% of GDP)	..	..	..
Central government cash surplus/deficit (% of GDP)	..	..	..
States and markets			
Starting a business (days)	..	..	58
Stock market capitalization (% of GDP)	..	..	..
Military expenditures (% of GDP)	..	1.8	0.9
Mobile cellular subscriptions (per 100 people)	0.0	9.7	117.3
Individuals using the Internet (% of population)	0.0	1.2	8.0
Paved roads (% of total)	8.2	9.9	12.0
High-technology exports (% of manufactured exports)	45	5	3
Global links			
Merchandise trade (% of GDP)	52	70	93
Net barter terms of trade index (2000 = 100)	157	100	219
Total external debt stocks ($ billions)	4.0	3.9	2.9
Total debt service (% of exports)	6.4	9.9	..
Net migration (thousands)	20.0	14.4	5.0
Remittances received ($ millions)	0.9	6.1	..
Foreign direct investment, net inflows ($ millions)	73	-43	728
Net official development assistance received ($ millions)	131	12	76

Gambia, The

Sub-Saharan Africa		Low income	
Population (millions)	1.8	Population growth (%)	2.7
Surface area (1,000 sq. km)	11	Population living below $1.25 a day (%)	29.8
GNI, Atlas ($ millions)	889.3	GNI per capita, Atlas ($)	500
GNI, PPP ($ millions)	3,102.9	GNI per capita, PPP ($)	1,750

	1990	2000	2011
People			
Share of poorest 20% in nat'l consumption/income (%)	..	4.8	..
Life expectancy at birth (years)	53	55	58
Total fertility rate (births per woman)	6.1	5.6	4.8
Adolescent fertility rate (births per 1,000 women 15–19)	..	114	69
Contraceptive prevalence (% of married women 15–49)	12	10	13
Births attended by skilled health staff (% of total)	44	55	57
Under-five mortality rate (per 1,000 live births)	165	130	101
Child malnutrition, underweight (% of under age 5)	..	15.4	15.8
Child immunization, measles (% of ages 12–23 mos.)	86	89	91
Primary completion rate, total (% of relevant age group)	42	67	66
Gross secondary enrollment, total (% of relevant age group)	16	..	54
Ratio of girls to boys in primary & secondary school (%)	58	..	99
HIV prevalence rate (% population of ages 15–49)	0.1	0.7	1.5
Environment			
Forests (1,000 sq. km)	4.4	4.6	4.8
Deforestation (avg. annual %, 1990–2000 and 2000–2010)		-0.4	-0.4
Freshwater use (% of internal resources)	..	2.4	2.4
Access to improved water source (% total pop.)	74	83	89
Access to improved sanitation facilities (% total pop.)	60	63	68
Energy use per capita (kilograms of oil equivalent)	64	..	..
Carbon dioxide emissions per capita (metric tons)	0.2	0.2	0.3
Electricity use per capita (kilowatt-hours)	..	..	..
Economy			
GDP ($ millions)	317	783	898
GDP growth (annual %)	3.6	5.5	-4.3
GDP implicit price deflator (annual % growth)	12.0	2.2	3.7
Value added in agriculture (% of GDP)	24	25	19
Value added in industry (% of GDP)	11	15	13
Value added in services (% of GDP)	65	61	68
Exports of goods and services (% of GDP)	60	26	29
Imports of goods and services (% of GDP)	72	31	47
Gross capital formation (% of GDP)	22	5	19
Central government revenue (% of GDP)	19.4	..	..
Central government cash surplus/deficit (% of GDP)	2.1	..	..
States and markets			
Starting a business (days)	..	..	27
Stock market capitalization (% of GDP)	..	..	..
Military expenditures (% of GDP)	1.1	0.4	..
Mobile cellular subscriptions (per 100 people)	0.0	0.4	78.9
Individuals using the Internet (% of population)	0.0	0.9	10.9
Paved roads (% of total)	..	19.3	..
High-technology exports (% of manufactured exports)	..	3	3
Global links			
Merchandise trade (% of GDP)	69	26	49
Net barter terms of trade index (2000 = 100)	100	100	92
Total external debt stocks ($ millions)	369	490	466
Total debt service (% of exports)	22.2	14.8	7.5
Net migration (thousands)	48.4	-26.4	-13.7
Remittances received ($ millions)	..	56.5	90.7
Foreign direct investment, net inflows ($ millions)	14.1	18.3	36.0
Net official development assistance received ($ millions)	97	50	135

Georgia

Europe & Central Asia | Lower middle income

Population (millions)	4.5	Population growth (%)		0.7
Surface area (1,000 sq. km)	70	Population living below $1.25 a day (%)		18.0
GNI, Atlas ($ billions)	12.8	GNI per capita, Atlas ($)		2,860
GNI, PPP ($ billions)	24.0	GNI per capita, PPP ($)		5,350

	1990	2000	2011
People			
Share of poorest 20% in nat'l consumption/income (%)	..	5.3	5.3
Life expectancy at birth (years)	70	72	73
Total fertility rate (births per woman)	2.2	1.6	1.6
Adolescent fertility rate (births per 1,000 women 15-19)	..	53	41
Contraceptive prevalence (% of married women 15-49)	..	41	53
Births attended by skilled health staff (% of total)	97	96	100
Under-five mortality rate (per 1,000 live births)	47	33	21
Child malnutrition, underweight (% of under age 5)	..	2.2	1.1
Child immunization, measles (% of ages 12-23 mos.)	16	73	94
Primary completion rate, total (% of relevant age group)	..	98	116
Gross secondary enrollment, total (% of relevant age group)	95	79	86
Ratio of girls to boys in primary & secondary school (%)	98	98	97
HIV prevalence rate (% population of ages 15-49)	0.1	0.1	0.2
Environment			
Forests (1,000 sq. km)	28	28	27
Deforestation (avg. annual %, 1990-2000 and 2000-2010)		0.0	0.1
Freshwater use (% of internal resources)	..	..	3.1
Access to improved water source (% total pop.)	81	89	98
Access to improved sanitation facilities (% total pop.)	96	95	95
Energy use per capita (kilograms of oil equivalent)	2,586	649	700
Carbon dioxide emissions per capita (metric tons)	3.1	1.0	1.3
Electricity use per capita (kilowatt-hours)	3,039	1,453	1,743
Economy			
GDP ($ billions)	7.7	3.1	14.4
GDP growth (annual %)	-14.8	1.8	7.0
GDP implicit price deflator (annual % growth)	22.4	4.7	9.2
Value added in agriculture (% of GDP)	32	22	9
Value added in industry (% of GDP)	33	22	23
Value added in services (% of GDP)	35	56	67
Exports of goods and services (% of GDP)	40	23	36
Imports of goods and services (% of GDP)	46	40	55
Gross capital formation (% of GDP)	31	27	26
Central government revenue (% of GDP)	..	10.4	25.3
Central government cash surplus/deficit (% of GDP)	..	-1.6	-1.2
States and markets			
Starting a business (days)	..	25	2
Stock market capitalization (% of GDP)	..	0.8	5.5
Military expenditures (% of GDP)	..	0.6	3.0
Mobile cellular subscriptions (per 100 people)	0.0	4.1	102.3
Individuals using the Internet (% of population)	0.0	0.5	36.6
Paved roads (% of total)	93.8	93.4	36.4
High-technology exports (% of manufactured exports)	..	11	2
Global links			
Merchandise trade (% of GDP)	..	34	64
Net barter terms of trade index (2000 = 100)	..	100	134
Total external debt stocks ($ billions)	0.1	1.8	11.1
Total debt service (% of exports)	..	12.5	26.9
Net migration (thousands)	-65	-390	-150
Remittances received ($ millions)	..	274	1,537
Foreign direct investment, net inflows ($ millions)	..	131	1,154
Net official development assistance received ($ millions)	0	169	550

Germany

Population (millions)	81.8	Population growth (%)	0.0
Surface area (1,000 sq. km)	357	Population living below $1.25 a day (%)	..
GNI, Atlas ($ billions)	3,617.7	GNI per capita, Atlas ($)	44,230
GNI, PPP ($ billions)	3,287.6	GNI per capita, PPP ($)	40,190

	1990	2000	2011
People			
Share of poorest 20% in nat'l consumption/income (%)	..	8.5	..
Life expectancy at birth (years)	75	78	81
Total fertility rate (births per woman)	1.5	1.4	1.4
Adolescent fertility rate (births per 1,000 women 15–19)	..	11	7
Contraceptive prevalence (% of married women 15–49)	70	..	..
Births attended by skilled health staff (% of total)	..	..	100
Under-five mortality rate (per 1,000 live births)	9	5	4
Child malnutrition, underweight (% of under age 5)	..	..	1.1
Child immunization, measles (% of ages 12–23 mos.)	75	92	99
Primary completion rate, total (% of relevant age group)	101	102	101
Gross secondary enrollment, total (% of relevant age group)	98	98	103
Ratio of girls to boys in primary & secondary school (%)	99	99	96
HIV prevalence rate (% population of ages 15–49)	0.1	0.1	0.2
Environment			
Forests (1,000 sq. km)	107	111	111
Deforestation (avg. annual %, 1990–2000 and 2000–2010)		-0.3	0.0
Freshwater use (% of internal resources)	..	36.6	30.2
Access to improved water source (% total pop.)	100	100	100
Access to improved sanitation facilities (% total pop.)	100	100	100
Energy use per capita (kilograms of oil equivalent)	4,421	4,094	3,755
Carbon dioxide emissions per capita (metric tons)	11.6	10.1	9.0
Electricity use per capita (kilowatt-hours)	6,640	6,635	7,215
Economy			
GDP ($ billions)	1,714	1,886	3,601
GDP growth (annual %)	5.3	3.1	3.0
GDP implicit price deflator (annual % growth)	3.4	-0.7	0.8
Value added in agriculture (% of GDP)	1	1	1
Value added in industry (% of GDP)	37	30	28
Value added in services (% of GDP)	61	68	71
Exports of goods and services (% of GDP)	25	33	50
Imports of goods and services (% of GDP)	25	33	45
Gross capital formation (% of GDP)	23	22	18
Central government revenue (% of GDP)	..	30.3	29.1
Central government cash surplus/deficit (% of GDP)	..	1.4	-0.4
States and markets			
Starting a business (days)	..	45	15
Stock market capitalization (% of GDP)	20.7	67.3	32.9
Military expenditures (% of GDP)	2.5	1.5	1.3
Mobile cellular subscriptions (per 100 people)	0.3	58.5	132.3
Individuals using the Internet (% of population)	0.1	30.2	83.0
Paved roads (% of total)	99.0	100.0	..
High-technology exports (% of manufactured exports)	12	19	15
Global links			
Merchandise trade (% of GDP)	45	56	76
Net barter terms of trade index (2000 = 100)	..	100	99
Total external debt stocks ($ millions)	..	..	..
Total debt service (% of exports)	..	..	..
Net migration (thousands)	1,621	839	550
Remittances received ($ billions)	4.9	3.6	13.2
Foreign direct investment, net inflows ($ billions)	3	210	39
Net official development assistance received ($ millions)	..	..	..

Ghana

Sub-Saharan Africa		Lower middle income	
Population (millions)	25.0	Population growth (%)	2.3
Surface area (1,000 sq. km)	239	Population living below $1.25 a day (%)	28.6
GNI, Atlas ($ billions)	35.1	GNI per capita, Atlas ($)	1,410
GNI, PPP ($ billions)	45.2	GNI per capita, PPP ($)	1,810

	1990	2000	2011
People			
Share of poorest 20% in nat'l consumption/income (%)	7.0	5.6	5.2
Life expectancy at birth (years)	57	58	64
Total fertility rate (births per woman)	5.6	4.7	4.1
Adolescent fertility rate (births per 1,000 women 15–19)	..	84	64
Contraceptive prevalence (% of married women 15–49)	17	22	34
Births attended by skilled health staff (% of total)	44	47	68
Under-five mortality rate (per 1,000 live births)	121	99	78
Child malnutrition, underweight (% of under age 5)	25.1	20.3	14.3
Child immunization, measles (% of ages 12–23 mos.)	61	90	91
Primary completion rate, total (% of relevant age group)	65	71	99
Gross secondary enrollment, total (% of relevant age group)	36	41	59
Ratio of girls to boys in primary & secondary school (%)	78	90	93
HIV prevalence rate (% population of ages 15–49)	1.0	2.2	1.5
Environment			
Forests (1,000 sq. km)	74	61	48
Deforestation (avg. annual %, 1990–2000 and 2000–2010)		2.0	2.1
Freshwater use (% of internal resources)	..	3.2	3.2
Access to improved water source (% total pop.)	53	71	86
Access to improved sanitation facilities (% total pop.)	7	10	14
Energy use per capita (kilograms of oil equivalent)	358	404	382
Carbon dioxide emissions per capita (metric tons)	0.3	0.3	0.3
Electricity use per capita (kilowatt-hours)	323	330	298
Economy			
GDP ($ billions)	5.9	5.0	39.2
GDP growth (annual %)	3.3	3.7	14.4
GDP implicit price deflator (annual % growth)	31.2	27.2	12.5
Value added in agriculture (% of GDP)	45	39	26
Value added in industry (% of GDP)	17	28	26
Value added in services (% of GDP)	38	32	49
Exports of goods and services (% of GDP)	17	49	38
Imports of goods and services (% of GDP)	26	67	51
Gross capital formation (% of GDP)	14	24	19
Central government revenue (% of GDP)	12.5	18.1	19.6
Central government cash surplus/deficit (% of GDP)	..	–6.5	–4.0
States and markets			
Starting a business (days)	..	22	12
Stock market capitalization (% of GDP)	1.2	10.1	7.9
Military expenditures (% of GDP)	0.5	1.0	0.3
Mobile cellular subscriptions (per 100 people)	0.0	0.7	84.8
Individuals using the Internet (% of population)	0.0	0.2	14.1
Paved roads (% of total)	19.6	29.6	12.6
High-technology exports (% of manufactured exports)	2	2	1
Global links			
Merchandise trade (% of GDP)	36	93	73
Net barter terms of trade index (2000 = 100)	100	100	185
Total external debt stocks ($ billions)	3.7	6.3	11.3
Total debt service (% of exports)	38.4	16.0	2.4
Net migration (thousands)	–30.0	–51.3	–51.3
Remittances received ($ millions)	6	32	152
Foreign direct investment, net inflows ($ millions)	15	166	3,222
Net official development assistance received ($ millions)	560	598	1,815

Greece

High income

Population (millions)	11.3	Population growth (%)		-0.1
Surface area (1,000 sq. km)	132	Population living below $1.25 a day (%)		..
GNI, Atlas ($ billions)	276.7	GNI per capita, Atlas ($)		24,490
GNI, PPP ($ billions)	283.7	GNI per capita, PPP ($)		25,110

	1990	2000	2011
People			
Share of poorest 20% in nat'l consumption/income (%)	..	6.7	..
Life expectancy at birth (years)	77	78	81
Total fertility rate (births per woman)	1.4	1.3	1.4
Adolescent fertility rate (births per 1,000 women 15–19)	..	11	10
Contraceptive prevalence (% of married women 15–49)	..	76	..
Births attended by skilled health staff (% of total)	..	..	..
Under-five mortality rate (per 1,000 live births)	13	8	4
Child malnutrition, underweight (% of under age 5)	..	..	1.1
Child immunization, measles (% of ages 12–23 mos.)	76	89	99
Primary completion rate, total (% of relevant age group)	98	..	99
Gross secondary enrollment, total (% of relevant age group)	94	89	109
Ratio of girls to boys in primary & secondary school (%)	99	103	98
HIV prevalence rate (% population of ages 15–49)	0.1	0.1	0.2
Environment			
Forests (1,000 sq. km)	33	36	39
Deforestation (avg. annual %, 1990–2000 and 2000–2010)		-0.9	-0.8
Freshwater use (% of internal resources)	12.1	17.1	16.3
Access to improved water source (% total pop.)	96	99	100
Access to improved sanitation facilities (% total pop.)	97	98	98
Energy use per capita (kilograms of oil equivalent)	2,111	2,481	2,349
Carbon dioxide emissions per capita (metric tons)	7.2	8.4	8.4
Electricity use per capita (kilowatt-hours)	3,234	4,539	5,242
Economy			
GDP ($ billions)	93	124	290
GDP growth (annual %)	0.0	4.5	-7.1
GDP implicit price deflator (annual % growth)	20.7	3.4	1.0
Value added in agriculture (% of GDP)	..	..	..
Value added in industry (% of GDP)	..	..	..
Value added in services (% of GDP)	..	..	..
Exports of goods and services (% of GDP)	18	26	25
Imports of goods and services (% of GDP)	31	40	33
Gross capital formation (% of GDP)	25	25	16
Central government revenue (% of GDP)	..	41.9	41.0
Central government cash surplus/deficit (% of GDP)	..	-3.8	-9.8
States and markets			
Starting a business (days)	..	38	11
Stock market capitalization (% of GDP)	16.3	89.1	11.6
Military expenditures (% of GDP)	3.4	3.6	2.8
Mobile cellular subscriptions (per 100 people)	0.0	54.0	106.5
Individuals using the Internet (% of population)	0.0	9.1	53.0
Paved roads (% of total)	91.7	91.8	35.4
High-technology exports (% of manufactured exports)	2	14	10
Global links			
Merchandise trade (% of GDP)	30	36	32
Net barter terms of trade index (2000 = 100)	..	100	94
Total external debt stocks ($ millions)	..	..	..
Total debt service (% of exports)	..	..	..
Net migration (thousands)	155	300	154
Remittances received ($ billions)	1.8	2.2	1.2
Foreign direct investment, net inflows ($ billions)	1.0	1.1	1.1
Net official development assistance received ($ millions)	..	..	..

Greenland

High income

Population (thousands)	57	Population growth (%)	-0.1
Surface area (1,000 sq. km)	410	Population living below $1.25 a day (%)	..
GNI, Atlas ($ billions)	1.5	GNI per capita, Atlas ($)	26,020
GNI, PPP ($ millions)	..	GNI per capita, PPP ($)	..

	1990	2000	2011
People			
Share of poorest 20% in nat'l consumption/income (%)	..	..	..
Life expectancy at birth (years)	65	66	70
Total fertility rate (births per woman)	2.4	2.3	2.1
Adolescent fertility rate (births per 1,000 women 15-19)	..	..	..
Contraceptive prevalence (% of married women 15-49)	..	..	..
Births attended by skilled health staff (% of total)	..	..	..
Under-five mortality rate (per 1,000 live births)	..	..	..
Child malnutrition, underweight (% of under age 5)	..	..	..
Child immunization, measles (% of ages 12-23 mos.)	..	..	..
Primary completion rate, total (% of relevant age group)	..	..	..
Gross secondary enrollment, total (% of relevant age group)	..	..	..
Ratio of girls to boys in primary & secondary school (%)	..	..	..
HIV prevalence rate (% population of ages 15-49)	..	..	..
Environment			
Forests (sq. km)	2.0	2.0	2.2
Deforestation (avg. annual %, 1990-2000 and 2000-2010)		0.0	0.0
Freshwater use (% of internal resources)	..	..	..
Access to improved water source (% total pop.)	100	100	100
Access to improved sanitation facilities (% total pop.)	100	100	100
Energy use per capita (kilograms of oil equivalent)	..	..	..
Carbon dioxide emissions per capita (metric tons)	10.0	9.5	10.2
Electricity use per capita (kilowatt-hours)	..	..	..
Economy			
GDP ($ millions)	1,019	1,068	1,268
GDP growth (annual %)	-11.7	7.1	-5.4
GDP implicit price deflator (annual % growth)	5.1	2.1	-19.0
Value added in agriculture (% of GDP)	..	..	..
Value added in industry (% of GDP)	..	..	..
Value added in services (% of GDP)	..	..	..
Exports of goods and services (% of GDP)	..	..	..
Imports of goods and services (% of GDP)	..	..	..
Gross capital formation (% of GDP)	..	..	..
Central government revenue (% of GDP)	..	..	..
Central government cash surplus/deficit (% of GDP)	..	..	..
States and markets			
Starting a business (days)	..	..	..
Stock market capitalization (% of GDP)	..	..	..
Military expenditures (% of GDP)	..	..	..
Mobile cellular subscriptions (per 100 people)	0.0	26.9	102.5
Individuals using the Internet (% of population)	0.0	31.7	64.0
Paved roads (% of total)	..	..	..
High-technology exports (% of manufactured exports)	10	37	..
Global links			
Merchandise trade (% of GDP)	88	60	86
Net barter terms of trade index (2000 = 100)	..	100	72
Total external debt stocks ($ millions)	..	..	..
Total debt service (% of exports)	..	..	..
Net migration (thousands)	..	..	..
Remittances received ($ millions)	..	..	..
Foreign direct investment, net inflows ($ millions)	..	..	..
Net official development assistance received ($ millions)	..	..	..

Grenada

Latin America & Caribbean | | **Upper middle income**

Population (thousands)	105	Population growth (%)	0.4
Surface area (sq. km)	340	Population living below $1.25 a day (%)	..
GNI, Atlas ($ millions)	770.9	GNI per capita, Atlas ($)	7,350
GNI, PPP ($ millions)	1,086.0	GNI per capita, PPP ($)	10,350

	1990	2000	2011
People			
Share of poorest 20% in nat'l consumption/income (%)	..	..	..
Life expectancy at birth (years)	69	73	76
Total fertility rate (births per woman)	3.8	2.6	2.2
Adolescent fertility rate (births per 1,000 women 15–19)	..	55	37
Contraceptive prevalence (% of married women 15–49)	54	54	54
Births attended by skilled health staff (% of total)	..	100	99
Under-five mortality rate (per 1,000 live births)	21	16	13
Child malnutrition, underweight (% of under age 5)	..	..	..
Child immunization, measles (% of ages 12–23 mos.)	85	92	95
Primary completion rate, total (% of relevant age group)	..	91	112
Gross secondary enrollment, total (% of relevant age group)	91	108	108
Ratio of girls to boys in primary & secondary school (%)	104	103	99
HIV prevalence rate (% population of ages 15–49)	..	..	..
Environment			
Forests (sq. km)	170	170	170
Deforestation (avg. annual %, 1990–2000 and 2000–2010)		0.0	0.0
Freshwater use (% of internal resources)	..	..	..
Access to improved water source (% total pop.)	94	94	..
Access to improved sanitation facilities (% total pop.)	97	97	97
Energy use per capita (kilograms of oil equivalent)	442	..	..
Carbon dioxide emissions per capita (metric tons)	1.1	1.9	2.4
Electricity use per capita (kilowatt-hours)	..	..	..
Economy			
GDP ($ millions)	221	523	816
GDP growth (annual %)	5.2	2.5	1.0
GDP implicit price deflator (annual % growth)	-1.4	34.5	3.1
Value added in agriculture (% of GDP)	13	6	5
Value added in industry (% of GDP)	18	21	17
Value added in services (% of GDP)	69	73	78
Exports of goods and services (% of GDP)	42	45	23
Imports of goods and services (% of GDP)	63	59	48
Gross capital formation (% of GDP)	38	38	21
Central government revenue (% of GDP)	..	21.4	19.3
Central government cash surplus/deficit (% of GDP)	..	-2.1	-3.0
States and markets			
Starting a business (days)	..	..	15
Stock market capitalization (% of GDP)	..	..	..
Military expenditures (% of GDP)	..	..	..
Mobile cellular subscriptions (per 100 people)	0.2	4.2	116.7
Individuals using the Internet (% of population)	0.0	4.1	33.5
Paved roads (% of total)	55.4	61.0	..
High-technology exports (% of manufactured exports)	4	30	11
Global links			
Merchandise trade (% of GDP)	60	55	45
Net barter terms of trade index (2000 = 100)	..	100	102
Total external debt stocks ($ millions)	112	203	567
Total debt service (% of exports)	4.3	6.0	13.3
Net migration (thousands)	-14.7	-5.5	-5.0
Remittances received ($ millions)	18.0	46.4	28.9
Foreign direct investment, net inflows ($ millions)	12.9	37.4	41.4
Net official development assistance received ($ millions)	13.8	16.5	12.8

Guam

Population (thousands)	182	Population growth (%)		1.2
Surface area (sq. km)	540	Population living below $1.25 a day (%)		..
GNI, Atlas ($ millions)	..	GNI per capita, Atlas ($)		..
GNI, PPP ($ millions)	..	GNI per capita, PPP ($)		..

	1990	2000	2011
People			
Share of poorest 20% in nat'l consumption/income (%)	..	..	..
Life expectancy at birth (years)	72	74	76
Total fertility rate (births per woman)	3.1	2.9	2.4
Adolescent fertility rate (births per 1,000 women 15–19)	..	64	50
Contraceptive prevalence (% of married women 15–49)	..	67	..
Births attended by skilled health staff (% of total)	..	99	..
Under-five mortality rate (per 1,000 live births)	..	..	..
Child malnutrition, underweight (% of under age 5)	..	..	..
Child immunization, measles (% of ages 12–23 mos.)	..	..	..
Primary completion rate, total (% of relevant age group)	..	..	..
Gross secondary enrollment, total (% of relevant age group)	..	..	..
Ratio of girls to boys in primary & secondary school (%)	..	..	..
HIV prevalence rate (% population of ages 15–49)	..	..	..
Environment			
Forests (sq. km)	259	259	259
Deforestation (avg. annual %, 1990–2000 and 2000–2010)		0.0	0.0
Freshwater use (% of internal resources)	..	..	..
Access to improved water source (% total pop.)	100	100	100
Access to improved sanitation facilities (% total pop.)	99	99	99
Energy use per capita (kilograms of oil equivalent)	..	..	..
Carbon dioxide emissions per capita (metric tons)	..	..	..
Electricity use per capita (kilowatt-hours)	..	..	..
Economy			
GDP ($ millions)	..	..	..
GDP growth (annual %)	..	..	..
GDP implicit price deflator (annual % growth)	..	..	..
Value added in agriculture (% of GDP)	..	..	..
Value added in industry (% of GDP)	..	..	..
Value added in services (% of GDP)	..	..	..
Exports of goods and services (% of GDP)	..	..	..
Imports of goods and services (% of GDP)	..	..	..
Gross capital formation (% of GDP)	..	..	..
Central government revenue (% of GDP)	..	..	..
Central government cash surplus/deficit (% of GDP)	..	..	..
States and markets			
Starting a business (days)	..	..	..
Stock market capitalization (% of GDP)	..	..	..
Military expenditures (% of GDP)	..	..	..
Mobile cellular subscriptions (per 100 people)	0.0	17.5	..
Individuals using the Internet (% of population)	0.0	16.1	50.6
Paved roads (% of total)	..	..	..
High-technology exports (% of manufactured exports)	..	..	..
Global links			
Merchandise trade (% of GDP)	..	..	..
Net barter terms of trade index (2000 = 100)	..	100	85
Total external debt stocks ($ millions)	..	..	..
Total debt service (% of exports)	..	..	..
Net migration (thousands)	0.5	-4.8	0.0
Remittances received ($ millions)	..	..	..
Foreign direct investment, net inflows ($ millions)	..	..	..
Net official development assistance received ($ millions)	..	..	..

Guatemala

Latin America & Caribbean		**Lower middle income**	
Population (millions)	14.8	Population growth (%)	2.5
Surface area (1,000 sq. km)	109	Population living below $1.25 a day (%)	13.5
GNI, Atlas ($ billions)	42.4	GNI per capita, Atlas ($)	2,870
GNI, PPP ($ billions)	70.3	GNI per capita, PPP ($)	4,760

	1990	2000	2011
People			
Share of poorest 20% in nat'l consumption/income (%)	2.2	3.5	3.1
Life expectancy at birth (years)	62	68	71
Total fertility rate (births per woman)	5.6	4.8	3.9
Adolescent fertility rate (births per 1,000 women 15–19)	..	118	103
Contraceptive prevalence (% of married women 15–49)	..	38	54
Births attended by skilled health staff (% of total)	..	41	52
Under-five mortality rate (per 1,000 live births)	78	48	30
Child malnutrition, underweight (% of under age 5)	20.7	19.6	13.0
Child immunization, measles (% of ages 12–23 mos.)	68	86	87
Primary completion rate, total (% of relevant age group)	..	58	86
Gross secondary enrollment, total (% of relevant age group)	23	38	64
Ratio of girls to boys in primary & secondary school (%)	87	89	95
HIV prevalence rate (% population of ages 15–49)	0.1	0.5	0.8
Environment			
Forests (1,000 sq. km)	47	42	36
Deforestation (avg. annual %, 1990–2000 and 2000–2010)		1.2	1.4
Freshwater use (% of internal resources)	..	2.7	2.7
Access to improved water source (% total pop.)	81	87	92
Access to improved sanitation facilities (% total pop.)	62	71	78
Energy use per capita (kilograms of oil equivalent)	495	627	713
Carbon dioxide emissions per capita (metric tons)	0.6	0.9	1.1
Electricity use per capita (kilowatt-hours)	208	343	567
Economy			
GDP ($ billions)	7.7	19.3	46.9
GDP growth (annual %)	3.1	3.6	3.9
GDP implicit price deflator (annual % growth)	40.5	6.8	5.5
Value added in agriculture (% of GDP)	..	15	11
Value added in industry (% of GDP)	..	29	68
Value added in services (% of GDP)	..	56	20
Exports of goods and services (% of GDP)	21	20	27
Imports of goods and services (% of GDP)	25	29	38
Gross capital formation (% of GDP)	14	18	14
Central government revenue (% of GDP)	7.9	10.2	11.6
Central government cash surplus/deficit (% of GDP)	-1.9	-1.8	-2.8
States and markets			
Starting a business (days)	..	39	40
Stock market capitalization (% of GDP)	..	0.9	..
Military expenditures (% of GDP)	1.5	0.8	0.4
Mobile cellular subscriptions (per 100 people)	0.0	7.6	140.4
Individuals using the Internet (% of population)	0.0	0.7	11.7
Paved roads (% of total)	24.9	34.5	59.1
High-technology exports (% of manufactured exports)	6	8	4
Global links			
Merchandise trade (% of GDP)	37	39	58
Net barter terms of trade index (2000 = 100)	115	100	91
Total external debt stocks ($ billions)	2.9	3.9	16.3
Total debt service (% of exports)	15.4	9.7	15.6
Net migration (thousands)	-300	-390	-200
Remittances received ($ millions)	119	596	4,508
Foreign direct investment, net inflows ($ millions)	48	230	1,081
Net official development assistance received ($ millions)	201	263	392

Guinea

Sub-Saharan Africa				**Low income**
Population (millions)	10.2	Population growth (%)		2.4
Surface area (1,000 sq. km)	246	Population living below $1.25 a day (%)		43.3
GNI, Atlas ($ billions)	4.4	GNI per capita, Atlas ($)		430
GNI, PPP ($ billions)	10.5	GNI per capita, PPP ($)		1,020

	1990	2000	2011
People			
Share of poorest 20% in nat'l consumption/income (%)	3.1	6.4	6.4
Life expectancy at birth (years)	44	48	54
Total fertility rate (births per woman)	6.7	6.0	5.2
Adolescent fertility rate (births per 1,000 women 15–19)	..	169	138
Contraceptive prevalence (% of married women 15–49)	2	6	..
Births attended by skilled health staff (% of total)	31	35	46
Under-five mortality rate (per 1,000 live births)	228	175	126
Child malnutrition, underweight (% of under age 5)	..	29.1	20.8
Child immunization, measles (% of ages 12–23 mos.)	35	42	58
Primary completion rate, total (% of relevant age group)	21	32	64
Gross secondary enrollment, total (% of relevant age group)	11	19	42
Ratio of girls to boys in primary & secondary school (%)	44	64	79
HIV prevalence rate (% population of ages 15–49)	0.7	1.5	1.4
Environment			
Forests (1,000 sq. km)	73	69	65
Deforestation (avg. annual %, 1990–2000 and 2000–2010)		0.5	0.5
Freshwater use (% of internal resources)	..	0.7	0.7
Access to improved water source (% total pop.)	51	63	74
Access to improved sanitation facilities (% total pop.)	10	14	18
Energy use per capita (kilograms of oil equivalent)	..	..	..
Carbon dioxide emissions per capita (metric tons)	0.2	0.2	0.1
Electricity use per capita (kilowatt-hours)	..	..	..
Economy			
GDP ($ billions)	2.7	3.0	5.1
GDP growth (annual %)	4.3	2.5	3.9
GDP implicit price deflator (annual % growth)	17.3	6.3	19.6
Value added in agriculture (% of GDP)	24	22	22
Value added in industry (% of GDP)	33	33	45
Value added in services (% of GDP)	43	44	33
Exports of goods and services (% of GDP)	31	25	30
Imports of goods and services (% of GDP)	33	29	48
Gross capital formation (% of GDP)	25	20	18
Central government revenue (% of GDP)	..	12.0	..
Central government cash surplus/deficit (% of GDP)	..	-2.4	..
States and markets			
Starting a business (days)	..	40	35
Stock market capitalization (% of GDP)	..	..	..
Military expenditures (% of GDP)	2.4	1.5	..
Mobile cellular subscriptions (per 100 people)	0.0	0.5	44.0
Individuals using the Internet (% of population)	0.0	0.1	1.3
Paved roads (% of total)	15.2	16.5	..
High-technology exports (% of manufactured exports)	..	0	0
Global links			
Merchandise trade (% of GDP)	52	43	73
Net barter terms of trade index (2000 = 100)	122	100	110
Total external debt stocks ($ billions)	2.5	3.1	3.1
Total debt service (% of exports)	20.1	20.7	11.2
Net migration (thousands)	162	-227	-300
Remittances received ($ millions)	18.0	1.2	64.5
Foreign direct investment, net inflows ($ millions)	18	10	896
Net official development assistance received ($ millions)	292	153	208

Guinea-Bissau

Sub-Saharan Africa   **Low income**

Population (millions)	1.5	Population growth (%)		2.1
Surface area (1,000 sq. km)	36	Population living below $1.25 a day (%)		48.9
GNI, Atlas ($ millions)	925.5	GNI per capita, Atlas ($)		600
GNI, PPP ($ millions)	1,910.6	GNI per capita, PPP ($)		1,230

	1990	2000	2011
People			
Share of poorest 20% in nat'l consumption/income (%)	2.1	7.3	..
Life expectancy at birth (years)	43	45	48
Total fertility rate (births per woman)	6.6	5.8	5.0
Adolescent fertility rate (births per 1,000 women 15–19)	..	137	99
Contraceptive prevalence (% of married women 15–49)	..	8	14
Births attended by skilled health staff (% of total)	..	35	44
Under-five mortality rate (per 1,000 live births)	210	186	161
Child malnutrition, underweight (% of under age 5)	..	21.9	17.2
Child immunization, measles (% of ages 12–23 mos.)	53	71	61
Primary completion rate, total (% of relevant age group)	6	30	68
Gross secondary enrollment, total (% of relevant age group)	5	19	..
Ratio of girls to boys in primary & secondary school (%)	55	66	..
HIV prevalence rate (% population of ages 15–49)	0.3	1.2	2.5
Environment			
Forests (1,000 sq. km)	22	21	20
Deforestation (avg. annual %, 1990–2000 and 2000–2010)		0.4	0.5
Freshwater use (% of internal resources)	0.1	1.1	1.1
Access to improved water source (% total pop.)	36	50	64
Access to improved sanitation facilities (% total pop.)	..	14	20
Energy use per capita (kilograms of oil equivalent)	73	..	..
Carbon dioxide emissions per capita (metric tons)	0.2	0.2	0.2
Electricity use per capita (kilowatt-hours)	..	..	..
Economy			
GDP ($ millions)	244	215	968
GDP growth (annual %)	6.1	3.6	5.7
GDP implicit price deflator (annual % growth)	30.2	7.1	4.4
Value added in agriculture (% of GDP)	61	56	..
Value added in industry (% of GDP)	19	13	..
Value added in services (% of GDP)	21	31	..
Exports of goods and services (% of GDP)	10	32	..
Imports of goods and services (% of GDP)	37	52	..
Gross capital formation (% of GDP)	30	11	..
Central government revenue (% of GDP)	..	..	..
Central government cash surplus/deficit (% of GDP)	..	..	..
States and markets			
Starting a business (days)	..	..	9
Stock market capitalization (% of GDP)	..	..	..
Military expenditures (% of GDP)	2.1	4.4	..
Mobile cellular subscriptions (per 100 people)	0.0	0.0	56.2
Individuals using the Internet (% of population)	0.0	0.2	2.7
Paved roads (% of total)	8.3	27.9	..
High-technology exports (% of manufactured exports)	..	..	..
Global links			
Merchandise trade (% of GDP)	43	56	55
Net barter terms of trade index (2000 = 100)	146	100	81
Total external debt stocks ($ millions)	695	949	284
Total debt service (% of exports)	32.3	7.1	6.4
Net migration (thousands)	-20.0	-20.0	-10.0
Remittances received ($ millions)	1.0	8.0	45.9
Foreign direct investment, net inflows ($ millions)	2.0	0.7	19.4
Net official development assistance received ($ millions)	126	81	119

Guyana

Latin America & Caribbean		Lower middle income	
Population (thousands)	756	Population growth (%)	0.2
Surface area (1,000 sq. km)	215	Population living below $1.25 a day (%)	..
GNI, Atlas ($ billions)	2.2	GNI per capita, Atlas ($)	2,900
GNI, PPP ($ billions)	2.6	GNI per capita, PPP ($)	3,460

	1990	2000	2011
People			
Share of poorest 20% in nat'l consumption/income (%)	4.3	4.5	..
Life expectancy at birth (years)	61	64	70
Total fertility rate (births per woman)	2.6	2.5	2.2
Adolescent fertility rate (births per 1,000 women 15–19)	..	79	57
Contraceptive prevalence (% of married women 15–49)	38	37	43
Births attended by skilled health staff (% of total)	..	86	92
Under-five mortality rate (per 1,000 live births)	63	49	36
Child malnutrition, underweight (% of under age 5)	16.1	11.9	11.1
Child immunization, measles (% of ages 12–23 mos.)	73	86	98
Primary completion rate, total (% of relevant age group)	97	103	85
Gross secondary enrollment, total (% of relevant age group)	..	98	93
Ratio of girls to boys in primary & secondary school (%)	..	98	107
HIV prevalence rate (% population of ages 15–49)	0.6	1.9	1.1

	1990	2000	2011
Environment			
Forests (1,000 sq. km)	152	152	152
Deforestation (avg. annual %, 1990–2000 and 2000–2010)		0.0	0.0
Freshwater use (% of internal resources)	0.6	0.7	0.7
Access to improved water source (% total pop.)	..	89	94
Access to improved sanitation facilities (% total pop.)	..	79	84
Energy use per capita (kilograms of oil equivalent)	527	..	..
Carbon dioxide emissions per capita (metric tons)	1.6	2.2	2.1
Electricity use per capita (kilowatt-hours)	..	..	..

	1990	2000	2011
Economy			
GDP ($ millions)	397	713	2,577
GDP growth (annual %)	-3.0	-1.4	4.4
GDP implicit price deflator (annual % growth)	56.4	6.6	6.7
Value added in agriculture (% of GDP)	38	31	21
Value added in industry (% of GDP)	25	29	34
Value added in services (% of GDP)	37	40	45
Exports of goods and services (% of GDP)	63	96	..
Imports of goods and services (% of GDP)	80	111	..
Gross capital formation (% of GDP)	31	24	24
Central government revenue (% of GDP)	..	..	..
Central government cash surplus/deficit (% of GDP)	..	..	..

	1990	2000	2011
States and markets			
Starting a business (days)	..	46	20
Stock market capitalization (% of GDP)	..	12.7	17.1
Military expenditures (% of GDP)	0.9	1.5	1.2
Mobile cellular subscriptions (per 100 people)	0.0	5.4	69.9
Individuals using the Internet (% of population)	0.0	6.6	32.0
Paved roads (% of total)	6.6	7.4	..
High-technology exports (% of manufactured exports)	..	2	0

	1990	2000	2011
Global links			
Merchandise trade (% of GDP)	143	150	113
Net barter terms of trade index (2000 = 100)	..	100	130
Total external debt stocks ($ billions)	2.0	1.4	1.8
Total debt service (% of exports)	18.7	10.2	2.7
Net migration (thousands)	-88.0	-42.5	-40.0
Remittances received ($ millions)	1	27	373
Foreign direct investment, net inflows ($ millions)	8	67	165
Net official development assistance received ($ millions)	168	116	159

Haiti

Latin America & Caribbean		Low income	
Population (millions)	10.1	Population growth (%)	1.3
Surface area (1,000 sq. km)	28	Population living below $1.25 a day (%)	61.7
GNI, Atlas ($ billions)	7.1	GNI per capita, Atlas ($)	700
GNI, PPP ($ billions)	11.9	GNI per capita, PPP ($)	1,180

	1990	2000	2011
People			
Share of poorest 20% in nat'l consumption/income (%)	..	2.4	..
Life expectancy at birth (years)	55	58	62
Total fertility rate (births per woman)	5.4	4.3	3.3
Adolescent fertility rate (births per 1,000 women 15–19)	..	56	42
Contraceptive prevalence (% of married women 15–49)	10	28	32
Births attended by skilled health staff (% of total)	23	24	26
Under-five mortality rate (per 1,000 live births)	143	102	70
Child malnutrition, underweight (% of under age 5)	23.7	13.9	18.9
Child immunization, measles (% of ages 12–23 mos.)	31	55	59
Primary completion rate, total (% of relevant age group)	..	..	..
Gross secondary enrollment, total (% of relevant age group)	..	..	..
Ratio of girls to boys in primary & secondary school (%)	..	..	..
HIV prevalence rate (% population of ages 15–49)	2.9	2.7	1.8
Environment			
Forests (1,000 sq. km)	1.2	1.1	1.0
Deforestation (avg. annual %, 1990–2000 and 2000–2010)		0.6	0.8
Freshwater use (% of internal resources)	7.5	9.2	9.2
Access to improved water source (% total pop.)	59	62	69
Access to improved sanitation facilities (% total pop.)	26	22	17
Energy use per capita (kilograms of oil equivalent)	219	233	229
Carbon dioxide emissions per capita (metric tons)	0.1	0.2	0.2
Electricity use per capita (kilowatt-hours)	58	35	24
Economy			
GDP ($ billions)	3.5	3.7	7.3
GDP growth (annual %)	-5.3	0.9	5.6
GDP implicit price deflator (annual % growth)	20.9	11.1	6.8
Value added in agriculture (% of GDP)	..	..	..
Value added in industry (% of GDP)	..	..	..
Value added in services (% of GDP)	..	..	..
Exports of goods and services (% of GDP)	10	13	14
Imports of goods and services (% of GDP)	29	33	55
Gross capital formation (% of GDP)	24	27	28
Central government revenue (% of GDP)	..	..	..
Central government cash surplus/deficit (% of GDP)	..	..	..
States and markets			
Starting a business (days)	..	202	105
Stock market capitalization (% of GDP)	..	..	..
Military expenditures (% of GDP)	0.1	..	..
Mobile cellular subscriptions (per 100 people)	0.0	0.6	41.5
Individuals using the Internet (% of population)	0.0	0.2	8.4
Paved roads (% of total)	21.9	24.3	..
High-technology exports (% of manufactured exports)	14	..	..
Global links			
Merchandise trade (% of GDP)	16	37	50
Net barter terms of trade index (2000 = 100)	132	100	65
Total external debt stocks ($ millions)	939	1,203	783
Total debt service (% of exports)	11.9	9.2	0.5
Net migration (thousands)	-131	-136	-240
Remittances received ($ millions)	123	578	1,551
Foreign direct investment, net inflows ($ millions)	8	13	181
Net official development assistance received ($ millions)	167	208	1,712

Honduras

Latin America & Caribbean		Lower middle income	
Population (millions)	7.8	Population growth (%)	2.0
Surface area (1,000 sq. km)	112	Population living below $1.25 a day (%)	17.9
GNI, Atlas ($ billions)	15.4	GNI per capita, Atlas ($)	1,980
GNI, PPP ($ billions)	29.7	GNI per capita, PPP ($)	3,820

	1990	2000	2011
People			
Share of poorest 20% in nat'l consumption/income (%)	2.8	2.7	2.0
Life expectancy at birth (years)	66	70	73
Total fertility rate (births per woman)	5.1	4.0	3.1
Adolescent fertility rate (births per 1,000 women 15–19)	..	107	87
Contraceptive prevalence (% of married women 15–49)	47	62	65
Births attended by skilled health staff (% of total)	47	56	67
Under-five mortality rate (per 1,000 live births)	55	35	21
Child malnutrition, underweight (% of under age 5)	15.8	12.5	8.6
Child immunization, measles (% of ages 12–23 mos.)	90	98	99
Primary completion rate, total (% of relevant age group)	65	..	101
Gross secondary enrollment, total (% of relevant age group)	33	..	74
Ratio of girls to boys in primary & secondary school (%)	104	..	107
HIV prevalence rate (% population of ages 15–49)	..	..	..
Environment			
Forests (1,000 sq. km)	81	64	51
Deforestation (avg. annual %, 1990–2000 and 2000–2010)		2.4	2.1
Freshwater use (% of internal resources)	..	1.2	1.2
Access to improved water source (% total pop.)	76	82	87
Access to improved sanitation facilities (% total pop.)	50	64	77
Energy use per capita (kilograms of oil equivalent)	487	481	601
Carbon dioxide emissions per capita (metric tons)	0.5	0.8	1.0
Electricity use per capita (kilowatt-hours)	373	516	671
Economy			
GDP ($ billions)	3.0	7.1	17.4
GDP growth (annual %)	0.1	5.7	3.6
GDP implicit price deflator (annual % growth)	21.2	30.8	9.3
Value added in agriculture (% of GDP)	22	16	15
Value added in industry (% of GDP)	26	32	27
Value added in services (% of GDP)	51	52	58
Exports of goods and services (% of GDP)	37	54	48
Imports of goods and services (% of GDP)	40	66	69
Gross capital formation (% of GDP)	23	28	27
Central government revenue (% of GDP)	..	20.0	21.2
Central government cash surplus/deficit (% of GDP)	..	–3.0	–2.6
States and markets			
Starting a business (days)	..	62	14
Stock market capitalization (% of GDP)	1.3	8.8	..
Military expenditures (% of GDP)	..	0.7	1.1
Mobile cellular subscriptions (per 100 people)	0.0	2.5	104.0
Individuals using the Internet (% of population)	0.0	1.2	15.9
Paved roads (% of total)	21.1	20.4	..
High-technology exports (% of manufactured exports)	1	0	1
Global links			
Merchandise trade (% of GDP)	61	103	101
Net barter terms of trade index (2000 = 100)	78	100	90
Total external debt stocks ($ billions)	3.8	5.5	4.6
Total debt service (% of exports)	38.3	9.9	13.8
Net migration (thousands)	–70	–180	–100
Remittances received ($ millions)	63	484	2,811
Foreign direct investment, net inflows ($ millions)	44	382	1,043
Net official development assistance received ($ millions)	448	448	624

Hong Kong SAR, China

High income

Population (millions)	7.1	Population growth (%)	0.1
Surface area (1,000 sq. km)	1.1	Population living below $1.25 a day (%)	..
GNI, Atlas ($ billions)	254.6	GNI per capita, Atlas ($)	36,010
GNI, PPP ($ billions)	370.2	GNI per capita, PPP ($)	52,350

	1990	2000	2011
People			
Share of poorest 20% in nat'l consumption/income (%)	..	..	..
Life expectancy at birth (years)	77	81	83
Total fertility rate (births per woman)	1.3	1.0	1.2
Adolescent fertility rate (births per 1,000 women 15–19)	..	4	4
Contraceptive prevalence (% of married women 15–49)	86	86	80
Births attended by skilled health staff (% of total)	..	..	..
Under-five mortality rate (per 1,000 live births)	..	..	..
Child malnutrition, underweight (% of under age 5)	..	..	..
Child immunization, measles (% of ages 12–23 mos.)	..	..	..
Primary completion rate, total (% of relevant age group)	102	97	91
Gross secondary enrollment, total (% of relevant age group)	76	77	80
Ratio of girls to boys in primary & secondary school (%)	102	98	103
HIV prevalence rate (% population of ages 15–49)	..	..	..
Environment			
Forests (sq. km)	..	..	..
Deforestation (avg. annual %, 1990–2000 and 2000–2010)		..	..
Freshwater use (% of internal resources)	..	..	..
Access to improved water source (% total pop.)	..	..	..
Access to improved sanitation facilities (% total pop.)	..	..	..
Energy use per capita (kilograms of oil equivalent)	1,518	2,009	1,951
Carbon dioxide emissions per capita (metric tons)	4.8	6.1	5.3
Electricity use per capita (kilowatt-hours)	4,178	5,447	5,923
Economy			
GDP ($ billions)	77	172	249
GDP growth (annual %)	3.8	7.7	4.9
GDP implicit price deflator (annual % growth)	7.6	-3.4	3.8
Value added in agriculture (% of GDP)	..	0	0
Value added in industry (% of GDP)	..	12	7
Value added in services (% of GDP)	..	88	93
Exports of goods and services (% of GDP)	131	142	225
Imports of goods and services (% of GDP)	122	137	222
Gross capital formation (% of GDP)	27	28	23
Central government revenue (% of GDP)	..	14.7	22.3
Central government cash surplus/deficit (% of GDP)	..	-6.7	4.1
States and markets			
Starting a business (days)	..	11	3
Stock market capitalization (% of GDP)	108.4	363.1	357.8
Military expenditures (% of GDP)	..	..	..
Mobile cellular subscriptions (per 100 people)	2.3	80.3	214.7
Individuals using the Internet (% of population)	0.0	27.8	74.5
Paved roads (% of total)	100.0	100.0	100.0
High-technology exports (% of manufactured exports)	17	23	14
Global links			
Merchandise trade (% of GDP)	217	243	389
Net barter terms of trade index (2000 = 100)	100	100	96
Total external debt stocks ($ millions)	..	..	..
Total debt service (% of exports)	..	..	..
Net migration (thousands)	160	551	176
Remittances received ($ millions)	..	136	357
Foreign direct investment, net inflows ($ billions)	..	61.9	95.4
Net official development assistance received ($ millions)	38.2	..	..

Hungary

High income

Population (millions)	10.0	Population growth (%)		-0.3
Surface area (1,000 sq. km)	93	Population living below $1.25 a day (%)		<2
GNI, Atlas ($ billions)	126.9	GNI per capita, Atlas ($)		12,730
GNI, PPP ($ billions)	202.5	GNI per capita, PPP ($)		20,310

	1990	2000	2011
People			
Share of poorest 20% in nat'l consumption/income (%)	10.4	9.6	8.4
Life expectancy at birth (years)	69	71	75
Total fertility rate (births per woman)	1.8	1.3	1.2
Adolescent fertility rate (births per 1,000 women 15–19)	..	22	14
Contraceptive prevalence (% of married women 15–49)	81	..	..
Births attended by skilled health staff (% of total)	99	100	100
Under-five mortality rate (per 1,000 live births)	19	11	6
Child malnutrition, underweight (% of under age 5)	2.3	..	..
Child immunization, measles (% of ages 12–23 mos.)	99	99	99
Primary completion rate, total (% of relevant age group)	86	97	98
Gross secondary enrollment, total (% of relevant age group)	88	95	100
Ratio of girls to boys in primary & secondary school (%)	100	100	98
HIV prevalence rate (% population of ages 15–49)	0.1	0.1	0.1
Environment			
Forests (1,000 sq. km)	18	19	20
Deforestation (avg. annual %, 1990–2000 and 2000–2010)		-0.6	-0.6
Freshwater use (% of internal resources)	..	97.3	93.2
Access to improved water source (% total pop.)	96	99	100
Access to improved sanitation facilities (% total pop.)	100	100	100
Energy use per capita (kilograms of oil equivalent)	2,772	2,448	2,514
Carbon dioxide emissions per capita (metric tons)	6.1	5.6	4.9
Electricity use per capita (kilowatt-hours)	3,427	3,309	3,876
Economy			
GDP ($ billions)	33.1	46.4	140.0
GDP growth (annual %)	-3.5	4.2	1.7
GDP implicit price deflator (annual % growth)	25.7	9.7	3.5
Value added in agriculture (% of GDP)	15	6	4
Value added in industry (% of GDP)	39	32	31
Value added in services (% of GDP)	46	62	65
Exports of goods and services (% of GDP)	31	75	92
Imports of goods and services (% of GDP)	29	78	85
Gross capital formation (% of GDP)	25	27	19
Central government revenue (% of GDP)	..	38.5	47.3
Central government cash surplus/deficit (% of GDP)	..	-2.8	3.6
States and markets			
Starting a business (days)	..	52	5
Stock market capitalization (% of GDP)	1.5	25.9	13.4
Military expenditures (% of GDP)	2.8	1.7	1.0
Mobile cellular subscriptions (per 100 people)	0.0	30.1	117.3
Individuals using the Internet (% of population)	0.0	7.0	59.0
Paved roads (% of total)	44.1	43.7	38.1
High-technology exports (% of manufactured exports)	4	27	23
Global links			
Merchandise trade (% of GDP)	62	130	153
Net barter terms of trade index (2000 = 100)	..	100	94
Total external debt stocks ($ millions)	..	..	..
Total debt service (% of exports)	..	..	..
Net migration (thousands)	-77.1	81.7	75.0
Remittances received ($ millions)	..	281	2,441
Foreign direct investment, net inflows ($ billions)	0.6	2.8	9.6
Net official development assistance received ($ millions)	..	..	..

Iceland

High income

Population (thousands)	319	Population growth (%)	0.3
Surface area (1,000 sq. km)	103[d]	Population living below $1.25 a day (%)	..
GNI, Atlas ($ billions)	11.1	GNI per capita, Atlas ($)	34,820
GNI, PPP ($ billions)	9.9	GNI per capita, PPP ($)	31,020

	1990	2000	2011
People			
Share of poorest 20% in nat'l consumption/income (%)	..	..	..
Life expectancy at birth (years)	78	80	82
Total fertility rate (births per woman)	2.3	2.1	2.0
Adolescent fertility rate (births per 1,000 women 15-19)	..	20	12
Contraceptive prevalence (% of married women 15-49)	..	..	..
Births attended by skilled health staff (% of total)	..	..	..
Under-five mortality rate (per 1,000 live births)	6	4	3
Child malnutrition, underweight (% of under age 5)	..	..	..
Child immunization, measles (% of ages 12–23 mos.)	99	91	93
Primary completion rate, total (% of relevant age group)	..	98	98
Gross secondary enrollment, total (% of relevant age group)	98	107	108
Ratio of girls to boys in primary & secondary school (%)	98	102	101
HIV prevalence rate (% population of ages 15–49)	0.1	0.2	0.3
Environment			
Forests (sq. km)	87	184	308
Deforestation (avg. annual %, 1990–2000 and 2000–2010)		-7.8	-5.0
Freshwater use (% of internal resources)	0.1	0.1	0.1
Access to improved water source (% total pop.)	100	100	100
Access to improved sanitation facilities (% total pop.)	100	100	100
Energy use per capita (kilograms of oil equivalent)	8,196	11,023	17,983
Carbon dioxide emissions per capita (metric tons)	7.8	7.7	6.4
Electricity use per capita (kilowatt-hours)	16,148	26,202	51,440
Economy			
GDP ($ billions)	6.4	8.7	14.0
GDP growth (annual %)	1.2	4.3	2.6
GDP implicit price deflator (annual % growth)	15.2	3.6	3.2
Value added in agriculture (% of GDP)	12	9	7
Value added in industry (% of GDP)	31	26	25
Value added in services (% of GDP)	57	65	68
Exports of goods and services (% of GDP)	34	34	59
Imports of goods and services (% of GDP)	32	41	51
Gross capital formation (% of GDP)	19	23	14
Central government revenue (% of GDP)	..	33.3	30.0
Central government cash surplus/deficit (% of GDP)	..	2.7	-5.3
States and markets			
Starting a business (days)	..	5	5
Stock market capitalization (% of GDP)	..	51.0	14.4
Military expenditures (% of GDP)	..	..	0.1
Mobile cellular subscriptions (per 100 people)	3.9	76.4	106.1
Individuals using the Internet (% of population)	0.0	44.5	95.0
Paved roads (% of total)	19.9	29.5	39.9
High-technology exports (% of manufactured exports)	10	13	21
Global links			
Merchandise trade (% of GDP)	51	52	73
Net barter terms of trade index (2000 = 100)	..	100	90
Total external debt stocks ($ millions)	..	..	..
Total debt service (% of exports)	..	..	..
Net migration (thousands)	0.3	2.0	10.4
Remittances received ($ millions)	62.3	87.6	21.1
Foreign direct investment, net inflows ($ millions)	22	155	1,107
Net official development assistance received ($ millions)	..	..	..

India

South Asia　　　　　　　　　　　　　　　　**Lower middle income**

Population (millions)	1,241.5	Population growth (%)	1.4
Surface area (1,000 sq. km)	3,287	Population living below $1.25 a day (%)	32.7
GNI, Atlas ($ billions)	1,766.2	GNI per capita, Atlas ($)	1,420
GNI, PPP ($ billions)	4,524.6	GNI per capita, PPP ($)	3,640

	1990	2000	2011
People			
Share of poorest 20% in nat'l consumption/income (%)	8.8	..	..
Life expectancy at birth (years)	58	62	65
Total fertility rate (births per woman)	3.9	3.1	2.6
Adolescent fertility rate (births per 1,000 women 15–19)	..	106	77
Contraceptive prevalence (% of married women 15–49)	41	47	55
Births attended by skilled health staff (% of total)	34	43	52
Under-five mortality rate (per 1,000 live births)	114	88	61
Child malnutrition, underweight (% of under age 5)	59.5	44.4	43.5
Child immunization, measles (% of ages 12–23 mos.)	56	55	74
Primary completion rate, total (% of relevant age group)	63	71	96
Gross secondary enrollment, total (% of relevant age group)	37	45	63
Ratio of girls to boys in primary & secondary school (%)	67	79	95
HIV prevalence rate (% population of ages 15–49)	..	..	..
Environment			
Forests (1,000 sq. km)	639	654	686
Deforestation (avg. annual %, 1990–2000 and 2000–2010)		-0.2	-0.5
Freshwater use (% of internal resources)	34.6	42.2	52.6
Access to improved water source (% total pop.)	69	81	92
Access to improved sanitation facilities (% total pop.)	18	25	34
Energy use per capita (kilograms of oil equivalent)	362	434	566
Carbon dioxide emissions per capita (metric tons)	0.8	1.1	1.6
Electricity use per capita (kilowatt-hours)	268	387	616
Economy			
GDP ($ billions)	327	475	1,873
GDP growth (annual %)	5.5	4.0	6.3
GDP implicit price deflator (annual % growth)	10.7	3.7	8.3
Value added in agriculture (% of GDP)	29	23	18
Value added in industry (% of GDP)	26	26	27
Value added in services (% of GDP)	44	51	56
Exports of goods and services (% of GDP)	7	13	24
Imports of goods and services (% of GDP)	8	14	30
Gross capital formation (% of GDP)	25	24	35
Central government revenue (% of GDP)	12.2	11.5	11.8
Central government cash surplus/deficit (% of GDP)	-3.3	-3.8	-3.7
States and markets			
Starting a business (days)	..	89	27
Stock market capitalization (% of GDP)	11.8	31.2	54.2
Military expenditures (% of GDP)	3.1	3.0	2.5
Mobile cellular subscriptions (per 100 people)	0.0	0.3	72.0
Individuals using the Internet (% of population)	0.0	0.5	10.1
Paved roads (% of total)	47.3	47.5	49.5
High-technology exports (% of manufactured exports)	4	6	7
Global links			
Merchandise trade (% of GDP)	13	20	41
Net barter terms of trade index (2000 = 100)	86	100	136
Total external debt stocks ($ billions)	86	101	334
Total debt service (% of exports)	34.9	17.5	6.5
Net migration (thousands)	-14	-513	-3,000
Remittances received ($ billions)	2.4	12.9	63.8
Foreign direct investment, net inflows ($ billions)	0.2	3.6	32.2
Net official development assistance received ($ billions)	1.4	1.4	3.2

Indonesia

East Asia & Pacific   **Lower middle income**

Population (millions)	242.3	Population growth (%)	1.0
Surface area (1,000 sq. km)	1,905	Population living below $1.25 a day (%)	18.1
GNI, Atlas ($ billions)	712.7	GNI per capita, Atlas ($)	2,940
GNI, PPP ($ billions)	1,091.4	GNI per capita, PPP ($)	4,500

	1990	2000	2011
People			
Share of poorest 20% in nat'l consumption/income (%)	9.4	9.6	..
Life expectancy at birth (years)	62	66	69
Total fertility rate (births per woman)	3.1	2.5	2.1
Adolescent fertility rate (births per 1,000 women 15–19)	..	49	43
Contraceptive prevalence (% of married women 15–49)	50	55	61
Births attended by skilled health staff (% of total)	41	67	82
Under-five mortality rate (per 1,000 live births)	82	53	32
Child malnutrition, underweight (% of under age 5)	31.0	24.8	18.6
Child immunization, measles (% of ages 12–23 mos.)	58	74	89
Primary completion rate, total (% of relevant age group)	92	93	109
Gross secondary enrollment, total (% of relevant age group)	46	53	77
Ratio of girls to boys in primary & secondary school (%)	92	96	101
HIV prevalence rate (% population of ages 15–49)	0.1	0.1	0.3
Environment			
Forests (1,000 sq. km)	1,185	994	937
Deforestation (avg. annual %, 1990–2000 and 2000–2010)		1.8	0.5
Freshwater use (% of internal resources)	3.7	5.6	5.6
Access to improved water source (% total pop.)	70	78	82
Access to improved sanitation facilities (% total pop.)	32	44	54
Energy use per capita (kilograms of oil equivalent)	535	727	867
Carbon dioxide emissions per capita (metric tons)	0.8	1.2	1.9
Electricity use per capita (kilowatt-hours)	160	387	641
Economy			
GDP ($ billions)	114	165	847
GDP growth (annual %)	9.0	4.9	6.5
GDP implicit price deflator (annual % growth)	7.7	20.4	8.4
Value added in agriculture (% of GDP)	19	16	15
Value added in industry (% of GDP)	39	46	47
Value added in services (% of GDP)	41	38	38
Exports of goods and services (% of GDP)	25	41	26
Imports of goods and services (% of GDP)	24	30	25
Gross capital formation (% of GDP)	31	22	33
Central government revenue (% of GDP)	16.6	18.3	16.2
Central government cash surplus/deficit (% of GDP)	0.7	-3.7	-1.1
States and markets			
Starting a business (days)	..	168	47
Stock market capitalization (% of GDP)	7.1	16.3	46.1
Military expenditures (% of GDP)	0.9	0.5	0.7
Mobile cellular subscriptions (per 100 people)	0.0	1.7	103.1
Individuals using the Internet (% of population)	0.0	0.9	18.0
Paved roads (% of total)	45.1	57.1	56.9
High-technology exports (% of manufactured exports)	2	16	8
Global links			
Merchandise trade (% of GDP)	42	66	45
Net barter terms of trade index (2000 = 100)	95	100	134
Total external debt stocks ($ billions)	70	144	214
Total debt service (% of exports)	33.5	22.8	14.5
Net migration (thousands)	-264	-776	-1,293
Remittances received ($ billions)	0.2	1.2	6.9
Foreign direct investment, net inflows ($ billions)	1.1	-4.6	18.2
Net official development assistance received ($ billions)	1.7	1.7	0.4

Iran, Islamic Rep.

Middle East & North Africa		Upper middle income	
Population (millions)	74.8	Population growth (%)	1.1
Surface area (1,000 sq. km)	1,745	Population living below $1.25 a day (%)	<2
GNI, Atlas ($ billions)	330.4	GNI per capita, Atlas ($)	4,520
GNI, PPP ($ billions)	835.5	GNI per capita, PPP ($)	11,420

	1990	2000	2011
People			
Share of poorest 20% in nat'l consumption/income (%)	5.2	5.2	..
Life expectancy at birth (years)	62	70	73
Total fertility rate (births per woman)	4.8	2.2	1.6
Adolescent fertility rate (births per 1,000 women 15–19)	..	39	26
Contraceptive prevalence (% of married women 15–49)	49	74	..
Births attended by skilled health staff (% of total)	..	90	..
Under-five mortality rate (per 1,000 live births)	61	44	25
Child malnutrition, underweight (% of under age 5)	..	4.6	..
Child immunization, measles (% of ages 12–23 mos.)	85	99	99
Primary completion rate, total (% of relevant age group)	87	93	106
Gross secondary enrollment, total (% of relevant age group)	54	80	86
Ratio of girls to boys in primary & secondary school (%)	82	94	97
HIV prevalence rate (% population of ages 15–49)	0.1	0.1	0.2
Environment			
Forests (1,000 sq. km)	111	111	111
Deforestation (avg. annual %, 1990–2000 and 2000–2010)		0.0	0.0
Freshwater use (% of internal resources)	..	69.8	72.6
Access to improved water source (% total pop.)	90	93	96
Access to improved sanitation facilities (% total pop.)	79	90	100
Energy use per capita (kilograms of oil equivalent)	1,264	1,882	2,817
Carbon dioxide emissions per capita (metric tons)	3.8	5.7	8.2
Electricity use per capita (kilowatt-hours)	967	1,553	2,652
Economy			
GDP ($ billions)	116	101	331
GDP growth (annual %)	13.7	5.1	1.8
GDP implicit price deflator (annual % growth)	20.6	26.4	0.6
Value added in agriculture (% of GDP)	19	14	..
Value added in industry (% of GDP)	29	37	..
Value added in services (% of GDP)	52	50	..
Exports of goods and services (% of GDP)	15	23	..
Imports of goods and services (% of GDP)	23	17	..
Gross capital formation (% of GDP)	37	33	..
Central government revenue (% of GDP)	18.7	23.4	31.9
Central government cash surplus/deficit (% of GDP)	-1.9	1.8	0.5
States and markets			
Starting a business (days)	..	29	13
Stock market capitalization (% of GDP)	2.2	7.3	19.1
Military expenditures (% of GDP)	2.1	3.7	1.9
Mobile cellular subscriptions (per 100 people)	0.0	1.5	74.9
Individuals using the Internet (% of population)	0.0	0.9	21.0
Paved roads (% of total)	..	64.8	80.6
High-technology exports (% of manufactured exports)	..	1	4
Global links			
Merchandise trade (% of GDP)	34	42	39
Net barter terms of trade index (2000 = 100)	..	100	181
Total external debt stocks ($ billions)	9.0	8.0	19.1
Total debt service (% of exports)	3.2	9.7	1.4
Net migration (thousands)	1,344	687	-186
Remittances received ($ millions)	1,200	536	1,330
Foreign direct investment, net inflows ($ millions)	-362	39	4,150
Net official development assistance received ($ millions)	106	130	102

Iraq

Middle East & North Africa		**Lower middle income**	
Population (millions)	33.0	Population growth (%)	2.9
Surface area (1,000 sq. km)	435	Population living below $1.25 a day (%)	2.8
GNI, Atlas ($ billions)	87.0	GNI per capita, Atlas ($)	2,640
GNI, PPP ($ billions)	123.5	GNI per capita, PPP ($)	3,750

	1990	2000	2011
People			
Share of poorest 20% in nat'l consumption/income (%)	..	..	8.7
Life expectancy at birth (years)	68	71	69
Total fertility rate (births per woman)	6.0	5.3	4.6
Adolescent fertility rate (births per 1,000 women 15–19)	..	66	88
Contraceptive prevalence (% of married women 15–49)	14	44	50
Births attended by skilled health staff (% of total)	54	72	80
Under-five mortality rate (per 1,000 live births)	46	43	38
Child malnutrition, underweight (% of under age 5)	10.4	12.9	7.1
Child immunization, measles (% of ages 12–23 mos.)	75	87	76
Primary completion rate, total (% of relevant age group)	59	56	..
Gross secondary enrollment, total (% of relevant age group)	47	38	..
Ratio of girls to boys in primary & secondary school (%)	77	77	..
HIV prevalence rate (% population of ages 15–49)	..	..	..
Environment			
Forests (1,000 sq. km)	8.0	8.2	8.3
Deforestation (avg. annual %, 1990-2000 and 2000-2010)		-0.2	-0.1
Freshwater use (% of internal resources)	121.6	187.5	187.5
Access to improved water source (% total pop.)	81	80	79
Access to improved sanitation facilities (% total pop.)	67	69	73
Energy use per capita (kilograms of oil equivalent)	1,083	1,067	1,180
Carbon dioxide emissions per capita (metric tons)	2.9	3.0	3.5
Electricity use per capita (kilowatt-hours)	1,253	1,199	1,183
Economy			
GDP ($ billions)	48.4	25.9	115.4
GDP growth (annual %)	..	-4.3	9.9
GDP implicit price deflator (annual % growth)	..	47.4	29.4
Value added in agriculture (% of GDP)	..	5	..
Value added in industry (% of GDP)	..	84	..
Value added in services (% of GDP)	..	10	..
Exports of goods and services (% of GDP)	..	..	..
Imports of goods and services (% of GDP)	..	..	..
Gross capital formation (% of GDP)	..	..	..
Central government revenue (% of GDP)	..	..	..
Central government cash surplus/deficit (% of GDP)	..	..	..
States and markets			
Starting a business (days)	..	..	74
Stock market capitalization (% of GDP)	..	..	..
Military expenditures (% of GDP)	..	..	5.1
Mobile cellular subscriptions (per 100 people)	0.0	0.0	78.1
Individuals using the Internet (% of population)	0.0	0.1	5.0
Paved roads (% of total)	77.9	84.3	..
High-technology exports (% of manufactured exports)	..	..	..
Global links			
Merchandise trade (% of GDP)	55	131	119
Net barter terms of trade index (2000 = 100)	..	100	212
Total external debt stocks ($ millions)	..	..	..
Total debt service (% of exports)	..	..	..
Net migration (thousands)	-630	-18	-150
Remittances received ($ millions)	..	..	386
Foreign direct investment, net inflows ($ millions)	0	-3	1,396
Net official development assistance received ($ millions)	63	102	1,904

Ireland

High income

Population (millions)	4.6	Population growth (%)		2.3
Surface area (1,000 sq. km)	70	Population living below $1.25 a day (%)		..
GNI, Atlas ($ billions)	179.2	GNI per capita, Atlas ($)		39,150
GNI, PPP ($ billions)	153.4	GNI per capita, PPP ($)		33,520

	1990	2000	2011
People			
Share of poorest 20% in nat'l consumption/income (%)	..	7.4	..
Life expectancy at birth (years)	75	77	80
Total fertility rate (births per woman)	2.1	1.9	2.1
Adolescent fertility rate (births per 1,000 women 15–19)	..	19	11
Contraceptive prevalence (% of married women 15–49)	..	75	..
Births attended by skilled health staff (% of total)	..	100	..
Under-five mortality rate (per 1,000 live births)	9	7	4
Child malnutrition, underweight (% of under age 5)	..	..	..
Child immunization, measles (% of ages 12–23 mos.)	78	79	92
Primary completion rate, total (% of relevant age group)	103	95	103
Gross secondary enrollment, total (% of relevant age group)	99	105	121
Ratio of girls to boys in primary & secondary school (%)	105	103	102
HIV prevalence rate (% population of ages 15–49)	0.1	0.2	0.3
Environment			
Forests (1,000 sq. km)	4.7	6.4	7.5
Deforestation (avg. annual %, 1990–2000 and 2000–2010)		-3.2	-1.5
Freshwater use (% of internal resources)	..	1.6	1.6
Access to improved water source (% total pop.)	100	100	100
Access to improved sanitation facilities (% total pop.)	99	99	99
Energy use per capita (kilograms of oil equivalent)	2,842	3,608	2,953
Carbon dioxide emissions per capita (metric tons)	8.9	10.8	9.3
Electricity use per capita (kilowatt-hours)	3,768	5,796	6,025
Economy			
GDP ($ billions)	48	98	217
GDP growth (annual %)	8.5	9.3	0.7
GDP implicit price deflator (annual % growth)	-0.7	7.0	-0.4
Value added in agriculture (% of GDP)	9	3	1
Value added in industry (% of GDP)	35	42	32
Value added in services (% of GDP)	57	55	67
Exports of goods and services (% of GDP)	57	97	107
Imports of goods and services (% of GDP)	52	84	84
Gross capital formation (% of GDP)	21	24	10
Central government revenue (% of GDP)	..	33.0	32.8
Central government cash surplus/deficit (% of GDP)	..	4.9	-13.5
States and markets			
Starting a business (days)	..	18	10
Stock market capitalization (% of GDP)	..	84.0	16.3
Military expenditures (% of GDP)	1.3	0.7	0.6
Mobile cellular subscriptions (per 100 people)	0.7	64.7	108.4
Individuals using the Internet (% of population)	0.0	17.9	76.8
Paved roads (% of total)	94.0	100.0	100.0
High-technology exports (% of manufactured exports)	41	48	21
Global links			
Merchandise trade (% of GDP)	93	132	89
Net barter terms of trade index (2000 = 100)	..	100	86
Total external debt stocks ($ millions)	..	..	..
Total debt service (% of exports)	..	..	..
Net migration (thousands)	-115	83	100
Remittances received ($ millions)	286	252	755
Foreign direct investment, net inflows ($ billions)	0.6	25.5	11.5
Net official development assistance received ($ millions)	..	..	..

Isle of Man

High income

Population (thousands)	83	Population growth (%)	0.6
Surface area (sq. km)	570	Population living below $1.25 a day (%)	..
GNI, Atlas ($ billions)	..	GNI per capita, Atlas ($)	..
GNI, PPP ($ millions)	..	GNI per capita, PPP ($)	..

	1990	2000	2011
People			
Share of poorest 20% in nat'l consumption/income (%)	..	..	..
Life expectancy at birth (years)	..	78	..
Total fertility rate (births per woman)	..	1.7	..
Adolescent fertility rate (births per 1,000 women 15-19)	..	..	..
Contraceptive prevalence (% of married women 15-49)	..	..	..
Births attended by skilled health staff (% of total)	..	..	..
Under-five mortality rate (per 1,000 live births)	..	..	..
Child malnutrition, underweight (% of under age 5)	..	..	..
Child immunization, measles (% of ages 12-23 mos.)	..	..	..
Primary completion rate, total (% of relevant age group)	..	..	..
Gross secondary enrollment, total (% of relevant age group)	..	..	..
Ratio of girls to boys in primary & secondary school (%)	..	..	..
HIV prevalence rate (% population of ages 15-49)	..	..	..
Environment			
Forests (sq. km)	35	35	35
Deforestation (avg. annual %, 1990-2000 and 2000-2010)		0.0	0.0
Freshwater use (% of internal resources)	..	..	..
Access to improved water source (% total pop.)	..	..	..
Access to improved sanitation facilities (% total pop.)	..	..	..
Energy use per capita (kilograms of oil equivalent)	..	..	..
Carbon dioxide emissions per capita (metric tons)	..	..	..
Electricity use per capita (kilowatt-hours)	..	..	..
Economy			
GDP ($ millions)	..	1,564	..
GDP growth (annual %)	4.2	5.3	..
GDP implicit price deflator (annual % growth)	9.0	3.3	..
Value added in agriculture (% of GDP)	..	..	..
Value added in industry (% of GDP)	..	..	..
Value added in services (% of GDP)	..	..	..
Exports of goods and services (% of GDP)	..	..	..
Imports of goods and services (% of GDP)	..	..	..
Gross capital formation (% of GDP)	..	..	..
Central government revenue (% of GDP)	..	..	..
Central government cash surplus/deficit (% of GDP)	..	..	..
States and markets			
Starting a business (days)	..	..	..
Stock market capitalization (% of GDP)	..	..	..
Military expenditures (% of GDP)	..	..	..
Mobile cellular subscriptions (per 100 people)	..	..	..
Individuals using the Internet (% of population)	..	..	..
Paved roads (% of total)	..	..	..
High-technology exports (% of manufactured exports)	..	..	..
Global links			
Merchandise trade (% of GDP)	..	..	..
Net barter terms of trade index (2000 = 100)	..	..	..
Total external debt stocks ($ millions)	..	..	..
Total debt service (% of exports)	..	..	..
Net migration (thousands)	..	..	..
Remittances received ($ millions)	..	..	..
Foreign direct investment, net inflows ($ millions)	..	..	..
Net official development assistance received ($ millions)	..	..	..

Israel

High income

Population (millions)	7.8	Population growth (%)	1.8
Surface area (1,000 sq. km)	22	Population living below $1.25 a day (%)	..
GNI, Atlas ($ billions)	224.7	GNI per capita, Atlas ($)	28,930
GNI, PPP ($ billions)	210.5	GNI per capita, PPP ($)	27,110

	1990	2000	2011
People			
Share of poorest 20% in nat'l consumption/income (%)	..	5.7	..
Life expectancy at birth (years)	77	79	82
Total fertility rate (births per woman)	2.8	3.0	3.0
Adolescent fertility rate (births per 1,000 women 15–19)	..	17	14
Contraceptive prevalence (% of married women 15–49)	68	..	..
Births attended by skilled health staff (% of total)	..	..	..
Under-five mortality rate (per 1,000 live births)	12	7	4
Child malnutrition, underweight (% of under age 5)	..	..	..
Child immunization, measles (% of ages 12–23 mos.)	91	97	98
Primary completion rate, total (% of relevant age group)	..	104	102
Gross secondary enrollment, total (% of relevant age group)	89	103	102
Ratio of girls to boys in primary & secondary school (%)	104	100	101
HIV prevalence rate (% population of ages 15–49)	0.1	0.2	0.2
Environment			
Forests (1,000 sq. km)	1.3	1.5	1.5
Deforestation (avg. annual %, 1990–2000 and 2000–2010)		-1.5	-0.1
Freshwater use (% of internal resources)	240.5	244.1	260.5
Access to improved water source (% total pop.)	100	100	100
Access to improved sanitation facilities (% total pop.)	100	100	100
Energy use per capita (kilograms of oil equivalent)	2,463	2,902	3,133
Carbon dioxide emissions per capita (metric tons)	7.2	10.0	9.0
Electricity use per capita (kilowatt-hours)	4,176	6,323	6,856
Economy			
GDP ($ billions)	52	125	243
GDP growth (annual %)	6.8	9.3	4.7
GDP implicit price deflator (annual % growth)	15.9	1.6	2.1
Value added in agriculture (% of GDP)	..	..	..
Value added in industry (% of GDP)	..	..	..
Value added in services (% of GDP)	..	..	..
Exports of goods and services (% of GDP)	35	37	37
Imports of goods and services (% of GDP)	45	37	38
Gross capital formation (% of GDP)	25	20	15
Central government revenue (% of GDP)	..	40.6	35.1
Central government cash surplus/deficit (% of GDP)	..	-3.6	-4.4
States and markets			
Starting a business (days)	..	20	21
Stock market capitalization (% of GDP)	6.3	51.3	59.7
Military expenditures (% of GDP)	12.9	8.0	6.8
Mobile cellular subscriptions (per 100 people)	0.3	73.2	121.7
Individuals using the Internet (% of population)	0.1	20.9	70.0
Paved roads (% of total)	100.0	100.0	100.0
High-technology exports (% of manufactured exports)	11	19	14
Global links			
Merchandise trade (% of GDP)	55	55	59
Net barter terms of trade index (2000 = 100)	..	100	95
Total external debt stocks ($ millions)	..	..	..
Total debt service (% of exports)	..	..	..
Net migration (thousands)	65	245	274
Remittances received ($ millions)	812	400	595
Foreign direct investment, net inflows ($ billions)	0.2	8.0	11.4
Net official development assistance received ($ billions)	1.4	..	..

Italy

Population (millions)	60.7	Population growth (%)	0.4
Surface area (1,000 sq. km)	301	Population living below $1.25 a day (%)	..
GNI, Atlas ($ billions)	2,144.7	GNI per capita, Atlas ($)	35,320
GNI, PPP ($ billions)	1,968.9	GNI per capita, PPP ($)	32,420

	1990	2000	2011
People			
Share of poorest 20% in nat'l consumption/income (%)	..	6.5	..
Life expectancy at birth (years)	77	79	82
Total fertility rate (births per woman)	1.3	1.3	1.4
Adolescent fertility rate (births per 1,000 women 15-19)	..	7	5
Contraceptive prevalence (% of married women 15-49)	..	..	..
Births attended by skilled health staff (% of total)	..	99	..
Under-five mortality rate (per 1,000 live births)	10	6	4
Child malnutrition, underweight (% of under age 5)	..	..	..
Child immunization, measles (% of ages 12-23 mos.)	43	74	90
Primary completion rate, total (% of relevant age group)	100	102	103
Gross secondary enrollment, total (% of relevant age group)	79	93	100
Ratio of girls to boys in primary & secondary school (%)	100	98	99
HIV prevalence rate (% population of ages 15-49)	0.4	0.4	0.4
Environment			
Forests (1,000 sq. km)	76	84	92
Deforestation (avg. annual %, 1990-2000 and 2000-2010)		-1.0	-0.9
Freshwater use (% of internal resources)	..	24.9	24.9
Access to improved water source (% total pop.)	100	100	100
Access to improved sanitation facilities (% total pop.)	..	..	..
Energy use per capita (kilograms of oil equivalent)	2,584	3,012	2,720
Carbon dioxide emissions per capita (metric tons)	7.5	7.9	6.7
Electricity use per capita (kilowatt-hours)	4,145	5,300	5,384
Economy			
GDP ($ billions)	1,138	1,104	2,194
GDP growth (annual %)	2.0	3.7	0.4
GDP implicit price deflator (annual % growth)	8.9	1.9	1.3
Value added in agriculture (% of GDP)	3	3	2
Value added in industry (% of GDP)	32	28	25
Value added in services (% of GDP)	65	69	73
Exports of goods and services (% of GDP)	19	27	29
Imports of goods and services (% of GDP)	19	26	30
Gross capital formation (% of GDP)	23	21	20
Central government revenue (% of GDP)	..	36.9	37.6
Central government cash surplus/deficit (% of GDP)	..	-0.8	-3.5
States and markets			
Starting a business (days)	..	23	6
Stock market capitalization (% of GDP)	13.1	69.6	19.7
Military expenditures (% of GDP)	2.1	2.0	1.6
Mobile cellular subscriptions (per 100 people)	0.5	74.1	157.9
Individuals using the Internet (% of population)	0.0	23.1	56.8
Paved roads (% of total)	100.0	100.0	..
High-technology exports (% of manufactured exports)	8	9	7
Global links			
Merchandise trade (% of GDP)	31	43	49
Net barter terms of trade index (2000 = 100)	..	100	96
Total external debt stocks ($ millions)	..	..	..
Total debt service (% of exports)	..	..	..
Net migration (thousands)	-10	225	1,999
Remittances received ($ billions)	5.1	1.9	7.0
Foreign direct investment, net inflows ($ billions)	6.4	13.2	28.0
Net official development assistance received ($ millions)	..	..	..

Jamaica

Latin America & Caribbean		Upper middle income	
Population (millions)	2.7	Population growth (%)	0.3
Surface area (1,000 sq. km)	11	Population living below $1.25 a day (%)	<2
GNI, Atlas ($ billions)	..	GNI per capita, Atlas ($)	..
GNI, PPP ($ billions)	..	GNI per capita, PPP ($)	..

	1990	2000	2011
People			
Share of poorest 20% in nat'l consumption/income (%)	5.9	5.5	..
Life expectancy at birth (years)	71	70	73
Total fertility rate (births per woman)	2.9	2.6	2.3
Adolescent fertility rate (births per 1,000 women 15–19)	..	89	71
Contraceptive prevalence (% of married women 15–49)	55	69	72
Births attended by skilled health staff (% of total)	92	96	98
Under-five mortality rate (per 1,000 live births)	35	26	18
Child malnutrition, underweight (% of under age 5)	4.0	3.8	1.9
Child immunization, measles (% of ages 12–23 mos.)	74	88	88
Primary completion rate, total (% of relevant age group)	97	88	73
Gross secondary enrollment, total (% of relevant age group)	70	87	93
Ratio of girls to boys in primary & secondary school (%)	102	100	99
HIV prevalence rate (% population of ages 15–49)	0.9	2.5	1.8
Environment			
Forests (1,000 sq. km)	3.4	3.4	3.4
Deforestation (avg. annual %, 1990–2000 and 2000–2010)		0.1	0.1
Freshwater use (% of internal resources)	..	6.2	6.2
Access to improved water source (% total pop.)	93	93	93
Access to improved sanitation facilities (% total pop.)	80	80	80
Energy use per capita (kilograms of oil equivalent)	1,166	1,478	1,131
Carbon dioxide emissions per capita (metric tons)	3.3	4.0	3.2
Electricity use per capita (kilowatt-hours)	879	2,334	1,223
Economy			
GDP ($ billions)	4.6	9.0	14.4
GDP growth (annual %)	4.2	0.9	..
GDP implicit price deflator (annual % growth)	25.1	10.6	..
Value added in agriculture (% of GDP)	8	7	7
Value added in industry (% of GDP)	37	26	22
Value added in services (% of GDP)	55	67	72
Exports of goods and services (% of GDP)	48	33	31
Imports of goods and services (% of GDP)	52	49	54
Gross capital formation (% of GDP)	26	27	21
Central government revenue (% of GDP)	..	31.8	30.2
Central government cash surplus/deficit (% of GDP)	..	-2.4	-5.1
States and markets			
Starting a business (days)	..	31	7
Stock market capitalization (% of GDP)	19.8	39.8	50.0
Military expenditures (% of GDP)	0.6	0.5	0.8
Mobile cellular subscriptions (per 100 people)	0.0	14.2	108.1
Individuals using the Internet (% of population)	0.0	3.1	31.5
Paved roads (% of total)	64.0	70.1	..
High-technology exports (% of manufactured exports)	0	0	1
Global links			
Merchandise trade (% of GDP)	67	51	57
Net barter terms of trade index (2000 = 100)	..	100	69
Total external debt stocks ($ millions)	4.8	4.8	14.5
Total debt service (% of exports)	28.6	18.7	36.5
Net migration (thousands)	-161	-73	-100
Remittances received ($ millions)	229	892	2,106
Foreign direct investment, net inflows ($ millions)	138	468	173
Net official development assistance received ($ millions)	271	9	54

Japan

Population (millions)	127.8	Population growth (%)		0.3
Surface area (1,000 sq. km)	378	Population living below $1.25 a day (%)		..
GNI, Atlas ($ billions)	5,739.5	GNI per capita, Atlas ($)		44,900
GNI, PPP ($ billions)	4,516.3	GNI per capita, PPP ($)		35,330

	1990	2000	2011
People			
Share of poorest 20% in nat'l consumption/income (%)	10.6	..	..
Life expectancy at birth (years)	79	81	83
Total fertility rate (births per woman)	1.5	1.4	1.4
Adolescent fertility rate (births per 1,000 women 15–19)	..	5	6
Contraceptive prevalence (% of married women 15–49)	58	56	..
Births attended by skilled health staff (% of total)	100	100	..
Under-five mortality rate (per 1,000 live births)	6	5	3
Child malnutrition, underweight (% of under age 5)	..	..	..
Child immunization, measles (% of ages 12–23 mos.)	73	96	94
Primary completion rate, total (% of relevant age group)	103	103	102
Gross secondary enrollment, total (% of relevant age group)	96	102	102
Ratio of girls to boys in primary & secondary school (%)	101	101	100
HIV prevalence rate (% population of ages 15–49)	0.1	0.1	0.1
Environment			
Forests (1,000 sq. km)	250	249	250
Deforestation (avg. annual %, 1990–2000 and 2000–2010)		0.0	-0.0
Freshwater use (% of internal resources)	21.3	20.9	20.9
Access to improved water source (% total pop.)	100	100	100
Access to improved sanitation facilities (% total pop.)	100	100	100
Energy use per capita (kilograms of oil equivalent)	3,556	4,091	3,584
Carbon dioxide emissions per capita (metric tons)	8.9	9.6	8.6
Electricity use per capita (kilowatt-hours)	6,486	7,974	8,394
Economy			
GDP ($ billions)	3,104	4,731	5,867
GDP growth (annual %)	5.6	2.3	-0.7
GDP implicit price deflator (annual % growth)	2.3	-1.2	-2.1
Value added in agriculture (% of GDP)	2	2	1
Value added in industry (% of GDP)	38	31	27
Value added in services (% of GDP)	60	67	71
Exports of goods and services (% of GDP)	10	11	15
Imports of goods and services (% of GDP)	9	9	16
Gross capital formation (% of GDP)	32	25	20
Central government revenue (% of GDP)	..	..	11.4
Central government cash surplus/deficit (% of GDP)	..	..	-8.3
States and markets			
Starting a business (days)	..	31	23
Stock market capitalization (% of GDP)	94.1	66.7	60.3
Military expenditures (% of GDP)	0.9	1.0	1.0
Mobile cellular subscriptions (per 100 people)	0.7	53.1	105.0
Individuals using the Internet (% of population)	0.0	30.0	79.5
Paved roads (% of total)	69.2	76.6	..
High-technology exports (% of manufactured exports)	24	29	17
Global links			
Merchandise trade (% of GDP)	17	18	29
Net barter terms of trade index (2000 = 100)	..	100	60
Total external debt stocks ($ millions)	..	..	..
Total debt service (% of exports)	..	..	..
Net migration (thousands)	-628	18	270
Remittances received ($ billions)	0.5	1.4	2.1
Foreign direct investment, net inflows ($ billions)	1.8	8.2	0.1
Net official development assistance received ($ millions)	..	..	..

Jordan

Middle East & North Africa		Upper middle income	
Population (millions)	6.2	Population growth (%)	2.2
Surface area (1,000 sq. km)	89	Population living below $1.25 a day (%)	<2
GNI, Atlas ($ billions)	27.1	GNI per capita, Atlas ($)	4,380
GNI, PPP ($ billions)	36.6	GNI per capita, PPP ($)	5,930

	1990	2000	2011
People			
Share of poorest 20% in nat'l consumption/income (%)	6.0	6.7	7.7
Life expectancy at birth (years)	70	72	73
Total fertility rate (births per woman)	5.8	3.9	3.7
Adolescent fertility rate (births per 1,000 women 15–19)	..	35	24
Contraceptive prevalence (% of married women 15–49)	40	56	59
Births attended by skilled health staff (% of total)	87	100	99
Under-five mortality rate (per 1,000 live births)	37	28	21
Child malnutrition, underweight (% of under age 5)	4.8	3.6	1.9
Child immunization, measles (% of ages 12–23 mos.)	87	94	98
Primary completion rate, total (% of relevant age group)	95	94	101
Gross secondary enrollment, total (% of relevant age group)	76	84	87
Ratio of girls to boys in primary & secondary school (%)	101	102	102
HIV prevalence rate (% population of ages 15–49)	..	..	..
Environment			
Forests (sq. km)	975	975	975
Deforestation (avg. annual %, 1990–2000 and 2000–2010)		0.0	0.0
Freshwater use (% of internal resources)	144.3	144.3	138.0
Access to improved water source (% total pop.)	97	96	97
Access to improved sanitation facilities (% total pop.)	97	98	98
Energy use per capita (kilograms of oil equivalent)	1,033	1,014	1,191
Carbon dioxide emissions per capita (metric tons)	3.3	3.2	3.8
Electricity use per capita (kilowatt-hours)	1,050	1,377	2,226
Economy			
GDP ($ billions)	4.0	8.5	28.8
GDP growth (annual %)	1.0	4.2	2.6
GDP implicit price deflator (annual % growth)	11.4	-0.4	6.4
Value added in agriculture (% of GDP)	8	2	3
Value added in industry (% of GDP)	28	26	31
Value added in services (% of GDP)	64	72	66
Exports of goods and services (% of GDP)	62	42	46
Imports of goods and services (% of GDP)	93	68	74
Gross capital formation (% of GDP)	32	22	25
Central government revenue (% of GDP)	26.1	25.1	20.5
Central government cash surplus/deficit (% of GDP)	-3.5	-2.0	-6.8
States and markets			
Starting a business (days)	..	79	12
Stock market capitalization (% of GDP)	49.7	58.4	94.3
Military expenditures (% of GDP)	8.0	6.2	4.7
Mobile cellular subscriptions (per 100 people)	0.0	8.1	118.2
Individuals using the Internet (% of population)	0.0	2.6	34.9
Paved roads (% of total)	100.0	100.0	100.0
High-technology exports (% of manufactured exports)	2	8	3
Global links			
Merchandise trade (% of GDP)	91	77	91
Net barter terms of trade index (2000 = 100)	94	100	76
Total external debt stocks ($ billions)	8.3	11.1	17.6
Total debt service (% of exports)	24.4	20.1	6.7
Net migration (thousands)	118	-188	203
Remittances received ($ billions)	0.5	1.8	3.5
Foreign direct investment, net inflows ($ millions)	38	913	1,469
Net official development assistance received ($ millions)	952	553	959

Kazakhstan

Population (millions)	16.6	Population growth (%)		1.4
Surface area (1,000 sq. km)	2,725	Population living below $1.25 a day (%)		<2
GNI, Atlas ($ billions)	136.7	GNI per capita, Atlas ($)		8,260
GNI, PPP ($ billions)	186.4	GNI per capita, PPP ($)		11,250

	1990	2000	2011
People			
Share of poorest 20% in nat'l consumption/income (%)	7.5	5.5	9.1
Life expectancy at birth (years)	68	66	69
Total fertility rate (births per woman)	2.7	1.8	2.6
Adolescent fertility rate (births per 1,000 women 15–19)	..	33	26
Contraceptive prevalence (% of married women 15–49)	..	66	51
Births attended by skilled health staff (% of total)	99	98	100
Under-five mortality rate (per 1,000 live births)	57	42	28
Child malnutrition, underweight (% of under age 5)	..	3.8	4.9
Child immunization, measles (% of ages 12–23 mos.)	89	99	99
Primary completion rate, total (% of relevant age group)	..	93	108
Gross secondary enrollment, total (% of relevant age group)	100	94	102
Ratio of girls to boys in primary & secondary school (%)	..	102	98
HIV prevalence rate (% population of ages 15–49)	0.1	0.1	0.2
Environment			
Forests (1,000 sq. km)	34	34	33
Deforestation (avg. annual %, 1990–2000 and 2000–2010)		0.2	0.2
Freshwater use (% of internal resources)	..	30.6	32.9
Access to improved water source (% total pop.)	96	96	95
Access to improved sanitation facilities (% total pop.)	96	97	97
Energy use per capita (kilograms of oil equivalent)	4,493	2,397	4,595
Carbon dioxide emissions per capita (metric tons)	15.9	8.6	14.0
Electricity use per capita (kilowatt-hours)	5,905	3,170	4,728
Economy			
GDP ($ billions)	26.9	18.3	188.0
GDP growth (annual %)	–11.0	9.8	7.5
GDP implicit price deflator (annual % growth)	96.4	17.4	17.6
Value added in agriculture (% of GDP)	27	9	6
Value added in industry (% of GDP)	45	40	40
Value added in services (% of GDP)	29	51	54
Exports of goods and services (% of GDP)	74	57	49
Imports of goods and services (% of GDP)	75	49	28
Gross capital formation (% of GDP)	32	18	22
Central government revenue (% of GDP)	..	11.3	23.9
Central government cash surplus/deficit (% of GDP)	..	0.1	7.7
States and markets			
Starting a business (days)	..	26	19
Stock market capitalization (% of GDP)	..	7.3	23.0
Military expenditures (% of GDP)	1.0	0.8	1.0
Mobile cellular subscriptions (per 100 people)	0.0	1.3	155.7
Individuals using the Internet (% of population)	0.0	0.7	45.0
Paved roads (% of total)	55.1	94.0	89.5
High-technology exports (% of manufactured exports)	..	4	30
Global links			
Merchandise trade (% of GDP)	..	76	67
Net barter terms of trade index (2000 = 100)	..	100	220
Total external debt stocks ($ billions)	0	13	124
Total debt service (% of exports)	..	32.4	34.6
Net migration (thousands)	–595	–1,320	7
Remittances received ($ millions)	..	122	180
Foreign direct investment, net inflows ($ billions)	0.1	1.3	13.2
Net official development assistance received ($ millions)	112	189	214

Kenya

Population (millions)	41.6	Population growth (%)	2.7
Surface area (1,000 sq. km)	580	Population living below $1.25 a day (%)	43.4
GNI, Atlas ($ billions)	34.1	GNI per capita, Atlas ($)	820
GNI, PPP ($ billions)	71.1	GNI per capita, PPP ($)	1,710

	1990	2000	2011
People			
Share of poorest 20% in nat'l consumption/income (%)	3.4	..	..
Life expectancy at birth (years)	59	52	57
Total fertility rate (births per woman)	6.0	5.0	4.7
Adolescent fertility rate (births per 1,000 women 15–19)	..	105	99
Contraceptive prevalence (% of married women 15–49)	27	39	46
Births attended by skilled health staff (% of total)	50	42	44
Under-five mortality rate (per 1,000 live births)	98	113	73
Child malnutrition, underweight (% of under age 5)	20.1	17.5	16.4
Child immunization, measles (% of ages 12–23 mos.)	78	78	87
Primary completion rate, total (% of relevant age group)	..	..	..
Gross secondary enrollment, total (% of relevant age group)	41	39	60
Ratio of girls to boys in primary & secondary school (%)	92	98	95
HIV prevalence rate (% population of ages 15–49)	2.5	8.9	6.2
Environment			
Forests (1,000 sq. km)	37	36	35
Deforestation (avg. annual %, 1990–2000 and 2000–2010)		0.4	0.3
Freshwater use (% of internal resources)	9.9	9.9	13.2
Access to improved water source (% total pop.)	44	52	59
Access to improved sanitation facilities (% total pop.)	25	28	32
Energy use per capita (kilograms of oil equivalent)	455	439	483
Carbon dioxide emissions per capita (metric tons)	0.2	0.3	0.3
Electricity use per capita (kilowatt-hours)	125	113	156
Economy			
GDP ($ billions)	8.6	12.7	33.6
GDP growth (annual %)	4.2	0.6	4.4
GDP implicit price deflator (annual % growth)	10.6	6.1	12.1
Value added in agriculture (% of GDP)	30	32	28
Value added in industry (% of GDP)	19	17	18
Value added in services (% of GDP)	51	51	54
Exports of goods and services (% of GDP)	26	22	29
Imports of goods and services (% of GDP)	31	32	46
Gross capital formation (% of GDP)	24	17	21
Central government revenue (% of GDP)	19.5	19.7	20.7
Central government cash surplus/deficit (% of GDP)	-2.8	2.0	-4.6
States and markets			
Starting a business (days)	..	60	32
Stock market capitalization (% of GDP)	5.3	10.1	30.3
Military expenditures (% of GDP)	2.9	1.3	1.5
Mobile cellular subscriptions (per 100 people)	0.0	0.4	67.5
Individuals using the Internet (% of population)	0.0	0.3	28.0
Paved roads (% of total)	12.8	12.1	14.3
High-technology exports (% of manufactured exports)	4	4	6
Global links			
Merchandise trade (% of GDP)	38	38	61
Net barter terms of trade index (2000 = 100)	70	100	91
Total external debt stocks ($ billions)	7.1	6.2	10.3
Total debt service (% of exports)	35.4	21.0	4.2
Net migration (thousands)	5	-21	-189
Remittances received ($ millions)	139	538	934
Foreign direct investment, net inflows ($ millions)	57	111	335
Net official development assistance received ($ billions)	1.2	0.5	2.5

Kiribati

East Asia & Pacific   **Lower middle income**

Population (thousands)	101	Population growth (%)	1.5
Surface area (sq. km)	810	Population living below $1.25 a day (%)	..
GNI, Atlas ($ millions)	204.8	GNI per capita, Atlas ($)	2,030
GNI, PPP ($ millions)	333.9	GNI per capita, PPP ($)	3,300

	1990	2000	2011
People			
Share of poorest 20% in nat'l consumption/income (%)	..	..	..
Life expectancy at birth (years)	58	60	..
Total fertility rate (births per woman)	3.8	3.6	..
Adolescent fertility rate (births per 1,000 women 15–19)	..	..	..
Contraceptive prevalence (% of married women 15–49)	..	36	22
Births attended by skilled health staff (% of total)	..	89	80
Under-five mortality rate (per 1,000 live births)	88	65	47
Child malnutrition, underweight (% of under age 5)	..	..	..
Child immunization, measles (% of ages 12–23 mos.)	75	80	90
Primary completion rate, total (% of relevant age group)	101	99	112
Gross secondary enrollment, total (% of relevant age group)	38	64	86
Ratio of girls to boys in primary & secondary school (%)	99	106	107
HIV prevalence rate (% population of ages 15–49)	..	..	..
Environment			
Forests (sq. km)	122	122	122
Deforestation (avg. annual %, 1990–2000 and 2000–2010)		0.0	0.0
Freshwater use (% of internal resources)	..	..	
Access to improved water source (% total pop.)	48	62	..
Access to improved sanitation facilities (% total pop.)	26	33	..
Energy use per capita (kilograms of oil equivalent)	99	..	..
Carbon dioxide emissions per capita (metric tons)	0.3	0.4	0.5
Electricity use per capita (kilowatt-hours)	..	..	..
Economy			
GDP ($ millions)	28.4	68.2	166.7
GDP growth (annual %)	2.1	7.2	1.8
GDP implicit price deflator (annual % growth)	-4.7	0.3	2.8
Value added in agriculture (% of GDP)	19	22	25
Value added in industry (% of GDP)	8	12	8
Value added in services (% of GDP)	74	66	67
Exports of goods and services (% of GDP)	12	7	..
Imports of goods and services (% of GDP)	147	47	..
Gross capital formation (% of GDP)	93	..	..
Central government revenue (% of GDP)	..	..	..
Central government cash surplus/deficit (% of GDP)	..	..	..
States and markets			
Starting a business (days)	..	21	31
Stock market capitalization (% of GDP)	..	..	..
Military expenditures (% of GDP)	..	..	..
Mobile cellular subscriptions (per 100 people)	0.0	0.4	13.6
Individuals using the Internet (% of population)	0.0	1.8	10.0
Paved roads (% of total)	..	..	..
High-technology exports (% of manufactured exports)	..	..	43
Global links			
Merchandise trade (% of GDP)	105	64	78
Net barter terms of trade index (2000 = 100)	..	100	90
Total external debt stocks ($ millions)	..	..	..
Total debt service (% of exports)	..	..	..
Net migration (thousands)	..	..	..
Remittances received ($ millions)	5.1	..	..
Foreign direct investment, net inflows ($ millions)	0.3	0.7	3.9
Net official development assistance received ($ millions)	20.2	17.9	64.0

Korea, Dem. People's Rep.

East Asia & Pacific   **Low income**

Population (millions)	24.5	Population growth (%)	0.4
Surface area (1,000 sq. km)	121	Population living below $1.25 a day (%)	..
GNI, Atlas ($ millions)	..	GNI per capita, Atlas ($)	..
GNI, PPP ($ millions)	..	GNI per capita, PPP ($)	..

	1990	2000	2011
People			
Share of poorest 20% in nat'l consumption/income (%)	..	..	..
Life expectancy at birth (years)	70	65	69
Total fertility rate (births per woman)	2.4	2.1	2.0
Adolescent fertility rate (births per 1,000 women 15–19)	..	1	1
Contraceptive prevalence (% of married women 15–49)	62	69	..
Births attended by skilled health staff (% of total)	..	97	100
Under-five mortality rate (per 1,000 live births)	45	58	33
Child malnutrition, underweight (% of under age 5)	..	24.7	18.8
Child immunization, measles (% of ages 12–23 mos.)	98	78	99
Primary completion rate, total (% of relevant age group)	..	..	..
Gross secondary enrollment, total (% of relevant age group)	..	..	..
Ratio of girls to boys in primary & secondary school (%)	..	..	..
HIV prevalence rate (% population of ages 15–49)	..	..	..
Environment			
Forests (1,000 sq. km)	82	69	55
Deforestation (avg. annual %, 1990–2000 and 2000–2010)		1.7	2.0
Freshwater use (% of internal resources)	..	..	12.9
Access to improved water source (% total pop.)	100	100	98
Access to improved sanitation facilities (% total pop.)	53	61	80
Energy use per capita (kilograms of oil equivalent)	1,649	861	761
Carbon dioxide emissions per capita (metric tons)	..	3.4	3.1
Electricity use per capita (kilowatt-hours)	1,247	713	749
Economy			
GDP ($ millions)	..	..	..
GDP growth (annual %)	..	..	..
GDP implicit price deflator (annual % growth)	..	..	..
Value added in agriculture (% of GDP)	..	..	..
Value added in industry (% of GDP)	..	..	..
Value added in services (% of GDP)	..	..	..
Exports of goods and services (% of GDP)	..	..	..
Imports of goods and services (% of GDP)	..	..	..
Gross capital formation (% of GDP)	..	..	..
Central government revenue (% of GDP)	..	..	..
Central government cash surplus/deficit (% of GDP)	..	..	..
States and markets			
Starting a business (days)	..	..	..
Stock market capitalization (% of GDP)	..	..	..
Military expenditures (% of GDP)	..	..	..
Mobile cellular subscriptions (per 100 people)	0.0	0.0	4.1
Individuals using the Internet (% of population)	0.0	0.0	0.0
Paved roads (% of total)	5.7	6.4	2.8
High-technology exports (% of manufactured exports)	..	..	..
Global links			
Merchandise trade (% of GDP)	..	..	..
Net barter terms of trade index (2000 = 100)	..	100	80
Total external debt stocks ($ millions)	..	..	..
Total debt service (% of exports)	..	..	..
Net migration (thousands)	0.0	0.0	0.0
Remittances received ($ millions)	..	..	..
Foreign direct investment, net inflows ($ millions)	-60.8	3.4	55.0
Net official development assistance received ($ millions)	8	73	118

Korea, Rep.

High income

Population (millions)	49.8	Population growth (%)	0.7
Surface area (1,000 sq. km)	100	Population living below $1.25 a day (%)	..
GNI, Atlas ($ billions)	1,039.0	GNI per capita, Atlas ($)	20,870
GNI, PPP ($ billions)	1,511.7	GNI per capita, PPP ($)	30,370

	1990	2000	2011
People			
Share of poorest 20% in nat'l consumption/income (%)	..	7.9	..
Life expectancy at birth (years)	71	76	81
Total fertility rate (births per woman)	1.6	1.5	1.2
Adolescent fertility rate (births per 1,000 women 15–19)	..	3	5
Contraceptive prevalence (% of married women 15–49)	79	79	80
Births attended by skilled health staff (% of total)	..	100	..
Under-five mortality rate (per 1,000 live births)	8	6	5
Child malnutrition, underweight (% of under age 5)	..	0.9	..
Child immunization, measles (% of ages 12–23 mos.)	93	95	99
Primary completion rate, total (% of relevant age group)	99	104	101
Gross secondary enrollment, total (% of relevant age group)	93	99	97
Ratio of girls to boys in primary & secondary school (%)	98	100	99
HIV prevalence rate (% population of ages 15–49)	0.1	0.1	0.1
Environment			
Forests (1,000 sq. km)	64	63	62
Deforestation (avg. annual %, 1990–2000 and 2000–2010)		0.1	0.1
Freshwater use (% of internal resources)	..	39.3	39.3
Access to improved water source (% total pop.)	90	93	98
Access to improved sanitation facilities (% total pop.)	100	100	100
Energy use per capita (kilograms of oil equivalent)	2,171	4,003	5,175
Carbon dioxide emissions per capita (metric tons)	5.8	9.5	10.4
Electricity use per capita (kilowatt-hours)	2,373	5,907	9,744
Economy			
GDP ($ billions)	264	533	1,116
GDP growth (annual %)	9.2	8.5	3.6
GDP implicit price deflator (annual % growth)	10.5	5.0	1.7
Value added in agriculture (% of GDP)	9	5	3
Value added in industry (% of GDP)	42	38	39
Value added in services (% of GDP)	49	57	58
Exports of goods and services (% of GDP)	28	39	56
Imports of goods and services (% of GDP)	29	36	54
Gross capital formation (% of GDP)	38	31	29
Central government revenue (% of GDP)	16.8	22.3	23.2
Central government cash surplus/deficit (% of GDP)	1.7	4.4	1.8
States and markets			
Starting a business (days)	..	17	7
Stock market capitalization (% of GDP)	42.1	32.2	89.1
Military expenditures (% of GDP)	3.8	2.6	2.8
Mobile cellular subscriptions (per 100 people)	0.2	58.3	108.5
Individuals using the Internet (% of population)	0.0	44.7	83.8
Paved roads (% of total)	71.5	74.5	79.3
High-technology exports (% of manufactured exports)	18	35	26
Global links			
Merchandise trade (% of GDP)	51	62	97
Net barter terms of trade index (2000 = 100)	133	100	63
Total external debt stocks ($ millions)	..	..	..
Total debt service (% of exports)	..	..	..
Net migration (thousands)	435	-515	-30
Remittances received ($ billions)	2.4	4.9	8.5
Foreign direct investment, net inflows ($ billions)	0.8	9.3	4.7
Net official development assistance received ($ millions)	52.0	-55.1	..

Kosovo

Europe & Central Asia		Lower middle income	
Population (millions)	1.8	Population growth (%)	1.5
Surface area (1,000 sq. km)	11	Population living below $1.25 a day (%)	..
GNI, Atlas ($ billions)	6.3	GNI per capita, Atlas ($)	3,510
GNI, PPP ($ millions)	..	GNI per capita, PPP ($)	..

	1990	2000	2011
People			
Share of poorest 20% in nat'l consumption/income (%)	..	..	..
Life expectancy at birth (years)	68	68	70
Total fertility rate (births per woman)	3.9	3.0	2.2
Adolescent fertility rate (births per 1,000 women 15–19)		..	..
Contraceptive prevalence (% of married women 15–49)	..	..	..
Births attended by skilled health staff (% of total)		..	..
Under-five mortality rate (per 1,000 live births)	..	..	..
Child malnutrition, underweight (% of under age 5)		..	..
Child immunization, measles (% of ages 12–23 mos.)	..	..	..
Primary completion rate, total (% of relevant age group)	..	..	..
Gross secondary enrollment, total (% of relevant age group)	..	..	..
Ratio of girls to boys in primary & secondary school (%)	..	..	..
HIV prevalence rate (% population of ages 15–49)	..	..	..
Environment			
Forests (sq. km)	..	..	..
Deforestation (avg. annual %, 1990–2000 and 2000–2010)		..	..
Freshwater use (% of internal resources)		..	..
Access to improved water source (% total pop.)	..	..	..
Access to improved sanitation facilities (% total pop.)	..	..	..
Energy use per capita (kilograms of oil equivalent)	..	870	*1,372*
Carbon dioxide emissions per capita (metric tons)		..	..
Electricity use per capita (kilowatt-hours)	..	1,557	*2,650*
Economy			
GDP ($ millions)	..	1,849	6,453
GDP growth (annual %)	..	27.0	5.0
GDP implicit price deflator (annual % growth)	..	11.4	4.8
Value added in agriculture (% of GDP)	..	..	12
Value added in industry (% of GDP)	..	..	20
Value added in services (% of GDP)	..	..	68
Exports of goods and services (% of GDP)	..	..	20
Imports of goods and services (% of GDP)	..	..	61
Gross capital formation (% of GDP)	..	..	31
Central government revenue (% of GDP)	..	..	..
Central government cash surplus/deficit (% of GDP)	..	..	..
States and markets			
Starting a business (days)	..	..	52
Stock market capitalization (% of GDP)	..	..	..
Military expenditures (% of GDP)	..	..	..
Mobile cellular subscriptions (per 100 people)	..	..	..
Individuals using the Internet (% of population)	..	..	..
Paved roads (% of total)	..	..	*26.0*
High-technology exports (% of manufactured exports)	..	..	..
Global links			
Merchandise trade (% of GDP)	..	..	..
Net barter terms of trade index (2000 = 100)	..	..	..
Total external debt stocks ($ millions)	..	72	1,531
Total debt service (% of exports)	..	..	8.9
Net migration (thousands)	..	..	..
Remittances received ($ millions)	..	..	1,122
Foreign direct investment, net inflows ($ millions)	..	..	546
Net official development assistance received ($ millions)	..	..	657

Kuwait

Population (millions)	2.8	Population growth (%)	2.9
Surface area (1,000 sq. km)	18	Population living below $1.25 a day (%)	..
GNI, Atlas ($ billions)	133.8	GNI per capita, Atlas ($)	48,900
GNI, PPP ($ billions)	147.0	GNI per capita, PPP ($)	53,720

	1990	2000	2011
People			
Share of poorest 20% in nat'l consumption/income (%)	..	..	..
Life expectancy at birth (years)	73	74	75
Total fertility rate (births per woman)	2.6	2.6	2.3
Adolescent fertility rate (births per 1,000 women 15-19)	..	20	14
Contraceptive prevalence (% of married women 15-49)	..	52	..
Births attended by skilled health staff (% of total)	..	100	100
Under-five mortality rate (per 1,000 live births)	17	13	11
Child malnutrition, underweight (% of under age 5)	..	2.2	1.7
Child immunization, measles (% of ages 12-23 mos.)	66	99	99
Primary completion rate, total (% of relevant age group)	56	103	..
Gross secondary enrollment, total (% of relevant age group)	76	108	101
Ratio of girls to boys in primary & secondary school (%)	93	103	105
HIV prevalence rate (% population of ages 15-49)	..	..	..
Environment			
Forests (sq. km)	35	49	64
Deforestation (avg. annual %, 1990-2000 and 2000-2010)		-3.5	-2.6
Freshwater use (% of internal resources)	..	..	..
Access to improved water source (% total pop.)	99	99	99
Access to improved sanitation facilities (% total pop.)	100	100	100
Energy use per capita (kilograms of oil equivalent)	4,364	9,690	12,204
Carbon dioxide emissions per capita (metric tons)	23.1	28.4	30.3
Electricity use per capita (kilowatt-hours)	8,253	14,822	18,320
Economy			
GDP ($ billions)	18.4	37.7	176.6
GDP growth (annual %)	25.9	4.7	8.2
GDP implicit price deflator (annual % growth)	-1.7	20.5	26.4
Value added in agriculture (% of GDP)	1	0	..
Value added in industry (% of GDP)	52	59	..
Value added in services (% of GDP)	47	40	..
Exports of goods and services (% of GDP)	45	56	66
Imports of goods and services (% of GDP)	58	30	21
Gross capital formation (% of GDP)	18	11	18
Central government revenue (% of GDP)	58.7	48.3	61.4
Central government cash surplus/deficit (% of GDP)	6.1	4.9	25.0
States and markets			
Starting a business (days)	..	35	32
Stock market capitalization (% of GDP)	40.8	55.1	57.1
Military expenditures (% of GDP)	48.7	7.1	3.2
Mobile cellular subscriptions (per 100 people)	1.0	24.5	175.1
Individuals using the Internet (% of population)	0.0	6.7	74.2
Paved roads (% of total)	72.9	80.6	..
High-technology exports (% of manufactured exports)	3	0	1
Global links			
Merchandise trade (% of GDP)	60	71	73
Net barter terms of trade index (2000 = 100)	..	100	219
Total external debt stocks ($ millions)	..	..	..
Total debt service (% of exports)	..	..	..
Net migration (thousands)	119	125	278
Remittances received ($ millions)	..	..	..
Foreign direct investment, net inflows ($ millions)	6	16	400
Net official development assistance received ($ millions)	12.9	..	..

Kyrgyz Republic

Europe & Central Asia		Low income
Population (millions)	5.5	Population growth (%)	1.2
Surface area (1,000 sq. km)	200	Population living below $1.25 a day (%)	6.7
GNI, Atlas ($ billions)	5.0	GNI per capita, Atlas ($)	900
GNI, PPP ($ billions)	12.7	GNI per capita, PPP ($)	2,290

	1990	2000	2011
People			
Share of poorest 20% in nat'l consumption/income (%)	2.5	8.4	6.8
Life expectancy at birth (years)	68	69	70
Total fertility rate (births per woman)	3.7	2.4	3.1
Adolescent fertility rate (births per 1,000 women 15–19)	..	34	33
Contraceptive prevalence (% of married women 15–49)	..	..	48
Births attended by skilled health staff (% of total)	99	99	99
Under-five mortality rate (per 1,000 live births)	70	47	31
Child malnutrition, underweight (% of under age 5)	..	..	2.7
Child immunization, measles (% of ages 12–23 mos.)	94	98	97
Primary completion rate, total (% of relevant age group)	..	93	96
Gross secondary enrollment, total (% of relevant age group)	102	84	88
Ratio of girls to boys in primary & secondary school (%)	100	101	99
HIV prevalence rate (% population of ages 15–49)	0.1	0.1	0.4
Environment			
Forests (1,000 sq. km)	8.4	8.6	9.7
Deforestation (avg. annual %, 1990–2000 and 2000–2010)		-0.3	-1.1
Freshwater use (% of internal resources)	..	20.6	20.6
Access to improved water source (% total pop.)	78	82	90
Access to improved sanitation facilities (% total pop.)	93	93	93
Energy use per capita (kilograms of oil equivalent)	1,705	490	536
Carbon dioxide emissions per capita (metric tons)	2.4	0.9	1.2
Electricity use per capita (kilowatt-hours)	2,331	1,911	1,375
Economy			
GDP ($ billions)	2.7	1.4	6.2
GDP growth (annual %)	5.7	5.4	6.0
GDP implicit price deflator (annual % growth)	7.9	27.2	22.5
Value added in agriculture (% of GDP)	34	37	19
Value added in industry (% of GDP)	35	31	31
Value added in services (% of GDP)	31	32	51
Exports of goods and services (% of GDP)	29	42	55
Imports of goods and services (% of GDP)	50	48	82
Gross capital formation (% of GDP)	24	20	24
Central government revenue (% of GDP)	15.5	14.2	21.1
Central government cash surplus/deficit (% of GDP)	..	-2.9	-4.8
States and markets			
Starting a business (days)	..	21	10
Stock market capitalization (% of GDP)	..	0.3	2.7
Military expenditures (% of GDP)	1.6	2.9	4.2
Mobile cellular subscriptions (per 100 people)	0.0	0.2	116.4
Individuals using the Internet (% of population)	0.0	1.0	20.0
Paved roads (% of total)	90.0	91.1	..
High-technology exports (% of manufactured exports)	..	15	3
Global links			
Merchandise trade (% of GDP)	..	77	101
Net barter terms of trade index (2000 = 100)	..	100	109
Total external debt stocks ($ billions)	0.0	1.9	5.5
Total debt service (% of exports)	0.4	30.2	11.8
Net migration (thousands)	-155	-27	-132
Remittances received ($ millions)	2	9	1,709
Foreign direct investment, net inflows ($ millions)	10	-2	694
Net official development assistance received ($ millions)	21	215	523

Lao PDR

East Asia & Pacific   **Lower middle income**

Population (millions)	6.3	Population growth (%)	1.4
Surface area (1,000 sq. km)	237	Population living below $1.25 a day (%)	33.9
GNI, Atlas ($ billions)	7.1	GNI per capita, Atlas ($)	1,130
GNI, PPP ($ billions)	16.2	GNI per capita, PPP ($)	2,580

	1990	2000	2011
People			
Share of poorest 20% in nat'l consumption/income (%)	9.3	8.6	7.6
Life expectancy at birth (years)	54	61	67
Total fertility rate (births per woman)	6.2	4.2	2.7
Adolescent fertility rate (births per 1,000 women 15-19)	..	53	32
Contraceptive prevalence (% of married women 15-49)	19	32	..
Births attended by skilled health staff (% of total)	..	19	37
Under-five mortality rate (per 1,000 live births)	148	81	42
Child malnutrition, underweight (% of under age 5)	39.8	36.4	31.6
Child immunization, measles (% of ages 12-23 mos.)	32	42	69
Primary completion rate, total (% of relevant age group)	44	69	93
Gross secondary enrollment, total (% of relevant age group)	24	35	46
Ratio of girls to boys in primary & secondary school (%)	77	81	91
HIV prevalence rate (% population of ages 15-49)	0.1	0.1	0.3
Environment			
Forests (1,000 sq. km)	173	165	157
Deforestation (avg. annual %, 1990-2000 and 2000-2010)		0.5	0.5
Freshwater use (% of internal resources)	..	..	2.2
Access to improved water source (% total pop.)	..	45	67
Access to improved sanitation facilities (% total pop.)	..	26	63
Energy use per capita (kilograms of oil equivalent)	..	..	..
Carbon dioxide emissions per capita (metric tons)	0.06	0.18	0.30
Electricity use per capita (kilowatt-hours)	..	..	..
Economy			
GDP ($ millions)	866	1,731	8,298
GDP growth (annual %)	6.7	5.8	8.0
GDP implicit price deflator (annual % growth)	37.9	24.8	4.4
Value added in agriculture (% of GDP)	61	45	31
Value added in industry (% of GDP)	15	17	35
Value added in services (% of GDP)	24	38	35
Exports of goods and services (% of GDP)	11	30	38
Imports of goods and services (% of GDP)	25	44	44
Gross capital formation (% of GDP)	14	14	27
Central government revenue (% of GDP)	..	..	15.0
Central government cash surplus/deficit (% of GDP)	..	..	-0.9
States and markets			
Starting a business (days)	..	153	92
Stock market capitalization (% of GDP)	..	..	..
Military expenditures (% of GDP)	9.0	0.8	0.2
Mobile cellular subscriptions (per 100 people)	0.0	0.2	87.2
Individuals using the Internet (% of population)	0.0	0.1	9.0
Paved roads (% of total)	24.0	14.1	13.7
High-technology exports (% of manufactured exports)	..	..	..
Global links			
Merchandise trade (% of GDP)	31	50	61
Net barter terms of trade index (2000 = 100)	..	100	125
Total external debt stocks ($ billions)	1.8	2.5	6.2
Total debt service (% of exports)	8.5	8.0	13.2
Net migration (thousands)	0.1	-87.5	-75.0
Remittances received ($ millions)	11	1	110
Foreign direct investment, net inflows ($ millions)	6	34	301
Net official development assistance received ($ millions)	149	281	397

Latvia

Population (millions)	2.1	Population growth (%)	-8.4
Surface area (1,000 sq. km)	64	Population living below $1.25 a day (%)	<2
GNI, Atlas ($ billions)	27.4	GNI per capita, Atlas ($)	13,320
GNI, PPP ($ billions)	39.3	GNI per capita, PPP ($)	19,090

	1990	2000	2011
People			
Share of poorest 20% in nat'l consumption/income (%)	9.6	6.9	6.6
Life expectancy at birth (years)	69	70	74
Total fertility rate (births per woman)	2.0	1.2	1.3
Adolescent fertility rate (births per 1,000 women 15–19)	..	19	14
Contraceptive prevalence (% of married women 15–49)	..	..	..
Births attended by skilled health staff (% of total)	100	100	100
Under-five mortality rate (per 1,000 live births)	21	17	8
Child malnutrition, underweight (% of under age 5)	..	..	..
Child immunization, measles (% of ages 12–23 mos.)	95	97	99
Primary completion rate, total (% of relevant age group)	..	92	93
Gross secondary enrollment, total (% of relevant age group)	95	91	96
Ratio of girls to boys in primary & secondary school (%)	101	101	98
HIV prevalence rate (% population of ages 15–49)	0.1	0.3	0.7
Environment			
Forests (1,000 sq. km)	32	32	34
Deforestation (avg. annual %, 1990–2000 and 2000–2010)		-0.2	-0.3
Freshwater use (% of internal resources)	..	2.5	2.5
Access to improved water source (% total pop.)	99	99	99
Access to improved sanitation facilities (% total pop.)	..	78	78
Energy use per capita (kilograms of oil equivalent)	2,958	1,565	1,971
Carbon dioxide emissions per capita (metric tons)	5.2	2.6	3.0
Electricity use per capita (kilowatt-hours)	3,397	2,078	3,026
Economy			
GDP ($ billions)	7.4	7.8	28.3
GDP growth (annual %)	-7.9	6.9	5.5
GDP implicit price deflator (annual % growth)	24.1	4.2	5.4
Value added in agriculture (% of GDP)	22	5	4
Value added in industry (% of GDP)	46	24	22
Value added in services (% of GDP)	32	72	74
Exports of goods and services (% of GDP)	48	42	59
Imports of goods and services (% of GDP)	49	49	63
Gross capital formation (% of GDP)	40	24	26
Central government revenue (% of GDP)	..	26.1	25.0
Central government cash surplus/deficit (% of GDP)	..	-2.2	-2.9
States and markets			
Starting a business (days)	..	16	16
Stock market capitalization (% of GDP)	..	7.2	3.8
Military expenditures (% of GDP)	0.8	0.9	1.0
Mobile cellular subscriptions (per 100 people)	0.0	16.8	102.9
Individuals using the Internet (% of population)	0.0	6.3	71.7
Paved roads (% of total)	..	100.0	20.9
High-technology exports (% of manufactured exports)	..	4	8
Global links			
Merchandise trade (% of GDP)	..	65	104
Net barter terms of trade index (2000 = 100)	..	100	110
Total external debt stocks ($ billions)	0.0	5.0	38.3
Total debt service (% of exports)	..	17.6	47.0
Net migration (thousands)	41.8	-40.0	-10.0
Remittances received ($ millions)	..	72	695
Foreign direct investment, net inflows ($ millions)	29	413	1,502
Net official development assistance received ($ millions)	..	..	..

Lebanon

Middle East & North Africa		Upper middle income	
Population (millions)	4.3	Population growth (%)	0.7
Surface area (1,000 sq. km)	10	Population living below $1.25 a day (%)	..
GNI, Atlas ($ billions)	38.9	GNI per capita, Atlas ($)	9,140
GNI, PPP ($ billions)	61.6	GNI per capita, PPP ($)	14,470

	1990	2000	2011
People			
Share of poorest 20% in nat'l consumption/income (%)	..	..	..
Life expectancy at birth (years)	69	71	73
Total fertility rate (births per woman)	3.1	2.4	1.8
Adolescent fertility rate (births per 1,000 women 15–19)	..	25	16
Contraceptive prevalence (% of married women 15–49)	..	63	54
Births attended by skilled health staff (% of total)	..	98	..
Under-five mortality rate (per 1,000 live births)	33	19	9
Child malnutrition, underweight (% of under age 5)	..	4.2	5.2
Child immunization, measles (% of ages 12–23 mos.)	61	71	79
Primary completion rate, total (% of relevant age group)	..	102	87
Gross secondary enrollment, total (% of relevant age group)	61	77	83
Ratio of girls to boys in primary & secondary school (%)	101	102	103
HIV prevalence rate (% population of ages 15–49)	0.1	0.1	0.1
Environment			
Forests (1,000 sq. km)	1.3	1.3	1.4
Deforestation (avg. annual %, 1990–2000 and 2000–2010)		0.0	-0.4
Freshwater use (% of internal resources)	..	29.9	27.3
Access to improved water source (% total pop.)	100	100	100
Access to improved sanitation facilities (% total pop.)	98	98	..
Energy use per capita (kilograms of oil equivalent)	663	1,311	1,526
Carbon dioxide emissions per capita (metric tons)	3.1	4.1	5.0
Electricity use per capita (kilowatt-hours)	475	2,610	3,569
Economy			
GDP ($ billions)	2.8	17.3	40.1
GDP growth (annual %)	26.5	1.3	3.0
GDP implicit price deflator (annual % growth)	15.5	-2.1	4.9
Value added in agriculture (% of GDP)	..	7	6
Value added in industry (% of GDP)	..	23	21
Value added in services (% of GDP)	..	70	74
Exports of goods and services (% of GDP)	18	14	24
Imports of goods and services (% of GDP)	100	36	50
Gross capital formation (% of GDP)	18	20	33
Central government revenue (% of GDP)	..	16.0	23.3
Central government cash surplus/deficit (% of GDP)	..	-18.4	-5.9
States and markets			
Starting a business (days)	..	46	9
Stock market capitalization (% of GDP)	..	9.2	25.3
Military expenditures (% of GDP)	7.6	5.4	4.4
Mobile cellular subscriptions (per 100 people)	0.0	19.9	78.6
Individuals using the Internet (% of population)	0.0	8.0	52.0
Paved roads (% of total)	95.0	84.9	..
High-technology exports (% of manufactured exports)	..	2	2
Global links			
Merchandise trade (% of GDP)	107	40	66
Net barter terms of trade index (2000 = 100)	..	100	98
Total external debt stocks ($ billions)	1.8	10.2	24.8
Total debt service (% of exports)	..	35.6	19.9
Net migration (thousands)	-220	0	-13
Remittances received ($ millions)	..	2,544	7,322
Foreign direct investment, net inflows ($ millions)	..	1,336	3,476
Net official development assistance received ($ millions)	286	200	432

Lesotho

Population (millions)	2.2	Population growth (%)	1.0
Surface area (1,000 sq. km)	30	Population living below $1.25 a day (%)	43.4
GNI, Atlas ($ billions)	2.7	GNI per capita, Atlas ($)	1,210
GNI, PPP ($ billions)	4.5	GNI per capita, PPP ($)	2,050

	1990	2000	2011
People			
Share of poorest 20% in nat'l consumption/income (%)	2.6	3.0	..
Life expectancy at birth (years)	59	48	48
Total fertility rate (births per woman)	4.9	4.1	3.1
Adolescent fertility rate (births per 1,000 women 15-19)	..	91	63
Contraceptive prevalence (% of married women 15-49)	23	30	47
Births attended by skilled health staff (% of total)	61	60	62
Under-five mortality rate (per 1,000 live births)	88	117	86
Child malnutrition, underweight (% of under age 5)	13.8	15.0	13.5
Child immunization, measles (% of ages 12-23 mos.)	80	74	85
Primary completion rate, total (% of relevant age group)	58	60	68
Gross secondary enrollment, total (% of relevant age group)	25	30	49
Ratio of girls to boys in primary & secondary school (%)	124	107	106
HIV prevalence rate (% population of ages 15-49)	0.8	23.4	23.3
Environment			
Forests (sq. km)	400	420	442
Deforestation (avg. annual %, 1990-2000 and 2000-2010)		-0.5	-0.5
Freshwater use (% of internal resources)	..	1.0	1.0
Access to improved water source (% total pop.)	80	80	78
Access to improved sanitation facilities (% total pop.)	..	25	26
Energy use per capita (kilograms of oil equivalent)	..	..	..
Carbon dioxide emissions per capita (metric tons)	..	..	..
Electricity use per capita (kilowatt-hours)	..	..	..
Economy			
GDP ($ millions)	545	771	2,426
GDP growth (annual %)	5.6	5.1	4.2
GDP implicit price deflator (annual % growth)	12.6	3.9	6.0
Value added in agriculture (% of GDP)	25	12	8
Value added in industry (% of GDP)	34	30	34
Value added in services (% of GDP)	41	58	59
Exports of goods and services (% of GDP)	18	35	46
Imports of goods and services (% of GDP)	122	135	113
Gross capital formation (% of GDP)	56	41	35
Central government revenue (% of GDP)	44.5	49.0	65.2
Central government cash surplus/deficit (% of GDP)	-0.6	-2.8	5.6
States and markets			
Starting a business (days)	..	93	24
Stock market capitalization (% of GDP)	..	..	..
Military expenditures (% of GDP)	5.1	4.0	2.4
Mobile cellular subscriptions (per 100 people)	0.0	1.1	56.2
Individuals using the Internet (% of population)	0.0	0.2	4.2
Paved roads (% of total)	18.0	18.3	..
High-technology exports (% of manufactured exports)	..	0	0
Global links			
Merchandise trade (% of GDP)	135	133	153
Net barter terms of trade index (2000 = 100)	100	100	74
Total external debt stocks ($ millions)	396	677	792
Total debt service (% of exports)	4.2	7.5	1.9
Net migration (thousands)	-50.9	-20.9	-20.0
Remittances received ($ millions)	428	478	649
Foreign direct investment, net inflows ($ millions)	17	32	132
Net official development assistance received ($ millions)	139	37	265

Liberia

Population (millions)	4.1	Population growth (%)	3.3
Surface area (1,000 sq. km)	111	Population living below $1.25 a day (%)	83.8
GNI, Atlas ($ billions)	1.4	GNI per capita, Atlas ($)	330
GNI, PPP ($ billions)	2.2	GNI per capita, PPP ($)	540

	1990	2000	2011
People			
Share of poorest 20% in nat'l consumption/income (%)	..	..	6.4
Life expectancy at birth (years)	42	46	57
Total fertility rate (births per woman)	6.5	5.8	5.2
Adolescent fertility rate (births per 1,000 women 15-19)	..	149	127
Contraceptive prevalence (% of married women 15-49)	..	10	11
Births attended by skilled health staff (% of total)	..	51	46
Under-five mortality rate (per 1,000 live births)	241	164	78
Child malnutrition, underweight (% of under age 5)	..	22.8	20.4
Child immunization, measles (% of ages 12-23 mos.)	..	63	40
Primary completion rate, total (% of relevant age group)	..	..	66
Gross secondary enrollment, total (% of relevant age group)	..	35	45
Ratio of girls to boys in primary & secondary school (%)	..	73	88
HIV prevalence rate (% population of ages 15-49)	0.7	2.5	1.0
Environment			
Forests (1,000 sq. km)	49	46	43
Deforestation (avg. annual %, 1990-2000 and 2000-2010)		0.6	0.7
Freshwater use (% of internal resources)	..	0.1	0.1
Access to improved water source (% total pop.)	..	61	73
Access to improved sanitation facilities (% total pop.)	..	12	18
Energy use per capita (kilograms of oil equivalent)	..	..	..
Carbon dioxide emissions per capita (metric tons)	0.2	0.2	0.1
Electricity use per capita (kilowatt-hours)	..	..	..
Economy			
GDP ($ millions)	384	529	1,545
GDP growth (annual %)	-51.0	25.7	9.4
GDP implicit price deflator (annual % growth)	-0.2	-6.9	10.5
Value added in agriculture (% of GDP)	54	76	53
Value added in industry (% of GDP)	17	4	10
Value added in services (% of GDP)	29	20	37
Exports of goods and services (% of GDP)	..	26	27
Imports of goods and services (% of GDP)	..	27	93
Gross capital formation (% of GDP)	..	7	25
Central government revenue (% of GDP)	..	..	0.3
Central government cash surplus/deficit (% of GDP)	..	..	0.0
States and markets			
Starting a business (days)	..	..	6
Stock market capitalization (% of GDP)	..	..	..
Military expenditures (% of GDP)	3.7	0.2	0.7
Mobile cellular subscriptions (per 100 people)	0.0	0.1	49.2
Individuals using the Internet (% of population)	0.0	0.0	3.0
Paved roads (% of total)	5.5	6.2	..
High-technology exports (% of manufactured exports)	..	..	..
Global links			
Merchandise trade (% of GDP)	374	188	91
Net barter terms of trade index (2000 = 100)	..	100	162
Total external debt stocks ($ billions)	2.1	2.8	0.4
Total debt service (% of exports)	..	..	1.4
Net migration (thousands)	-368	453	300
Remittances received ($ millions)	..	..	360
Foreign direct investment, net inflows ($ millions)	225	21	1,313
Net official development assistance received ($ millions)	114	67	765

Libya

Middle East & North Africa		Upper middle income	
Population (millions)	6.4	Population growth (%)	1.1
Surface area (1,000 sq. km)	1,760	Population living below $1.25 a day (%)	..
GNI, Atlas ($ billions)	77.1	GNI per capita, Atlas ($)	12,320
GNI, PPP ($ billions)	105.2	GNI per capita, PPP ($)	16,800

	1990	2000	2011
People			
Share of poorest 20% in nat'l consumption/income (%)	..	..	..
Life expectancy at birth (years)	68	73	75
Total fertility rate (births per woman)	4.8	3.1	2.5
Adolescent fertility rate (births per 1,000 women 15–19)	..	4	3
Contraceptive prevalence (% of married women 15–49)	..	..	..
Births attended by skilled health staff (% of total)	..	99	100
Under-five mortality rate (per 1,000 live births)	44	27	16
Child malnutrition, underweight (% of under age 5)	..	..	5.6
Child immunization, measles (% of ages 12–23 mos.)	89	93	98
Primary completion rate, total (% of relevant age group)	..	..	..
Gross secondary enrollment, total (% of relevant age group)	..	110	..
Ratio of girls to boys in primary & secondary school (%)	..	103	..
HIV prevalence rate (% population of ages 15–49)	..	..	..
Environment			
Forests (1,000 sq. km)	2.2	2.2	2.2
Deforestation (avg. annual %, 1990–2000 and 2000–2010)		0.0	0.0
Freshwater use (% of internal resources)	680.0	618.0	618.0
Access to improved water source (% total pop.)	54	54	..
Access to improved sanitation facilities (% total pop.)	97	97	97
Energy use per capita (kilograms of oil equivalent)	2,614	3,560	3,013
Carbon dioxide emissions per capita (metric tons)	8.5	9.0	10.0
Electricity use per capita (kilowatt-hours)	1,614	2,276	4,270
Economy			
GDP ($ billions)	28.9	33.9	62.4
GDP growth (annual %)	..	3.7	2.1
GDP implicit price deflator (annual % growth)	..	18.4	−32.8
Value added in agriculture (% of GDP)	..	5	2
Value added in industry (% of GDP)	..	66	78
Value added in services (% of GDP)	..	29	20
Exports of goods and services (% of GDP)	40	36	67
Imports of goods and services (% of GDP)	31	15	27
Gross capital formation (% of GDP)	19	13	28
Central government revenue (% of GDP)	..	..	..
Central government cash surplus/deficit (% of GDP)	..	..	..
States and markets			
Starting a business (days)	..	..	..
Stock market capitalization (% of GDP)	..	..	..
Military expenditures (% of GDP)	..	3.2	1.2
Mobile cellular subscriptions (per 100 people)	0.0	0.8	155.7
Individuals using the Internet (% of population)	0.0	0.2	17.0
Paved roads (% of total)	51.7	57.2	..
High-technology exports (% of manufactured exports)	..	..	..
Global links			
Merchandise trade (% of GDP)	64	50	76
Net barter terms of trade index (2000 = 100)	..	100	185
Total external debt stocks ($ millions)	..	..	..
Total debt service (% of exports)	..	..	..
Net migration (thousands)	−20.3	−20.3	−20.3
Remittances received ($ millions)	..	9.0	..
Foreign direct investment, net inflows ($ millions)	159	141	200
Net official development assistance received ($ millions)	8	5	642

Liechtenstein

Population (thousands)	36	Population growth (%)		0.8
Surface area (sq. km)	160	Population living below $1.25 a day (%)		..
GNI, Atlas ($ billions)	4.9	GNI per capita, Atlas ($)		137,070
GNI, PPP ($ billions)	..	GNI per capita, PPP ($)		..

	1990	2000	2011
People			
Share of poorest 20% in nat'l consumption/income (%)	..	..	..
Life expectancy at birth (years)	..	..	..
Total fertility rate (births per woman)	..	1.6	1.7
Adolescent fertility rate (births per 1,000 women 15–19)	..	..	..
Contraceptive prevalence (% of married women 15–49)	..	..	..
Births attended by skilled health staff (% of total)	..	..	..
Under-five mortality rate (per 1,000 live births)	10	6	2
Child malnutrition, underweight (% of under age 5)	..	..	..
Child immunization, measles (% of ages 12–23 mos.)	..	..	..
Primary completion rate, total (% of relevant age group)	..	90	101
Gross secondary enrollment, total (% of relevant age group)	..	112	111
Ratio of girls to boys in primary & secondary school (%)	..	92	89
HIV prevalence rate (% population of ages 15–49)	..	..	..
Environment			
Forests (sq. km)	65	69	69
Deforestation (avg. annual %, 1990–2000 and 2000–2010)		-0.6	0.0
Freshwater use (% of internal resources)	..	..	..
Access to improved water source (% total pop.)	..	..	..
Access to improved sanitation facilities (% total pop.)	..	..	..
Energy use per capita (kilograms of oil equivalent)	..	..	..
Carbon dioxide emissions per capita (metric tons)	..	..	..
Electricity use per capita (kilowatt-hours)	..	..	..
Economy			
GDP ($ billions)	1.4	2.5	4.8
GDP growth (annual %)	2.3	3.2	-1.2
GDP implicit price deflator (annual % growth)	5.4	1.6	-0.5
Value added in agriculture (% of GDP)	..	..	..
Value added in industry (% of GDP)	..	..	..
Value added in services (% of GDP)	..	..	..
Exports of goods and services (% of GDP)	..	..	..
Imports of goods and services (% of GDP)	..	..	..
Gross capital formation (% of GDP)	..	..	..
Central government revenue (% of GDP)	..	..	..
Central government cash surplus/deficit (% of GDP)	..	..	..
States and markets			
Starting a business (days)	..	..	..
Stock market capitalization (% of GDP)	..	..	..
Military expenditures (% of GDP)	..	..	..
Mobile cellular subscriptions (per 100 people)	0.0	30.4	101.8
Individuals using the Internet (% of population)	0.0	36.5	85.0
Paved roads (% of total)	..	..	..
High-technology exports (% of manufactured exports)	..	..	..
Global links			
Merchandise trade (% of GDP)	..	..	..
Net barter terms of trade index (2000 = 100)	..	..	..
Total external debt stocks ($ millions)	..	..	..
Total debt service (% of exports)	..	..	..
Net migration (thousands)	..	..	..
Remittances received ($ millions)	..	..	..
Foreign direct investment, net inflows ($ millions)	..	..	..
Net official development assistance received ($ millions)	..	..	..

Lithuania

Population (millions)	3.0	Population growth (%)		-8.1
Surface area (1,000 sq. km)	65	Population living below $1.25 a day (%)		<2
GNI, Atlas ($ billions)	39.3	GNI per capita, Atlas ($)		12,980
GNI, PPP ($ billions)	62.9	GNI per capita, PPP ($)		20,760

	1990	2000	2011
People			
Share of poorest 20% in nat'l consumption/income (%)	8.0	7.9	6.6
Life expectancy at birth (years)	71	72	74
Total fertility rate (births per woman)	2.0	1.4	1.8
Adolescent fertility rate (births per 1,000 women 15–19)	..	25	17
Contraceptive prevalence (% of married women 15–49)	..	..	..
Births attended by skilled health staff (% of total)	100	100	100
Under-five mortality rate (per 1,000 live births)	17	12	6
Child malnutrition, underweight (% of under age 5)	..	..	..
Child immunization, measles (% of ages 12–23 mos.)	89	97	94
Primary completion rate, total (% of relevant age group)	..	97	95
Gross secondary enrollment, total (% of relevant age group)	95	98	99
Ratio of girls to boys in primary & secondary school (%)	96	99	98
HIV prevalence rate (% population of ages 15–49)	0.1	0.1	0.1
Environment			
Forests (1,000 sq. km)	19	20	22
Deforestation (avg. annual %, 1990–2000 and 2000–2010)		-0.4	-0.7
Freshwater use (% of internal resources)	..	17.7	15.3
Access to improved water source (% total pop.)	..	92	92
Access to improved sanitation facilities (% total pop.)	..	86	86
Energy use per capita (kilograms of oil equivalent)	4,345	2,037	2,107
Carbon dioxide emissions per capita (metric tons)	6.0	3.5	3.8
Electricity use per capita (kilowatt-hours)	4,023	2,517	3,271
Economy			
GDP ($ billions)	10.5	11.4	42.7
GDP growth (annual %)	-5.7	3.3	5.9
GDP implicit price deflator (annual % growth)	228.3	0.9	5.8
Value added in agriculture (% of GDP)	27	6	4
Value added in industry (% of GDP)	31	30	28
Value added in services (% of GDP)	42	64	68
Exports of goods and services (% of GDP)	52	45	78
Imports of goods and services (% of GDP)	61	51	79
Gross capital formation (% of GDP)	33	19	19
Central government revenue (% of GDP)	..	25.9	26.4
Central government cash surplus/deficit (% of GDP)	..	-2.8	-5.2
States and markets			
Starting a business (days)	..	26	20
Stock market capitalization (% of GDP)	..	13.9	9.5
Military expenditures (% of GDP)	0.8	1.7	1.0
Mobile cellular subscriptions (per 100 people)	0.0	15.0	151.3
Individuals using the Internet (% of population)	0.0	6.4	65.1
Paved roads (% of total)	..	..	29.3
High-technology exports (% of manufactured exports)	0	4	10
Global links			
Merchandise trade (% of GDP)	..	81	139
Net barter terms of trade index (2000 = 100)	..	100	102
Total external debt stocks ($ billions)	0.0	4.9	30.0
Total debt service (% of exports)	0.3	21.1	20.1
Net migration (thousands)	33	-106	-35
Remittances received ($ millions)	0	50	1,956
Foreign direct investment, net inflows ($ millions)	30	379	1,443
Net official development assistance received ($ millions)	..	..	..

Luxembourg

Population (thousands)	518	Population growth (%)	2.2
Surface area (1,000 sq. km)	2.6	Population living below $1.25 a day (%)	..
GNI, Atlas ($ billions)	40.1	GNI per capita, Atlas ($)	77,390
GNI, PPP ($ billions)	33.2	GNI per capita, PPP ($)	64,110

	1990	2000	2011
People			
Share of poorest 20% in nat'l consumption/income (%)	..	8.4	..
Life expectancy at birth (years)	75	78	81
Total fertility rate (births per woman)	1.6	1.8	1.5
Adolescent fertility rate (births per 1,000 women 15–19)	..	11	9
Contraceptive prevalence (% of married women 15–49)	..	..	..
Births attended by skilled health staff (% of total)	..	100	..
Under-five mortality rate (per 1,000 live births)	8	5	3
Child malnutrition, underweight (% of under age 5)	..	..	..
Child immunization, measles (% of ages 12–23 mos.)	80	91	96
Primary completion rate, total (% of relevant age group)	..	..	83
Gross secondary enrollment, total (% of relevant age group)	69	97	101
Ratio of girls to boys in primary & secondary school (%)	102	104	102
HIV prevalence rate (% population of ages 15–49)	0.1	0.3	0.3
Environment			
Forests (sq. km)	860	868	868
Deforestation (avg. annual %, 1990–2000 and 2000–2010)		-0.1	0.0
Freshwater use (% of internal resources)	5.9	6.0	6.0
Access to improved water source (% total pop.)	100	100	100
Access to improved sanitation facilities (% total pop.)	100	100	100
Energy use per capita (kilograms of oil equivalent)	8,932	7,618	8,008
Carbon dioxide emissions per capita (metric tons)	26.2	18.9	20.4
Electricity use per capita (kilowatt-hours)	13,668	15,668	16,834
Economy			
GDP ($ billions)	12.7	20.3	59.2
GDP growth (annual %)	5.3	8.4	1.7
GDP implicit price deflator (annual % growth)	2.5	2.0	5.1
Value added in agriculture (% of GDP)	1	1	0
Value added in industry (% of GDP)	27	18	13
Value added in services (% of GDP)	71	81	86
Exports of goods and services (% of GDP)	102	150	176
Imports of goods and services (% of GDP)	88	129	145
Gross capital formation (% of GDP)	24	23	21
Central government revenue (% of GDP)	..	39.8	38.7
Central government cash surplus/deficit (% of GDP)	..	5.5	-0.4
States and markets			
Starting a business (days)	..	..	19
Stock market capitalization (% of GDP)	82.9	167.8	114.2
Military expenditures (% of GDP)	0.8	0.6	..
Mobile cellular subscriptions (per 100 people)	0.2	69.6	148.3
Individuals using the Internet (% of population)	0.0	22.9	90.9
Paved roads (% of total)	99.1	100.0	100.0
High-technology exports (% of manufactured exports)	..	17	10
Global links			
Merchandise trade (% of GDP)	..	97	85
Net barter terms of trade index (2000 = 100)	..	100	98
Total external debt stocks ($ millions)	..	..	..
Total debt service (% of exports)	..	..	..
Net migration (thousands)	11.9	19.9	42.5
Remittances received ($ millions)	..	579	1,740
Foreign direct investment, net inflows ($ billions)	..	1.0	18.4
Net official development assistance received ($ millions)	..	..	..

Macao SAR, China

High income

Population (thousands)	556	Population growth (%)	2.2
Surface area (sq. km)	28	Population living below $1.25 a day (%)	..
GNI, Atlas ($ billions)	24.7	GNI per capita, Atlas ($)	45,460
GNI, PPP ($ billions)	31.0	GNI per capita, PPP ($)	56,950

	1990	2000	2011
People			
Share of poorest 20% in nat'l consumption/income (%)	..	..	..
Life expectancy at birth (years)	76	79	81
Total fertility rate (births per woman)	1.7	0.9	1.1
Adolescent fertility rate (births per 1,000 women 15–19)	..	5	4
Contraceptive prevalence (% of married women 15–49)	..	..	..
Births attended by skilled health staff (% of total)	..	100	..
Under-five mortality rate (per 1,000 live births)	..	..	..
Child malnutrition, underweight (% of under age 5)	..	..	..
Child immunization, measles (% of ages 12-23 mos.)	..	..	..
Primary completion rate, total (% of relevant age group)	97	99	97
Gross secondary enrollment, total (% of relevant age group)	61	83	96
Ratio of girls to boys in primary & secondary school (%)	99	100	97
HIV prevalence rate (% population of ages 15–49)	..	..	..
Environment			
Forests (sq. km)	..	..	..
Deforestation (avg. annual %, 1990–2000 and 2000–2010)	..	..	..
Freshwater use (% of internal resources)	..	..	..
Access to improved water source (% total pop.)	..	..	..
Access to improved sanitation facilities (% total pop.)	..	..	..
Energy use per capita (kilograms of oil equivalent)	..	..	..
Carbon dioxide emissions per capita (metric tons)	2.9	3.8	2.8
Electricity use per capita (kilowatt-hours)	..	..	..
Economy			
GDP ($ billions)	3.0	6.1	36.4
GDP growth (annual %)	8.0	5.7	20.7
GDP implicit price deflator (annual % growth)	11.5	-2.0	6.9
Value added in agriculture (% of GDP)	0	0	0
Value added in industry (% of GDP)	21	15	7
Value added in services (% of GDP)	79	85	93
Exports of goods and services (% of GDP)	110	100	112
Imports of goods and services (% of GDP)	84	65	54
Gross capital formation (% of GDP)	25	12	13
Central government revenue (% of GDP)	..	19.9	40.3
Central government cash surplus/deficit (% of GDP)	..	1.6	25.0
States and markets			
Starting a business (days)	..	..	..
Stock market capitalization (% of GDP)	..	..	..
Military expenditures (% of GDP)	..	..	..
Mobile cellular subscriptions (per 100 people)	0.6	32.7	243.5
Individuals using the Internet (% of population)	0.0	13.6	58.0
Paved roads (% of total)	100.0	100.0	100.0
High-technology exports (% of manufactured exports)	2	1	0
Global links			
Merchandise trade (% of GDP)	108	85	24
Net barter terms of trade index (2000 = 100)	..	100	87
Total external debt stocks ($ millions)	..	..	..
Total debt service (% of exports)	..	..	..
Net migration (thousands)	36.9	19.8	50.6
Remittances received ($ millions)	..	208	48
Foreign direct investment, net inflows ($ millions)	0	-1	2,116
Net official development assistance received ($ millions)	0.2	0.3	..

Macedonia, FYR

Europe & Central Asia   **Upper middle income**

Population (millions)	2.1	Population growth (%)	0.2
Surface area (1,000 sq. km)	26	Population living below $1.25 a day (%)	<2
GNI, Atlas ($ billions)	9.9	GNI per capita, Atlas ($)	4,810
GNI, PPP ($ billions)	23.5	GNI per capita, PPP ($)	11,370

	1990	2000	2011
People			
Share of poorest 20% in nat'l consumption/income (%)	..	6.5	5.1
Life expectancy at birth (years)	71	73	75
Total fertility rate (births per woman)	2.1	1.7	1.4
Adolescent fertility rate (births per 1,000 women 15-19)	..	29	19
Contraceptive prevalence (% of married women 15-49)	..	..	..
Births attended by skilled health staff (% of total)	89	98	100
Under-five mortality rate (per 1,000 live births)	38	16	10
Child malnutrition, underweight (% of under age 5)	..	1.9	..
Child immunization, measles (% of ages 12-23 mos.)	98	97	98
Primary completion rate, total (% of relevant age group)	98	100	92
Gross secondary enrollment, total (% of relevant age group)	76	84	84
Ratio of girls to boys in primary & secondary school (%)	99	98	100
HIV prevalence rate (% population of ages 15-49)	..	..	..
Environment			
Forests (1,000 sq. km)	9	10	10
Deforestation (avg. annual %, 1990-2000 and 2000-2010)		-0.5	-0.4
Freshwater use (% of internal resources)	..	12.9	19.0
Access to improved water source (% total pop.)	100	100	100
Access to improved sanitation facilities (% total pop.)	..	88	88
Energy use per capita (kilograms of oil equivalent)	1,298	1,327	1,402
Carbon dioxide emissions per capita (metric tons)	5.6	6.0	5.5
Electricity use per capita (kilowatt-hours)	2,789	2,933	3,591
Economy			
GDP ($ billions)	4.5	3.6	10.4
GDP growth (annual %)	-6.2	4.5	2.8
GDP implicit price deflator (annual % growth)	93.7	8.2	3.4
Value added in agriculture (% of GDP)	9	12	11
Value added in industry (% of GDP)	44	34	28
Value added in services (% of GDP)	47	54	61
Exports of goods and services (% of GDP)	26	49	55
Imports of goods and services (% of GDP)	36	64	74
Gross capital formation (% of GDP)	19	22	27
Central government revenue (% of GDP)	..	..	32.9
Central government cash surplus/deficit (% of GDP)	..	..	-0.8
States and markets			
Starting a business (days)	..	48	2
Stock market capitalization (% of GDP)	..	0.2	24.0
Military expenditures (% of GDP)	..	1.9	1.3
Mobile cellular subscriptions (per 100 people)	0.0	5.8	107.2
Individuals using the Internet (% of population)	0.0	2.5	56.7
Paved roads (% of total)	58.9	63.8	57.6
High-technology exports (% of manufactured exports)	..	1	4
Global links			
Merchandise trade (% of GDP)	104	95	110
Net barter terms of trade index (2000 = 100)	..	100	87
Total external debt stocks ($ billions)	1.0	1.5	6.3
Total debt service (% of exports)	..	8.3	18.9
Net migration (thousands)	-15.0	-9.0	2.0
Remittances received ($ millions)	..	81	434
Foreign direct investment, net inflows ($ millions)	..	215	495
Net official development assistance received ($ millions)	3	250	165

Madagascar

Sub-Saharan Africa		Low income
Population (millions)	21.3	Population growth (%)	2.9
Surface area (1,000 sq. km)	587	Population living below $1.25 a day (%)	81.3
GNI, Atlas ($ billions)	9.1	GNI per capita, Atlas ($)	430
GNI, PPP ($ billions)	20.2	GNI per capita, PPP ($)	950

	1990	2000	2011
People			
Share of poorest 20% in nat'l consumption/income (%)	5.1	4.9	5.4
Life expectancy at birth (years)	51	60	67
Total fertility rate (births per woman)	6.3	5.5	4.6
Adolescent fertility rate (births per 1,000 women 15-19)	..	152	125
Contraceptive prevalence (% of married women 15-49)	17	19	40
Births attended by skilled health staff (% of total)	57	46	44
Under-five mortality rate (per 1,000 live births)	161	104	62
Child malnutrition, underweight (% of under age 5)	35.5	36.8	..
Child immunization, measles (% of ages 12-23 mos.)	47	56	70
Primary completion rate, total (% of relevant age group)	36	37	73
Gross secondary enrollment, total (% of relevant age group)	19	..	31
Ratio of girls to boys in primary & secondary school (%)	96	..	97
HIV prevalence rate (% population of ages 15-49)	0.1	0.3	0.3
Environment			
Forests (1,000 sq. km)	137	131	125
Deforestation (avg. annual %, 1990-2000 and 2000-2010)		0.4	0.4
Freshwater use (% of internal resources)	..	4.4	4.4
Access to improved water source (% total pop.)	29	38	46
Access to improved sanitation facilities (% total pop.)	9	12	15
Energy use per capita (kilograms of oil equivalent)	..	..	..
Carbon dioxide emissions per capita (metric tons)	0.09	0.12	0.09
Electricity use per capita (kilowatt-hours)	..	..	..
Economy			
GDP ($ billions)	3.1	3.9	9.9
GDP growth (annual %)	3.1	4.8	1.0
GDP implicit price deflator (annual % growth)	11.5	7.2	7.6
Value added in agriculture (% of GDP)	29	29	29
Value added in industry (% of GDP)	13	14	16
Value added in services (% of GDP)	59	57	55
Exports of goods and services (% of GDP)	17	31	26
Imports of goods and services (% of GDP)	28	38	37
Gross capital formation (% of GDP)	17	15	33
Central government revenue (% of GDP)	..	11.7	14.2
Central government cash surplus/deficit (% of GDP)	..	-2.0	-1.9
States and markets			
Starting a business (days)	..	67	8
Stock market capitalization (% of GDP)	..	..	..
Military expenditures (% of GDP)	1.2	1.2	0.7
Mobile cellular subscriptions (per 100 people)	0.0	0.4	40.7
Individuals using the Internet (% of population)	0.0	0.2	1.9
Paved roads (% of total)	15.4	11.6	16.3
High-technology exports (% of manufactured exports)	8	1	8
Global links			
Merchandise trade (% of GDP)	31	50	45
Net barter terms of trade index (2000 = 100)	81	100	75
Total external debt stocks ($ billions)	3.7	4.7	2.8
Total debt service (% of exports)	45.9	9.7	2.1
Net migration (thousands)	-8.0	-6.0	-5.0
Remittances received ($ millions)	7.9	11.3	..
Foreign direct investment, net inflows ($ millions)	22	83	907
Net official development assistance received ($ millions)	397	320	409

Malawi

Population (millions)	15.4	Population growth (%)	3.2
Surface area (1,000 sq. km)	118	Population living below $1.25 a day (%)	73.9
GNI, Atlas ($ billions)	5.6	GNI per capita, Atlas ($)	360
GNI, PPP ($ billions)	13.4	GNI per capita, PPP ($)	870

	1990	2000	2011
People			
Share of poorest 20% in nat'l consumption/income (%)	..	7.0	..
Life expectancy at birth (years)	47	46	54
Total fertility rate (births per woman)	6.8	6.1	6.0
Adolescent fertility rate (births per 1,000 women 15-19)	..	160	108
Contraceptive prevalence (% of married women 15-49)	13	31	46
Births attended by skilled health staff (% of total)	55	56	71
Under-five mortality rate (per 1,000 live births)	227	164	83
Child malnutrition, underweight (% of under age 5)	24.4	21.5	13.8
Child immunization, measles (% of ages 12-23 mos.)	81	73	96
Primary completion rate, total (% of relevant age group)	28	65	71
Gross secondary enrollment, total (% of relevant age group)	16	32	34
Ratio of girls to boys in primary & secondary school (%)	81	93	102
HIV prevalence rate (% population of ages 15-49)	7.8	13.8	10.0
Environment			
Forests (1,000 sq. km)	39	36	32
Deforestation (avg. annual %, 1990-2000 and 2000-2010)		0.9	1.0
Freshwater use (% of internal resources)	..	6.0	6.0
Access to improved water source (% total pop.)	41	62	83
Access to improved sanitation facilities (% total pop.)	39	46	51
Energy use per capita (kilograms of oil equivalent)	..	..	..
Carbon dioxide emissions per capita (metric tons)	0.07	0.08	0.07
Electricity use per capita (kilowatt-hours)	..	..	..
Economy			
GDP ($ millions)	1,881	1,744	5,621
GDP growth (annual %)	5.7	1.6	4.3
GDP implicit price deflator (annual % growth)	10.7	30.5	3.8
Value added in agriculture (% of GDP)	45	40	30
Value added in industry (% of GDP)	29	18	19
Value added in services (% of GDP)	26	43	50
Exports of goods and services (% of GDP)	24	26	30
Imports of goods and services (% of GDP)	33	35	39
Gross capital formation (% of GDP)	23	14	16
Central government revenue (% of GDP)	..	..	..
Central government cash surplus/deficit (% of GDP)	..	..	..
States and markets			
Starting a business (days)	..	45	39
Stock market capitalization (% of GDP)	..	3.6	24.6
Military expenditures (% of GDP)	1.3	0.7	..
Mobile cellular subscriptions (per 100 people)	0.0	0.4	25.7
Individuals using the Internet (% of population)	0.0	0.1	3.3
Paved roads (% of total)	..	45.0	..
High-technology exports (% of manufactured exports)	0	2	3
Global links			
Merchandise trade (% of GDP)	53	52	69
Net barter terms of trade index (2000 = 100)	148	100	98
Total external debt stocks ($ billions)	1.6	2.7	1.2
Total debt service (% of exports)	29.3	13.5	1.3
Net migration (thousands)	846	-106	-20
Remittances received ($ millions)	..	0.7	17.4
Foreign direct investment, net inflows ($ millions)	23.3	26.0	92.4
Net official development assistance received ($ millions)	500	446	798

Malaysia

Population (millions)	28.9	Population growth (%)	1.6
Surface area (1,000 sq. km)	331	Population living below $1.25 a day (%)	<2
GNI, Atlas ($ billions)	253.0	GNI per capita, Atlas ($)	8,770
GNI, PPP ($ billions)	451.7	GNI per capita, PPP ($)	15,650

	1990	2000	2011
People			
Share of poorest 20% in nat'l consumption/income (%)	5.1	6.5	4.5
Life expectancy at birth (years)	70	72	74
Total fertility rate (births per woman)	3.5	3.1	2.6
Adolescent fertility rate (births per 1,000 women 15–19)	..	15	11
Contraceptive prevalence (% of married women 15–49)	50	..	..
Births attended by skilled health staff (% of total)	93	97	99
Under-five mortality rate (per 1,000 live births)	17	11	7
Child malnutrition, underweight (% of under age 5)	22.1	16.7	12.9
Child immunization, measles (% of ages 12–23 mos.)	70	88	95
Primary completion rate, total (% of relevant age group)	88	95	..
Gross secondary enrollment, total (% of relevant age group)	55	66	69
Ratio of girls to boys in primary & secondary school (%)	102	104	..
HIV prevalence rate (% population of ages 15–49)	0.1	0.4	0.4
Environment			
Forests (1,000 sq. km)	224	216	204
Deforestation (avg. annual %, 1990–2000 and 2000–2010)		0.4	0.5
Freshwater use (% of internal resources)	1.7	1.3	2.3
Access to improved water source (% total pop.)	88	97	100
Access to improved sanitation facilities (% total pop.)	84	92	96
Energy use per capita (kilograms of oil equivalent)	1,183	2,012	2,558
Carbon dioxide emissions per capita (metric tons)	3.1	5.4	7.1
Electricity use per capita (kilowatt-hours)	1,146	2,721	4,117
Economy			
GDP ($ billions)	44	94	288
GDP growth (annual %)	9.0	8.9	5.1
GDP implicit price deflator (annual % growth)	3.8	8.9	5.5
Value added in agriculture (% of GDP)	15	9	12
Value added in industry (% of GDP)	42	48	40
Value added in services (% of GDP)	43	43	48
Exports of goods and services (% of GDP)	75	120	92
Imports of goods and services (% of GDP)	72	101	76
Gross capital formation (% of GDP)	32	27	24
Central government revenue (% of GDP)	..	17.5	21.0
Central government cash surplus/deficit (% of GDP)	..	–4.1	–4.8
States and markets			
Starting a business (days)	..	37	6
Stock market capitalization (% of GDP)	110.4	124.7	137.2
Military expenditures (% of GDP)	2.6	1.6	1.6
Mobile cellular subscriptions (per 100 people)	0.5	21.9	127.0
Individuals using the Internet (% of population)	0.0	21.4	61.0
Paved roads (% of total)	70.0	76.2	80.4
High-technology exports (% of manufactured exports)	38	60	43
Global links			
Merchandise trade (% of GDP)	133	192	144
Net barter terms of trade index (2000 = 100)	103	100	101
Total external debt stocks ($ billions)	15.3	41.9	94.5
Total debt service (% of exports)	12.6	5.6	3.9
Net migration (thousands)	461	422	84
Remittances received ($ millions)	185	342	1,198
Foreign direct investment, net inflows ($ billions)	2.3	3.8	12.0
Net official development assistance received ($ millions)	468	46	31

Maldives

South Asia		Upper middle income
Population (thousands)	320	Population growth (%)	1.3
Surface area (sq. km)	300	Population living below $1.25 a day (%)	<2
GNI, Atlas ($ billions)	1.8	GNI per capita, Atlas ($)	5,720
GNI, PPP ($ billions)	2.4	GNI per capita, PPP ($)	7,430

	1990	2000	2011
People			
Share of poorest 20% in nat'l consumption/income (%)	..	6.5	..
Life expectancy at birth (years)	61	70	77
Total fertility rate (births per woman)	6.1	2.9	1.7
Adolescent fertility rate (births per 1,000 women 15–19)	..	32	11
Contraceptive prevalence (% of married women 15–49)	29	42	35
Births attended by skilled health staff (% of total)	..	70	95
Under-five mortality rate (per 1,000 live births)	105	53	11
Child malnutrition, underweight (% of under age 5)	..	25.7	17.8
Child immunization, measles (% of ages 12–23 mos.)	96	99	96
Primary completion rate, total (% of relevant age group)	..	..	107
Gross secondary enrollment, total (% of relevant age group)	..	53	..
Ratio of girls to boys in primary & secondary school (%)	..	101	..
HIV prevalence rate (% population of ages 15–49)	0.1	0.1	0.1
Environment			
Forests (sq. km)	9.0	9.0	9.0
Deforestation (avg. annual %, 1990–2000 and 2000–2010)		0.0	0.0
Freshwater use (% of internal resources)	..	11.3	19.7
Access to improved water source (% total pop.)	93	95	98
Access to improved sanitation facilities (% total pop.)	68	79	97
Energy use per capita (kilograms of oil equivalent)	232	..	..
Carbon dioxide emissions per capita (metric tons)	0.7	1.8	3.3
Electricity use per capita (kilowatt-hours)	..	..	..
Economy			
GDP ($ millions)	215	624	2,050
GDP growth (annual %)	..	4.8	7.5
GDP implicit price deflator (annual % growth)	..	1.1	4.9
Value added in agriculture (% of GDP)	..	9	6
Value added in industry (% of GDP)	..	15	13
Value added in services (% of GDP)	..	76	82
Exports of goods and services (% of GDP)	85	89	114
Imports of goods and services (% of GDP)	83	72	110
Gross capital formation (% of GDP)	..	26	..
Central government revenue (% of GDP)	22.1	30.0	23.9
Central government cash surplus/deficit (% of GDP)	-7.5	-5.0	-16.7
States and markets			
Starting a business (days)	..	13	9
Stock market capitalization (% of GDP)	..	..	..
Military expenditures (% of GDP)	..	..	..
Mobile cellular subscriptions (per 100 people)	0.0	2.8	165.7
Individuals using the Internet (% of population)	0.0	2.2	34.0
Paved roads (% of total)	..	..	..
High-technology exports (% of manufactured exports)	..	..	..
Global links			
Merchandise trade (% of GDP)	100	80	88
Net barter terms of trade index (2000 = 100)	..	100	100
Total external debt stocks ($ millions)	78	206	983
Total debt service (% of exports)	4.8	4.2	8.9
Net migration (thousands)	-2.6	-1.1	-0.1
Remittances received ($ millions)	1.7	2.2	3.0
Foreign direct investment, net inflows ($ millions)	6	22	282
Net official development assistance received ($ millions)	20.9	19.2	46.0

Mali

Sub-Saharan Africa		Low income	
Population (millions)	15.8	Population growth (%)	3.0
Surface area (1,000 sq. km)	1,240	Population living below $1.25 a day (%)	50.4
GNI, Atlas ($ billions)	9.7	GNI per capita, Atlas ($)	610
GNI, PPP ($ billions)	16.8	GNI per capita, PPP ($)	1,060

	1990	2000	2011
People			
Share of poorest 20% in nat'l consumption/income (%)	..	6.1	8.0
Life expectancy at birth (years)	44	47	51
Total fertility rate (births per woman)	7.1	6.8	6.2
Adolescent fertility rate (births per 1,000 women 15–19)	..	190	172
Contraceptive prevalence (% of married women 15–49)	..	8	8
Births attended by skilled health staff (% of total)	..	41	49
Under-five mortality rate (per 1,000 live births)	257	214	176
Child malnutrition, underweight (% of under age 5)	..	30.1	27.9
Child immunization, measles (% of ages 12–23 mos.)	43	49	56
Primary completion rate, total (% of relevant age group)	9	29	55
Gross secondary enrollment, total (% of relevant age group)	7	17	39
Ratio of girls to boys in primary & secondary school (%)	59	71	83
HIV prevalence rate (% population of ages 15–49)	1.1	1.7	1.1
Environment			
Forests (1,000 sq. km)	141	133	124
Deforestation (avg. annual %, 1990–2000 and 2000–2010)		0.6	0.6
Freshwater use (% of internal resources)	..	10.9	10.9
Access to improved water source (% total pop.)	28	46	64
Access to improved sanitation facilities (% total pop.)	15	18	22
Energy use per capita (kilograms of oil equivalent)	..	..	..
Carbon dioxide emissions per capita (metric tons)	0.05	0.05	0.04
Electricity use per capita (kilowatt-hours)	..	..	..
Economy			
GDP ($ billions)	2.4	2.4	10.8
GDP growth (annual %)	-1.9	3.2	2.7
GDP implicit price deflator (annual % growth)	4.9	5.6	6.6
Value added in agriculture (% of GDP)	46	42	39
Value added in industry (% of GDP)	16	21	21
Value added in services (% of GDP)	39	38	40
Exports of goods and services (% of GDP)	17	27	25
Imports of goods and services (% of GDP)	34	39	36
Gross capital formation (% of GDP)	23	25	22
Central government revenue (% of GDP)	..	13.4	17.3
Central government cash surplus/deficit (% of GDP)	..	-3.4	-2.5
States and markets			
Starting a business (days)	..	41	8
Stock market capitalization (% of GDP)	..	..	..
Military expenditures (% of GDP)	2.2	2.4	1.8
Mobile cellular subscriptions (per 100 people)	0.0	0.1	68.3
Individuals using the Internet (% of population)	0.0	0.1	2.0
Paved roads (% of total)	10.9	12.1	24.6
High-technology exports (% of manufactured exports)	..	15	2
Global links			
Merchandise trade (% of GDP)	40	56	52
Net barter terms of trade index (2000 = 100)	135	100	177
Total external debt stocks ($ billions)	2.5	3.0	2.9
Total debt service (% of exports)	15.3	14.1	2.5
Net migration (thousands)	-481	-142	-101
Remittances received ($ millions)	107	73	473
Foreign direct investment, net inflows ($ millions)	6	82	178
Net official development assistance received ($ millions)	479	288	1,271

Malta

Population (thousands)	416	Population growth (%)	-0.1
Surface area (sq. km)	320	Population living below $1.25 a day (%)	..
GNI, Atlas ($ billions)	7.7	GNI per capita, Atlas ($)	18,620
GNI, PPP ($ billions)	10.2	GNI per capita, PPP ($)	24,480

	1990	2000	2011
People			
Share of poorest 20% in nat'l consumption/income (%)	..	..	..
Life expectancy at birth (years)	75	78	82
Total fertility rate (births per woman)	2.1	1.7	1.4
Adolescent fertility rate (births per 1,000 women 15-19)	..	16	13
Contraceptive prevalence (% of married women 15-49)	86	..	..
Births attended by skilled health staff (% of total)	98	..	100
Under-five mortality rate (per 1,000 live births)	11	8	6
Child malnutrition, underweight (% of under age 5)	..	..	..
Child immunization, measles (% of ages 12-23 mos.)	80	74	84
Primary completion rate, total (% of relevant age group)	98	100	97
Gross secondary enrollment, total (% of relevant age group)	83	85	101
Ratio of girls to boys in primary & secondary school (%)	95	100	94
HIV prevalence rate (% population of ages 15-49)	0.1	0.1	0.1
Environment			
Forests (sq. km)	3.0	3.0	3.0
Deforestation (avg. annual %, 1990-2000 and 2000-2010)		0.0	0.0
Freshwater use (% of internal resources)	..	106.7	106.7
Access to improved water source (% total pop.)	100	100	100
Access to improved sanitation facilities (% total pop.)	100	100	100
Energy use per capita (kilograms of oil equivalent)	1,962	1,771	2,013
Carbon dioxide emissions per capita (metric tons)	6.2	5.4	6.0
Electricity use per capita (kilowatt-hours)	2,824	4,410	4,151
Economy			
GDP ($ billions)	2.5	4.0	8.9
GDP growth (annual %)	6.3	6.8	2.1
GDP implicit price deflator (annual % growth)	3.2	4.2	1.6
Value added in agriculture (% of GDP)	3	2	2
Value added in industry (% of GDP)	56	51	33
Value added in services (% of GDP)	41	47	65
Exports of goods and services (% of GDP)	76	91	98
Imports of goods and services (% of GDP)	89	98	93
Gross capital formation (% of GDP)	31	25	13
Central government revenue (% of GDP)	..	36.3	38.3
Central government cash surplus/deficit (% of GDP)	..	-9.6	-2.8
States and markets			
Starting a business (days)	..	..	40
Stock market capitalization (% of GDP)	..	51.7	38.5
Military expenditures (% of GDP)	0.8	0.6	0.7
Mobile cellular subscriptions (per 100 people)	0.0	28.8	124.9
Individuals using the Internet (% of population)	0.0	13.1	69.2
Paved roads (% of total)	..	88.0	87.5
High-technology exports (% of manufactured exports)	45	72	47
Global links			
Merchandise trade (% of GDP)	122	148	120
Net barter terms of trade index (2000 = 100)	..	100	54
Total external debt stocks ($ millions)	..	..	..
Total debt service (% of exports)	..	..	..
Net migration (thousands)	2.3	2.2	5.0
Remittances received ($ millions)	58.2	20.0	36.7
Foreign direct investment, net inflows ($ millions)	46	601	467
Net official development assistance received ($ millions)	5.3	21.2	..

Marshall Islands

Lower middle income

Population (thousands)	55	Population growth (%)	1.4
Surface area (sq. km)	180	Population living below $1.25 a day (%)	..
GNI, Atlas ($ millions)	214.3	GNI per capita, Atlas ($)	3,910
GNI, PPP ($ millions)	..	GNI per capita, PPP ($)	..

	1990	2000	2011
People			
Share of poorest 20% in nat'l consumption/income (%)	..	..	..
Life expectancy at birth (years)	..	65	..
Total fertility rate (births per woman)	..	5.7	..
Adolescent fertility rate (births per 1,000 women 15-19)	..	..	..
Contraceptive prevalence (% of married women 15-49)	..	34	45
Births attended by skilled health staff (% of total)	..	95	99
Under-five mortality rate (per 1,000 live births)	52	38	26
Child malnutrition, underweight (% of under age 5)	..	..	..
Child immunization, measles (% of ages 12-23 mos.)	52	94	97
Primary completion rate, total (% of relevant age group)	..	93	97
Gross secondary enrollment, total (% of relevant age group)	..	68	99
Ratio of girls to boys in primary & secondary school (%)	..	102	101
HIV prevalence rate (% population of ages 15-49)	..	..	..
Environment			
Forests (sq. km)	130	126	126
Deforestation (avg. annual %, 1990-2000 and 2000-2010)		0.0	0.0
Freshwater use (% of internal resources)	..	..	..
Access to improved water source (% total pop.)	95	95	94
Access to improved sanitation facilities (% total pop.)	64	70	75
Energy use per capita (kilograms of oil equivalent)	..	..	..
Carbon dioxide emissions per capita (metric tons)	1.0	1.5	1.9
Electricity use per capita (kilowatt-hours)	..	..	..
Economy			
GDP ($ millions)	78.5	110.9	173.7
GDP growth (annual %)	2.7	5.9	5.0
GDP implicit price deflator (annual % growth)	5.0	-3.0	1.5
Value added in agriculture (% of GDP)	..	..	..
Value added in industry (% of GDP)	..	..	..
Value added in services (% of GDP)	..	..	..
Exports of goods and services (% of GDP)	..	..	..
Imports of goods and services (% of GDP)	..	..	..
Gross capital formation (% of GDP)	..	..	..
Central government revenue (% of GDP)	..	..	..
Central government cash surplus/deficit (% of GDP)	..	..	..
States and markets			
Starting a business (days)	..	17	17
Stock market capitalization (% of GDP)	..	..	..
Military expenditures (% of GDP)	..	..	..
Mobile cellular subscriptions (per 100 people)	0.0	0.9	..
Individuals using the Internet (% of population)	0.0	1.5	3.5
Paved roads (% of total)	..	..	..
High-technology exports (% of manufactured exports)	..	..	..
Global links			
Merchandise trade (% of GDP)	..	58	101
Net barter terms of trade index (2000 = 100)	..	100	107
Total external debt stocks ($ millions)	..	..	..
Total debt service (% of exports)	..	..	..
Net migration (thousands)	..	..	..
Remittances received ($ millions)	..	..	..
Foreign direct investment, net inflows ($ millions)	1	125	7
Net official development assistance received ($ millions)	0.3	57.2	82.3

Mauritania

Sub-Saharan Africa		Low income	
Population (millions)	3.5	Population growth (%)	2.3
Surface area (1,000 sq. km)	1,031	Population living below $1.25 a day (%)	23.4
GNI, Atlas ($ billions)	3.6	GNI per capita, Atlas ($)	1,030
GNI, PPP ($ billions)	8.9	GNI per capita, PPP ($)	2,530

	1990	2000	2011
People			
Share of poorest 20% in nat'l consumption/income (%)	5.2	6.2	6.0
Life expectancy at birth (years)	56	57	59
Total fertility rate (births per woman)	5.9	5.2	4.5
Adolescent fertility rate (births per 1,000 women 15-19)	..	91	73
Contraceptive prevalence (% of married women 15-49)	4	8	9
Births attended by skilled health staff (% of total)	40	57	61
Under-five mortality rate (per 1,000 live births)	125	118	112
Child malnutrition, underweight (% of under age 5)	43.3	30.4	15.9
Child immunization, measles (% of ages 12-23 mos.)	38	62	67
Primary completion rate, total (% of relevant age group)	29	46	70
Gross secondary enrollment, total (% of relevant age group)	13	18	27
Ratio of girls to boys in primary & secondary school (%)	67	93	101
HIV prevalence rate (% population of ages 15-49)	0.3	0.6	1.1
Environment			
Forests (1,000 sq. km)	4.2	3.2	2.4
Deforestation (avg. annual %, 1990-2000 and 2000-2010)		2.7	2.7
Freshwater use (% of internal resources)	..	400.3	400.3
Access to improved water source (% total pop.)	30	40	50
Access to improved sanitation facilities (% total pop.)	16	21	26
Energy use per capita (kilograms of oil equivalent)	..	..	..
Carbon dioxide emissions per capita (metric tons)	1.3	0.5	0.6
Electricity use per capita (kilowatt-hours)	..	..	..
Economy			
GDP ($ millions)	1,020	1,294	4,213
GDP growth (annual %)	-1.8	-0.4	4.0
GDP implicit price deflator (annual % growth)	2.6	5.4	12.1
Value added in agriculture (% of GDP)	30	37	13
Value added in industry (% of GDP)	29	28	50
Value added in services (% of GDP)	42	35	37
Exports of goods and services (% of GDP)	46	30	66
Imports of goods and services (% of GDP)	61	45	59
Gross capital formation (% of GDP)	20	21	31
Central government revenue (% of GDP)	..	..	..
Central government cash surplus/deficit (% of GDP)	..	..	..
States and markets			
Starting a business (days)	..	82	19
Stock market capitalization (% of GDP)	..	..	..
Military expenditures (% of GDP)	3.9	2.9	3.8
Mobile cellular subscriptions (per 100 people)	0.0	0.6	93.6
Individuals using the Internet (% of population)	0.0	0.2	4.5
Paved roads (% of total)	..	32.6	29.7
High-technology exports (% of manufactured exports)	..	..	..
Global links			
Merchandise trade (% of GDP)	84	63	124
Net barter terms of trade index (2000 = 100)	97	100	131
Total external debt stocks ($ billions)	2.1	2.4	2.7
Total debt service (% of exports)	30.7	27.8	3.6
Net migration (thousands)	-30.3	9.9	9.9
Remittances received ($ millions)	13.7	2.2	..
Foreign direct investment, net inflows ($ millions)	6.7	40.1	45.2
Net official development assistance received ($ millions)	236	223	370

Mauritius

Population (millions)	1.3	Population growth (%)		0.4
Surface area (1,000 sq. km)	2.0	Population living below $1.25 a day (%)		..
GNI, Atlas ($ billions)	10.3	GNI per capita, Atlas ($)		8,040
GNI, PPP ($ billions)	18.4	GNI per capita, PPP ($)		14,330

	1990	2000	2011
People			
Share of poorest 20% in nat'l consumption/income (%)	..	..	..
Life expectancy at birth (years)	69	72	73
Total fertility rate (births per woman)	2.3	2.0	1.5
Adolescent fertility rate (births per 1,000 women 15–19)	..	36	33
Contraceptive prevalence (% of married women 15–49)	75	76	..
Births attended by skilled health staff (% of total)	91	99	..
Under-five mortality rate (per 1,000 live births)	24	19	15
Child malnutrition, underweight (% of under age 5)	..	..	..
Child immunization, measles (% of ages 12-23 mos.)	76	84	99
Primary completion rate, total (% of relevant age group)	111	88	..
Gross secondary enrollment, total (% of relevant age group)	52	75	91
Ratio of girls to boys in primary & secondary school (%)	101	101	..
HIV prevalence rate (% population of ages 15–49)	0.1	0.8	1.0
Environment			
Forests (sq. km)	388	387	350
Deforestation (avg. annual %, 1990–2000 and 2000–2010)		0.0	1.0
Freshwater use (% of internal resources)	20.6	22.2	26.4
Access to improved water source (% total pop.)	99	99	99
Access to improved sanitation facilities (% total pop.)	89	89	89
Energy use per capita (kilograms of oil equivalent)	453	..	..
Carbon dioxide emissions per capita (metric tons)	1.4	2.3	3.0
Electricity use per capita (kilowatt-hours)	..	..	..
Economy			
GDP ($ billions)	2.7	4.6	11.3
GDP growth (annual %)	7.2	9.0	4.1
GDP implicit price deflator (annual % growth)	10.1	2.1	3.9
Value added in agriculture (% of GDP)	13	7	4
Value added in industry (% of GDP)	33	31	26
Value added in services (% of GDP)	54	62	70
Exports of goods and services (% of GDP)	65	61	54
Imports of goods and services (% of GDP)	72	62	66
Gross capital formation (% of GDP)	30	26	25
Central government revenue (% of GDP)	..	..	22.4
Central government cash surplus/deficit (% of GDP)	..	..	-1.1
States and markets			
Starting a business (days)	..	46	6
Stock market capitalization (% of GDP)	10.1	29.0	58.1
Military expenditures (% of GDP)	0.3	0.2	0.1
Mobile cellular subscriptions (per 100 people)	0.2	15.0	99.0
Individuals using the Internet (% of population)	0.0	7.3	35.0
Paved roads (% of total)	93.0	97.0	98.0
High-technology exports (% of manufactured exports)	1	1	1
Global links			
Merchandise trade (% of GDP)	106	80	69
Net barter terms of trade index (2000 = 100)	93	100	71
Total external debt stocks ($ millions)	932	967	1,435
Total debt service (% of exports)	8.5	17.0	1.4
Net migration (thousands)	-35.9	-8.8	0.0
Remittances received ($ millions)	..	177	1
Foreign direct investment, net inflows ($ millions)	41	266	273
Net official development assistance received ($ millions)	88	20	192

Mexico

Latin America & Caribbean   **Upper middle income**

Population (millions)	114.8	Population growth (%)	1.2
Surface area (1,000 sq. km)	1,964	Population living below $1.25 a day (%)	<2
GNI, Atlas ($ billions)	1,081.8	GNI per capita, Atlas ($)	9,420
GNI, PPP ($ billions)	1,766.4	GNI per capita, PPP ($)	15,390

	1990	2000	2011
People			
Share of poorest 20% in nat'l consumption/income (%)	6.4	4.0	4.7
Life expectancy at birth (years)	71	74	77
Total fertility rate (births per woman)	3.4	2.6	2.3
Adolescent fertility rate (births per 1,000 women 15–19)	..	76	67
Contraceptive prevalence (% of married women 15–49)	63	70	73
Births attended by skilled health staff (% of total)	84	95	95
Under-five mortality rate (per 1,000 live births)	49	29	16
Child malnutrition, underweight (% of under age 5)	13.9	6.0	3.4
Child immunization, measles (% of ages 12-23 mos.)	75	96	98
Primary completion rate, total (% of relevant age group)	89	99	104
Gross secondary enrollment, total (% of relevant age group)	55	73	91
Ratio of girls to boys in primary & secondary school (%)	97	100	102
HIV prevalence rate (% population of ages 15–49)	0.2	0.2	0.3
Environment			
Forests (1,000 sq. km)	703	668	646
Deforestation (avg. annual %, 1990–2000 and 2000–2010)		0.5	0.3
Freshwater use (% of internal resources)	..	17.8	19.5
Access to improved water source (% total pop.)	85	90	96
Access to improved sanitation facilities (% total pop.)	64	75	85
Energy use per capita (kilograms of oil equivalent)	1,453	1,452	1,629
Carbon dioxide emissions per capita (metric tons)	3.7	3.8	4.0
Electricity use per capita (kilowatt-hours)	1,180	1,766	1,990
Economy			
GDP ($ billions)	263	581	1,153
GDP growth (annual %)	5.1	6.6	3.9
GDP implicit price deflator (annual % growth)	28.1	12.1	5.6
Value added in agriculture (% of GDP)	8	4	4
Value added in industry (% of GDP)	28	28	37
Value added in services (% of GDP)	64	68	60
Exports of goods and services (% of GDP)	19	31	32
Imports of goods and services (% of GDP)	20	33	33
Gross capital formation (% of GDP)	23	24	25
Central government revenue (% of GDP)	15.3	14.7	..
Central government cash surplus/deficit (% of GDP)	-2.5	-1.2	..
States and markets			
Starting a business (days)	..	58	9
Stock market capitalization (% of GDP)	12.4	21.5	35.4
Military expenditures (% of GDP)	0.5	0.6	0.5
Mobile cellular subscriptions (per 100 people)	0.1	14.1	82.4
Individuals using the Internet (% of population)	0.0	5.1	36.2
Paved roads (% of total)	35.1	32.8	36.4
High-technology exports (% of manufactured exports)	8	22	17
Global links			
Merchandise trade (% of GDP)	32	59	62
Net barter terms of trade index (2000 = 100)	102	100	108
Total external debt stocks ($ billions)	105	152	287
Total debt service (% of exports)	21.8	31.6	11.2
Net migration (millions)	-1.3	-1.4	-1.8
Remittances received ($ billions)	3.1	7.5	23.6
Foreign direct investment, net inflows ($ billions)	2.5	18.1	20.8
Net official development assistance received ($ millions)	156	-58	882

Micronesia, Fed. Sts.

East Asia & Pacific		Lower middle income	
Population (thousands)	112	Population growth (%)	0.4
Surface area (sq. km)	700	Population living below $1.25 a day (%)	*31.2*
GNI, Atlas ($ millions)	318.6	GNI per capita, Atlas ($)	2,860
GNI, PPP ($ millions)	398.9	GNI per capita, PPP ($)	3,580

	1990	2000	2011
People			
Share of poorest 20% in nat'l consumption/income (%)	..	1.6	..
Life expectancy at birth (years)	66	67	69
Total fertility rate (births per woman)	5.0	4.3	3.4
Adolescent fertility rate (births per 1,000 women 15-19)	..	38	20
Contraceptive prevalence (% of married women 15-49)	..	23	55
Births attended by skilled health staff (% of total)	..	88	100
Under-five mortality rate (per 1,000 live births)	56	49	42
Child malnutrition, underweight (% of under age 5)	..	..	..
Child immunization, measles (% of ages 12-23 mos.)	81	85	92
Primary completion rate, total (% of relevant age group)	..	..	..
Gross secondary enrollment, total (% of relevant age group)	..	..	..
Ratio of girls to boys in primary & secondary school (%)	..	..	..
HIV prevalence rate (% population of ages 15-49)	..	..	..
Environment			
Forests (sq. km)	640	639	642
Deforestation (avg. annual %, 1990-2000 and 2000-2010)		0.0	0.0
Freshwater use (% of internal resources)	..	..	..
Access to improved water source (% total pop.)	89	92	..
Access to improved sanitation facilities (% total pop.)	29	26	..
Energy use per capita (kilograms of oil equivalent)	..	..	..
Carbon dioxide emissions per capita (metric tons)	..	0.5	0.6
Electricity use per capita (kilowatt-hours)	..	..	..
Economy			
GDP ($ millions)	147	233	310
GDP growth (annual %)	3.7	4.6	2.1
GDP implicit price deflator (annual % growth)	4.9	1.1	3.4
Value added in agriculture (% of GDP)	..	..	..
Value added in industry (% of GDP)	..	..	..
Value added in services (% of GDP)	..	..	..
Exports of goods and services (% of GDP)	..	..	..
Imports of goods and services (% of GDP)	..	..	..
Gross capital formation (% of GDP)	..	..	..
Central government revenue (% of GDP)	..	..	..
Central government cash surplus/deficit (% of GDP)	..	..	..
States and markets			
Starting a business (days)	..	*16*	16
Stock market capitalization (% of GDP)	..	..	..
Military expenditures (% of GDP)	..	..	..
Mobile cellular subscriptions (per 100 people)	0.0	0.0	24.8
Individuals using the Internet (% of population)	0.0	3.7	*20.0*
Paved roads (% of total)	15.9	17.5	..
High-technology exports (% of manufactured exports)	..	..	..
Global links			
Merchandise trade (% of GDP)	..	55	63
Net barter terms of trade index (2000 = 100)	..	100	97
Total external debt stocks ($ millions)	..	..	..
Total debt service (% of exports)	..	..	..
Net migration (thousands)	-2.5	-13.6	-9.0
Remittances received ($ millions)	..	..	..
Foreign direct investment, net inflows ($ millions)	..	-0.2	7.8
Net official development assistance received ($ millions)	0	102	134

Moldova

Europe & Central Asia　　　　　　　　　　　**Lower middle income**

Population (millions)	3.6	Population growth (%)	-0.1
Surface area (1,000 sq. km)	34	Population living below $1.25 a day (%)	<2
GNI, Atlas ($ billions)	7.1	GNI per capita, Atlas ($)	1,980
GNI, PPP ($ billions)	13.0	GNI per capita, PPP ($)	3,640

	1990	2000	2011
People			
Share of poorest 20% in nat'l consumption/income (%)	6.9	6.7	7.8
Life expectancy at birth (years)	67	67	69
Total fertility rate (births per woman)	2.4	1.6	1.5
Adolescent fertility rate (births per 1,000 women 15-19)	..	46	30
Contraceptive prevalence (% of married women 15-49)	..	62	..
Births attended by skilled health staff (% of total)	100	98	100
Under-five mortality rate (per 1,000 live births)	35	24	16
Child malnutrition, underweight (% of under age 5)	..	..	..
Child immunization, measles (% of ages 12-23 mos.)	73	89	91
Primary completion rate, total (% of relevant age group)	..	98	91
Gross secondary enrollment, total (% of relevant age group)	94	82	88
Ratio of girls to boys in primary & secondary school (%)	105	101	101
HIV prevalence rate (% population of ages 15-49)	0.1	0.4	0.5
Environment			
Forests (1,000 sq. km)	3.2	3.2	3.9
Deforestation (avg. annual %, 1990-2000 and 2000-2010)		-0.2	-1.8
Freshwater use (% of internal resources)	296.3	191.5	191.5
Access to improved water source (% total pop.)	93	93	96
Access to improved sanitation facilities (% total pop.)	76	79	85
Energy use per capita (kilograms of oil equivalent)	2,669	688	731
Carbon dioxide emissions per capita (metric tons)	5.7	1.0	1.3
Electricity use per capita (kilowatt-hours)	3,235	1,005	1,049
Economy			
GDP ($ billions)	3.6	1.3	7.0
GDP growth (annual %)	-2.4	2.1	6.4
GDP implicit price deflator (annual % growth)	13.5	27.3	7.4
Value added in agriculture (% of GDP)	36	29	15
Value added in industry (% of GDP)	37	22	14
Value added in services (% of GDP)	27	49	71
Exports of goods and services (% of GDP)	48	50	45
Imports of goods and services (% of GDP)	51	75	86
Gross capital formation (% of GDP)	25	24	24
Central government revenue (% of GDP)	..	24.5	30.8
Central government cash surplus/deficit (% of GDP)	..	-1.5	-1.8
States and markets			
Starting a business (days)	..	42	9
Stock market capitalization (% of GDP)	..	3.2	..
Military expenditures (% of GDP)	0.5	0.4	0.3
Mobile cellular subscriptions (per 100 people)	0.0	3.4	104.8
Individuals using the Internet (% of population)	0.0	1.3	38.0
Paved roads (% of total)	87.1	86.1	86.2
High-technology exports (% of manufactured exports)	..	3	6
Global links			
Merchandise trade (% of GDP)	..	97	106
Net barter terms of trade index (2000 = 100)	..	100	106
Total external debt stocks ($ billions)	0.0	1.8	5.5
Total debt service (% of exports)	..	20.0	12.8
Net migration (thousands)	-89	-253	-172
Remittances received ($ millions)	..	179	1,600
Foreign direct investment, net inflows ($ millions)	17	128	294
Net official development assistance received ($ millions)	..	123	451

Monaco

Population (thousands)	35	Population growth (%)	0.1
Surface area (sq. km)	2.0	Population living below $1.25 a day (%)	..
GNI, Atlas ($ billions)	6.5	GNI per capita, Atlas ($)	183,150
GNI, PPP ($ millions)	..	GNI per capita, PPP ($)	..

	1990	2000	2011
People			
Share of poorest 20% in nat'l consumption/income (%)	..	..	..
Life expectancy at birth (years)	..	..	..
Total fertility rate (births per woman)	..	..	..
Adolescent fertility rate (births per 1,000 women 15–19)	..	..	..
Contraceptive prevalence (% of married women 15–49)	..	..	..
Births attended by skilled health staff (% of total)	..	..	..
Under-five mortality rate (per 1,000 live births)	8	5	4
Child malnutrition, underweight (% of under age 5)	..	..	..
Child immunization, measles (% of ages 12–23 mos.)	99	99	99
Primary completion rate, total (% of relevant age group)	..	..	..
Gross secondary enrollment, total (% of relevant age group)	..	..	..
Ratio of girls to boys in primary & secondary school (%)	..	..	..
HIV prevalence rate (% population of ages 15–49)	..	..	..
Environment			
Forests (sq. km)	0.0	0.0	0.0
Deforestation (avg. annual %, 1990–2000 and 2000–2010)		0.0	0.0
Freshwater use (% of internal resources)	..	..	..
Access to improved water source (% total pop.)	100	100	100
Access to improved sanitation facilities (% total pop.)	100	100	100
Energy use per capita (kilograms of oil equivalent)	..	..	..
Carbon dioxide emissions per capita (metric tons)	..	..	..
Electricity use per capita (kilowatt-hours)	..	..	..
Economy			
GDP ($ billions)	2.5	2.6	6.1
GDP growth (annual %)	2.6	3.9	-2.6
GDP implicit price deflator (annual % growth)	2.6	1.4	0.5
Value added in agriculture (% of GDP)	..	..	..
Value added in industry (% of GDP)	..	..	..
Value added in services (% of GDP)	..	..	..
Exports of goods and services (% of GDP)	..	..	..
Imports of goods and services (% of GDP)	..	..	..
Gross capital formation (% of GDP)	..	..	..
Central government revenue (% of GDP)	..	..	..
Central government cash surplus/deficit (% of GDP)	..	..	..
States and markets			
Starting a business (days)	..	..	..
Stock market capitalization (% of GDP)	..	..	..
Military expenditures (% of GDP)	..	..	..
Mobile cellular subscriptions (per 100 people)	0.0	39.6	89.7
Individuals using the Internet (% of population)	0.0	42.2	75.0
Paved roads (% of total)	100.0	100.0	100.0
High-technology exports (% of manufactured exports)	..	..	..
Global links			
Merchandise trade (% of GDP)	..	..	..
Net barter terms of trade index (2000 = 100)	..	..	..
Total external debt stocks ($ millions)	..	..	..
Total debt service (% of exports)	..	..	..
Net migration (thousands)	..	..	..
Remittances received ($ millions)	..	..	..
Foreign direct investment, net inflows ($ millions)	..	..	..
Net official development assistance received ($ millions)	..	..	..

Mongolia

East Asia & Pacific | **Lower middle income**

Population (millions)	2.8	Population growth (%)	1.6
Surface area (1,000 sq. km)	1,564	Population living below $1.25 a day (%)	..
GNI, Atlas ($ billions)	6.5	GNI per capita, Atlas ($)	2,310
GNI, PPP ($ billions)	12.0	GNI per capita, PPP ($)	4,290

	1990	2000	2011
People			
Share of poorest 20% in nat'l consumption/income (%)	..	7.5	7.1
Life expectancy at birth (years)	61	63	68
Total fertility rate (births per woman)	4.1	2.2	2.5
Adolescent fertility rate (births per 1,000 women 15-19)	..	26	19
Contraceptive prevalence (% of married women 15-49)	..	67	55
Births attended by skilled health staff (% of total)	..	97	99
Under-five mortality rate (per 1,000 live births)	107	63	31
Child malnutrition, underweight (% of under age 5)	10.8	11.6	..
Child immunization, measles (% of ages 12-23 mos.)	92	92	98
Primary completion rate, total (% of relevant age group)	..	86	115
Gross secondary enrollment, total (% of relevant age group)	89	65	93
Ratio of girls to boys in primary & secondary school (%)	106	111	102
HIV prevalence rate (% population of ages 15-49)	0.1	0.1	0.1
Environment			
Forests (1,000 sq. km)	125	117	108
Deforestation (avg. annual %, 1990-2000 and 2000-2010)		0.7	0.7
Freshwater use (% of internal resources)	..	1.2	1.2
Access to improved water source (% total pop.)	54	65	82
Access to improved sanitation facilities (% total pop.)	..	49	51
Energy use per capita (kilograms of oil equivalent)	1,558	994	1,189
Carbon dioxide emissions per capita (metric tons)	4.6	3.1	5.3
Electricity use per capita (kilowatt-hours)	1,540	1,070	1,530
Economy			
GDP ($ billions)	2.6	1.1	8.8
GDP growth (annual %)	-3.2	1.1	17.5
GDP implicit price deflator (annual % growth)	23.2	12.0	12.1
Value added in agriculture (% of GDP)	13	31	14
Value added in industry (% of GDP)	42	25	36
Value added in services (% of GDP)	45	44	49
Exports of goods and services (% of GDP)	18	54	62
Imports of goods and services (% of GDP)	40	68	87
Gross capital formation (% of GDP)	29	29	63
Central government revenue (% of GDP)	15.4	24.4	34.0
Central government cash surplus/deficit (% of GDP)	-0.5	0.2	-3.1
States and markets			
Starting a business (days)	..	20	12
Stock market capitalization (% of GDP)	..	3.2	18.0
Military expenditures (% of GDP)	4.6	2.1	0.9
Mobile cellular subscriptions (per 100 people)	0.0	6.4	105.1
Individuals using the Internet (% of population)	0.0	1.3	20.0
Paved roads (% of total)	..	3.5	..
High-technology exports (% of manufactured exports)	..	0	..
Global links			
Merchandise trade (% of GDP)	62	101	129
Net barter terms of trade index (2000 = 100)	..	100	227
Total external debt stocks ($ millions)	25	960	2,564
Total debt service (% of exports)	17.3	6.6	2.1
Net migration (thousands)	0.0	-57.7	-15.0
Remittances received ($ millions)	..	12	279
Foreign direct investment, net inflows ($ millions)	11	54	4,715
Net official development assistance received ($ millions)	13	217	340

Montenegro

Europe & Central Asia		Upper middle income	

Population (thousands)	632	Population growth (%)	0.1
Surface area (1,000 sq. km)	14	Population living below $1.25 a day (%)	<2
GNI, Atlas ($ billions)	4.5	GNI per capita, Atlas ($)	7,140
GNI, PPP ($ billions)	8.7	GNI per capita, PPP ($)	13,700

	1990	2000	2011
People			
Share of poorest 20% in nat'l consumption/income (%)	..	..	8.5
Life expectancy at birth (years)	75	75	75
Total fertility rate (births per woman)	1.9	1.8	1.6
Adolescent fertility rate (births per 1,000 women 15-19)	..	22	15
Contraceptive prevalence (% of married women 15-49)	..	53	39
Births attended by skilled health staff (% of total)	..	99	100
Under-five mortality rate (per 1,000 live births)	18	13	7
Child malnutrition, underweight (% of under age 5)	..	..	..
Child immunization, measles (% of ages 12-23 mos.)	..	..	91
Primary completion rate, total (% of relevant age group)	..	..	99
Gross secondary enrollment, total (% of relevant age group)	..	86	95
Ratio of girls to boys in primary & secondary school (%)	..	100	101
HIV prevalence rate (% population of ages 15-49)	..	..	..
Environment			
Forests (1,000 sq. km)	5.4	5.4	5.4
Deforestation (avg. annual %, 1990-2000 and 2000-2010)		0.0	0.0
Freshwater use (% of internal resources)	..	..	..
Access to improved water source (% total pop.)	97	98	98
Access to improved sanitation facilities (% total pop.)	..	90	90
Energy use per capita (kilograms of oil equivalent)	..	..	1,303
Carbon dioxide emissions per capita (metric tons)	..	..	4.8
Electricity use per capita (kilowatt-hours)	..	..	5,547
Economy			
GDP ($ millions)	..	984	4,496
GDP growth (annual %)	..	3.1	3.2
GDP implicit price deflator (annual % growth)	..	20.2	1.0
Value added in agriculture (% of GDP)	..	12	9
Value added in industry (% of GDP)	..	23	19
Value added in services (% of GDP)	..	64	71
Exports of goods and services (% of GDP)	..	37	40
Imports of goods and services (% of GDP)	..	51	66
Gross capital formation (% of GDP)	..	22	20
Central government revenue (% of GDP)	..	..	..
Central government cash surplus/deficit (% of GDP)	..	..	..
States and markets			
Starting a business (days)	..	..	10
Stock market capitalization (% of GDP)	..	..	73.9
Military expenditures (% of GDP)	..	..	2.0
Mobile cellular subscriptions (per 100 people)	..	..	185.3
Individuals using the Internet (% of population)	..	..	40.0
Paved roads (% of total)	..	..	69.1
High-technology exports (% of manufactured exports)	..	..	..
Global links			
Merchandise trade (% of GDP)	..	..	71
Net barter terms of trade index (2000 = 100)	..	..	..
Total external debt stocks ($ millions)	0	34	2,093
Total debt service (% of exports)	..	..	10.2
Net migration (thousands)	17.7	-32.5	-2.5
Remittances received ($ millions)	..	..	343
Foreign direct investment, net inflows ($ millions)	..	..	558
Net official development assistance received ($ millions)	..	8.1	73.7

Morocco

Middle East & North Africa	Lower middle income

Population (millions)	32.3	Population growth (%)	1.0
Surface area (1,000 sq. km)	447	Population living below $1.25 a day (%)	2.5
GNI, Atlas ($ billions)	97.6	GNI per capita, Atlas ($)	2,970
GNI, PPP ($ billions)	160.1	GNI per capita, PPP ($)	4,880

	1990	2000	2011
People			
Share of poorest 20% in nat'l consumption/income (%)	6.6	6.5	6.5
Life expectancy at birth (years)	64	69	72
Total fertility rate (births per woman)	4.0	2.7	2.2
Adolescent fertility rate (births per 1,000 women 15-19)	..	23	12
Contraceptive prevalence (% of married women 15-49)	42	63	67
Births attended by skilled health staff (% of total)	31	63	74
Under-five mortality rate (per 1,000 live births)	81	53	33
Child malnutrition, underweight (% of under age 5)	8.1	9.9	3.1
Child immunization, measles (% of ages 12-23 mos.)	79	93	95
Primary completion rate, total (% of relevant age group)	52	57	99
Gross secondary enrollment, total (% of relevant age group)	37	38	70
Ratio of girls to boys in primary & secondary school (%)	69	83	91
HIV prevalence rate (% population of ages 15-49)	0.1	0.1	0.2
Environment			
Forests (1,000 sq. km)	50	50	51
Deforestation (avg. annual %, 1990-2000 and 2000-2010)		0.1	-0.2
Freshwater use (% of internal resources)	38.1	43.5	43.5
Access to improved water source (% total pop.)	73	78	83
Access to improved sanitation facilities (% total pop.)	53	64	70
Energy use per capita (kilograms of oil equivalent)	280	356	517
Carbon dioxide emissions per capita (metric tons)	1.0	1.2	1.5
Electricity use per capita (kilowatt-hours)	360	490	781
Economy			
GDP ($ billions)	25.8	37.0	100.2
GDP growth (annual %)	4.0	1.6	4.5
GDP implicit price deflator (annual % growth)	5.5	-0.6	1.5
Value added in agriculture (% of GDP)	18	15	15
Value added in industry (% of GDP)	33	29	30
Value added in services (% of GDP)	48	56	55
Exports of goods and services (% of GDP)	26	28	35
Imports of goods and services (% of GDP)	32	33	48
Gross capital formation (% of GDP)	25	26	35
Central government revenue (% of GDP)	..	30.0	33.1
Central government cash surplus/deficit (% of GDP)	..	-3.1	-4.1
States and markets			
Starting a business (days)	..	36	12
Stock market capitalization (% of GDP)	3.7	29.4	60.0
Military expenditures (% of GDP)	4.1	2.3	3.3
Mobile cellular subscriptions (per 100 people)	0.0	8.1	113.3
Individuals using the Internet (% of population)	0.0	0.7	51.0
Paved roads (% of total)	49.1	56.4	70.4
High-technology exports (% of manufactured exports)	3	11	8
Global links			
Merchandise trade (% of GDP)	43	51	66
Net barter terms of trade index (2000 = 100)	85	100	141
Total external debt stocks ($ billions)	25.0	20.8	29.0
Total debt service (% of exports)	28.4	25.3	9.9
Net migration (thousands)	-250	-500	-675
Remittances received ($ billions)	2.0	2.2	7.3
Foreign direct investment, net inflows ($ millions)	165	221	2,521
Net official development assistance received ($ billions)	1.2	0.4	1.2

Mozambique

Population (millions)	23.9	Population growth (%)	2.3
Surface area (1,000 sq. km)	799	Population living below $1.25 a day (%)	59.6
GNI, Atlas ($ billions)	11.1	GNI per capita, Atlas ($)	460
GNI, PPP ($ billions)	22.9	GNI per capita, PPP ($)	960

	1990	2000	2011
People			
Share of poorest 20% in nat'l consumption/income (%)	..	5.4	5.2
Life expectancy at birth (years)	43	47	50
Total fertility rate (births per woman)	6.2	5.7	4.8
Adolescent fertility rate (births per 1,000 women 15–19)	..	153	129
Contraceptive prevalence (% of married women 15–49)	..	17	12
Births attended by skilled health staff (% of total)	..	48	55
Under-five mortality rate (per 1,000 live births)	226	172	103
Child malnutrition, underweight (% of under age 5)	..	23.0	18.3
Child immunization, measles (% of ages 12–23 mos.)	59	71	82
Primary completion rate, total (% of relevant age group)	27	16	56
Gross secondary enrollment, total (% of relevant age group)	7	6	26
Ratio of girls to boys in primary & secondary school (%)	73	75	90
HIV prevalence rate (% population of ages 15–49)	0.4	9.0	11.3
Environment			
Forests (1,000 sq. km)	434	412	388
Deforestation (avg. annual %, 1990–2000 and 2000–2010)		0.5	0.5
Freshwater use (% of internal resources)	0.6	0.7	0.7
Access to improved water source (% total pop.)	36	42	47
Access to improved sanitation facilities (% total pop.)	11	14	18
Energy use per capita (kilograms of oil equivalent)	437	394	436
Carbon dioxide emissions per capita (metric tons)	0.07	0.07	0.11
Electricity use per capita (kilowatt-hours)	40	122	444
Economy			
GDP ($ billions)	2.5	4.3	12.8
GDP growth (annual %)	1.0	1.1	7.1
GDP implicit price deflator (annual % growth)	34.1	12.0	10.7
Value added in agriculture (% of GDP)	37	24	30
Value added in industry (% of GDP)	18	25	23
Value added in services (% of GDP)	44	51	47
Exports of goods and services (% of GDP)	8	16	29
Imports of goods and services (% of GDP)	36	37	46
Gross capital formation (% of GDP)	22	31	24
Central government revenue (% of GDP)	..	..	..
Central government cash surplus/deficit (% of GDP)	..	..	..
States and markets			
Starting a business (days)	..	153	13
Stock market capitalization (% of GDP)	..	..	..
Military expenditures (% of GDP)	3.4	1.3	0.9
Mobile cellular subscriptions (per 100 people)	0.0	0.3	32.8
Individuals using the Internet (% of population)	0.0	0.1	4.3
Paved roads (% of total)	16.8	18.7	20.8
High-technology exports (% of manufactured exports)	..	9	26
Global links			
Merchandise trade (% of GDP)	40	35	78
Net barter terms of trade index (2000 = 100)	175	100	107
Total external debt stocks ($ billions)	4.6	7.3	4.1
Total debt service (% of exports)	26.2	13.4	1.6
Net migration (thousands)	–1,300	75	–20
Remittances received ($ millions)	70	37	157
Foreign direct investment, net inflows ($ millions)	9	139	2,079
Net official development assistance received ($ millions)	998	906	2,047

Myanmar

East Asia & Pacific			Low income
Population (millions)	48.3	Population growth (%)	0.8
Surface area (1,000 sq. km)	677	Population living below $1.25 a day (%)	..
GNI, Atlas ($ millions)	..	GNI per capita, Atlas ($)	..
GNI, PPP ($ millions)	..	GNI per capita, PPP ($)	..

	1990	2000	2011
People			
Share of poorest 20% in nat'l consumption/income (%)	..	..	..
Life expectancy at birth (years)	57	62	65
Total fertility rate (births per woman)	3.4	2.4	2.0
Adolescent fertility rate (births per 1,000 women 15-19)	..	21	13
Contraceptive prevalence (% of married women 15-49)	17	37	46
Births attended by skilled health staff (% of total)	46	57	71
Under-five mortality rate (per 1,000 live births)	107	84	62
Child malnutrition, underweight (% of under age 5)	28.8	30.1	22.6
Child immunization, measles (% of ages 12-23 mos.)	68	84	99
Primary completion rate, total (% of relevant age group)	..	81	104
Gross secondary enrollment, total (% of relevant age group)	21	40	54
Ratio of girls to boys in primary & secondary school (%)	94	101	102
HIV prevalence rate (% population of ages 15-49)	0.2	0.7	0.6
Environment			
Forests (1,000 sq. km)	392	349	315
Deforestation (avg. annual %, 1990-2000 and 2000-2010)		1.2	0.9
Freshwater use (% of internal resources)	..	3.3	3.3
Access to improved water source (% total pop.)	56	67	83
Access to improved sanitation facilities (% total pop.)	54	62	76
Energy use per capita (kilograms of oil equivalent)	272	286	292
Carbon dioxide emissions per capita (metric tons)	0.1	0.2	0.2
Electricity use per capita (kilowatt-hours)	46	78	131
Economy			
GDP ($ millions)	..	..	..
GDP growth (annual %)	2.8	13.7	..
GDP implicit price deflator (annual % growth)	18.5	2.5	..
Value added in agriculture (% of GDP)	57	57	..
Value added in industry (% of GDP)	11	10	..
Value added in services (% of GDP)	32	33	..
Exports of goods and services (% of GDP)	2	0	..
Imports of goods and services (% of GDP)	4	1	..
Gross capital formation (% of GDP)	13	12	..
Central government revenue (% of GDP)	10.5	5.3	..
Central government cash surplus/deficit (% of GDP)	..	-2.7	..
States and markets			
Starting a business (days)	..	..	..
Stock market capitalization (% of GDP)	..	..	..
Military expenditures (% of GDP)	3.4	2.3	..
Mobile cellular subscriptions (per 100 people)	0.0	0.0	2.6
Individuals using the Internet (% of population)	0.0	0.0	1.0
Paved roads (% of total)	10.9	11.4	..
High-technology exports (% of manufactured exports)	0	..	0
Global links			
Merchandise trade (% of GDP)	..	..	..
Net barter terms of trade index (2000 = 100)	252	100	105
Total external debt stocks ($ billions)	4.7	5.8	7.8
Total debt service (% of exports)	18.2	1.2	7.1
Net migration (thousands)	-137	4	-500
Remittances received ($ millions)	6	104	127
Foreign direct investment, net inflows ($ millions)	163	258	1,001
Net official development assistance received ($ millions)	161	106	376

Namibia

Sub-Saharan Africa		Upper middle income
Population (millions)	2.3	Population growth (%)	1.8
Surface area (1,000 sq. km)	824	Population living below $1.25 a day (%)	31.9
GNI, Atlas ($ billions)	10.9	GNI per capita, Atlas ($)	4,700
GNI, PPP ($ billions)	15.4	GNI per capita, PPP ($)	6,610

	1990	2000	2011
People			
Share of poorest 20% in nat'l consumption/income (%)	1.5	3.2	..
Life expectancy at birth (years)	61	58	62
Total fertility rate (births per woman)	5.2	4.0	3.2
Adolescent fertility rate (births per 1,000 women 15–19)	..	85	58
Contraceptive prevalence (% of married women 15–49)	41	44	55
Births attended by skilled health staff (% of total)	68	76	81
Under-five mortality rate (per 1,000 live births)	73	74	42
Child malnutrition, underweight (% of under age 5)	21.5	20.3	17.5
Child immunization, measles (% of ages 12–23 mos.)	57	69	74
Primary completion rate, total (% of relevant age group)	74	91	81
Gross secondary enrollment, total (% of relevant age group)	38	60	..
Ratio of girls to boys in primary & secondary school (%)	111	104	..
HIV prevalence rate (% population of ages 15–49)	1.8	14.6	13.4
Environment			
Forests (1,000 sq. km)	88	80	72
Deforestation (avg. annual %, 1990–2000 and 2000–2010)		0.9	1.0
Freshwater use (% of internal resources)	4.0	4.9	4.9
Access to improved water source (% total pop.)	64	81	93
Access to improved sanitation facilities (% total pop.)	24	28	32
Energy use per capita (kilograms of oil equivalent)	426	516	702
Carbon dioxide emissions per capita (metric tons)	0.01	0.93	1.60
Electricity use per capita (kilowatt-hours)	1,050	1,179	1,479
Economy			
GDP ($ billions)	2.4	3.9	12.5
GDP growth (annual %)	2.5	3.5	4.8
GDP implicit price deflator (annual % growth)	4.3	26.7	6.8
Value added in agriculture (% of GDP)	12	12	8
Value added in industry (% of GDP)	38	28	31
Value added in services (% of GDP)	50	60	61
Exports of goods and services (% of GDP)	52	41	45
Imports of goods and services (% of GDP)	67	45	52
Gross capital formation (% of GDP)	34	17	20
Central government revenue (% of GDP)	31.3	30.1	..
Central government cash surplus/deficit (% of GDP)	-2.6	-1.6	..
States and markets			
Starting a business (days)	..	85	66
Stock market capitalization (% of GDP)	0.7	8.0	9.2
Military expenditures (% of GDP)	8.4	2.4	3.4
Mobile cellular subscriptions (per 100 people)	0.0	4.3	96.4
Individuals using the Internet (% of population)	0.0	1.6	12.0
Paved roads (% of total)	10.8	13.6	14.5
High-technology exports (% of manufactured exports)	..	2	2
Global links			
Merchandise trade (% of GDP)	96	73	86
Net barter terms of trade index (2000 = 100)	93	100	117
Total external debt stocks ($ millions)	..	..	..
Total debt service (% of exports)	..	..	..
Net migration (thousands)	74.8	35.5	-1.5
Remittances received ($ millions)	13.5	9.5	15.5
Foreign direct investment, net inflows ($ millions)	30	119	969
Net official development assistance received ($ millions)	120	152	285

Nepal

South Asia			Low income

Population (millions)	30.5	Population growth (%)	1.7
Surface area (1,000 sq. km)	147	Population living below $1.25 a day (%)	24.8
GNI, Atlas ($ billions)	16.6	GNI per capita, Atlas ($)	540
GNI, PPP ($ billions)	38.4	GNI per capita, PPP ($)	1,260

	1990	2000	2011
People			
Share of poorest 20% in nat'l consumption/income (%)	..	6.5	8.3
Life expectancy at birth (years)	54	62	69
Total fertility rate (births per woman)	5.2	4.1	2.7
Adolescent fertility rate (births per 1,000 women 15-19)	..	124	90
Contraceptive prevalence (% of married women 15-49)	24	37	50
Births attended by skilled health staff (% of total)	7	12	36
Under-five mortality rate (per 1,000 live births)	135	83	48
Child malnutrition, underweight (% of under age 5)	..	43.0	29.1
Child immunization, measles (% of ages 12-23 mos.)	57	71	88
Primary completion rate, total (% of relevant age group)	52	66	..
Gross secondary enrollment, total (% of relevant age group)	32	35	..
Ratio of girls to boys in primary & secondary school (%)	57	77	..
HIV prevalence rate (% population of ages 15-49)	0.1	0.3	0.3
Environment			
Forests (1,000 sq. km)	48	39	36
Deforestation (avg. annual %, 1990-2000 and 2000-2010)		2.1	0.7
Freshwater use (% of internal resources)	..	5.0	4.9
Access to improved water source (% total pop.)	76	83	89
Access to improved sanitation facilities (% total pop.)	10	20	31
Energy use per capita (kilograms of oil equivalent)	303	332	341
Carbon dioxide emissions per capita (metric tons)	0.03	0.13	0.12
Electricity use per capita (kilowatt-hours)	35	58	93
Economy			
GDP ($ billions)	3.6	5.5	18.9
GDP growth (annual %)	4.6	6.2	3.9
GDP implicit price deflator (annual % growth)	10.7	4.5	10.4
Value added in agriculture (% of GDP)	52	41	32
Value added in industry (% of GDP)	16	22	15
Value added in services (% of GDP)	32	37	53
Exports of goods and services (% of GDP)	11	23	9
Imports of goods and services (% of GDP)	22	32	33
Gross capital formation (% of GDP)	18	24	33
Central government revenue (% of GDP)	8.4	10.6	14.9
Central government cash surplus/deficit (% of GDP)	..	..	-1.0
States and markets			
Starting a business (days)	..	31	29
Stock market capitalization (% of GDP)	..	14.4	24.0
Military expenditures (% of GDP)	1.1	1.0	1.4
Mobile cellular subscriptions (per 100 people)	0.0	0.0	43.8
Individuals using the Internet (% of population)	0.0	0.2	9.0
Paved roads (% of total)	37.5	53.9	53.9
High-technology exports (% of manufactured exports)	..	0	0
Global links			
Merchandise trade (% of GDP)	24	43	35
Net barter terms of trade index (2000 = 100)	..	100	78
Total external debt stocks ($ billions)	1.6	2.9	4.0
Total debt service (% of exports)	15.2	7.5	9.5
Net migration (thousands)	-145	-99	-100
Remittances received ($ millions)	55	111	4,217
Foreign direct investment, net inflows ($ millions)	5.9	-0.5	94.0
Net official development assistance received ($ millions)	423	386	892

Netherlands

High income

Population (millions)	16.7	Population growth (%)	0.5
Surface area (1,000 sq. km)	42	Population living below $1.25 a day (%)	..
GNI, Atlas ($ billions)	829.0	GNI per capita, Atlas ($)	49,660
GNI, PPP ($ billions)	720.3	GNI per capita, PPP ($)	43,150

	1990	2000	2011
People			
Share of poorest 20% in nat'l consumption/income (%)	..	7.6	..
Life expectancy at birth (years)	77	78	81
Total fertility rate (births per woman)	1.6	1.7	1.8
Adolescent fertility rate (births per 1,000 women 15–19)	..	7	4
Contraceptive prevalence (% of married women 15–49)	79	67	69
Births attended by skilled health staff (% of total)	..	100	..
Under-five mortality rate (per 1,000 live births)	8	6	4
Child malnutrition, underweight (% of under age 5)	..	..	..
Child immunization, measles (% of ages 12–23 mos.)	94	96	96
Primary completion rate, total (% of relevant age group)	..	98	..
Gross secondary enrollment, total (% of relevant age group)	116	123	121
Ratio of girls to boys in primary & secondary school (%)	97	97	99
HIV prevalence rate (% population of ages 15–49)	0.1	0.2	0.2
Environment			
Forests (1,000 sq. km)	3.5	3.6	3.7
Deforestation (avg. annual %, 1990–2000 and 2000–2010)		-0.4	-0.1
Freshwater use (% of internal resources)	72.6	81.3	96.5
Access to improved water source (% total pop.)	100	100	100
Access to improved sanitation facilities (% total pop.)	100	100	100
Energy use per capita (kilograms of oil equivalent)	4,393	4,598	4,646
Carbon dioxide emissions per capita (metric tons)	11.0	10.4	10.3
Electricity use per capita (kilowatt-hours)	5,218	6,560	7,010
Economy			
GDP ($ billions)	295	385	836
GDP growth (annual %)	4.2	3.9	1.0
GDP implicit price deflator (annual % growth)	1.6	4.1	1.2
Value added in agriculture (% of GDP)	4	3	2
Value added in industry (% of GDP)	29	25	24
Value added in services (% of GDP)	66	72	74
Exports of goods and services (% of GDP)	56	70	83
Imports of goods and services (% of GDP)	53	65	74
Gross capital formation (% of GDP)	23	22	18
Central government revenue (% of GDP)	..	40.7	40.6
Central government cash surplus/deficit (% of GDP)	..	2.0	-3.9
States and markets			
Starting a business (days)	..	9	5
Stock market capitalization (% of GDP)	40.7	166.3	71.1
Military expenditures (% of GDP)	2.5	1.6	1.4
Mobile cellular subscriptions (per 100 people)	0.5	67.8	115.4
Individuals using the Internet (% of population)	0.3	44.0	92.3
Paved roads (% of total)	88.0	90.0	..
High-technology exports (% of manufactured exports)	16	36	20
Global links			
Merchandise trade (% of GDP)	87	117	151
Net barter terms of trade index (2000 = 100)	..	100	102
Total external debt stocks ($ millions)	..	..	..
Total debt service (% of exports)	..	..	..
Net migration (thousands)	134	154	50
Remittances received ($ billions)	0.7	1.2	1.8
Foreign direct investment, net inflows ($ billions)	10.7	63.1	13.9
Net official development assistance received ($ millions)	..	..	..

New Caledonia

Population (thousands)	254	Population growth (%)	1.6
Surface area (1,000 sq. km)	19	Population living below $1.25 a day (%)	..
GNI, Atlas ($ billions)	..	GNI per capita, Atlas ($)	..
GNI, PPP ($ millions)	..	GNI per capita, PPP ($)	..

	1990	2000	2011
People			
Share of poorest 20% in nat'l consumption/income (%)	..	..	..
Life expectancy at birth (years)	70	75	77
Total fertility rate (births per woman)	3.2	2.6	2.1
Adolescent fertility rate (births per 1,000 women 15-19)	..	18	20
Contraceptive prevalence (% of married women 15-49)	..	..	..
Births attended by skilled health staff (% of total)	..	..	..
Under-five mortality rate (per 1,000 live births)	..	..	..
Child malnutrition, underweight (% of under age 5)	..	..	..
Child immunization, measles (% of ages 12-23 mos.)	..	..	..
Primary completion rate, total (% of relevant age group)	..	..	..
Gross secondary enrollment, total (% of relevant age group)	..	..	..
Ratio of girls to boys in primary & secondary school (%)	..	..	..
HIV prevalence rate (% population of ages 15-49)	..	..	..
Environment			
Forests (1,000 sq. km)	8.4	8.4	8.4
Deforestation (avg. annual %, 1990-2000 and 2000-2010)		0.0	0.0
Freshwater use (% of internal resources)	..	..	..
Access to improved water source (% total pop.)	..	..	..
Access to improved sanitation facilities (% total pop.)	..	..	..
Energy use per capita (kilograms of oil equivalent)	..	..	..
Carbon dioxide emissions per capita (metric tons)	9.7	10.8	12.1
Electricity use per capita (kilowatt-hours)	..	..	..
Economy			
GDP ($ billions)	2.5	2.7	..
GDP growth (annual %)	3.6	2.1	..
GDP implicit price deflator (annual % growth)	-4.6	-0.6	..
Value added in agriculture (% of GDP)	4	..	..
Value added in industry (% of GDP)	23	..	..
Value added in services (% of GDP)	73	..	..
Exports of goods and services (% of GDP)	18	13	..
Imports of goods and services (% of GDP)	35	33	..
Gross capital formation (% of GDP)	31	..	..
Central government revenue (% of GDP)	..	..	..
Central government cash surplus/deficit (% of GDP)	..	..	..
States and markets			
Starting a business (days)	..	..	..
Stock market capitalization (% of GDP)	..	..	..
Military expenditures (% of GDP)	..	..	..
Mobile cellular subscriptions (per 100 people)	0.0	23.6	89.2
Individuals using the Internet (% of population)	0.0	13.9	50.0
Paved roads (% of total)	..	..	..
High-technology exports (% of manufactured exports)	..	1	15
Global links			
Merchandise trade (% of GDP)	53	57	..
Net barter terms of trade index (2000 = 100)	..	100	230
Total external debt stocks ($ millions)	..	..	..
Total debt service (% of exports)	..	..	..
Net migration (thousands)	0.6	6.2	6.4
Remittances received ($ millions)	..	333	519
Foreign direct investment, net inflows ($ millions)	31	-41	1,745
Net official development assistance received ($ millions)	302	315	..

New Zealand

Population (millions)	4.4	Population growth (%)	0.9
Surface area (1,000 sq. km)	268	Population living below $1.25 a day (%)	..
GNI, Atlas ($ billions)	127.3	GNI per capita, Atlas ($)	29,140
GNI, PPP ($ billions)	126.3	GNI per capita, PPP ($)	28,930

	1990	2000	2011
People			
Share of poorest 20% in nat'l consumption/income (%)	..	..	..
Life expectancy at birth (years)	75	79	81
Total fertility rate (births per woman)	2.2	2.0	2.1
Adolescent fertility rate (births per 1,000 women 15–19)	..	29	21
Contraceptive prevalence (% of married women 15–49)	..	..	..
Births attended by skilled health staff (% of total)	..	97	..
Under-five mortality rate (per 1,000 live births)	11	7	6
Child malnutrition, underweight (% of under age 5)	..	..	..
Child immunization, measles (% of ages 12–23 mos.)	90	85	93
Primary completion rate, total (% of relevant age group)	..	..	..
Gross secondary enrollment, total (% of relevant age group)	89	111	119
Ratio of girls to boys in primary & secondary school (%)	99	103	103
HIV prevalence rate (% population of ages 15–49)	0.1	0.1	0.1
Environment			
Forests (1,000 sq. km)	77	83	83
Deforestation (avg. annual %, 1990–2000 and 2000–2010)		-0.7	0.0
Freshwater use (% of internal resources)	..	1.5	1.5
Access to improved water source (% total pop.)	100	100	100
Access to improved sanitation facilities (% total pop.)	..	..	..
Energy use per capita (kilograms of oil equivalent)	3,865	4,422	4,086
Carbon dioxide emissions per capita (metric tons)	7.1	8.5	7.4
Electricity use per capita (kilowatt-hours)	8,972	9,384	9,566
Economy			
GDP ($ billions)	44.5	51.6	159.7
GDP growth (annual %)	0.0	2.6	1.0
GDP implicit price deflator (annual % growth)	2.5	3.0	2.1
Value added in agriculture (% of GDP)	7	9	..
Value added in industry (% of GDP)	28	25	..
Value added in services (% of GDP)	65	66	..
Exports of goods and services (% of GDP)	27	35	30
Imports of goods and services (% of GDP)	26	33	29
Gross capital formation (% of GDP)	20	21	19
Central government revenue (% of GDP)	..	33.7	35.6
Central government cash surplus/deficit (% of GDP)	..	1.7	-7.3
States and markets			
Starting a business (days)	..	12	1
Stock market capitalization (% of GDP)	19.9	36.6	44.9
Military expenditures (% of GDP)	1.8	1.2	1.1
Mobile cellular subscriptions (per 100 people)	1.6	40.0	109.2
Individuals using the Internet (% of population)	0.0	47.4	86.0
Paved roads (% of total)	57.0	62.8	66.2
High-technology exports (% of manufactured exports)	4	10	9
Global links			
Merchandise trade (% of GDP)	42	53	47
Net barter terms of trade index (2000 = 100)	..	100	133
Total external debt stocks ($ millions)	..	..	..
Total debt service (% of exports)	..	..	..
Net migration (thousands)	-8.6	43.0	65.0
Remittances received ($ millions)	762	236	875
Foreign direct investment, net inflows ($ billions)	1.7	3.8	4.3
Net official development assistance received ($ millions)	..	..	..

Nicaragua

Latin America & Caribbean   **Lower middle income**

Population (millions)	5.9	Population growth (%)	1.4
Surface area (1,000 sq. km)	130	Population living below $1.25 a day (%)	11.9
GNI, Atlas ($ billions)	8.9	GNI per capita, Atlas ($)	1,510
GNI, PPP ($ billions)	21.9	GNI per capita, PPP ($)	3,730

	1990	2000	2011
People			
Share of poorest 20% in nat'l consumption/income (%)	4.2	5.6	..
Life expectancy at birth (years)	64	70	74
Total fertility rate (births per woman)	4.8	3.3	2.6
Adolescent fertility rate (births per 1,000 women 15-19)	..	125	106
Contraceptive prevalence (% of married women 15-49)	49	69	72
Births attended by skilled health staff (% of total)	61	67	74
Under-five mortality rate (per 1,000 live births)	66	42	26
Child malnutrition, underweight (% of under age 5)	9.6	7.8	5.7
Child immunization, measles (% of ages 12-23 mos.)	82	86	99
Primary completion rate, total (% of relevant age group)	40	66	81
Gross secondary enrollment, total (% of relevant age group)	37	53	69
Ratio of girls to boys in primary & secondary school (%)	119	105	102
HIV prevalence rate (% population of ages 15-49)	0.1	0.1	0.2
Environment			
Forests (1,000 sq. km)	45	38	30
Deforestation (avg. annual %, 1990-2000 and 2000-2010)		1.7	2.0
Freshwater use (% of internal resources)	..	0.7	0.7
Access to improved water source (% total pop.)	74	80	85
Access to improved sanitation facilities (% total pop.)	43	48	52
Energy use per capita (kilograms of oil equivalent)	508	536	542
Carbon dioxide emissions per capita (metric tons)	0.6	0.7	0.8
Electricity use per capita (kilowatt-hours)	310	345	473
Economy			
GDP ($ billions)	1.0	5.1	9.3
GDP growth (annual %)	-0.1	4.1	5.1
GDP implicit price deflator (annual % growth)	5,018.1	8.6	10.5
Value added in agriculture (% of GDP)	..	19	20
Value added in industry (% of GDP)	..	22	26
Value added in services (% of GDP)	..	58	54
Exports of goods and services (% of GDP)	25	20	41
Imports of goods and services (% of GDP)	46	41	60
Gross capital formation (% of GDP)	19	30	28
Central government revenue (% of GDP)	30.0	11.6	16.5
Central government cash surplus/deficit (% of GDP)	-34.2	-2.8	0.5
States and markets			
Starting a business (days)	..	46	39
Stock market capitalization (% of GDP)	..	..	..
Military expenditures (% of GDP)	4.0	0.6	0.6
Mobile cellular subscriptions (per 100 people)	0.0	1.8	82.2
Individuals using the Internet (% of population)	0.0	1.0	10.6
Paved roads (% of total)	10.5	11.1	12.9
High-technology exports (% of manufactured exports)	6	5	5
Global links			
Merchandise trade (% of GDP)	96	48	80
Net barter terms of trade index (2000 = 100)	155	100	83
Total external debt stocks ($ billions)	10.8	6.8	7.1
Total debt service (% of exports)	5.0	25.6	14.8
Net migration (thousands)	-156	-158	-200
Remittances received ($ millions)	10	320	914
Foreign direct investment, net inflows ($ millions)	1	267	968
Net official development assistance received ($ millions)	330	560	695

Niger

Population (millions)	16.1	Population growth (%)	3.5
Surface area (1,000 sq. km)	1,267	Population living below $1.25 a day (%)	43.6
GNI, Atlas ($ billions)	5.8	GNI per capita, Atlas ($)	360
GNI, PPP ($ billions)	11.6	GNI per capita, PPP ($)	720

	1990	2000	2011
People			
Share of poorest 20% in nat'l consumption/income (%)	7.5	..	8.1
Life expectancy at birth (years)	41	48	55
Total fertility rate (births per woman)	7.8	7.5	7.0
Adolescent fertility rate (births per 1,000 women 15–19)	..	216	196
Contraceptive prevalence (% of married women 15–49)	4	14	18
Births attended by skilled health staff (% of total)	15	16	18
Under-five mortality rate (per 1,000 live births)	314	216	125
Child malnutrition, underweight (% of under age 5)	41.0	43.6	39.9
Child immunization, measles (% of ages 12–23 mos.)	25	37	76
Primary completion rate, total (% of relevant age group)	17	19	46
Gross secondary enrollment, total (% of relevant age group)	6	7	14
Ratio of girls to boys in primary & secondary school (%)	53	65	79
HIV prevalence rate (% population of ages 15–49)	0.4	0.8	0.8
Environment			
Forests (1,000 sq. km)	19	13	12
Deforestation (avg. annual %, 1990–2000 and 2000–2010)		3.7	1.0
Freshwater use (% of internal resources)	14.3	67.5	67.5
Access to improved water source (% total pop.)	35	42	49
Access to improved sanitation facilities (% total pop.)	5	7	9
Energy use per capita (kilograms of oil equivalent)	..	..	..
Carbon dioxide emissions per capita (metric tons)	0.11	0.07	0.08
Electricity use per capita (kilowatt-hours)	..	..	..
Economy			
GDP ($ billions)	2.5	1.8	6.0
GDP growth (annual %)	-1.3	-1.4	2.3
GDP implicit price deflator (annual % growth)	-1.6	4.5	3.6
Value added in agriculture (% of GDP)	35	38	..
Value added in industry (% of GDP)	16	18	..
Value added in services (% of GDP)	49	44	..
Exports of goods and services (% of GDP)	15	18	..
Imports of goods and services (% of GDP)	22	26	..
Gross capital formation (% of GDP)	8	11	..
Central government revenue (% of GDP)	..	..	..
Central government cash surplus/deficit (% of GDP)	..	..	..
States and markets			
Starting a business (days)	..	35	17
Stock market capitalization (% of GDP)	..	..	..
Military expenditures (% of GDP)	..	1.1	0.9
Mobile cellular subscriptions (per 100 people)	0.0	0.0	29.5
Individuals using the Internet (% of population)	0.0	0.0	1.3
Paved roads (% of total)	29.0	25.7	20.6
High-technology exports (% of manufactured exports)	..	16	5
Global links			
Merchandise trade (% of GDP)	27	38	61
Net barter terms of trade index (2000 = 100)	165	100	164
Total external debt stocks ($ billions)	1.8	1.7	1.4
Total debt service (% of exports)	17.8	8.0	3.8
Net migration (thousands)	-91.9	24.1	-28.5
Remittances received ($ millions)	14	14	102
Foreign direct investment, net inflows ($ millions)	41	8	1,014
Net official development assistance received ($ millions)	388	209	649

Nigeria

Sub-Saharan Africa		Lower middle income	
Population (millions)	162.5	Population growth (%)	2.5
Surface area (1,000 sq. km)	924	Population living below $1.25 a day (%)	68.0
GNI, Atlas ($ billions)	207.3	GNI per capita, Atlas ($)	1,280
GNI, PPP ($ billions)	372.8	GNI per capita, PPP ($)	2,290

	1990	2000	2011
People			
Share of poorest 20% in nat'l consumption/income (%)	4.0	5.1	4.4
Life expectancy at birth (years)	46	46	52
Total fertility rate (births per woman)	6.4	5.9	5.5
Adolescent fertility rate (births per 1,000 women 15–19)	..	130	113
Contraceptive prevalence (% of married women 15–49)	6	15	15
Births attended by skilled health staff (% of total)	31	42	39
Under-five mortality rate (per 1,000 live births)	214	188	124
Child malnutrition, underweight (% of under age 5)	35.1	27.3	26.7
Child immunization, measles (% of ages 12–23 mos.)	54	33	71
Primary completion rate, total (% of relevant age group)	..	..	74
Gross secondary enrollment, total (% of relevant age group)	24	24	44
Ratio of girls to boys in primary & secondary school (%)	79	82	90
HIV prevalence rate (% population of ages 15–49)	0.5	3.7	3.7
Environment			
Forests (1,000 sq. km)	172	131	86
Deforestation (avg. annual %, 1990–2000 and 2000–2010)		2.7	3.7
Freshwater use (% of internal resources)	..	4.7	4.7
Access to improved water source (% total pop.)	47	53	58
Access to improved sanitation facilities (% total pop.)	37	34	31
Energy use per capita (kilograms of oil equivalent)	724	732	714
Carbon dioxide emissions per capita (metric tons)	0.5	0.6	0.5
Electricity use per capita (kilowatt-hours)	85	74	136
Economy			
GDP ($ billions)	28	46	244
GDP growth (annual %)	8.2	5.4	7.4
GDP implicit price deflator (annual % growth)	7.2	38.2	2.3
Value added in agriculture (% of GDP)	..	49	..
Value added in industry (% of GDP)	..	31	..
Value added in services (% of GDP)	..	21	..
Exports of goods and services (% of GDP)	43	54	40
Imports of goods and services (% of GDP)	29	32	36
Gross capital formation (% of GDP)	..	..	..
Central government revenue (% of GDP)	..	..	9.7
Central government cash surplus/deficit (% of GDP)	..	..	-1.7
States and markets			
Starting a business (days)	..	44	34
Stock market capitalization (% of GDP)	4.8	9.2	16.1
Military expenditures (% of GDP)	0.8	0.8	1.0
Mobile cellular subscriptions (per 100 people)	0.0	0.0	58.6
Individuals using the Internet (% of population)	0.0	0.1	28.4
Paved roads (% of total)	..	15.0	..
High-technology exports (% of manufactured exports)	..	1	1
Global links			
Merchandise trade (% of GDP)	68	65	70
Net barter terms of trade index (2000 = 100)	89	100	211
Total external debt stocks ($ billions)	33.4	31.6	13.1
Total debt service (% of exports)	22.6	8.8	0.4
Net migration (thousands)	-91	-95	-300
Remittances received ($ billions)	0.0	1.4	20.6
Foreign direct investment, net inflows ($ billions)	0.6	1.1	8.8
Net official development assistance received ($ millions)	255	174	1,813

Northern Mariana Islands

High income

Population (thousands)	61	Population growth (%)		0.4
Surface area (sq. km)	460	Population living below $1.25 a day (%)		..
GNI, Atlas ($ millions)	..	GNI per capita, Atlas ($)		..
GNI, PPP ($ millions)	..	GNI per capita, PPP ($)		..

	1990	2000	2011
People			
Share of poorest 20% in nat'l consumption/income (%)	..	..	..
Life expectancy at birth (years)	..	..	..
Total fertility rate (births per woman)	..	..	..
Adolescent fertility rate (births per 1,000 women 15–19)	..	..	..
Contraceptive prevalence (% of married women 15–49)	..	..	..
Births attended by skilled health staff (% of total)	..	100	..
Under-five mortality rate (per 1,000 live births)	..	..	..
Child malnutrition, underweight (% of under age 5)	..	..	..
Child immunization, measles (% of ages 12–23 mos.)	..	..	..
Primary completion rate, total (% of relevant age group)	..	..	..
Gross secondary enrollment, total (% of relevant age group)	..	..	..
Ratio of girls to boys in primary & secondary school (%)	..	..	..
HIV prevalence rate (% population of ages 15–49)	..	..	..
Environment			
Forests (sq. km)	340	320	302
Deforestation (avg. annual %, 1990–2000 and 2000–2010)		0.5	0.5
Freshwater use (% of internal resources)	..	..	
Access to improved water source (% total pop.)	98	98	98
Access to improved sanitation facilities (% total pop.)	84	92	..
Energy use per capita (kilograms of oil equivalent)	..	..	..
Carbon dioxide emissions per capita (metric tons)	..	..	..
Electricity use per capita (kilowatt-hours)	..	..	..
Economy			
GDP ($ millions)	..	..	..
GDP growth (annual %)	..	..	..
GDP implicit price deflator (annual % growth)	..	..	..
Value added in agriculture (% of GDP)	..	..	..
Value added in industry (% of GDP)	..	..	..
Value added in services (% of GDP)	..	..	..
Exports of goods and services (% of GDP)	..	..	..
Imports of goods and services (% of GDP)	..	..	..
Gross capital formation (% of GDP)	..	..	..
Central government revenue (% of GDP)	..	..	..
Central government cash surplus/deficit (% of GDP)	..	..	..
States and markets			
Starting a business (days)	..	..	..
Stock market capitalization (% of GDP)	..	..	..
Military expenditures (% of GDP)	..	..	..
Mobile cellular subscriptions (per 100 people)	0.0	4.4	..
Individuals using the Internet (% of population)	0.0	..	..
Paved roads (% of total)	..	..	..
High-technology exports (% of manufactured exports)	..	..	..
Global links			
Merchandise trade (% of GDP)	..	..	..
Net barter terms of trade index (2000 = 100)	..	100	86
Total external debt stocks ($ millions)	..	..	..
Total debt service (% of exports)	..	..	..
Net migration (thousands)	..	..	..
Remittances received ($ millions)	..	..	..
Foreign direct investment, net inflows ($ millions)	124	12	0
Net official development assistance received ($ millions)	63.1	0.1	..

Norway

Population (millions)	5.0	Population growth (%)	1.3
Surface area (1,000 sq. km)	324	Population living below $1.25 a day (%)	..
GNI, Atlas ($ billions)	440.2	GNI per capita, Atlas ($)	88,870
GNI, PPP ($ billions)	304.4	GNI per capita, PPP ($)	61,450

	1990	2000	2011
People			
Share of poorest 20% in nat'l consumption/income (%)	..	9.6	..
Life expectancy at birth (years)	77	79	81
Total fertility rate (births per woman)	1.9	1.9	1.9
Adolescent fertility rate (births per 1,000 women 15-19)	..	11	8
Contraceptive prevalence (% of married women 15-49)	74	87	..
Births attended by skilled health staff (% of total)	100	..	..
Under-five mortality rate (per 1,000 live births)	8	5	3
Child malnutrition, underweight (% of under age 5)	..	..	..
Child immunization, measles (% of ages 12-23 mos.)	87	88	93
Primary completion rate, total (% of relevant age group)	95	98	99
Gross secondary enrollment, total (% of relevant age group)	101	116	111
Ratio of girls to boys in primary & secondary school (%)	102	101	99
HIV prevalence rate (% population of ages 15-49)	0.1	0.1	0.2
Environment			
Forests (1,000 sq. km)	91	93	101
Deforestation (avg. annual %, 1990-2000 and 2000-2010)		-0.2	-0.8
Freshwater use (% of internal resources)		0.6	0.8
Access to improved water source (% total pop.)	100	100	100
Access to improved sanitation facilities (% total pop.)	100	100	100
Energy use per capita (kilograms of oil equivalent)	4,952	5,810	6,032
Carbon dioxide emissions per capita (metric tons)	7.4	8.6	9.7
Electricity use per capita (kilowatt-hours)	23,354	24,994	25,175
Economy			
GDP ($ billions)	118	168	486
GDP growth (annual %)	1.9	3.3	1.4
GDP implicit price deflator (annual % growth)	3.8	15.7	6.3
Value added in agriculture (% of GDP)	3	2	2
Value added in industry (% of GDP)	34	42	40
Value added in services (% of GDP)	63	56	58
Exports of goods and services (% of GDP)	40	47	42
Imports of goods and services (% of GDP)	34	29	28
Gross capital formation (% of GDP)	23	20	23
Central government revenue (% of GDP)	..	48.4	50.0
Central government cash surplus/deficit (% of GDP)	..	15.7	14.7
States and markets			
Starting a business (days)	..	18	7
Stock market capitalization (% of GDP)	22.2	38.6	45.1
Military expenditures (% of GDP)	2.9	1.7	1.6
Mobile cellular subscriptions (per 100 people)	4.6	71.8	115.6
Individuals using the Internet (% of population)	0.7	52.0	94.0
Paved roads (% of total)	69.0	76.0	80.7
High-technology exports (% of manufactured exports)	11	17	18
Global links			
Merchandise trade (% of GDP)	52	56	51
Net barter terms of trade index (2000 = 100)	..	100	157
Total external debt stocks ($ millions)	..	..	..
Total debt service (% of exports)	..	..	..
Net migration (thousands)	34	59	171
Remittances received ($ millions)	158	270	765
Foreign direct investment, net inflows ($ billions)	1.0	7.0	7.3
Net official development assistance received ($ millions)	..	..	..

Oman

High income

Population (millions)	2.8	Population growth (%)		2.3
Surface area (1,000 sq. km)	310	Population living below $1.25 a day (%)		..
GNI, Atlas ($ billions)	53.6	GNI per capita, Atlas ($)		19,260
GNI, PPP ($ billions)	71.6	GNI per capita, PPP ($)		25,720

	1990	2000	2011
People			
Share of poorest 20% in nat'l consumption/income (%)	..	..	..
Life expectancy at birth (years)	71	74	73
Total fertility rate (births per woman)	7.2	3.6	2.2
Adolescent fertility rate (births per 1,000 women 15–19)	..	28	9
Contraceptive prevalence (% of married women 15–49)	9	32	24
Births attended by skilled health staff (% of total)	..	95	99
Under-five mortality rate (per 1,000 live births)	48	22	9
Child malnutrition, underweight (% of under age 5)	21.4	11.3	8.6
Child immunization, measles (% of ages 12–23 mos.)	98	99	99
Primary completion rate, total (% of relevant age group)	62	78	107
Gross secondary enrollment, total (% of relevant age group)	40	75	104
Ratio of girls to boys in primary & secondary school (%)	85	99	98
HIV prevalence rate (% population of ages 15–49)	..	..	..
Environment			
Forests (sq. km)	20	20	20
Deforestation (avg. annual %, 1990–2000 and 2000–2010)		0.0	0.0
Freshwater use (% of internal resources)	87.4	97.1	94.4
Access to improved water source (% total pop.)	80	83	89
Access to improved sanitation facilities (% total pop.)	82	90	99
Energy use per capita (kilograms of oil equivalent)	2,258	3,570	7,188
Carbon dioxide emissions per capita (metric tons)	6.1	10.0	15.2
Electricity use per capita (kilowatt-hours)	2,121	3,207	5,933
Economy			
GDP ($ billions)	11.7	19.9	71.8
GDP growth (annual %)	-0.1	5.4	5.5
GDP implicit price deflator (annual % growth)	24.8	20.0	17.6
Value added in agriculture (% of GDP)	3	2	..
Value added in industry (% of GDP)	54	57	..
Value added in services (% of GDP)	43	41	..
Exports of goods and services (% of GDP)	47	59	53
Imports of goods and services (% of GDP)	28	31	41
Gross capital formation (% of GDP)	12	12	30
Central government revenue (% of GDP)	35.0	29.4	38.3
Central government cash surplus/deficit (% of GDP)	-0.3	-5.2	-0.8
States and markets			
Starting a business (days)	..	35	8
Stock market capitalization (% of GDP)	8.5	17.4	27.5
Military expenditures (% of GDP)	16.5	10.6	6.0
Mobile cellular subscriptions (per 100 people)	0.1	7.2	169.0
Individuals using the Internet (% of population)	0.0	3.5	68.0
Paved roads (% of total)	21.0	30.0	46.0
High-technology exports (% of manufactured exports)	15	3	3
Global links			
Merchandise trade (% of GDP)	71	83	99
Net barter terms of trade index (2000 = 100)	..	100	231
Total external debt stocks ($ millions)	..	..	..
Total debt service (% of exports)	..	..	..
Net migration (thousands)	9	-229	153
Remittances received ($ millions)	39.0	39.0	39.0
Foreign direct investment, net inflows ($ millions)	142	82	788
Net official development assistance received ($ millions)	68.2	79.7	-40.3

Pakistan

South Asia   **Lower middle income**

Population (millions)	176.7	Population growth (%)	1.8
Surface area (1,000 sq. km)	796	Population living below $1.25 a day (%)	21.0
GNI, Atlas ($ billions)	198.0	GNI per capita, Atlas ($)	1,120
GNI, PPP ($ billions)	507.2	GNI per capita, PPP ($)	2,870

	1990	2000	2011
People			
Share of poorest 20% in nat'l consumption/income (%)	8.1	8.7	9.6
Life expectancy at birth (years)	61	63	65
Total fertility rate (births per woman)	6.0	4.5	3.3
Adolescent fertility rate (births per 1,000 women 15-19)	..	49	29
Contraceptive prevalence (% of married women 15-49)	15	28	27
Births attended by skilled health staff (% of total)	19	23	43
Under-five mortality rate (per 1,000 live births)	122	95	72
Child malnutrition, underweight (% of under age 5)	39.0	31.3	30.9
Child immunization, measles (% of ages 12-23 mos.)	50	59	80
Primary completion rate, total (% of relevant age group)	..	..	67
Gross secondary enrollment, total (% of relevant age group)	21	28	35
Ratio of girls to boys in primary & secondary school (%)	49	73	79
HIV prevalence rate (% population of ages 15-49)	0.1	0.1	0.1
Environment			
Forests (1,000 sq. km)	25	21	16
Deforestation (avg. annual %, 1990-2000 and 2000-2010)		1.8	2.2
Freshwater use (% of internal resources)	282.9	313.8	333.6
Access to improved water source (% total pop.)	85	89	92
Access to improved sanitation facilities (% total pop.)	27	37	48
Energy use per capita (kilograms of oil equivalent)	381	439	487
Carbon dioxide emissions per capita (metric tons)	0.6	0.7	0.9
Electricity use per capita (kilowatt-hours)	267	357	457
Economy			
GDP ($ billions)	40	74	210
GDP growth (annual %)	4.5	4.3	3.0
GDP implicit price deflator (annual % growth)	6.5	24.9	18.3
Value added in agriculture (% of GDP)	26	26	22
Value added in industry (% of GDP)	25	23	25
Value added in services (% of GDP)	49	51	53
Exports of goods and services (% of GDP)	16	13	14
Imports of goods and services (% of GDP)	23	15	19
Gross capital formation (% of GDP)	19	17	13
Central government revenue (% of GDP)	19.1	13.9	12.4
Central government cash surplus/deficit (% of GDP)	-2.5	-4.1	-6.5
States and markets			
Starting a business (days)	..	24	21
Stock market capitalization (% of GDP)	7.1	8.9	15.6
Military expenditures (% of GDP)	6.8	4.0	3.0
Mobile cellular subscriptions (per 100 people)	0.0	0.2	61.6
Individuals using the Internet (% of population)	0.0	1.3	9.0
Paved roads (% of total)	54.0	56.0	72.2
High-technology exports (% of manufactured exports)	0	0	2
Global links			
Merchandise trade (% of GDP)	33	27	33
Net barter terms of trade index (2000 = 100)	109	100	52
Total external debt stocks ($ billions)	20.6	33.0	60.2
Total debt service (% of exports)	27.4	28.0	9.2
Net migration (thousands)	140	-187	-2,000
Remittances received ($ billions)	2.0	1.1	12.3
Foreign direct investment, net inflows ($ millions)	245	308	1,309
Net official development assistance received ($ billions)	1.1	0.7	3.5

Palau

East Asia & Pacific		Upper middle income	
Population (thousands)	21	Population growth (%)	0.7
Surface area (sq. km)	460	Population living below $1.25 a day (%)	..
GNI, Atlas ($ millions)	134.2	GNI per capita, Atlas ($)	6,510
GNI, PPP ($ millions)	228.4	GNI per capita, PPP ($)	11,080

	1990	2000	2011
People			
Share of poorest 20% in nat'l consumption/income (%)	..	..	..
Life expectancy at birth (years)	69	70	..
Total fertility rate (births per woman)	2.8	1.5	..
Adolescent fertility rate (births per 1,000 women 15–19)	..	..	..
Contraceptive prevalence (% of married women 15–49)	..	17	22
Births attended by skilled health staff (% of total)	99	100	100
Under-five mortality rate (per 1,000 live births)	32	25	19
Child malnutrition, underweight (% of under age 5)	..	..	..
Child immunization, measles (% of ages 12–23 mos.)	98	83	85
Primary completion rate, total (% of relevant age group)	..	99	..
Gross secondary enrollment, total (% of relevant age group)	..	86	..
Ratio of girls to boys in primary & secondary school (%)	..	100	..
HIV prevalence rate (% population of ages 15–49)	..	..	..
Environment			
Forests (sq. km)	380	396	403
Deforestation (avg. annual %, 1990–2000 and 2000–2010)		−0.4	−0.2
Freshwater use (% of internal resources)	..	..	..
Access to improved water source (% total pop.)	80	83	85
Access to improved sanitation facilities (% total pop.)	65	84	100
Energy use per capita (kilograms of oil equivalent)	4,869	..	..
Carbon dioxide emissions per capita (metric tons)	15.6	6.1	10.3
Electricity use per capita (kilowatt-hours)	..	..	..
Economy			
GDP ($ millions)	76.9	119.9	165.5
GDP growth (annual %)	−6.4	0.3	5.8
GDP implicit price deflator (annual % growth)	5.0	5.3	0.2
Value added in agriculture (% of GDP)	19	4	..
Value added in industry (% of GDP)	13	15	..
Value added in services (% of GDP)	69	81	..
Exports of goods and services (% of GDP)	20	10	103
Imports of goods and services (% of GDP)	39	106	94
Gross capital formation (% of GDP)	..	..	..
Central government revenue (% of GDP)	..	..	..
Central government cash surplus/deficit (% of GDP)	..	..	..
States and markets			
Starting a business (days)	..	24	28
Stock market capitalization (% of GDP)	..	..	..
Military expenditures (% of GDP)	..	..	..
Mobile cellular subscriptions (per 100 people)	..	12.6	74.9
Individuals using the Internet (% of population)	0.0	20.2	..
Paved roads (% of total)	..	..	..
High-technology exports (% of manufactured exports)	..	..	..
Global links			
Merchandise trade (% of GDP)	..	113	76
Net barter terms of trade index (2000 = 100)	..	100	104
Total external debt stocks ($ millions)	..	..	..
Total debt service (% of exports)	..	..	..
Net migration (thousands)	..	..	..
Remittances received ($ millions)	..	..	..
Foreign direct investment, net inflows ($ millions)	1.0	14.9	2.0
Net official development assistance received ($ millions)	0.0	39.1	27.6

Panama

Latin America & Caribbean		Upper middle income	
Population (millions)	3.6	Population growth (%)	1.5
Surface area (1,000 sq. km)	75	Population living below $1.25 a day (%)	6.6
GNI, Atlas ($ billions)	26.7	GNI per capita, Atlas ($)	7,470
GNI, PPP ($ billions)	51.8	GNI per capita, PPP ($)	14,510

	1990	2000	2011
People			
Share of poorest 20% in nat'l consumption/income (%)	1.2	1.9	3.3
Life expectancy at birth (years)	72	74	76
Total fertility rate (births per woman)	3.0	2.7	2.5
Adolescent fertility rate (births per 1,000 women 15-19)	..	91	77
Contraceptive prevalence (% of married women 15-49)	..	..	52
Births attended by skilled health staff (% of total)	86	93	89
Under-five mortality rate (per 1,000 live births)	33	26	20
Child malnutrition, underweight (% of under age 5)	..	5.1	3.9
Child immunization, measles (% of ages 12-23 mos.)	73	97	97
Primary completion rate, total (% of relevant age group)	86	94	101
Gross secondary enrollment, total (% of relevant age group)	61	67	74
Ratio of girls to boys in primary & secondary school (%)	99	100	102
HIV prevalence rate (% population of ages 15–49)	0.8	1.5	0.8
Environment			
Forests (1,000 sq. km)	38	34	32
Deforestation (avg. annual %, 1990–2000 and 2000–2010)		1.2	0.4
Freshwater use (% of internal resources)	1.1	0.3	0.3
Access to improved water source (% total pop.)	84	90	93
Access to improved sanitation facilities (% total pop.)	58	65	69
Energy use per capita (kilograms of oil equivalent)	617	872	1,073
Carbon dioxide emissions per capita (metric tons)	1.3	2.0	2.3
Electricity use per capita (kilowatt-hours)	852	1,298	1,832
Economy			
GDP ($ billions)	5.3	11.6	26.8
GDP growth (annual %)	8.1	2.7	10.6
GDP implicit price deflator (annual % growth)	0.6	-1.2	-9.6
Value added in agriculture (% of GDP)	10	7	4
Value added in industry (% of GDP)	15	19	17
Value added in services (% of GDP)	75	74	79
Exports of goods and services (% of GDP)	87	73	81
Imports of goods and services (% of GDP)	79	70	84
Gross capital formation (% of GDP)	17	24	28
Central government revenue (% of GDP)	25.6	23.1	..
Central government cash surplus/deficit (% of GDP)	2.0	-0.8	..
States and markets			
Starting a business (days)	..	18	7
Stock market capitalization (% of GDP)	3.4	24.0	39.9
Military expenditures (% of GDP)	1.4	1.0	..
Mobile cellular subscriptions (per 100 people)	0.0	13.9	188.6
Individuals using the Internet (% of population)	0.0	6.6	42.7
Paved roads (% of total)	32.0	34.6	42.0
High-technology exports (% of manufactured exports)	..	1	35
Global links			
Merchandise trade (% of GDP)	35	36	136
Net barter terms of trade index (2000 = 100)	69	100	86
Total external debt stocks ($ billions)	6.5	6.6	12.6
Total debt service (% of exports)	6.2	9.4	3.6
Net migration (thousands)	-15.0	11.0	11.0
Remittances received ($ millions)	110	16	388
Foreign direct investment, net inflows ($ millions)	136	624	3,223
Net official development assistance received ($ millions)	99.3	15.4	97.9

Papua New Guinea

Population (millions)	7.0	Population growth (%)		2.2
Surface area (1,000 sq. km)	463	Population living below $1.25 a day (%)		..
GNI, Atlas ($ billions)	10.4	GNI per capita, Atlas ($)		1,480
GNI, PPP ($ billions)	18.0	GNI per capita, PPP ($)		2,570

	1990	2000	2011
People			
Share of poorest 20% in nat'l consumption/income (%)	..	..	..
Life expectancy at birth (years)	56	59	63
Total fertility rate (births per woman)	4.8	4.5	3.9
Adolescent fertility rate (births per 1,000 women 15–19)	..	73	63
Contraceptive prevalence (% of married women 15–49)	..	..	32
Births attended by skilled health staff (% of total)	..	41	53
Under-five mortality rate (per 1,000 live births)	88	72	58
Child malnutrition, underweight (% of under age 5)	..	..	..
Child immunization, measles (% of ages 12–23 mos.)	67	62	60
Primary completion rate, total (% of relevant age group)	45	55	..
Gross secondary enrollment, total (% of relevant age group)	11	19	..
Ratio of girls to boys in primary & secondary school (%)	82	84	..
HIV prevalence rate (% population of ages 15–49)	0.2	0.8	0.7
Environment			
Forests (1,000 sq. km)	315	301	286
Deforestation (avg. annual %, 1990–2000 and 2000–2010)		0.5	0.5
Freshwater use (% of internal resources)	..	0.0	0.0
Access to improved water source (% total pop.)	41	39	40
Access to improved sanitation facilities (% total pop.)	47	46	45
Energy use per capita (kilograms of oil equivalent)	..	..	..
Carbon dioxide emissions per capita (metric tons)	0.5	0.5	0.5
Electricity use per capita (kilowatt-hours)	..	..	..
Economy			
GDP ($ billions)	3.2	3.5	12.9
GDP growth (annual %)	-3.0	-2.5	9.0
GDP implicit price deflator (annual % growth)	4.1	13.1	9.2
Value added in agriculture (% of GDP)	31	36	36
Value added in industry (% of GDP)	32	41	45
Value added in services (% of GDP)	37	23	20
Exports of goods and services (% of GDP)	41	66	51
Imports of goods and services (% of GDP)	49	49	48
Gross capital formation (% of GDP)	24	22	16
Central government revenue (% of GDP)	25.2	24.2	..
Central government cash surplus/deficit (% of GDP)	-2.2	-1.9	..
States and markets			
Starting a business (days)	..	51	51
Stock market capitalization (% of GDP)	..	49.3	69.6
Military expenditures (% of GDP)	2.1	0.9	0.5
Mobile cellular subscriptions (per 100 people)	0.0	0.2	34.2
Individuals using the Internet (% of population)	0.0	0.8	2.0
Paved roads (% of total)	3.2	3.5	..
High-technology exports (% of manufactured exports)	..	19	..
Global links			
Merchandise trade (% of GDP)	74	92	88
Net barter terms of trade index (2000 = 100)	..	100	166
Total external debt stocks ($ billions)	2.6	2.3	12.6
Total debt service (% of exports)	37.2	12.9	15.8
Net migration (thousands)	0.0	0.0	0.0
Remittances received ($ millions)	5.4	7.2	10.8
Foreign direct investment, net inflows ($ millions)	155	96	-309
Net official development assistance received ($ millions)	412	275	612

Paraguay

Latin America & Caribbean   **Lower middle income**

Population (millions)	6.6	Population growth (%)		1.7
Surface area (1,000 sq. km)	407	Population living below $1.25 a day (%)		7.2
GNI, Atlas ($ billions)	19.8	GNI per capita, Atlas ($)		3,020
GNI, PPP ($ billions)	35.4	GNI per capita, PPP ($)		5,390

	1990	2000	2011
People			
Share of poorest 20% in nat'l consumption/income (%)	5.8	2.7	3.3
Life expectancy at birth (years)	68	70	72
Total fertility rate (births per woman)	4.5	3.7	2.9
Adolescent fertility rate (births per 1,000 women 15-19)	..	86	68
Contraceptive prevalence (% of married women 15-49)	48	73	79
Births attended by skilled health staff (% of total)	66	77	82
Under-five mortality rate (per 1,000 live births)	53	35	22
Child malnutrition, underweight (% of under age 5)	2.8	..	..
Child immunization, measles (% of ages 12-23 mos.)	69	92	93
Primary completion rate, total (% of relevant age group)	65	92	91
Gross secondary enrollment, total (% of relevant age group)	31	61	68
Ratio of girls to boys in primary & secondary school (%)	97	98	99
HIV prevalence rate (% population of ages 15-49)	0.1	0.1	0.3
Environment			
Forests (1,000 sq. km)	212	194	174
Deforestation (avg. annual %, 1990-2000 and 2000-2010)		0.9	1.0
Freshwater use (% of internal resources)	..	0.5	0.5
Access to improved water source (% total pop.)	52	74	86
Access to improved sanitation facilities (% total pop.)	37	58	71
Energy use per capita (kilograms of oil equivalent)	724	721	742
Carbon dioxide emissions per capita (metric tons)	0.5	0.7	0.7
Electricity use per capita (kilowatt-hours)	502	881	1,134
Economy			
GDP ($ billions)	5.3	7.1	23.8
GDP growth (annual %)	3.1	-3.3	6.9
GDP implicit price deflator (annual % growth)	36.3	12.1	7.5
Value added in agriculture (% of GDP)	28	17	23
Value added in industry (% of GDP)	25	23	20
Value added in services (% of GDP)	47	60	57
Exports of goods and services (% of GDP)	33	38	49
Imports of goods and services (% of GDP)	39	46	57
Gross capital formation (% of GDP)	23	18	18
Central government revenue (% of GDP)	12.3	17.0	18.1
Central government cash surplus/deficit (% of GDP)	2.9	-3.9	1.1
States and markets			
Starting a business (days)	..	74	35
Stock market capitalization (% of GDP)	0.3	3.5	4.0
Military expenditures (% of GDP)	1.2	1.1	1.1
Mobile cellular subscriptions (per 100 people)	0.0	15.4	99.4
Individuals using the Internet (% of population)	0.0	0.7	23.9
Paved roads (% of total)	..	50.8	15.2
High-technology exports (% of manufactured exports)	0	3	7
Global links			
Merchandise trade (% of GDP)	44	43	75
Net barter terms of trade index (2000 = 100)	103	100	107
Total external debt stocks ($ billions)	2.2	3.1	6.0
Total debt service (% of exports)	8.4	11.2	3.6
Net migration (thousands)	-16.9	-43.0	-40.0
Remittances received ($ millions)	34	278	893
Foreign direct investment, net inflows ($ millions)	77	104	412
Net official development assistance received ($ millions)	57.2	81.6	93.7

Peru

Latin America & Caribbean		Upper middle income	
Population (millions)	29.4	Population growth (%)	1.1
Surface area (1,000 sq. km)	1,285	Population living below $1.25 a day (%)	4.9
GNI, Atlas ($ billions)	151.4	GNI per capita, Atlas ($)	5,150
GNI, PPP ($ billions)	277.6	GNI per capita, PPP ($)	9,440

	1990	2000	2011
People			
Share of poorest 20% in nat'l consumption/income (%)	..	3.4	3.9
Life expectancy at birth (years)	66	70	74
Total fertility rate (births per woman)	3.8	2.9	2.5
Adolescent fertility rate (births per 1,000 women 15–19)	..	65	50
Contraceptive prevalence (% of married women 15–49)	59	69	75
Births attended by skilled health staff (% of total)	53	59	85
Under-five mortality rate (per 1,000 live births)	75	39	18
Child malnutrition, underweight (% of under age 5)	8.8	5.2	4.5
Child immunization, measles (% of ages 12–23 mos.)	64	97	96
Primary completion rate, total (% of relevant age group)	..	103	97
Gross secondary enrollment, total (% of relevant age group)	68	86	91
Ratio of girls to boys in primary & secondary school (%)	96	97	99
HIV prevalence rate (% population of ages 15–49)	0.2	0.5	0.4
Environment			
Forests (1,000 sq. km)	702	692	678
Deforestation (avg. annual %, 1990–2000 and 2000–2010)		0.1	0.2
Freshwater use (% of internal resources)	1.2	1.2	1.2
Access to improved water source (% total pop.)	75	81	85
Access to improved sanitation facilities (% total pop.)	54	63	71
Energy use per capita (kilograms of oil equivalent)	449	473	667
Carbon dioxide emissions per capita (metric tons)	1.0	1.2	1.6
Electricity use per capita (kilowatt-hours)	550	682	1,106
Economy			
GDP ($ billions)	26.3	53.3	176.9
GDP growth (annual %)	-5.1	3.0	6.8
GDP implicit price deflator (annual % growth)	6,836.9	3.7	4.8
Value added in agriculture (% of GDP)	9	8	6
Value added in industry (% of GDP)	27	30	36
Value added in services (% of GDP)	64	62	57
Exports of goods and services (% of GDP)	16	16	29
Imports of goods and services (% of GDP)	14	18	25
Gross capital formation (% of GDP)	16	20	25
Central government revenue (% of GDP)	12.5	17.4	20.0
Central government cash surplus/deficit (% of GDP)	-8.1	-2.1	1.3
States and markets			
Starting a business (days)	..	98	26
Stock market capitalization (% of GDP)	3.1	19.8	44.8
Military expenditures (% of GDP)	0.1	1.8	1.2
Mobile cellular subscriptions (per 100 people)	0.0	4.9	110.4
Individuals using the Internet (% of population)	0.0	3.1	36.5
Paved roads (% of total)	9.9	13.4	13.9
High-technology exports (% of manufactured exports)	1	4	6
Global links			
Merchandise trade (% of GDP)	22	27	48
Net barter terms of trade index (2000 = 100)	114	100	159
Total external debt stocks ($ billions)	20.2	28.8	44.9
Total debt service (% of exports)	11.1	27.9	6.5
Net migration (thousands)	-180	-350	-725
Remittances received ($ millions)	87	718	2,697
Foreign direct investment, net inflows ($ millions)	41	810	8,233
Net official development assistance received ($ millions)	397	397	624

Philippines

Lower middle income

Population (millions)	94.9	Population growth (%)	1.7
Surface area (1,000 sq. km)	300	Population living below $1.25 a day (%)	18.4
GNI, Atlas ($ billions)	209.7	GNI per capita, Atlas ($)	2,210
GNI, PPP ($ billions)	393.0	GNI per capita, PPP ($)	4,140

	1990	2000	2011
People			
Share of poorest 20% in nat'l consumption/income (%)	5.9	5.4	6.0
Life expectancy at birth (years)	65	67	69
Total fertility rate (births per woman)	4.3	3.8	3.1
Adolescent fertility rate (births per 1,000 women 15–19)	..	52	48
Contraceptive prevalence (% of married women 15–49)	40	47	49
Births attended by skilled health staff (% of total)	53	58	72
Under-five mortality rate (per 1,000 live births)	57	39	25
Child malnutrition, underweight (% of under age 5)	29.9	20.7	20.7
Child immunization, measles (% of ages 12–23 mos.)	85	78	79
Primary completion rate, total (% of relevant age group)	89	101	92
Gross secondary enrollment, total (% of relevant age group)	72	75	85
Ratio of girls to boys in primary & secondary school (%)	100	103	101
HIV prevalence rate (% population of ages 15–49)	0.1	0.1	0.1
Environment			
Forests (1,000 sq. km)	66	71	77
Deforestation (avg. annual %, 1990–2000 and 2000–2010)		-0.8	-0.7
Freshwater use (% of internal resources)	..	..	17.0
Access to improved water source (% total pop.)	85	89	92
Access to improved sanitation facilities (% total pop.)	57	65	74
Energy use per capita (kilograms of oil equivalent)	464	516	434
Carbon dioxide emissions per capita (metric tons)	0.7	0.9	0.7
Electricity use per capita (kilowatt-hours)	363	504	643
Economy			
GDP ($ billions)	44	81	225
GDP growth (annual %)	3.0	4.4	3.9
GDP implicit price deflator (annual % growth)	13.0	5.7	4.1
Value added in agriculture (% of GDP)	22	14	13
Value added in industry (% of GDP)	34	34	31
Value added in services (% of GDP)	44	52	56
Exports of goods and services (% of GDP)	28	51	31
Imports of goods and services (% of GDP)	33	53	36
Gross capital formation (% of GDP)	24	18	22
Central government revenue (% of GDP)	16.2	14.2	14.0
Central government cash surplus/deficit (% of GDP)	-2.8	-3.7	-1.8
States and markets			
Starting a business (days)	..	49	36
Stock market capitalization (% of GDP)	13.4	32.0	73.6
Military expenditures (% of GDP)	2.1	1.6	1.1
Mobile cellular subscriptions (per 100 people)	0.0	8.3	99.3
Individuals using the Internet (% of population)	0.0	2.0	29.0
Paved roads (% of total)	..	20.0	..
High-technology exports (% of manufactured exports)	32	73	46
Global links			
Merchandise trade (% of GDP)	48	95	50
Net barter terms of trade index (2000 = 100)	87	100	65
Total external debt stocks ($ billions)	30.6	58.5	76.0
Total debt service (% of exports)	27.6	16.0	17.6
Net migration (thousands)	-299	-776	-1,233
Remittances received ($ billions)	1.5	7.0	23.0
Foreign direct investment, net inflows ($ billions)	0.5	2.2	1.9
Net official development assistance received ($ millions)	1,271	572	-192

Poland

Population (millions)	38.5	Population growth (%)		0.9
Surface area (1,000 sq. km)	313	Population living below $1.25 a day (%)		<2
GNI, Atlas ($ billions)	477.0	GNI per capita, Atlas ($)		12,380
GNI, PPP ($ billions)	780.8	GNI per capita, PPP ($)		20,260

	1990	2000	2011
People			
Share of poorest 20% in nat'l consumption/income (%)	9.2	7.8	7.7
Life expectancy at birth (years)	71	74	77
Total fertility rate (births per woman)	2.0	1.4	1.3
Adolescent fertility rate (births per 1,000 women 15–19)	..	17	13
Contraceptive prevalence (% of married women 15–49)	73	..	..
Births attended by skilled health staff (% of total)	100	100	..
Under-five mortality rate (per 1,000 live births)	17	10	6
Child malnutrition, underweight (% of under age 5)	..	..	..
Child immunization, measles (% of ages 12–23 mos.)	95	97	98
Primary completion rate, total (% of relevant age group)	98	95	95
Gross secondary enrollment, total (% of relevant age group)	88	101	97
Ratio of girls to boys in primary & secondary school (%)	101	98	99
HIV prevalence rate (% population of ages 15–49)	0.1	0.1	0.1
Environment			
Forests (1,000 sq. km)	89	91	94
Deforestation (avg. annual %, 1990–2000 and 2000–2010)		-0.2	-0.3
Freshwater use (% of internal resources)	28.3	23.9	22.3
Access to improved water source (% total pop.)	..	..	..
Access to improved sanitation facilities (% total pop.)	..	90	90
Energy use per capita (kilograms of oil equivalent)	2,705	2,317	2,663
Carbon dioxide emissions per capita (metric tons)	9.6	7.8	7.8
Electricity use per capita (kilowatt-hours)	3,272	3,240	3,783
Economy			
GDP ($ billions)	65	171	514
GDP growth (annual %)	-7.0	4.3	4.3
GDP implicit price deflator (annual % growth)	55.3	7.3	3.2
Value added in agriculture (% of GDP)	8	5	4
Value added in industry (% of GDP)	50	32	32
Value added in services (% of GDP)	42	63	65
Exports of goods and services (% of GDP)	26	27	42
Imports of goods and services (% of GDP)	20	34	43
Gross capital formation (% of GDP)	24	25	21
Central government revenue (% of GDP)	..	31.5	30.6
Central government cash surplus/deficit (% of GDP)	..	-2.8	-4.3
States and markets			
Starting a business (days)	..	31	32
Stock market capitalization (% of GDP)	0.2	18.3	26.9
Military expenditures (% of GDP)	2.4	1.8	1.9
Mobile cellular subscriptions (per 100 people)	0.0	17.6	131.0
Individuals using the Internet (% of population)	0.0	7.3	64.9
Paved roads (% of total)	61.6	68.3	69.9
High-technology exports (% of manufactured exports)	3	3	6
Global links			
Merchandise trade (% of GDP)	40	47	77
Net barter terms of trade index (2000 = 100)	..	100	100
Total external debt stocks ($ millions)	..	..	..
Total debt service (% of exports)	..	..	..
Net migration (thousands)	-250	-199	56
Remittances received ($ billions)	..	1.5	7.6
Foreign direct investment, net inflows ($ billions)	0.1	9.3	15.3
Net official development assistance received ($ millions)	..	..	..

Portugal

High income

Population (millions)	10.6	Population growth (%)		-0.8
Surface area (1,000 sq. km)	92	Population living below $1.25 a day (%)		..
GNI, Atlas ($ billions)	225.6	GNI per capita, Atlas ($)		21,370
GNI, PPP ($ billions)	259.9	GNI per capita, PPP ($)		24,620

	1990	2000	2011
People			
Share of poorest 20% in nat'l consumption/income (%)	..	..	..
Life expectancy at birth (years)	74	76	81
Total fertility rate (births per woman)	1.4	1.6	1.4
Adolescent fertility rate (births per 1,000 women 15-19)	..	20	13
Contraceptive prevalence (% of married women 15-49)	..	..	67
Births attended by skilled health staff (% of total)	98	100	..
Under-five mortality rate (per 1,000 live births)	15	7	3
Child malnutrition, underweight (% of under age 5)	..	0.1	..
Child immunization, measles (% of ages 12-23 mos.)	85	87	96
Primary completion rate, total (% of relevant age group)	..	..	..
Gross secondary enrollment, total (% of relevant age group)	60	105	109
Ratio of girls to boys in primary & secondary school (%)	97	101	100
HIV prevalence rate (% population of ages 15-49)	0.1	0.6	0.7
Environment			
Forests (1,000 sq. km)	33	34	35
Deforestation (avg. annual %, 1990-2000 and 2000-2010)		-0.3	-0.1
Freshwater use (% of internal resources)	..	22.3	22.3
Access to improved water source (% total pop.)	96	99	99
Access to improved sanitation facilities (% total pop.)	92	98	100
Energy use per capita (kilograms of oil equivalent)	1,677	2,413	2,193
Carbon dioxide emissions per capita (metric tons)	4.2	6.2	5.4
Electricity use per capita (kilowatt-hours)	2,542	4,014	4,929
Economy			
GDP ($ billions)	78	117	237
GDP growth (annual %)	4.0	3.9	-1.7
GDP implicit price deflator (annual % growth)	13.1	3.3	0.7
Value added in agriculture (% of GDP)	9	4	2
Value added in industry (% of GDP)	29	28	23
Value added in services (% of GDP)	63	68	74
Exports of goods and services (% of GDP)	30	29	36
Imports of goods and services (% of GDP)	37	40	39
Gross capital formation (% of GDP)	27	28	17
Central government revenue (% of GDP)	..	34.6	39.9
Central government cash surplus/deficit (% of GDP)	..	-2.6	-4.0
States and markets			
Starting a business (days)	..	78	5
Stock market capitalization (% of GDP)	11.8	51.7	26.0
Military expenditures (% of GDP)	2.4	1.9	2.0
Mobile cellular subscriptions (per 100 people)	0.1	64.5	115.4
Individuals using the Internet (% of population)	0.0	16.4	55.3
Paved roads (% of total)	..	86.0	..
High-technology exports (% of manufactured exports)	4	6	4
Global links			
Merchandise trade (% of GDP)	54	55	59
Net barter terms of trade index (2000 = 100)	..	100	87
Total external debt stocks ($ millions)	..	..	..
Total debt service (% of exports)	..	..	..
Net migration (thousands)	-148	174	150
Remittances received ($ billions)	4.5	3.5	3.8
Foreign direct investment, net inflows ($ billions)	2.6	6.7	13.1
Net official development assistance received ($ millions)	..	..	..

Puerto Rico

High income

Population (millions)	3.7	Population growth (%)	-0.4
Surface area (1,000 sq. km)	8.9	Population living below $1.25 a day (%)	..
GNI, Atlas ($ billions)	61.6	GNI per capita, Atlas ($)	16,560
GNI, PPP ($ billions)	..	GNI per capita, PPP ($)	..

	1990	2000	2011
People			
Share of poorest 20% in nat'l consumption/income (%)	..	..	
Life expectancy at birth (years)	74	77	79
Total fertility rate (births per woman)	2.2	2.0	1.8
Adolescent fertility rate (births per 1,000 women 15–19)	..	68	51
Contraceptive prevalence (% of married women 15–49)	..	84	..
Births attended by skilled health staff (% of total)	..	100	..
Under-five mortality rate (per 1,000 live births)	..	..	..
Child malnutrition, underweight (% of under age 5)	..	..	..
Child immunization, measles (% of ages 12–23 mos.)	..	..	..
Primary completion rate, total (% of relevant age group)	..	..	..
Gross secondary enrollment, total (% of relevant age group)	..	..	77
Ratio of girls to boys in primary & secondary school (%)	..	..	104
HIV prevalence rate (% population of ages 15–49)	..	..	..
Environment			
Forests (1,000 sq. km)	2.9	4.6	5.6
Deforestation (avg. annual %, 1990–2000 and 2000–2010)		-4.9	-1.8
Freshwater use (% of internal resources)	11.2	12.1	14.0
Access to improved water source (% total pop.)	..	..	..
Access to improved sanitation facilities (% total pop.)	..	..	..
Energy use per capita (kilograms of oil equivalent)	..	..	..
Carbon dioxide emissions per capita (metric tons)	..	..	..
Electricity use per capita (kilowatt-hours)	..	..	..
Economy			
GDP ($ billions)	30.6	61.7	96.3
GDP growth (annual %)	3.8	3.3	-2.1
GDP implicit price deflator (annual % growth)	4.3	3.3	3.2
Value added in agriculture (% of GDP)	1	1	1
Value added in industry (% of GDP)	42	42	50
Value added in services (% of GDP)	57	57	49
Exports of goods and services (% of GDP)	72	75	78
Imports of goods and services (% of GDP)	70	98	92
Gross capital formation (% of GDP)	17	18	9
Central government revenue (% of GDP)	..	..	..
Central government cash surplus/deficit (% of GDP)	..	..	..
States and markets			
Starting a business (days)	..	7	6
Stock market capitalization (% of GDP)	..	..	..
Military expenditures (% of GDP)	..	..	..
Mobile cellular subscriptions (per 100 people)	0.6	34.6	83.0
Individuals using the Internet (% of population)	0.0	10.5	48.0
Paved roads (% of total)	..	94.0	..
High-technology exports (% of manufactured exports)	..	..	..
Global links			
Merchandise trade (% of GDP)	..	..	..
Net barter terms of trade index (2000 = 100)	..	..	..
Total external debt stocks ($ millions)	..	..	..
Total debt service (% of exports)	..	..	..
Net migration (thousands)	-55	-25	-145
Remittances received ($ millions)	..	..	..
Foreign direct investment, net inflows ($ millions)	..	..	..
Net official development assistance received ($ millions)	..	..	..

Qatar

Population (millions)	1.9	Population growth (%)	6.1
Surface area (1,000 sq. km)	12	Population living below $1.25 a day (%)	..
GNI, Atlas ($ billions)	150.4	GNI per capita, Atlas ($)	80,440
GNI, PPP ($ billions)	161.6	GNI per capita, PPP ($)	86,440

	1990	2000	2011
People			
Share of poorest 20% in nat'l consumption/income (%)	..	..	3.9
Life expectancy at birth (years)	74	76	78
Total fertility rate (births per woman)	4.2	3.1	2.2
Adolescent fertility rate (births per 1,000 women 15–19)	..	21	16
Contraceptive prevalence (% of married women 15–49)	..	43	..
Births attended by skilled health staff (% of total)	..	100	100
Under-five mortality rate (per 1,000 live births)	20	13	8
Child malnutrition, underweight (% of under age 5)	..	..	..
Child immunization, measles (% of ages 12–23 mos.)	79	91	99
Primary completion rate, total (% of relevant age group)	74	93	96
Gross secondary enrollment, total (% of relevant age group)	81	88	102
Ratio of girls to boys in primary & secondary school (%)	106	109	103
HIV prevalence rate (% population of ages 15–49)	0.1	0.1	0.1
Environment			
Forests (sq. km)	0.0	0.0	0.0
Deforestation (avg. annual %, 1990–2000 and 2000–2010)		0.0	0.0
Freshwater use (% of internal resources)	..	524.8	792.9
Access to improved water source (% total pop.)	100	100	100
Access to improved sanitation facilities (% total pop.)	100	100	100
Energy use per capita (kilograms of oil equivalent)	13,020	17,620	12,799
Carbon dioxide emissions per capita (metric tons)	24.9	58.8	44.0
Electricity use per capita (kilowatt-hours)	9,643	14,385	14,997
Economy			
GDP ($ billions)	7.4	17.8	173.0
GDP growth (annual %)	..	3.3	18.8
GDP implicit price deflator (annual % growth)	..	-4.4	14.4
Value added in agriculture (% of GDP)	..	..	..
Value added in industry (% of GDP)	..	..	..
Value added in services (% of GDP)	..	..	..
Exports of goods and services (% of GDP)	..	67	47
Imports of goods and services (% of GDP)	..	22	31
Gross capital formation (% of GDP)	..	20	39
Central government revenue (% of GDP)	..	..	33.6
Central government cash surplus/deficit (% of GDP)	..	..	2.9
States and markets			
Starting a business (days)	..	..	9
Stock market capitalization (% of GDP)	..	29.0	72.5
Military expenditures (% of GDP)	..	4.7	2.2
Mobile cellular subscriptions (per 100 people)	0.8	20.5	123.1
Individuals using the Internet (% of population)	0.0	4.9	86.2
Paved roads (% of total)	85.6	90.0	..
High-technology exports (% of manufactured exports)	0	0	0
Global links			
Merchandise trade (% of GDP)	76	84	83
Net barter terms of trade index (2000 = 100)	..	100	213
Total external debt stocks ($ millions)	..	..	..
Total debt service (% of exports)	..	..	..
Net migration (thousands)	58	43	857
Remittances received ($ millions)	..	..	574
Foreign direct investment, net inflows ($ millions)	5	252	-87
Net official development assistance received ($ millions)	3.0	..	..

Romania

Europe & Central Asia		Upper middle income	
Population (millions)	21.4	Population growth (%)	–0.2
Surface area (1,000 sq. km)	238	Population living below $1.25 a day (%)	<2
GNI, Atlas ($ billions)	174.0	GNI per capita, Atlas ($)	8,140
GNI, PPP ($ billions)	337.4	GNI per capita, PPP ($)	15,780

	1990	2000	2011
People			
Share of poorest 20% in nat'l consumption/income (%)	9.9	8.2	8.3
Life expectancy at birth (years)	70	71	75
Total fertility rate (births per woman)	1.8	1.3	1.3
Adolescent fertility rate (births per 1,000 women 15-19)	..	38	29
Contraceptive prevalence (% of married women 15-49)	57	64	..
Births attended by skilled health staff (% of total)	100	99	99
Under-five mortality rate (per 1,000 live births)	37	27	13
Child malnutrition, underweight (% of under age 5)	5.0	3.7	..
Child immunization, measles (% of ages 12-23 mos.)	92	98	93
Primary completion rate, total (% of relevant age group)	92	95	92
Gross secondary enrollment, total (% of relevant age group)	103	82	97
Ratio of girls to boys in primary & secondary school (%)	98	100	99
HIV prevalence rate (% population of ages 15-49)	0.1	0.1	0.1
Environment			
Forests (1,000 sq. km)	64	64	66
Deforestation (avg. annual %, 1990-2000 and 2000-2010)		0.0	–0.3
Freshwater use (% of internal resources)	48.3	21.2	16.3
Access to improved water source (% total pop.)	75	84	89
Access to improved sanitation facilities (% total pop.)	71	72	73
Energy use per capita (kilograms of oil equivalent)	2,682	1,613	1,632
Carbon dioxide emissions per capita (metric tons)	6.8	4.0	3.7
Electricity use per capita (kilowatt-hours)	2,925	1,988	2,392
Economy			
GDP ($ billions)	38.3	37.1	189.8
GDP growth (annual %)	–5.6	2.1	2.5
GDP implicit price deflator (annual % growth)	13.6	44.3	8.1
Value added in agriculture (% of GDP)	24	13	7
Value added in industry (% of GDP)	50	36	41
Value added in services (% of GDP)	26	51	52
Exports of goods and services (% of GDP)	17	33	38
Imports of goods and services (% of GDP)	26	38	43
Gross capital formation (% of GDP)	30	20	29
Central government revenue (% of GDP)	..	25.8	29.0
Central government cash surplus/deficit (% of GDP)	..	-2.0	-4.9
States and markets			
Starting a business (days)	..	29	10
Stock market capitalization (% of GDP)	..	2.9	11.2
Military expenditures (% of GDP)	4.5	2.5	1.1
Mobile cellular subscriptions (per 100 people)	0.0	11.3	109.2
Individuals using the Internet (% of population)	0.0	3.6	44.0
Paved roads (% of total)	51.0	49.5	56.5
High-technology exports (% of manufactured exports)	3	6	10
Global links			
Merchandise trade (% of GDP)	33	64	73
Net barter terms of trade index (2000 = 100)	..	100	98
Total external debt stocks ($ billions)	1	11	130
Total debt service (% of exports)	0.3	20.1	27.5
Net migration (thousands)	-121	-300	-100
Remittances received ($ millions)	..	96	3,889
Foreign direct investment, net inflows ($ billions)	0.0	1.0	2.6
Net official development assistance received ($ millions)	..	..	..

Russian Federation

Upper middle income

Population (millions)	143.0	Population growth (%)	0.4
Surface area (1,000 sq. km)	17,098	Population living below $1.25 a day (%)	<2
GNI, Atlas ($ billions)	1,522.3	GNI per capita, Atlas ($)	10,650
GNI, PPP ($ billions)	2,917.7	GNI per capita, PPP ($)	20,410

	1990	2000	2011
People			
Share of poorest 20% in nat'l consumption/income (%)	4.4	6.1	6.5
Life expectancy at birth (years)	69	65	69
Total fertility rate (births per woman)	1.9	1.2	1.5
Adolescent fertility rate (births per 1,000 women 15-19)	..	31	25
Contraceptive prevalence (% of married women 15-49)	63	84	80
Births attended by skilled health staff (% of total)	99	99	100
Under-five mortality rate (per 1,000 live births)	27	21	12
Child malnutrition, underweight (% of under age 5)	..	2.9	..
Child immunization, measles (% of ages 12-23 mos.)	83	97	98
Primary completion rate, total (% of relevant age group)	..	91	98
Gross secondary enrollment, total (% of relevant age group)	96	92	89
Ratio of girls to boys in primary & secondary school (%)	..	100	98
HIV prevalence rate (% population of ages 15-49)	..	..	..
Environment			
Forests (1,000 sq. km)	8,090	8,093	8,092
Deforestation (avg. annual %, 1990-2000 and 2000-2010)		0.0	0.0
Freshwater use (% of internal resources)	..	1.5	1.5
Access to improved water source (% total pop.)	93	95	97
Access to improved sanitation facilities (% total pop.)	74	72	70
Energy use per capita (kilograms of oil equivalent)	5,929	4,233	4,927
Carbon dioxide emissions per capita (metric tons)	14.4	10.6	11.1
Electricity use per capita (kilowatt-hours)	6,673	5,209	6,431
Economy			
GDP ($ billions)	517	260	1,858
GDP growth (annual %)	-3.0	10.0	4.3
GDP implicit price deflator (annual % growth)	15.9	37.7	15.8
Value added in agriculture (% of GDP)	17	6	4
Value added in industry (% of GDP)	48	38	37
Value added in services (% of GDP)	35	56	59
Exports of goods and services (% of GDP)	18	44	31
Imports of goods and services (% of GDP)	18	24	22
Gross capital formation (% of GDP)	30	19	25
Central government revenue (% of GDP)	..	31.8	32.1
Central government cash surplus/deficit (% of GDP)	..	7.0	3.4
States and markets			
Starting a business (days)	..	43	18
Stock market capitalization (% of GDP)	0.0	15.0	42.9
Military expenditures (% of GDP)	19.1	3.7	3.9
Mobile cellular subscriptions (per 100 people)	0.0	2.2	179.3
Individuals using the Internet (% of population)	0.0	2.0	49.0
Paved roads (% of total)	74.2	67.4	..
High-technology exports (% of manufactured exports)	..	16	8
Global links			
Merchandise trade (% of GDP)	..	58	46
Net barter terms of trade index (2000 = 100)	..	100	234
Total external debt stocks ($ billions)	59	147	543
Total debt service (% of exports)	..	9.7	10.5
Net migration (millions)	0.9	2.2	1.1
Remittances received ($ billions)	..	1.3	5.0
Foreign direct investment, net inflows ($ billions)	1.2	2.7	52.9
Net official development assistance received ($ millions)	..	..	..

Rwanda

Sub-Sahran Africa		Low income
Population (millions)	10.9	Population growth (%)	3.0
Surface area (1,000 sq. km)	26	Population living below $1.25 a day (%)	63.2
GNI, Atlas ($ billions)	6.2	GNI per capita, Atlas ($)	570
GNI, PPP ($ billions)	13.9	GNI per capita, PPP ($)	1,270

	1990	2000	2011
People			
Share of poorest 20% in nat'l consumption/income (%)	..	4.8	5.2
Life expectancy at birth (years)	33	47	55
Total fertility rate (births per woman)	7.0	5.8	5.3
Adolescent fertility rate (births per 1,000 women 15–19)	..	48	36
Contraceptive prevalence (% of married women 15–49)	21	13	52
Births attended by skilled health staff (% of total)	26	31	69
Under-five mortality rate (per 1,000 live births)	156	183	54
Child malnutrition, underweight (% of under age 5)	24.3	20.3	11.7
Child immunization, measles (% of ages 12–23 mos.)	83	74	95
Primary completion rate, total (% of relevant age group)	45	23	70
Gross secondary enrollment, total (% of relevant age group)	16	11	36
Ratio of girls to boys in primary & secondary school (%)	95	97	103
HIV prevalence rate (% population of ages 15–49)	5.8	4.4	2.9
Environment			
Forests (1,000 sq. km)	3.2	3.4	4.5
Deforestation (avg. annual %, 1990–2000 and 2000–2010)		-0.8	-2.4
Freshwater use (% of internal resources)	..	1.6	1.6
Access to improved water source (% total pop.)	66	66	65
Access to improved sanitation facilities (% total pop.)	36	47	55
Energy use per capita (kilograms of oil equivalent)	..	..	..
Carbon dioxide emissions per capita (metric tons)	0.10	0.08	0.07
Electricity use per capita (kilowatt-hours)	..	..	..
Economy			
GDP ($ billions)	2.6	1.7	6.4
GDP growth (annual %)	-2.4	8.3	8.3
GDP implicit price deflator (annual % growth)	13.5	2.8	7.8
Value added in agriculture (% of GDP)	33	37	32
Value added in industry (% of GDP)	25	14	16
Value added in services (% of GDP)	43	49	52
Exports of goods and services (% of GDP)	6	6	13
Imports of goods and services (% of GDP)	14	25	32
Gross capital formation (% of GDP)	15	13	21
Central government revenue (% of GDP)	10.8	..	..
Central government cash surplus/deficit (% of GDP)	-5.4	..	..
States and markets			
Starting a business (days)	..	18	3
Stock market capitalization (% of GDP)	..	..	..
Military expenditures (% of GDP)	3.7	3.5	1.2
Mobile cellular subscriptions (per 100 people)	0.0	0.5	40.6
Individuals using the Internet (% of population)	0.0	0.1	7.0
Paved roads (% of total)	9.0	19.0	..
High-technology exports (% of manufactured exports)	..	2	3
Global links			
Merchandise trade (% of GDP)	16	15	35
Net barter terms of trade index (2000 = 100)	40	100	226
Total external debt stocks ($ billions)	0.7	1.3	1.1
Total debt service (% of exports)	14.3	25.7	2.4
Net migration (thousands)	15	1,816	15
Remittances received ($ millions)	3	7	103
Foreign direct investment, net inflows ($ millions)	8	8	106
Net official development assistance received ($ millions)	288	321	1,278

Samoa

East Asia & Pacific **Lower middle income**

Population (thousands)	184	Population growth (%)	0.4
Surface area (1,000 sq. km)	2.8	Population living below $1.25 a day (%)	..
GNI, Atlas ($ millions)	580.5	GNI per capita, Atlas ($)	3,160
GNI, PPP ($ millions)	784.2	GNI per capita, PPP ($)	4,270

	1990	2000	2011
People			
Share of poorest 20% in nat'l consumption/income (%)	..	..	..
Life expectancy at birth (years)	65	69	73
Total fertility rate (births per woman)	4.8	4.6	3.8
Adolescent fertility rate (births per 1,000 women 15–19)	..	40	26
Contraceptive prevalence (% of married women 15–49)	..	25	29
Births attended by skilled health staff (% of total)	76	100	81
Under-five mortality rate (per 1,000 live births)	30	23	19
Child malnutrition, underweight (% of under age 5)	..	1.7	..
Child immunization, measles (% of ages 12–23 mos.)	89	93	67
Primary completion rate, total (% of relevant age group)	..	94	98
Gross secondary enrollment, total (% of relevant age group)	..	78	82
Ratio of girls to boys in primary & secondary school (%)	..	106	109
HIV prevalence rate (% population of ages 15–49)	..	..	..
Environment			
Forests (1,000 sq. km)	1.3	1.7	1.7
Deforestation (avg. annual %, 1990–2000 and 2000–2010)		-2.8	0.0
Freshwater use (% of internal resources)	..	..	..
Access to improved water source (% total pop.)	89	92	96
Access to improved sanitation facilities (% total pop.)	99	98	98
Energy use per capita (kilograms of oil equivalent)	268	..	..
Carbon dioxide emissions per capita (metric tons)	0.8	0.8	0.9
Electricity use per capita (kilowatt-hours)	..	..	..
Economy			
GDP ($ millions)	112	246	641
GDP growth (annual %)	-4.4	7.0	2.0
GDP implicit price deflator (annual % growth)	9.0	2.8	2.2
Value added in agriculture (% of GDP)	..	17	10
Value added in industry (% of GDP)	..	26	27
Value added in services (% of GDP)	..	57	63
Exports of goods and services (% of GDP)	..	34	31
Imports of goods and services (% of GDP)	..	57	58
Gross capital formation (% of GDP)	..	..	..
Central government revenue (% of GDP)	..	..	..
Central government cash surplus/deficit (% of GDP)	..	..	..
States and markets			
Starting a business (days)	..	42	9
Stock market capitalization (% of GDP)	..	..	..
Military expenditures (% of GDP)	..	..	..
Mobile cellular subscriptions (per 100 people)	0.0	1.4	91.4
Individuals using the Internet (% of population)	0.0	0.6	7.0
Paved roads (% of total)	..	14.2	..
High-technology exports (% of manufactured exports)	..	1	0
Global links			
Merchandise trade (% of GDP)	80	70	62
Net barter terms of trade index (2000 = 100)	..	100	78
Total external debt stocks ($ millions)	92	139	368
Total debt service (% of exports)	10.6	5.7	5.8
Net migration (thousands)	-16.4	-15.0	-15.7
Remittances received ($ millions)	43	45	139
Foreign direct investment, net inflows ($ millions)	6.6	-1.5	14.9
Net official development assistance received ($ millions)	48	27	101

San Marino

Population (thousands)	32
Surface area (sq. km)	60
GNI, Atlas ($ billions)	1.6
GNI, PPP ($ millions)	..

Population growth (%)	0.6
Population living below $1.25 a day (%)	..
GNI per capita, Atlas ($)	50,400
GNI per capita, PPP ($)	..

	1990	2000	2011
People			
Share of poorest 20% in nat'l consumption/income (%)	..	..	..
Life expectancy at birth (years)	..	81	83
Total fertility rate (births per woman)	..	..	..
Adolescent fertility rate (births per 1,000 women 15-19)	..	..	..
Contraceptive prevalence (% of married women 15-49)	..	..	..
Births attended by skilled health staff (% of total)	..	..	..
Under-five mortality rate (per 1,000 live births)	12	5	2
Child malnutrition, underweight (% of under age 5)	..	..	..
Child immunization, measles (% of ages 12–23 mos.)	99	74	83
Primary completion rate, total (% of relevant age group)			93
Gross secondary enrollment, total (% of relevant age group)	..	..	95
Ratio of girls to boys in primary & secondary school (%)	..	..	100
HIV prevalence rate (% population of ages 15–49)	..	..	..
Environment			
Forests (sq. km)	0.0	0.0	0.0
Deforestation (avg. annual %, 1990–2000 and 2000–2010)		0.0	0.0
Freshwater use (% of internal resources)			..
Access to improved water source (% total pop.)	..	..	..
Access to improved sanitation facilities (% total pop.)	..	..	..
Energy use per capita (kilograms of oil equivalent)	..	..	..
Carbon dioxide emissions per capita (metric tons)	..	..	..
Electricity use per capita (kilowatt-hours)	..	..	..
Economy			
GDP ($ millions)	..	774	1,900
GDP growth (annual %)	2.1	2.2	1.9
GDP implicit price deflator (annual % growth)	8.4	2.6	3.2
Value added in agriculture (% of GDP)	..	..	..
Value added in industry (% of GDP)	..	..	..
Value added in services (% of GDP)	..	..	..
Exports of goods and services (% of GDP)	..	..	..
Imports of goods and services (% of GDP)	..	..	..
Gross capital formation (% of GDP)	..	..	..
Central government revenue (% of GDP)	..	46.4	45.6
Central government cash surplus/deficit (% of GDP)	..	1.3	6.9
States and markets			
Starting a business (days)	..	..	..
Stock market capitalization (% of GDP)	..	..	..
Military expenditures (% of GDP)	..	..	..
Mobile cellular subscriptions (per 100 people)	0.0	53.8	111.8
Individuals using the Internet (% of population)	0.0	48.8	49.6
Paved roads (% of total)	..	..	..
High-technology exports (% of manufactured exports)	..	..	..
Global links			
Merchandise trade (% of GDP)	..	..	..
Net barter terms of trade index (2000 = 100)	..	..	..
Total external debt stocks ($ millions)	..	..	..
Total debt service (% of exports)	..	..	..
Net migration (thousands)	..	..	..
Remittances received ($ millions)	..	..	..
Foreign direct investment, net inflows ($ millions)	..	..	..
Net official development assistance received ($ millions)	..	..	..

São Tomé and Príncipe

Sub-Saharan Africa   **Lower middle income**

Population (thousands)	169	Population growth (%)	1.9
Surface area (sq. km)	960	Population living below $1.25 a day (%)	28.2
GNI, Atlas ($ millions)	226.9	GNI per capita, Atlas ($)	1,350
GNI, PPP ($ millions)	350.3	GNI per capita, PPP ($)	2,080

	1990	2000	2011
People			
Share of poorest 20% in nat'l consumption/income (%)	..	5.2	..
Life expectancy at birth (years)	61	62	65
Total fertility rate (births per woman)	5.4	4.6	3.6
Adolescent fertility rate (births per 1,000 women 15–19)	..	86	58
Contraceptive prevalence (% of married women 15–49)	..	29	38
Births attended by skilled health staff (% of total)	..	79	82
Under-five mortality rate (per 1,000 live births)	96	93	89
Child malnutrition, underweight (% of under age 5)	..	10.1	14.4
Child immunization, measles (% of ages 12–23 mos.)	71	69	91
Primary completion rate, total (% of relevant age group)	79	46	115
Gross secondary enrollment, total (% of relevant age group)	36	38	69
Ratio of girls to boys in primary & secondary school (%)	96	100	102
HIV prevalence rate (% population of ages 15–49)	0.2	0.8	1.0
Environment			
Forests (sq. km)	270	270	270
Deforestation (avg. annual %, 1990–2000 and 2000–2010)		0.0	0.0
Freshwater use (% of internal resources)	..	0.3	0.3
Access to improved water source (% total pop.)	..	79	89
Access to improved sanitation facilities (% total pop.)	..	21	26
Energy use per capita (kilograms of oil equivalent)	202	..	..
Carbon dioxide emissions per capita (metric tons)	0.6	0.6	0.8
Electricity use per capita (kilowatt-hours)	..	..	..
Economy			
GDP ($ millions)	..	77	248
GDP growth (annual %)	..	2.0	4.9
GDP implicit price deflator (annual % growth)	..	19.6	12.1
Value added in agriculture (% of GDP)	..	12	..
Value added in industry (% of GDP)	..	10	..
Value added in services (% of GDP)	..	77	..
Exports of goods and services (% of GDP)	..	21	11
Imports of goods and services (% of GDP)	..	57	57
Gross capital formation (% of GDP)	..	..	..
Central government revenue (% of GDP)	..	..	..
Central government cash surplus/deficit (% of GDP)	..	..	..
States and markets			
Starting a business (days)	..	192	7
Stock market capitalization (% of GDP)	..	..	..
Military expenditures (% of GDP)	..	..	..
Mobile cellular subscriptions (per 100 people)	0.0	0.0	68.3
Individuals using the Internet (% of population)	0.0	4.6	20.2
Paved roads (% of total)	61.6	68.1	..
High-technology exports (% of manufactured exports)	..	1	14
Global links			
Merchandise trade (% of GDP)	..	43	55
Net barter terms of trade index (2000 = 100)	101	100	120
Total external debt stocks ($ millions)	150	305	231
Total debt service (% of exports)	34.8	25.4	5.4
Net migration (thousands)	-3.2	-4.9	-6.5
Remittances received ($ millions)	0.3	0.5	6.9
Foreign direct investment, net inflows ($ millions)	-0.1	3.8	35.0
Net official development assistance received ($ millions)	54.1	34.9	75.1

Saudi Arabia

High income

Population (millions)	28.1	Population growth (%)	2.3
Surface area (1,000 sq. km)	2,150	Population living below $1.25 a day (%)	..
GNI, Atlas ($ billions)	500.5	GNI per capita, Atlas ($)	17,820
GNI, PPP ($ billions)	693.7	GNI per capita, PPP ($)	24,700

	1990	2000	2011
People			
Share of poorest 20% in nat'l consumption/income (%)	..	..	..
Life expectancy at birth (years)	69	71	74
Total fertility rate (births per woman)	5.8	4.0	2.7
Adolescent fertility rate (births per 1,000 women 15–19)	..	27	20
Contraceptive prevalence (% of married women 15–49)	..	21	24
Births attended by skilled health staff (% of total)	..	96	97
Under-five mortality rate (per 1,000 live births)	43	21	9
Child malnutrition, underweight (% of under age 5)	..	..	..
Child immunization, measles (% of ages 12–23 mos.)	88	94	98
Primary completion rate, total (% of relevant age group)	..	..	106
Gross secondary enrollment, total (% of relevant age group)	..	..	97
Ratio of girls to boys in primary & secondary school (%)	..	..	94
HIV prevalence rate (% population of ages 15–49)	..	..	..
Environment			
Forests (1,000 sq. km)	9.8	9.8	9.8
Deforestation (avg. annual %, 1990–2000 and 2000–2010)		0.0	0.0
Freshwater use (% of internal resources)	709.2	709.2	986.3
Access to improved water source (% total pop.)	89	90	..
Access to improved sanitation facilities (% total pop.)	..	..	..
Energy use per capita (kilograms of oil equivalent)	3,703	5,055	6,168
Carbon dioxide emissions per capita (metric tons)	13.5	14.8	16.1
Electricity use per capita (kilowatt-hours)	4,041	5,840	7,967
Economy			
GDP ($ billions)	117	188	577
GDP growth (annual %)	8.3	4.9	6.8
GDP implicit price deflator (annual % growth)	13.1	11.6	19.8
Value added in agriculture (% of GDP)	6	5	2
Value added in industry (% of GDP)	49	54	60
Value added in services (% of GDP)	45	41	38
Exports of goods and services (% of GDP)	41	44	62
Imports of goods and services (% of GDP)	32	25	31
Gross capital formation (% of GDP)	15	19	19
Central government revenue (% of GDP)	..	..	..
Central government cash surplus/deficit (% of GDP)	..	..	..
States and markets			
Starting a business (days)	..	74	21
Stock market capitalization (% of GDP)	36.7	35.6	58.7
Military expenditures (% of GDP)	14.0	10.6	8.4
Mobile cellular subscriptions (per 100 people)	0.1	6.9	191.2
Individuals using the Internet (% of population)	0.0	2.2	47.5
Paved roads (% of total)	40.6	29.9	..
High-technology exports (% of manufactured exports)	0	0	1
Global links			
Merchandise trade (% of GDP)	59	57	86
Net barter terms of trade index (2000 = 100)	..	100	216
Total external debt stocks ($ millions)	..	..	..
Total debt service (% of exports)	..	..	..
Net migration (thousands)	538	-877	1,056
Remittances received ($ millions)	..	..	244
Foreign direct investment, net inflows ($ billions)	1.9	-1.9	16.3
Net official development assistance received ($ millions)	14.7	22.0	..

Senegal

Sub-Saharan Africa   **Lower middle income**

Population (millions)	12.8	Population growth (%)	2.6
Surface area (1,000 sq. km)	197	Population living below $1.25 a day (%)	29.6
GNI, Atlas ($ billions)	13.7	GNI per capita, Atlas ($)	1,070
GNI, PPP ($ billions)	24.8	GNI per capita, PPP ($)	1,940

	1990	2000	2011
People			
Share of poorest 20% in nat'l consumption/income (%)	3.5	6.6	..
Life expectancy at birth (years)	53	56	59
Total fertility rate (births per woman)	6.6	5.5	4.7
Adolescent fertility rate (births per 1,000 women 15–19)	..	110	93
Contraceptive prevalence (% of married women 15–49)	7	11	13
Births attended by skilled health staff (% of total)	47	58	65
Under-five mortality rate (per 1,000 live births)	136	130	65
Child malnutrition, underweight (% of under age 5)	19.0	20.3	19.2
Child immunization, measles (% of ages 12–23 mos.)	51	48	82
Primary completion rate, total (% of relevant age group)	43	40	63
Gross secondary enrollment, total (% of relevant age group)	15	16	42
Ratio of girls to boys in primary & secondary school (%)	68	82	102
HIV prevalence rate (% population of ages 15–49)	0.1	0.4	0.7
Environment			
Forests (1,000 sq. km)	93	89	84
Deforestation (avg. annual %, 1990–2000 and 2000–2010)		0.5	0.5
Freshwater use (% of internal resources)	..	8.6	8.6
Access to improved water source (% total pop.)	61	66	72
Access to improved sanitation facilities (% total pop.)	38	45	52
Energy use per capita (kilograms of oil equivalent)	233	252	272
Carbon dioxide emissions per capita (metric tons)	0.4	0.4	0.4
Electricity use per capita (kilowatt-hours)	108	106	195
Economy			
GDP ($ billions)	5.7	4.7	14.3
GDP growth (annual %)	-0.7	3.2	2.6
GDP implicit price deflator (annual % growth)	0.0	1.9	3.2
Value added in agriculture (% of GDP)	20	19	15
Value added in industry (% of GDP)	22	23	24
Value added in services (% of GDP)	58	58	61
Exports of goods and services (% of GDP)	25	28	25
Imports of goods and services (% of GDP)	32	37	44
Gross capital formation (% of GDP)	9	20	31
Central government revenue (% of GDP)	..	16.9	..
Central government cash surplus/deficit (% of GDP)	..	-0.9	..
States and markets			
Starting a business (days)	..	58	5
Stock market capitalization (% of GDP)	..	..	..
Military expenditures (% of GDP)	2.0	1.3	1.6
Mobile cellular subscriptions (per 100 people)	0.0	2.6	73.3
Individuals using the Internet (% of population)	0.0	0.4	17.5
Paved roads (% of total)	27.2	29.3	35.5
High-technology exports (% of manufactured exports)	..	7	1
Global links			
Merchandise trade (% of GDP)	35	52	59
Net barter terms of trade index (2000 = 100)	172	100	105
Total external debt stocks ($ billions)	3.8	3.7	4.3
Total debt service (% of exports)	21.1	16.3	6.1
Net migration (thousands)	-48	-168	-133
Remittances received ($ millions)	142	233	1,478
Foreign direct investment, net inflows ($ millions)	57	63	286
Net official development assistance received ($ millions)	812	431	1,052

Serbia

Europe & Central Asia		Upper middle income

Population (millions)	7.3	Population growth (%)	-0.4
Surface area (1,000 sq. km)	88	Population living below $1.25 a day (%)	<2
GNI, Atlas ($ billions)	41.3	GNI per capita, Atlas ($)	5,690
GNI, PPP ($ billions)	83.8	GNI per capita, PPP ($)	11,550

	1990	2000	2011
People			
Share of poorest 20% in nat'l consumption/income (%)	..	8.0	8.9
Life expectancy at birth (years)	71	72	75
Total fertility rate (births per woman)	1.8	1.5	1.4
Adolescent fertility rate (births per 1,000 women 15–19)	..	27	20
Contraceptive prevalence (% of married women 15–49)	..	59	61
Births attended by skilled health staff (% of total)	..	98	100
Under-five mortality rate (per 1,000 live births)	29	13	7
Child malnutrition, underweight (% of under age 5)	..	..	..
Child immunization, measles (% of ages 12–23 mos.)	83	89	95
Primary completion rate, total (% of relevant age group)	..	..	99
Gross secondary enrollment, total (% of relevant age group)	..	90	91
Ratio of girls to boys in primary & secondary school (%)	..	101	101
HIV prevalence rate (% population of ages 15–49)	0.1	0.1	0.1
Environment			
Forests (1,000 sq. km)	23	25	28
Deforestation (avg. annual %, 1990–2000 and 2000–2010)		-0.6	-1.0
Freshwater use (% of internal resources)	..	..	49.0
Access to improved water source (% total pop.)	99	99	99
Access to improved sanitation facilities (% total pop.)	..	92	92
Energy use per capita (kilograms of oil equivalent)	2,550	1,771	2,141
Carbon dioxide emissions per capita (metric tons)	..	..	6.3
Electricity use per capita (kilowatt-hours)	4,629	4,199	4,359
Economy			
GDP ($ billions)	..	6.1	45.8
GDP growth (annual %)	-8.0	5.3	2.0
GDP implicit price deflator (annual % growth)	..	77.4	10.3
Value added in agriculture (% of GDP)	..	20	9
Value added in industry (% of GDP)	..	30	27
Value added in services (% of GDP)	..	50	64
Exports of goods and services (% of GDP)	..	24	36
Imports of goods and services (% of GDP)	..	40	51
Gross capital formation (% of GDP)	..	9	25
Central government revenue (% of GDP)	..	..	35.5
Central government cash surplus/deficit (% of GDP)	..	..	-4.2
States and markets			
Starting a business (days)	..	56	12
Stock market capitalization (% of GDP)	..	4.9	18.3
Military expenditures (% of GDP)	..	5.5	2.1
Mobile cellular subscriptions (per 100 people)	..	..	125.4
Individuals using the Internet (% of population)	..	..	42.2
Paved roads (% of total)	..	62.7	63.3
High-technology exports (% of manufactured exports)	..	..	..
Global links			
Merchandise trade (% of GDP)	..	..	70
Net barter terms of trade index (2000 = 100)	..	..	..
Total external debt stocks ($ billions)	17.8e	11.6e	31.6
Total debt service (% of exports)	..	..	31.5
Net migration (thousands)	27	-148	0
Remittances received ($ millions)	..	..	3,271
Foreign direct investment, net inflows ($ millions)	126e	52e	2,700
Net official development assistance received ($ millions)	..	1,134e	596

Seychelles

Sub-Saharan Africa		Upper middle income	
Population (thousands)	86	Population growth (%)	-0.6
Surface area (sq. km)	460	Population living below $1.25 a day (%)	<2
GNI, Atlas ($ millions)	969.3	GNI per capita, Atlas ($)	11,270
GNI, PPP ($ millions)	2,260.1	GNI per capita, PPP ($)	26,280

	1990	2000	2011
People			
Share of poorest 20% in nat'l consumption/income (%)	..	5.7	3.7
Life expectancy at birth (years)	71	73	73
Total fertility rate (births per woman)	2.7	2.1	2.1
Adolescent fertility rate (births per 1,000 women 15-19)	..	..	..
Contraceptive prevalence (% of married women 15-49)	..	..	..
Births attended by skilled health staff (% of total)	..	..	..
Under-five mortality rate (per 1,000 live births)	17	14	14
Child malnutrition, underweight (% of under age 5)	5.0	..	..
Child immunization, measles (% of ages 12–23 mos.)	86	97	99
Primary completion rate, total (% of relevant age group)	114	107	125
Gross secondary enrollment, total (% of relevant age group)	122	105	124
Ratio of girls to boys in primary & secondary school (%)	98	103	105
HIV prevalence rate (% population of ages 15–49)	..	..	..
Environment			
Forests (sq. km)	407	407	407
Deforestation (avg. annual %, 1990–2000 and 2000–2010)		0.0	0.0
Freshwater use (% of internal resources)	..	..	..
Access to improved water source (% total pop.)	..	..	..
Access to improved sanitation facilities (% total pop.)	..	..	..
Energy use per capita (kilograms of oil equivalent)	537	..	..
Carbon dioxide emissions per capita (metric tons)	1.6	7.0	8.4
Electricity use per capita (kilowatt-hours)	..	..	..
Economy			
GDP ($ millions)	369	615	1,060
GDP growth (annual %)	7.5	4.2	5.0
GDP implicit price deflator (annual % growth)	6.4	1.3	6.4
Value added in agriculture (% of GDP)	5	3	2
Value added in industry (% of GDP)	16	29	14
Value added in services (% of GDP)	79	68	84
Exports of goods and services (% of GDP)	15	32	46
Imports of goods and services (% of GDP)	51	55	99
Gross capital formation (% of GDP)	..	..	..
Central government revenue (% of GDP)	51.6	38.7	35.7
Central government cash surplus/deficit (% of GDP)	-4.9	-13.9	5.6
States and markets			
Starting a business (days)	..	..	39
Stock market capitalization (% of GDP)	..	..	..
Military expenditures (% of GDP)	4.0	1.7	0.9
Mobile cellular subscriptions (per 100 people)	0.0	33.0	145.7
Individuals using the Internet (% of population)	0.0	7.4	43.2
Paved roads (% of total)	56.9	96.0	96.5
High-technology exports (% of manufactured exports)	1	2	3
Global links			
Merchandise trade (% of GDP)	66	87	116
Net barter terms of trade index (2000 = 100)	78	100	75
Total external debt stocks ($ millions)	185	304	1,779
Total debt service (% of exports)	9.1	4.2	3.2
Net migration (thousands)	..	..	..
Remittances received ($ millions)	7.5	3.2	25.5
Foreign direct investment, net inflows ($ millions)	20	24	139
Net official development assistance received ($ millions)	35.6	23.1	21.3

Sierra Leone

Population (millions)	6.0	Population growth (%)	2.2
Surface area (1,000 sq. km)	72	Population living below $1.25 a day (%)	53.4
GNI, Atlas ($ billions)	2.8	GNI per capita, Atlas ($)	460
GNI, PPP ($ billions)	6.8	GNI per capita, PPP ($)	1,140

	1990	2000	2011
People			
Share of poorest 20% in nat'l consumption/income (%)	..	6.1	..
Life expectancy at birth (years)	39	40	48
Total fertility rate (births per woman)	5.7	5.7	4.9
Adolescent fertility rate (births per 1,000 women 15–19)	..	146	112
Contraceptive prevalence (% of married women 15–49)	3	4	11
Births attended by skilled health staff (% of total)	..	42	63
Under-five mortality rate (per 1,000 live births)	267	241	185
Child malnutrition, underweight (% of under age 5)	25.4	24.7	21.3
Child immunization, measles (% of ages 12–23 mos.)	..	37	80
Primary completion rate, total (% of relevant age group)	..	..	74
Gross secondary enrollment, total (% of relevant age group)	17	28	..
Ratio of girls to boys in primary & secondary school (%)	62	68	..
HIV prevalence rate (% population of ages 15–49)	0.1	0.8	1.6
Environment			
Forests (1,000 sq. km)	31	29	27
Deforestation (avg. annual %, 1990–2000 and 2000–2010)		0.7	0.7
Freshwater use (% of internal resources)	..	0.3	0.3
Access to improved water source (% total pop.)	38	46	55
Access to improved sanitation facilities (% total pop.)	11	11	13
Energy use per capita (kilograms of oil equivalent)	..	..	..
Carbon dioxide emissions per capita (metric tons)	0.10	0.10	0.25
Electricity use per capita (kilowatt-hours)	..	..	..
Economy			
GDP ($ millions)	650	636	2,973
GDP growth (annual %)	3.3	6.7	6.0
GDP implicit price deflator (annual % growth)	70.6	3.3	17.7
Value added in agriculture (% of GDP)	47	58	58
Value added in industry (% of GDP)	19	28	8
Value added in services (% of GDP)	34	13	34
Exports of goods and services (% of GDP)	35	18	17
Imports of goods and services (% of GDP)	34	39	54
Gross capital formation (% of GDP)	13	1	41
Central government revenue (% of GDP)	5.6	11.4	11.6
Central government cash surplus/deficit (% of GDP)	..	-9.3	-4.6
States and markets			
Starting a business (days)	..	26	12
Stock market capitalization (% of GDP)	..	..	..
Military expenditures (% of GDP)	1.4	3.7	0.9
Mobile cellular subscriptions (per 100 people)	0.0	0.3	35.6
Individuals using the Internet (% of population)	0.0	0.1	0.3
Paved roads (% of total)	10.6	7.9	..
High-technology exports (% of manufactured exports)	..	28	..
Global links			
Merchandise trade (% of GDP)	44	25	69
Net barter terms of trade index (2000 = 100)	..	100	62
Total external debt stocks ($ billions)	1.2	1.2	1.0
Total debt service (% of exports)	10.0	76.4	3.8
Net migration (thousands)	63	-150	60
Remittances received ($ millions)	0.0	7.1	58.8
Foreign direct investment, net inflows ($ millions)	32	39	715
Net official development assistance received ($ millions)	59	181	429

Singapore

High income

Population (millions)	5.2	Population growth (%)	2.1
Surface area (sq. km)	710	Population living below $1.25 a day (%)	..
GNI, Atlas ($ billions)	222.6	GNI per capita, Atlas ($)	42,930
GNI, PPP ($ billions)	307.8	GNI per capita, PPP ($)	59,380

	1990	2000	2011
People			
Share of poorest 20% in nat'l consumption/income (%)	..	5.0	..
Life expectancy at birth (years)	76	78	82
Total fertility rate (births per woman)	1.9	1.4	1.2
Adolescent fertility rate (births per 1,000 women 15–19)	..	7	6
Contraceptive prevalence (% of married women 15–49)	65	..	..
Births attended by skilled health staff (% of total)	..	100	..
Under-five mortality rate (per 1,000 live births)	8	4	3
Child malnutrition, underweight (% of under age 5)	..	3.3	..
Child immunization, measles (% of ages 12–23 mos.)	84	96	95
Primary completion rate, total (% of relevant age group)	..	..	..
Gross secondary enrollment, total (% of relevant age group)	..	..	..
Ratio of girls to boys in primary & secondary school (%)	..	..	..
HIV prevalence rate (% population of ages 15–49)	0.1	0.1	0.1
Environment			
Forests (sq. km)	23	23	23
Deforestation (avg. annual %, 1990–2000 and 2000–2010)		0.0	0.0
Freshwater use (% of internal resources)	..	31.7	31.7
Access to improved water source (% total pop.)	100	100	100
Access to improved sanitation facilities (% total pop.)	99	100	100
Energy use per capita (kilograms of oil equivalent)	3,779	4,647	6,456
Carbon dioxide emissions per capita (metric tons)	15.4	11.8	6.4
Electricity use per capita (kilowatt-hours)	4,983	7,575	8,307
Economy			
GDP ($ billions)	36	96	240
GDP growth (annual %)	10.1	9.0	4.9
GDP implicit price deflator (annual % growth)	4.4	3.6	0.5
Value added in agriculture (% of GDP)	0	0	0
Value added in industry (% of GDP)	32	35	27
Value added in services (% of GDP)	68	65	73
Exports of goods and services (% of GDP)	177	192	209
Imports of goods and services (% of GDP)	167	179	182
Gross capital formation (% of GDP)	35	33	22
Central government revenue (% of GDP)	25.4	26.2	18.3
Central government cash surplus/deficit (% of GDP)	10.5	11.2	9.8
States and markets			
Starting a business (days)	..	8	3
Stock market capitalization (% of GDP)	95.0	159.3	128.6
Military expenditures (% of GDP)	4.6	4.6	3.6
Mobile cellular subscriptions (per 100 people)	1.7	70.1	150.2
Individuals using the Internet (% of population)	0.0	36.0	71.0
Paved roads (% of total)	97.1	100.0	100.0
High-technology exports (% of manufactured exports)	40	63	45
Global links			
Merchandise trade (% of GDP)	314	284	323
Net barter terms of trade index (2000 = 100)	116	100	81
Total external debt stocks ($ millions)	..	..	..
Total debt service (% of exports)	..	..	..
Net migration (thousands)	121	254	722
Remittances received ($ millions)	..	..	..
Foreign direct investment, net inflows ($ billions)	5.6	16.5	64.0
Net official development assistance received ($ millions)	-3.1	..	..

Sint Maarten (Dutch part)

High income

Population (thousands)	37	Population growth (%)		-3.3
Surface area (sq. km)	..	Population living below $1.25 a day (%)		..
GNI, Atlas ($ millions)	..	GNI per capita, Atlas ($)		..
GNI, PPP ($ millions)	..	GNI per capita, PPP ($)		..

	1990	2000	2011
People			
Share of poorest 20% in nat'l consumption/income (%)	..	..	..
Life expectancy at birth (years)	..	..	76
Total fertility rate (births per woman)	..	..	1.7
Adolescent fertility rate (births per 1,000 women 15–19)	..	..	..
Contraceptive prevalence (% of married women 15–49)	..	..	..
Births attended by skilled health staff (% of total)	..	..	..
Under-five mortality rate (per 1,000 live births)	..	..	..
Child malnutrition, underweight (% of under age 5)	..	..	..
Child immunization, measles (% of ages 12–23 mos.)	..	..	..
Primary completion rate, total (% of relevant age group)	..	..	..
Gross secondary enrollment, total (% of relevant age group)	..	..	..
Ratio of girls to boys in primary & secondary school (%)	..	..	..
HIV prevalence rate (% population of ages 15–49)	..	..	..
Environment			
Forests (sq. km)	..	..	..
Deforestation (avg. annual %, 1990–2000 and 2000–2010)		..	..
Freshwater use (% of internal resources)		..	..
Access to improved water source (% total pop.)	..	..	..
Access to improved sanitation facilities (% total pop.)	..	..	..
Energy use per capita (kilograms of oil equivalent)	..	..	..
Carbon dioxide emissions per capita (metric tons)	..	..	..
Electricity use per capita (kilowatt-hours)	..	..	..
Economy			
GDP ($ millions)	..	..	..
GDP growth (annual %)	..	..	..
GDP implicit price deflator (annual % growth)	..	..	..
Value added in agriculture (% of GDP)	..	..	..
Value added in industry (% of GDP)	..	..	..
Value added in services (% of GDP)	..	..	..
Exports of goods and services (% of GDP)	..	..	..
Imports of goods and services (% of GDP)	..	..	..
Gross capital formation (% of GDP)	..	..	..
Central government revenue (% of GDP)	..	..	..
Central government cash surplus/deficit (% of GDP)	..	..	..
States and markets			
Starting a business (days)	..	..	..
Stock market capitalization (% of GDP)	..	..	..
Military expenditures (% of GDP)	..	..	..
Mobile cellular subscriptions (per 100 people)	..	..	..
Individuals using the Internet (% of population)	..	..	..
Paved roads (% of total)	..	..	..
High-technology exports (% of manufactured exports)	..	..	..
Global links			
Merchandise trade (% of GDP)	..	..	..
Net barter terms of trade index (2000 = 100)	..	..	..
Total external debt stocks ($ millions)	..	..	..
Total debt service (% of exports)	..	..	..
Net migration (thousands)	..	..	..
Remittances received ($ millions)	..	..	11.3
Foreign direct investment, net inflows ($ millions)	..	..	-48.5
Net official development assistance received ($ millions)	..	..	..

Slovak Republic

High income

Population (millions)	5.4	Population growth (%)		-0.6
Surface area (1,000 sq. km)	49	Population living below $1.25 a day (%)		<2
GNI, Atlas ($ billions)	87.4	GNI per capita, Atlas ($)		16,190
GNI, PPP ($ billions)	120.4	GNI per capita, PPP ($)		22,300

	1990	2000	2011
People			
Share of poorest 20% in nat'l consumption/income (%)	11.9	9.2	10.1
Life expectancy at birth (years)	71	73	76
Total fertility rate (births per woman)	2.1	1.3	1.5
Adolescent fertility rate (births per 1,000 women 15–19)	..	23	17
Contraceptive prevalence (% of married women 15–49)	74	..	..
Births attended by skilled health staff (% of total)	100	100	100
Under-five mortality rate (per 1,000 live births)	18	12	8
Child malnutrition, underweight (% of under age 5)	..	..	..
Child immunization, measles (% of ages 12–23 mos.)	..	98	98
Primary completion rate, total (% of relevant age group)	96	94	99
Gross secondary enrollment, total (% of relevant age group)	88	85	90
Ratio of girls to boys in primary & secondary school (%)	102	101	100
HIV prevalence rate (% population of ages 15–49)	0.1	0.1	0.1
Environment			
Forests (1,000 sq. km)	19	19	19
Deforestation (avg. annual %, 1990-2000 and 2000-2010)		0.0	-0.1
Freshwater use (% of internal resources)	..	9.3	5.5
Access to improved water source (% total pop.)	100	100	100
Access to improved sanitation facilities (% total pop.)	100	100	100
Energy use per capita (kilograms of oil equivalent)	4,025	3,293	3,138
Carbon dioxide emissions per capita (metric tons)	8.6	6.8	6.3
Electricity use per capita (kilowatt-hours)	5,542	4,956	5,164
Economy			
GDP ($ billions)	11.7	28.7	96.0
GDP growth (annual %)	-2.7	1.4	3.3
GDP implicit price deflator (annual % growth)	6.9	9.4	1.6
Value added in agriculture (% of GDP)	7	4	4
Value added in industry (% of GDP)	59	36	35
Value added in services (% of GDP)	33	59	61
Exports of goods and services (% of GDP)	27	70	89
Imports of goods and services (% of GDP)	36	73	86
Gross capital formation (% of GDP)	33	26	22
Central government revenue (% of GDP)	..	35.3	28.4
Central government cash surplus/deficit (% of GDP)	..	-3.2	-4.9
States and markets			
Starting a business (days)	..	103	16
Stock market capitalization (% of GDP)	..	4.2	4.9
Military expenditures (% of GDP)	2.0	1.7	1.1
Mobile cellular subscriptions (per 100 people)	0.0	23.0	109.3
Individuals using the Internet (% of population)	0.0	9.4	74.4
Paved roads (% of total)	..	87.0	87.1
High-technology exports (% of manufactured exports)	..	4	7
Global links			
Merchandise trade (% of GDP)	91	86	163
Net barter terms of trade index (2000 = 100)	..	100	87
Total external debt stocks ($ millions)	..	..	..
Total debt service (% of exports)	..	..	..
Net migration (thousands)	-35.3	2.6	36.7
Remittances received ($ millions)	79	18	1,753
Foreign direct investment, net inflows ($ billions)	0.2	2.1	3.7
Net official development assistance received ($ millions)	..	..	..

Slovenia

High income

Population (millions)	2.1	
Surface area (1,000 sq. km)	20	
GNI, Atlas ($ billions)	48.5	
GNI, PPP ($ billions)	54.4	

Population growth (%)	0.2
Population living below $1.25 a day (%)	<2
GNI per capita, Atlas ($)	23,600
GNI per capita, PPP ($)	26,500

	1990	2000	2011
People			
Share of poorest 20% in nat'l consumption/income (%)	9.3	8.7	..
Life expectancy at birth (years)	73	75	80
Total fertility rate (births per woman)	1.5	1.3	1.6
Adolescent fertility rate (births per 1,000 women 15–19)	..	10	5
Contraceptive prevalence (% of married women 15–49)	..	..	..
Births attended by skilled health staff (% of total)	100	100	100
Under-five mortality rate (per 1,000 live births)	10	5	3
Child malnutrition, underweight (% of under age 5)	..	..	..
Child immunization, measles (% of ages 12–23 mos.)	90	95	95
Primary completion rate, total (% of relevant age group)	96	96	96
Gross secondary enrollment, total (% of relevant age group)	88	101	97
Ratio of girls to boys in primary & secondary school (%)	103	103	99
HIV prevalence rate (% population of ages 15–49)	0.1	0.1	0.1
Environment			
Forests (1,000 sq. km)	12	12	13
Deforestation (avg. annual %, 1990–2000 and 2000–2010)		-0.4	-0.2
Freshwater use (% of internal resources)	..	..	5.0
Access to improved water source (% total pop.)	100	100	99
Access to improved sanitation facilities (% total pop.)	100	100	100
Energy use per capita (kilograms of oil equivalent)	2,858	3,224	3,527
Carbon dioxide emissions per capita (metric tons)	6.2	7.2	7.5
Electricity use per capita (kilowatt-hours)	5,335	5,778	6,521
Economy			
GDP ($ billions)	17.4	20.0	49.5
GDP growth (annual %)	-8.9	4.3	-0.2
GDP implicit price deflator (annual % growth)	94.9	5.2	0.8
Value added in agriculture (% of GDP)	6	3	2
Value added in industry (% of GDP)	42	36	32
Value added in services (% of GDP)	52	61	66
Exports of goods and services (% of GDP)	91	54	72
Imports of goods and services (% of GDP)	79	57	71
Gross capital formation (% of GDP)	17	27	22
Central government revenue (% of GDP)	39.8	38.9	37.5
Central government cash surplus/deficit (% of GDP)	3.2	-1.1	-6.0
States and markets			
Starting a business (days)	..	60	6
Stock market capitalization (% of GDP)	..	12.7	12.8
Military expenditures (% of GDP)	2.2	1.1	1.4
Mobile cellular subscriptions (per 100 people)	0.0	61.2	106.6
Individuals using the Internet (% of population)	0.0	15.1	72.0
Paved roads (% of total)	72.0	100.0	100.0
High-technology exports (% of manufactured exports)	3	5	6
Global links			
Merchandise trade (% of GDP)	102	95	142
Net barter terms of trade index (2000 = 100)	..	100	86
Total external debt stocks ($ millions)	..	..	..
Total debt service (% of exports)	..	..	..
Net migration (thousands)	20.8	24.2	22.0
Remittances received ($ millions)	38	205	433
Foreign direct investment, net inflows ($ millions)	111	136	818
Net official development assistance received ($ millions)	7.1	60.8	..

Solomon Islands

East Asia & Pacific		Lower middle income	
Population (thousands)	552	Population growth (%)	2.6
Surface area (1,000 sq. km)	29	Population living below $1.25 a day (%)	..
GNI, Atlas ($ millions)	615.2	GNI per capita, Atlas ($)	1,110
GNI, PPP ($ millions)	1,296.9	GNI per capita, PPP ($)	2,350

	1990	2000	2011
People			
Share of poorest 20% in nat'l consumption/income (%)	..	..	..
Life expectancy at birth (years)	57	63	68
Total fertility rate (births per woman)	5.9	4.7	4.2
Adolescent fertility rate (births per 1,000 women 15–19)	..	71	66
Contraceptive prevalence (% of married women 15–49)	..	7	35
Births attended by skilled health staff (% of total)	..	85	86
Under-five mortality rate (per 1,000 live births)	42	31	22
Child malnutrition, underweight (% of under age 5)	16.3	..	11.5
Child immunization, measles (% of ages 12–23 mos.)	70	85	73
Primary completion rate, total (% of relevant age group)	60	..	..
Gross secondary enrollment, total (% of relevant age group)	14	21	48
Ratio of girls to boys in primary & secondary school (%)	84	90	96
HIV prevalence rate (% population of ages 15–49)	..	..	..
Environment			
Forests (1,000 sq. km)	23	23	22
Deforestation (avg. annual %, 1990–2000 and 2000–2010)		0.2	0.2
Freshwater use (% of internal resources)	..	..	..
Access to improved water source (% total pop.)	69	70	..
Access to improved sanitation facilities (% total pop.)	29	31	..
Energy use per capita (kilograms of oil equivalent)	172	..	..
Carbon dioxide emissions per capita (metric tons)	0.5	0.4	0.4
Electricity use per capita (kilowatt-hours)	..	..	..
Economy			
GDP ($ millions)	303	435	838
GDP growth (annual %)	6.0	-14.3	9.0
GDP implicit price deflator (annual % growth)	7.2	10.7	7.3
Value added in agriculture (% of GDP)	29	35	39
Value added in industry (% of GDP)	5	13	6
Value added in services (% of GDP)	66	53	55
Exports of goods and services (% of GDP)	30	24	26
Imports of goods and services (% of GDP)	65	39	50
Gross capital formation (% of GDP)	20	7	..
Central government revenue (% of GDP)	..	..	..
Central government cash surplus/deficit (% of GDP)	..	..	..
States and markets			
Starting a business (days)	..	56	9
Stock market capitalization (% of GDP)	..	..	..
Military expenditures (% of GDP)	..	..	..
Mobile cellular subscriptions (per 100 people)	0.0	0.3	49.8
Individuals using the Internet (% of population)	0.0	0.5	6.0
Paved roads (% of total)	2.1	2.4	..
High-technology exports (% of manufactured exports)	..	..	72
Global links			
Merchandise trade (% of GDP)	53	37	105
Net barter terms of trade index (2000 = 100)	85	100	88
Total external debt stocks ($ millions)	120	156	256
Total debt service (% of exports)	11.8	7.1	2.0
Net migration (thousands)	-1.9	-0.7	0.0
Remittances received ($ millions)	..	4.3	1.7
Foreign direct investment, net inflows ($ millions)	10	13	146
Net official development assistance received ($ millions)	46	68	334

Somalia

Sub-Saharan Africa		Low income
Population (millions)	9.6	Population growth (%)	2.4
Surface area (1,000 sq. km)	638	Population living below $1.25 a day (%)	..
GNI, Atlas ($ millions)	..	GNI per capita, Atlas ($)	..
GNI, PPP ($ millions)	..	GNI per capita, PPP ($)	..

	1990	2000	2011
People			
Share of poorest 20% in nat'l consumption/income (%)	..	..	..
Life expectancy at birth (years)	45	48	51
Total fertility rate (births per woman)	6.6	6.5	6.3
Adolescent fertility rate (births per 1,000 women 15–19)	..	72	68
Contraceptive prevalence (% of married women 15–49)	..	8	15
Births attended by skilled health staff (% of total)	..	34	33
Under-five mortality rate (per 1,000 live births)	180	180	180
Child malnutrition, underweight (% of under age 5)	..	22.8	32.8
Child immunization, measles (% of ages 12–23 mos.)	30	24	46
Primary completion rate, total (% of relevant age group)	..	..	..
Gross secondary enrollment, total (% of relevant age group)	..	..	..
Ratio of girls to boys in primary & secondary school (%)	..	..	..
HIV prevalence rate (% population of ages 15–49)	0.5	0.9	0.7
Environment			
Forests (1,000 sq. km)	83	75	67
Deforestation (avg. annual %, 1990–2000 and 2000–2010)		1.0	1.1
Freshwater use (% of internal resources)	..	54.8	55.0
Access to improved water source (% total pop.)	19	22	29
Access to improved sanitation facilities (% total pop.)	21	22	23
Energy use per capita (kilograms of oil equivalent)	..	..	..
Carbon dioxide emissions per capita (metric tons)	0.00	0.07	0.07
Electricity use per capita (kilowatt-hours)	..	..	..
Economy			
GDP ($ millions)	917	..	..
GDP growth (annual %)	–1.5	..	..
GDP implicit price deflator (annual % growth)	215.5	..	..
Value added in agriculture (% of GDP)	65	..	..
Value added in industry (% of GDP)	..	..	..
Value added in services (% of GDP)	..	..	..
Exports of goods and services (% of GDP)	10	..	..
Imports of goods and services (% of GDP)	38	..	..
Gross capital formation (% of GDP)	16	..	..
Central government revenue (% of GDP)	..	..	..
Central government cash surplus/deficit (% of GDP)	..	..	..
States and markets			
Starting a business (days)	..	..	..
Stock market capitalization (% of GDP)	..	..	..
Military expenditures (% of GDP)	..	..	..
Mobile cellular subscriptions (per 100 people)	0.0	1.1	6.9
Individuals using the Internet (% of population)	0.0	0.0	1.3
Paved roads (% of total)	11.1	11.8	..
High-technology exports (% of manufactured exports)	..	..	..
Global links			
Merchandise trade (% of GDP)	..	..	..
Net barter terms of trade index (2000 = 100)	..	100	100
Total external debt stocks ($ billions)	2.4	2.6	3.1
Total debt service (% of exports)	47.6	..	..
Net migration (thousands)	–632	–100	–300
Remittances received ($ millions)	..	..	..
Foreign direct investment, net inflows ($ millions)	6	0	102
Net official development assistance received ($ millions)	515	102	1,096

South Africa

Sub-Saharan Africa		Upper middle income	
Population (millions)	50.6	Population growth (%)	1.2
Surface area (1,000 sq. km)	1,219	Population living below $1.25 a day (%)	13.8
GNI, Atlas ($ billions)	352.0	GNI per capita, Atlas ($)	6,960
GNI, PPP ($ billions)	542.0	GNI per capita, PPP ($)	10,710

	1990	2000	2011
People			
Share of poorest 20% in nat'l consumption/income (%)	3.0	3.1	2.7
Life expectancy at birth (years)	62	55	53
Total fertility rate (births per woman)	3.7	2.9	2.4
Adolescent fertility rate (births per 1,000 women 15–19)	..	75	52
Contraceptive prevalence (% of married women 15–49)	57	60	..
Births attended by skilled health staff (% of total)	..	91	..
Under-five mortality rate (per 1,000 live births)	62	74	47
Child malnutrition, underweight (% of under age 5)	..	10.1	8.7
Child immunization, measles (% of ages 12–23 mos.)	79	72	78
Primary completion rate, total (% of relevant age group)	76	86	..
Gross secondary enrollment, total (% of relevant age group)	66	85	94
Ratio of girls to boys in primary & secondary school (%)	103	100	99
HIV prevalence rate (% population of ages 15–49)	0.5	14.8	17.3
Environment			
Forests (1,000 sq. km)	92	92	92
Deforestation (avg. annual %, 1990–2000 and 2000–2010)		0.0	0.0
Freshwater use (% of internal resources)	29.7	27.9	27.9
Access to improved water source (% total pop.)	83	86	91
Access to improved sanitation facilities (% total pop.)	71	75	79
Energy use per capita (kilograms of oil equivalent)	2,584	2,483	2,738
Carbon dioxide emissions per capita (metric tons)	9.5	8.4	10.1
Electricity use per capita (kilowatt-hours)	4,431	4,681	4,803
Economy			
GDP ($ billions)	112	133	408
GDP growth (annual %)	-0.3	4.2	3.1
GDP implicit price deflator (annual % growth)	15.5	8.8	8.0
Value added in agriculture (% of GDP)	5	3	2
Value added in industry (% of GDP)	40	32	31
Value added in services (% of GDP)	55	65	67
Exports of goods and services (% of GDP)	24	28	29
Imports of goods and services (% of GDP)	19	25	29
Gross capital formation (% of GDP)	18	16	20
Central government revenue (% of GDP)	..	26.3	28.5
Central government cash surplus/deficit (% of GDP)	..	-2.0	-4.4
States and markets			
Starting a business (days)	..	38	19
Stock market capitalization (% of GDP)	123.2	154.2	209.6
Military expenditures (% of GDP)	3.7	1.5	1.3
Mobile cellular subscriptions (per 100 people)	0.0	18.6	126.8
Individuals using the Internet (% of population)	0.0	5.3	21.0
Paved roads (% of total)	..	20.3	..
High-technology exports (% of manufactured exports)	7	7	5
Global links			
Merchandise trade (% of GDP)	37	45	54
Net barter terms of trade index (2000 = 100)	104	100	154
Total external debt stocks ($ billions)	0	25	114
Total debt service (% of exports)	..	9.9	5.3
Net migration (thousands)	-123	200	700
Remittances received ($ millions)	136	344	1,158
Foreign direct investment, net inflows ($ millions)	-76	969	5,889
Net official development assistance received ($ millions)	270	486	1,274

South Sudan

Sub-Saharan Africa		Lower middle income	
Population (millions)	10.3	Population growth (%)	3.6
Surface area (1,000 sq. km)	644	Population living below $1.25 a day (%)	..
GNI, Atlas ($ millions)	..	GNI per capita, Atlas ($)	..
GNI, PPP ($ millions)	..	GNI per capita, PPP ($)	..

	1990	2000	2011
People			
Share of poorest 20% in nat'l consumption/income (%)	..	..	..
Life expectancy at birth (years)	..	..	62
Total fertility rate (births per woman)	..	..	3.9
Adolescent fertility rate (births per 1,000 women 15–19)	..	..	..
Contraceptive prevalence (% of married women 15–49)	..	..	4
Births attended by skilled health staff (% of total)	..	..	19
Under-five mortality rate (per 1,000 live births)	217	165	121
Child malnutrition, underweight (% of under age 5)	..	..	..
Child immunization, measles (% of ages 12–23 mos.)	..	..	64
Primary completion rate, total (% of relevant age group)	..	..	..
Gross secondary enrollment, total (% of relevant age group)	..	..	..
Ratio of girls to boys in primary & secondary school (%)	..	..	..
HIV prevalence rate (% population of ages 15–49)	..	..	3.1
Environment			
Forests (1,000 sq. km)	..	..	148
Deforestation (avg. annual %, 1990–2000 and 2000–2010)	..	..	..
Freshwater use (% of internal resources)	..	..	..
Access to improved water source (% total pop.)	..	..	..
Access to improved sanitation facilities (% total pop.)	..	..	..
Energy use per capita (kilograms of oil equivalent)	..	..	..
Carbon dioxide emissions per capita (metric tons)	..	..	..
Electricity use per capita (kilowatt-hours)	..	..	..
Economy			
GDP ($ billions)	..	..	19.2
GDP growth (annual %)	..	..	1.9
GDP implicit price deflator (annual % growth)	..	..	54.2
Value added in agriculture (% of GDP)	..	..	..
Value added in industry (% of GDP)	..	..	..
Value added in services (% of GDP)	..	..	..
Exports of goods and services (% of GDP)	..	..	65
Imports of goods and services (% of GDP)	..	..	27
Gross capital formation (% of GDP)	..	..	..
Central government revenue (% of GDP)	..	..	..
Central government cash surplus/deficit (% of GDP)	..	..	..
States and markets			
Starting a business (days)	..	..	..
Stock market capitalization (% of GDP)	..	..	..
Military expenditures (% of GDP)	..	..	2.9
Mobile cellular subscriptions (per 100 people)	..	..	..
Individuals using the Internet (% of population)	..	..	..
Paved roads (% of total)	..	..	..
High-technology exports (% of manufactured exports)	..	..	..
Global links			
Merchandise trade (% of GDP)	..	..	..
Net barter terms of trade index (2000 = 100)	..	..	..
Total external debt stocks ($ millions)	..	..	..
Total debt service (% of exports)	..	..	..
Net migration (thousands)	..	..	..
Remittances received ($ millions)	..	..	..
Foreign direct investment, net inflows ($ millions)	..	..	..
Net official development assistance received ($ millions)	..	..	..

Spain

Population (millions)	46.2	Population growth (%)	0.2
Surface area (1,000 sq. km)	506	Population living below $1.25 a day (%)	..
GNI, Atlas ($ billions)	1,428.3	GNI per capita, Atlas ($)	30,930
GNI, PPP ($ billions)	1,451.7	GNI per capita, PPP ($)	31,440

	1990	2000	2011
People			
Share of poorest 20% in nat'l consumption/income (%)	..	7.0	..
Life expectancy at birth (years)	77	79	82
Total fertility rate (births per woman)	1.3	1.2	1.4
Adolescent fertility rate (births per 1,000 women 15–19)	..	9	11
Contraceptive prevalence (% of married women 15–49)	..	72	66
Births attended by skilled health staff (% of total)	..	..	..
Under-five mortality rate (per 1,000 live births)	11	7	4
Child malnutrition, underweight (% of under age 5)	..	1.6	..
Child immunization, measles (% of ages 12–23 mos.)	99	94	95
Primary completion rate, total (% of relevant age group)	101	..	103
Gross secondary enrollment, total (% of relevant age group)	102	111	125
Ratio of girls to boys in primary & secondary school (%)	103	103	101
HIV prevalence rate (% population of ages 15–49)	0.4	0.5	0.4
Environment			
Forests (1,000 sq. km)	138	170	183
Deforestation (avg. annual %, 1990–2000 and 2000–2010)		-2.1	-0.7
Freshwater use (% of internal resources)	33.2	33.0	29.2
Access to improved water source (% total pop.)	100	100	100
Access to improved sanitation facilities (% total pop.)	100	100	100
Energy use per capita (kilograms of oil equivalent)	2,319	3,029	2,727
Carbon dioxide emissions per capita (metric tons)	5.6	7.3	6.3
Electricity use per capita (kilowatt-hours)	3,538	5,207	6,155
Economy			
GDP ($ billions)	521	580	1,477
GDP growth (annual %)	3.8	5.0	0.4
GDP implicit price deflator (annual % growth)	7.3	3.4	1.0
Value added in agriculture (% of GDP)	6	4	3
Value added in industry (% of GDP)	34	29	26
Value added in services (% of GDP)	61	66	71
Exports of goods and services (% of GDP)	16	29	30
Imports of goods and services (% of GDP)	19	32	31
Gross capital formation (% of GDP)	26	26	22
Central government revenue (% of GDP)	..	31.1	23.2
Central government cash surplus/deficit (% of GDP)	..	-0.5	-3.5
States and markets			
Starting a business (days)	..	114	28
Stock market capitalization (% of GDP)	21.3	86.9	69.8
Military expenditures (% of GDP)	1.7	1.2	1.0
Mobile cellular subscriptions (per 100 people)	0.1	60.2	113.2
Individuals using the Internet (% of population)	0.0	13.6	67.6
Paved roads (% of total)	99.0	99.0	..
High-technology exports (% of manufactured exports)	7	8	6
Global links			
Merchandise trade (% of GDP)	28	47	46
Net barter terms of trade index (2000 = 100)	..	100	99
Total external debt stocks ($ millions)	..	..	..
Total debt service (% of exports)	..	..	..
Net migration (thousands)	-68	796	2,250
Remittances received ($ billions)	2.2	4.9	9.9
Foreign direct investment, net inflows ($ billions)	14.0	38.8	31.4
Net official development assistance received ($ millions)	..	..	..

Sri Lanka

South Asia		**Lower middle income**	
Population (millions)	20.9	Population growth (%)	1.0
Surface area (1,000 sq. km)	66	Population living below $1.25 a day (%)	4.1
GNI, Atlas ($ billions)	53.8	GNI per capita, Atlas ($)	2,580
GNI, PPP ($ billions)	115.2	GNI per capita, PPP ($)	5,520

	1990	2000	2011
People			
Share of poorest 20% in nat'l consumption/income (%)	8.7	6.8	6.9
Life expectancy at birth (years)	70	71	75
Total fertility rate (births per woman)	2.5	2.2	2.3
Adolescent fertility rate (births per 1,000 women 15-19)	..	28	22
Contraceptive prevalence (% of married women 15-49)	66	70	68
Births attended by skilled health staff (% of total)	94	96	99
Under-five mortality rate (per 1,000 live births)	29	19	12
Child malnutrition, underweight (% of under age 5)	33.8	22.8	21.6
Child immunization, measles (% of ages 12-23 mos.)	80	99	99
Primary completion rate, total (% of relevant age group)	97	107	101
Gross secondary enrollment, total (% of relevant age group)	72	..	100
Ratio of girls to boys in primary & secondary school (%)	102	..	102
HIV prevalence rate (% population of ages 15-49)	0.1	0.1	0.1
Environment			
Forests (1,000 sq. km)	24	21	18
Deforestation (avg. annual %, 1990-2000 and 2000-2010)		1.2	1.1
Freshwater use (% of internal resources)	18.5	24.6	24.5
Access to improved water source (% total pop.)	67	80	91
Access to improved sanitation facilities (% total pop.)	70	82	92
Energy use per capita (kilograms of oil equivalent)	324	436	478
Carbon dioxide emissions per capita (metric tons)	0.2	0.5	0.6
Electricity use per capita (kilowatt-hours)	154	290	449
Economy			
GDP ($ billions)	8.0	16.3	59.2
GDP growth (annual %)	6.4	6.0	8.3
GDP implicit price deflator (annual % growth)	20.1	7.3	7.8
Value added in agriculture (% of GDP)	26	20	12
Value added in industry (% of GDP)	26	27	30
Value added in services (% of GDP)	48	53	58
Exports of goods and services (% of GDP)	30	39	23
Imports of goods and services (% of GDP)	38	50	38
Gross capital formation (% of GDP)	22	28	30
Central government revenue (% of GDP)	21.0	16.8	14.3
Central government cash surplus/deficit (% of GDP)	-5.2	-8.4	-6.4
States and markets			
Starting a business (days)	..	58	7
Stock market capitalization (% of GDP)	11.4	6.6	32.8
Military expenditures (% of GDP)	2.3	5.0	2.6
Mobile cellular subscriptions (per 100 people)	0.0	2.3	87.0
Individuals using the Internet (% of population)	0.0	0.6	15.0
Paved roads (% of total)	..	85.8	14.9
High-technology exports (% of manufactured exports)	1	3	1
Global links			
Merchandise trade (% of GDP)	57	77	52
Net barter terms of trade index (2000 = 100)	82	100	72
Total external debt stocks ($ billions)	5.9	9.2	24.0
Total debt service (% of exports)	16.1	12.1	9.3
Net migration (thousands)	-137	-400	-250
Remittances received ($ billions)	0.4	1.2	5.2
Foreign direct investment, net inflows ($ millions)	43	173	956
Net official development assistance received ($ millions)	728	275	611

St. Kitts and Nevis

High income

Population (thousands)	53	Population growth (%)	1.2
Surface area (sq. km)	260	Population living below $1.25 a day (%)	..
GNI, Atlas ($ millions)	668.9	GNI per capita, Atlas ($)	12,610
GNI, PPP ($ millions)	874.0	GNI per capita, PPP ($)	16,470

	1990	2000	2011
People			
Share of poorest 20% in nat'l consumption/income (%)	..	..	..
Life expectancy at birth (years)	68	71	..
Total fertility rate (births per woman)	2.6	2.1	..
Adolescent fertility rate (births per 1,000 women 15-19)	..	..	..
Contraceptive prevalence (% of married women 15-49)	..	..	54
Births attended by skilled health staff (% of total)	..	99	100
Under-five mortality rate (per 1,000 live births)	28	16	7
Child malnutrition, underweight (% of under age 5)	..	..	..
Child immunization, measles (% of ages 12-23 mos.)	99	99	99
Primary completion rate, total (% of relevant age group)	117	101	93
Gross secondary enrollment, total (% of relevant age group)	83	97	94
Ratio of girls to boys in primary & secondary school (%)	101	100	103
HIV prevalence rate (% population of ages 15-49)	..	..	..
Environment			
Forests (sq. km)	110	110	110
Deforestation (avg. annual %, 1990-2000 and 2000-2010)		0.0	0.0
Freshwater use (% of internal resources)	..	..	..
Access to improved water source (% total pop.)	99	99	99
Access to improved sanitation facilities (% total pop.)	96	96	96
Energy use per capita (kilograms of oil equivalent)	514	..	..
Carbon dioxide emissions per capita (metric tons)	1.6	2.3	5.0
Electricity use per capita (kilowatt-hours)	..	..	..
Economy			
GDP ($ millions)	159	417	697
GDP growth (annual %)	2.3	0.7	2.1
GDP implicit price deflator (annual % growth)	8.7	27.0	1.4
Value added in agriculture (% of GDP)	6	2	2
Value added in industry (% of GDP)	29	31	23
Value added in services (% of GDP)	65	68	75
Exports of goods and services (% of GDP)	52	36	33
Imports of goods and services (% of GDP)	83	60	45
Gross capital formation (% of GDP)	55	43	32
Central government revenue (% of GDP)	28.3	23.2	34.5
Central government cash surplus/deficit (% of GDP)	0.6	-8.2	2.6
States and markets			
Starting a business (days)	..	..	19
Stock market capitalization (% of GDP)	..	53.1	85.8
Military expenditures (% of GDP)	..	..	..
Mobile cellular subscriptions (per 100 people)	0.0	2.6	152.7
Individuals using the Internet (% of population)	0.0	5.9	76.0
Paved roads (% of total)	38.5	42.5	..
High-technology exports (% of manufactured exports)	5	1	0
Global links			
Merchandise trade (% of GDP)	87	55	42
Net barter terms of trade index (2000 = 100)	..	100	67
Total external debt stocks ($ millions)	..	..	..
Total debt service (% of exports)	..	..	..
Net migration (thousands)	..	..	..
Remittances received ($ millions)	19.3	27.1	47.5
Foreign direct investment, net inflows ($ millions)	49	96	114
Net official development assistance received ($ millions)	8.1	3.9	16.5

St. Vincent and Grenadines

Latin America & Caribbean		Upper middle income	
Population (thousands)	109	Population growth (%)	0.0
Surface area (sq. km)	390	Population living below $1.25 a day (%)	..
GNI, Atlas ($ millions)	663.9	GNI per capita, Atlas ($)	6,070
GNI, PPP ($ millions)	1,141.9	GNI per capita, PPP ($)	10,440

	1990	2000	2011
People			
Share of poorest 20% in nat'l consumption/income (%)	..	..	..
Life expectancy at birth (years)	69	70	72
Total fertility rate (births per woman)	3.0	2.4	2.0
Adolescent fertility rate (births per 1,000 women 15–19)	..	69	55
Contraceptive prevalence (% of married women 15–49)	58	58	48
Births attended by skilled health staff (% of total)	..	100	99
Under-five mortality rate (per 1,000 live births)	27	22	21
Child malnutrition, underweight (% of under age 5)	..	..	..
Child immunization, measles (% of ages 12–23 mos.)	96	95	99
Primary completion rate, total (% of relevant age group)	..	93	94
Gross secondary enrollment, total (% of relevant age group)	60	82	107
Ratio of girls to boys in primary & secondary school (%)	107	106	97
HIV prevalence rate (% population of ages 15–49)	..	..	..
Environment			
Forests (sq. km)	253	260	268
Deforestation (avg. annual %, 1990–2000 and 2000–2010)		-0.3	-0.3
Freshwater use (% of internal resources)	..	..	..
Access to improved water source (% total pop.)	..	..	..
Access to improved sanitation facilities (% total pop.)	..	..	..
Energy use per capita (kilograms of oil equivalent)	274	..	..
Carbon dioxide emissions per capita (metric tons)	0.8	1.5	1.8
Electricity use per capita (kilowatt-hours)	..	..	..
Economy			
GDP ($ millions)	198	397	688
GDP growth (annual %)	5.0	-0.6	0.1
GDP implicit price deflator (annual % growth)	6.4	20.4	1.8
Value added in agriculture (% of GDP)	21	9	6
Value added in industry (% of GDP)	23	20	20
Value added in services (% of GDP)	56	72	74
Exports of goods and services (% of GDP)	66	45	27
Imports of goods and services (% of GDP)	77	50	56
Gross capital formation (% of GDP)	30	23	25
Central government revenue (% of GDP)	25.6	25.9	24.5
Central government cash surplus/deficit (% of GDP)	..	-1.4	-3.7
States and markets			
Starting a business (days)	..	..	10
Stock market capitalization (% of GDP)	..	..	..
Military expenditures (% of GDP)	..	..	..
Mobile cellular subscriptions (per 100 people)	0.0	2.2	120.5
Individuals using the Internet (% of population)	0.0	3.2	43.0
Paved roads (% of total)	..	68.0	..
High-technology exports (% of manufactured exports)	0	0	0
Global links			
Merchandise trade (% of GDP)	110	53	54
Net barter terms of trade index (2000 = 100)	..	100	107
Total external debt stocks ($ millions)	63	195	283
Total debt service (% of exports)	3.3	7.2	15.2
Net migration (thousands)	-6.7	-7.6	-5.0
Remittances received ($ millions)	15.6	22.5	29.5
Foreign direct investment, net inflows ($ millions)	8	38	110
Net official development assistance received ($ millions)	15.4	6.2	18.8

Sudan

Sub-Saharan Africa		Lower middle income	
Population (millions)	34.3[f]	Population growth (%)	2.1[f]
Surface area (1,000 sq. km)	1,861[f]	Population living below $1.25 a day (%)	19.8
GNI, Atlas ($ billions)	58.3[f]	GNI per capita, Atlas ($)	1,310[g]
GNI, PPP ($ billions)	94.7[g]	GNI per capita, PPP ($)	2,120[g]

	1990	2000	2011
People			
Share of poorest 20% in nat'l consumption/income (%)	..	..	6.8
Life expectancy at birth (years)	53	57	61
Total fertility rate (births per woman)	6.0	5.3	4.3
Adolescent fertility rate (births per 1,000 women 15–19)	..	79	55
Contraceptive prevalence (% of married women 15–49)	9	7	9
Births attended by skilled health staff (% of total)	69	..	23[f]
Under-five mortality rate (per 1,000 live births)[f]	123	104	86
Child malnutrition, underweight (% of under age 5)	31.8	38.4	31.7
Child immunization, measles (% of ages 12–23 mos.)	57	58	87
Primary completion rate, total (% of relevant age group)	..	37	58
Gross secondary enrollment, total (% of relevant age group)	21	25	39
Ratio of girls to boys in primary & secondary school (%)	78	88	90
HIV prevalence rate (% population of ages 15–49)	0.2	0.6	0.4
Environment			
Forests (1,000 sq. km)	764	705	699
Deforestation (avg. annual %, 1990–2000 and 2000–2010)		0.8	0.1
Freshwater use (% of internal resources)	51.7	123.8	123.8
Access to improved water source (% total pop.)	65	62	58
Access to improved sanitation facilities (% total pop.)	27	27	26
Energy use per capita (kilograms of oil equivalent)	401	390	371
Carbon dioxide emissions per capita (metric tons)	0.2	0.2	0.3
Electricity use per capita (kilowatt-hours)	48	63	141
Economy			
GDP ($ billions)	12.4	12.3	64.1[g]
GDP growth (annual %)	-5.5	8.4	4.7[g]
GDP implicit price deflator (annual % growth)	66.2	7.8	9.2[g]
Value added in agriculture (% of GDP)	41	42	24[g]
Value added in industry (% of GDP)	15	21	28[g]
Value added in services (% of GDP)	44	37	47[g]
Exports of goods and services (% of GDP)	4	16	18[g]
Imports of goods and services (% of GDP)	7	13	16[g]
Gross capital formation (% of GDP)	11	25	22[g]
Central government revenue (% of GDP)	..	8.0	..
Central government cash surplus/deficit (% of GDP)	..	-0.4	..
States and markets			
Starting a business (days)	..	..	36
Stock market capitalization (% of GDP)	..	..	..
Military expenditures (% of GDP)	2.6	4.8	..
Mobile cellular subscriptions (per 100 people)	0.0	0.1	56.1
Individuals using the Internet (% of population)	0.0	0.0	19.0
Paved roads (% of total)	33.8	36.3	..
High-technology exports (% of manufactured exports)	..	4	29
Global links			
Merchandise trade (% of GDP)	8	27	30
Net barter terms of trade index (2000 = 100)	100	100	229
Total external debt stocks ($ billions)	14.8	16.1	21.2
Total debt service (% of exports)	9.7	13.5	4.2
Net migration (thousands)	-459	-227	135
Remittances received ($ millions)	62	641	1,420
Foreign direct investment, net inflows ($ millions)	-31	392	1,936
Net official development assistance received ($ millions)	848	225	1,138

Sweden

High income

Population (millions)	9.4	Population growth (%)		0.8
Surface area (1,000 sq. km)	450	Population living below $1.25 a day (%)		..
GNI, Atlas ($ billions)	502.5	GNI per capita, Atlas ($)		53,170
GNI, PPP ($ billions)	398.9	GNI per capita, PPP ($)		42,210

	1990	2000	2011
People			
Share of poorest 20% in nat'l consumption/income (%)	..	9.1	..
Life expectancy at birth (years)	78	80	82
Total fertility rate (births per woman)	2.1	1.5	1.9
Adolescent fertility rate (births per 1,000 women 15–19)	..	8	6
Contraceptive prevalence (% of married women 15–49)	..	..	..
Births attended by skilled health staff (% of total)	..	..	..
Under-five mortality rate (per 1,000 live births)	7	4	3
Child malnutrition, underweight (% of under age 5)	..	..	..
Child immunization, measles (% of ages 12–23 mos.)	96	91	96
Primary completion rate, total (% of relevant age group)	97	100	97
Gross secondary enrollment, total (% of relevant age group)	90	152	99
Ratio of girls to boys in primary & secondary school (%)	102	115	99
HIV prevalence rate (% population of ages 15–49)	0.1	0.2	0.2
Environment			
Forests (1,000 sq. km)	273	274	282
Deforestation (avg. annual %, 1990–2000 and 2000–2010)		0.0	-0.3
Freshwater use (% of internal resources)	1.7	1.6	1.5
Access to improved water source (% total pop.)	100	100	100
Access to improved sanitation facilities (% total pop.)	100	100	100
Energy use per capita (kilograms of oil equivalent)	5,515	5,360	5,228
Carbon dioxide emissions per capita (metric tons)	6.0	5.6	4.7
Electricity use per capita (kilowatt-hours)	15,836	15,682	14,939
Economy			
GDP ($ billions)	244	247	540
GDP growth (annual %)	1.0	4.5	3.9
GDP implicit price deflator (annual % growth)	8.7	1.4	1.0
Value added in agriculture (% of GDP)	4	2	2
Value added in industry (% of GDP)	31	29	26
Value added in services (% of GDP)	65	69	72
Exports of goods and services (% of GDP)	30	47	50
Imports of goods and services (% of GDP)	30	40	44
Gross capital formation (% of GDP)	24	19	20
Central government revenue (% of GDP)	..	39.6	32.4
Central government cash surplus/deficit (% of GDP)	..	3.5	0.5
States and markets			
Starting a business (days)	..	16	16
Stock market capitalization (% of GDP)	40.1	132.8	87.1
Military expenditures (% of GDP)	2.5	2.0	1.3
Mobile cellular subscriptions (per 100 people)	5.4	71.9	118.6
Individuals using the Internet (% of population)	0.6	45.7	91.0
Paved roads (% of total)	..	31.2	23.4
High-technology exports (% of manufactured exports)	13	23	13
Global links			
Merchandise trade (% of GDP)	46	65	67
Net barter terms of trade index (2000 = 100)	..	100	87
Total external debt stocks ($ millions)	..	..	..
Total debt service (% of exports)	..	..	..
Net migration (thousands)	132	49	266
Remittances received ($ millions)	153	438	776
Foreign direct investment, net inflows ($ billions)	2.0	23.9	3.1
Net official development assistance received ($ millions)	..	..	..

Switzerland

High income

Population (millions)	7.9
Surface area (1,000 sq. km)	41
GNI, Atlas ($ billions)	604.1
GNI, PPP ($ billions)	415.6

Population growth (%)	1.1
Population living below $1.25 a day (%)	..
GNI per capita, Atlas ($)	76,350
GNI per capita, PPP ($)	52,530

	1990	2000	2011
People			
Share of poorest 20% in nat'l consumption/income (%)	..	7.6	..
Life expectancy at birth (years)	77	80	83
Total fertility rate (births per woman)	1.6	1.5	1.5
Adolescent fertility rate (births per 1,000 women 15–19)	..	5	4
Contraceptive prevalence (% of married women 15–49)	..	..	..
Births attended by skilled health staff (% of total)	..	..	100
Under-five mortality rate (per 1,000 live births)	8	6	4
Child malnutrition, underweight (% of under age 5)	..	..	..
Child immunization, measles (% of ages 12–23 mos.)	90	81	92
Primary completion rate, total (% of relevant age group)	51	96	96
Gross secondary enrollment, total (% of relevant age group)	96	95	95
Ratio of girls to boys in primary & secondary school (%)	97	97	98
HIV prevalence rate (% population of ages 15–49)	0.2	0.3	0.4
Environment			
Forests (1,000 sq. km)	12	12	12
Deforestation (avg. annual %, 1990–2000 and 2000–2010)		-0.4	-0.4
Freshwater use (% of internal resources)	..	6.5	6.5
Access to improved water source (% total pop.)	100	100	100
Access to improved sanitation facilities (% total pop.)	100	100	100
Energy use per capita (kilograms of oil equivalent)	3,621	3,481	3,225
Carbon dioxide emissions per capita (metric tons)	6.4	5.4	5.4
Electricity use per capita (kilowatt-hours)	7,503	7,845	8,175
Economy			
GDP ($ billions)	244	256	659
GDP growth (annual %)	3.7	3.7	1.9
GDP implicit price deflator (annual % growth)	4.6	1.5	0.2
Value added in agriculture (% of GDP)	..	..	..
Value added in industry (% of GDP)	31	27	26
Value added in services (% of GDP)	..	..	..
Exports of goods and services (% of GDP)	36	45	51
Imports of goods and services (% of GDP)	35	40	40
Gross capital formation (% of GDP)	30	23	21
Central government revenue (% of GDP)	19.6	23.7	17.6
Central government cash surplus/deficit (% of GDP)		2.1	1.3
States and markets			
Starting a business (days)	..	20	18
Stock market capitalization (% of GDP)	65.6	309.4	141.4
Military expenditures (% of GDP)	1.7	1.1	0.8
Mobile cellular subscriptions (per 100 people)	1.9	64.7	131.4
Individuals using the Internet (% of population)	0.6	47.1	85.2
Paved roads (% of total)	..	100.0	100.0
High-technology exports (% of manufactured exports)	16	22	24
Global links			
Merchandise trade (% of GDP)	55	64	67
Net barter terms of trade index (2000 = 100)	..	100	80
Total external debt stocks ($ millions)	..	..	..
Total debt service (% of exports)	..	..	..
Net migration (thousands)	131	65	183
Remittances received ($ billions)	0.9	1.1	3.3
Foreign direct investment, net inflows ($ billions)	5.5	19.8	10.1
Net official development assistance received ($ millions)	..	..	..

Tanzania

Sub-Saharan Africa		Low income	
Population (millions)	46.2	Population growth (%)	3.0
Surface area (1,000 sq. km)	947	Population living below $1.25 a day (%)	67.9
GNI, Atlas ($ billions)	24.2	GNI per capita, Atlas ($)	540
GNI, PPP ($ billions)	67.1	GNI per capita, PPP ($)	1,500

	1990	2000	2011
People			
Share of poorest 20% in nat'l consumption/income (%)	7.4	7.3	6.8
Life expectancy at birth (years)	51	50	58
Total fertility rate (births per woman)	6.2	5.7	5.5
Adolescent fertility rate (births per 1,000 women 15–19)	..	133	129
Contraceptive prevalence (% of married women 15–49)	10	25	34
Births attended by skilled health staff (% of total)	44	36	49
Under-five mortality rate (per 1,000 live births)	158	126	68
Child malnutrition, underweight (% of under age 5)	25.1	25.3	16.2
Child immunization, measles (% of ages 12–23 mos.)	80	78	93
Primary completion rate, total (% of relevant age group)	48	55	81
Gross secondary enrollment, total (% of relevant age group)	5	..	35
Ratio of girls to boys in primary & secondary school (%)	97	..	100
HIV prevalence rate (% population of ages 15–49)	5.0	7.5	5.8
Environment			
Forests (1,000 sq. km)	415	375	330
Deforestation (avg. annual %, 1990–2000 and 2000–2010)		1.0	1.1
Freshwater use (% of internal resources)	..	6.2	6.2
Access to improved water source (% total pop.)	55	54	53
Access to improved sanitation facilities (% total pop.)	7	9	10
Energy use per capita (kilograms of oil equivalent)	382	393	448
Carbon dioxide emissions per capita (metric tons)	0.09	0.08	0.16
Electricity use per capita (kilowatt-hours)	51	58	78
Economy			
GDP ($ billions)	4.3	10.2	23.9
GDP growth (annual %)	7.0	4.9	6.4
GDP implicit price deflator (annual % growth)	22.4	7.6	9.2
Value added in agriculture (% of GDP)	46	33	28
Value added in industry (% of GDP)	18	19	25
Value added in services (% of GDP)	36	47	47
Exports of goods and services (% of GDP)	13	13	31
Imports of goods and services (% of GDP)	37	20	50
Gross capital formation (% of GDP)	26	17	37
Central government revenue (% of GDP)	..	..	..
Central government cash surplus/deficit (% of GDP)	..	..	..
States and markets			
Starting a business (days)	..	28	26
Stock market capitalization (% of GDP)	..	2.3	6.4
Military expenditures (% of GDP)	2.0	1.3	1.1
Mobile cellular subscriptions (per 100 people)	0.0	0.3	55.5
Individuals using the Internet (% of population)	0.0	0.1	12.0
Paved roads (% of total)	..	8.6	14.9
High-technology exports (% of manufactured exports)	..	1	5
Global links			
Merchandise trade (% of GDP)	32	22	66
Net barter terms of trade index (2000 = 100)	107	100	151
Total external debt stocks ($ billions)	6.4	7.2	10.0
Total debt service (% of exports)	32.9	11.9	2.0
Net migration (thousands)	68	-206	-300
Remittances received ($ millions)	..	8.0	75.8
Foreign direct investment, net inflows ($ millions)	0	463	1,095
Net official development assistance received ($ billions)	1.2	1.1	2.4

Thailand

East Asia & Pacific		Upper middle income	
Population (millions)	69.5	Population growth (%)	0.6
Surface area (1,000 sq. km)	513	Population living below $1.25 a day (%)	<2
GNI, Atlas ($ billions)	308.3	GNI per capita, Atlas ($)	4,440
GNI, PPP ($ billions)	581.4	GNI per capita, PPP ($)	8,360

	1990	2000	2011
People			
Share of poorest 20% in nat'l consumption/income (%)	5.9	6.2	6.7
Life expectancy at birth (years)	72	73	74
Total fertility rate (births per woman)	2.1	1.7	1.6
Adolescent fertility rate (births per 1,000 women 15–19)	..	44	38
Contraceptive prevalence (% of married women 15–49)	66	79	80
Births attended by skilled health staff (% of total)	..	99	100
Under-five mortality rate (per 1,000 live births)	35	19	12
Child malnutrition, underweight (% of under age 5)	16.3	..	7.0
Child immunization, measles (% of ages 12–23 mos.)	80	94	98
Primary completion rate, total (% of relevant age group)	..	88	..
Gross secondary enrollment, total (% of relevant age group)	28	62	79
Ratio of girls to boys in primary & secondary school (%)	98	98	103
HIV prevalence rate (% population of ages 15–49)	1.0	1.8	1.2
Environment			
Forests (1,000 sq. km)	195	190	190
Deforestation (avg. annual %, 1990–2000 and 2000–2010)		0.3	0.0
Freshwater use (% of internal resources)	..	..	25.5
Access to improved water source (% total pop.)	86	92	96
Access to improved sanitation facilities (% total pop.)	84	94	96
Energy use per capita (kilograms of oil equivalent)	735	1,145	1,699
Carbon dioxide emissions per capita (metric tons)	1.7	3.2	4.0
Electricity use per capita (kilowatt-hours)	703	1,443	2,243
Economy			
GDP ($ billions)	85	123	346
GDP growth (annual %)	11.2	4.8	0.1
GDP implicit price deflator (annual % growth)	5.8	1.3	4.2
Value added in agriculture (% of GDP)	12	9	12
Value added in industry (% of GDP)	37	42	41
Value added in services (% of GDP)	50	49	46
Exports of goods and services (% of GDP)	34	67	77
Imports of goods and services (% of GDP)	42	58	72
Gross capital formation (% of GDP)	41	23	27
Central government revenue (% of GDP)	..	19.5	21.3
Central government cash surplus/deficit (% of GDP)	..	1.5	-1.2
States and markets			
Starting a business (days)	..	33	29
Stock market capitalization (% of GDP)	28.0	24.0	77.7
Military expenditures (% of GDP)	2.7	1.5	1.6
Mobile cellular subscriptions (per 100 people)	0.1	4.8	111.6
Individuals using the Internet (% of population)	0.0	3.7	23.7
Paved roads (% of total)	88.4	98.5	..
High-technology exports (% of manufactured exports)	21	33	21
Global links			
Merchandise trade (% of GDP)	66	107	132
Net barter terms of trade index (2000 = 100)	119	100	94
Total external debt stocks ($ billions)	28.1	79.8	80.0
Total debt service (% of exports)	16.9	16.3	3.8
Net migration (thousands)	505	596	492
Remittances received ($ billions)	1.0	1.7	4.6
Foreign direct investment, net inflows ($ billions)	2.4	3.4	7.8
Net official development assistance received ($ millions)	796	697	-153

Tonga

East Asia & Pacific **Lower middle income**

Population (thousands)	105	Population growth (%)	0.4
Surface area (sq. km)	750	Population living below $1.25 a day (%)	..
GNI, Atlas ($ millions)	399.0	GNI per capita, Atlas ($)	3,820
GNI, PPP ($ millions)	522.7	GNI per capita, PPP ($)	5,000

	1990	2000	2011
People			
Share of poorest 20% in nat'l consumption/income (%)	..	..	..
Life expectancy at birth (years)	70	71	72
Total fertility rate (births per woman)	4.6	4.3	3.9
Adolescent fertility rate (births per 1,000 women 15-19)	..	22	19
Contraceptive prevalence (% of married women 15-49)	..	33	32
Births attended by skilled health staff (% of total)	92	95	98
Under-five mortality rate (per 1,000 live births)	25	20	15
Child malnutrition, underweight (% of under age 5)	..	..	..
Child immunization, measles (% of ages 12-23 mos.)	86	95	99
Primary completion rate, total (% of relevant age group)	128	107	..
Gross secondary enrollment, total (% of relevant age group)	98	106	..
Ratio of girls to boys in primary & secondary school (%)	99	102	..
HIV prevalence rate (% population of ages 15-49)	..	..	..
Environment			
Forests (sq. km)	90	90	90
Deforestation (avg. annual %, 1990-2000 and 2000-2010)		0.0	0.0
Freshwater use (% of internal resources)	..	..	..
Access to improved water source (% total pop.)	100	100	100
Access to improved sanitation facilities (% total pop.)	96	96	96
Energy use per capita (kilograms of oil equivalent)	266	..	..
Carbon dioxide emissions per capita (metric tons)	0.8	1.2	1.7
Electricity use per capita (kilowatt-hours)	..	..	..
Economy			
GDP ($ millions)	114	189	434
GDP growth (annual %)	-2.0	3.4	4.9
GDP implicit price deflator (annual % growth)	12.2	3.1	5.2
Value added in agriculture (% of GDP)	36	23	20
Value added in industry (% of GDP)	14	21	22
Value added in services (% of GDP)	50	56	58
Exports of goods and services (% of GDP)	34	15	18
Imports of goods and services (% of GDP)	65	47	61
Gross capital formation (% of GDP)	18	22	38
Central government revenue (% of GDP)	..	..	..
Central government cash surplus/deficit (% of GDP)	..	..	..
States and markets			
Starting a business (days)	..	32	16
Stock market capitalization (% of GDP)	..	..	..
Military expenditures (% of GDP)	..	..	..
Mobile cellular subscriptions (per 100 people)	0.0	0.2	52.6
Individuals using the Internet (% of population)	0.0	2.4	25.0
Paved roads (% of total)	..	27.0	..
High-technology exports (% of manufactured exports)	..	0	0
Global links			
Merchandise trade (% of GDP)	64	42	45
Net barter terms of trade index (2000 = 100)	..	100	81
Total external debt stocks ($ millions)	44	74	191
Total debt service (% of exports)	3.5	8.9	8.8
Net migration (thousands)	-10.9	-8.7	-8.2
Remittances received ($ millions)	24.0	52.5	71.5
Foreign direct investment, net inflows ($ millions)	0.2	4.8	10.4
Net official development assistance received ($ millions)	29.8	18.8	93.7

Trinidad and Tobago

High income

Population (millions)	1.3	Population growth (%)	0.4
Surface area (1,000 sq. km)	5.1	Population living below $1.25 a day (%)	..
GNI, Atlas ($ billions)	21.3	GNI per capita, Atlas ($)	15,840
GNI, PPP ($ billions)	32.7	GNI per capita, PPP ($)	24,350

	1990	2000	2011
People			
Share of poorest 20% in nat'l consumption/income (%)	5.5	..	..
Life expectancy at birth (years)	69	68	70
Total fertility rate (births per woman)	2.4	1.6	1.6
Adolescent fertility rate (births per 1,000 women 15–19)	..	38	32
Contraceptive prevalence (% of married women 15–49)	..	38	43
Births attended by skilled health staff (% of total)	..	96	98
Under-five mortality rate (per 1,000 live births)	37	32	28
Child malnutrition, underweight (% of under age 5)	..	4.4	..
Child immunization, measles (% of ages 12–23 mos.)	70	90	92
Primary completion rate, total (% of relevant age group)	102	87	91
Gross secondary enrollment, total (% of relevant age group)	85	76	90
Ratio of girls to boys in primary & secondary school (%)	102	103	101
HIV prevalence rate (% population of ages 15–49)	0.2	1.3	1.5
Environment			
Forests (1,000 sq. km)	2.4	2.3	2.3
Deforestation (avg. annual %, 1990–2000 and 2000–2010)		0.3	0.3
Freshwater use (% of internal resources)	..	6.0	6.0
Access to improved water source (% total pop.)	88	91	94
Access to improved sanitation facilities (% total pop.)	93	92	92
Energy use per capita (kilograms of oil equivalent)	4,926	8,260	15,913
Carbon dioxide emissions per capita (metric tons)	14.0	19.0	35.8
Electricity use per capita (kilowatt-hours)	2,697	3,916	5,894
Economy			
GDP ($ billions)	5.1	8.2	22.5
GDP growth (annual %)	1.5	6.1	-4.1
GDP implicit price deflator (annual % growth)	15.5	12.9	12.8
Value added in agriculture (% of GDP)	3	1	1
Value added in industry (% of GDP)	47	49	60
Value added in services (% of GDP)	50	49	40
Exports of goods and services (% of GDP)	45	59	58
Imports of goods and services (% of GDP)	29	45	33
Gross capital formation (% of GDP)	13	20	11
Central government revenue (% of GDP)	28.1	27.1	33.4
Central government cash surplus/deficit (% of GDP)	-0.2	2.0	-4.8
States and markets			
Starting a business (days)	..	..	41
Stock market capitalization (% of GDP)	13.7	53.1	65.5
Military expenditures (% of GDP)	0.1	..	..
Mobile cellular subscriptions (per 100 people)	0.0	12.5	135.6
Individuals using the Internet (% of population)	0.0	7.7	55.2
Paved roads (% of total)	46.2	51.1	..
High-technology exports (% of manufactured exports)	0	1	0
Global links			
Merchandise trade (% of GDP)	61	93	102
Net barter terms of trade index (2000 = 100)	100	100	153
Total external debt stocks ($ millions)	..	..	..
Total debt service (% of exports)	..	..	..
Net migration (thousands)	-62.1	-19.8	-19.8
Remittances received ($ millions)	3.4	38.1	90.9
Foreign direct investment, net inflows ($ millions)	109	680	574
Net official development assistance received ($ millions)	17.8	-1.5	4.3

Tunisia

Middle East & North Africa			Upper middle income

Population (millions)	10.7	Population growth (%)	1.2
Surface area (1,000 sq. km)	164	Population living below $1.25 a day (%)	<2
GNI, Atlas ($ billions)	42.9	GNI per capita, Atlas ($)	4,020
GNI, PPP ($ billions)	96.0	GNI per capita, PPP ($)	8,990

	1990	2000	2011
People			
Share of poorest 20% in nat'l consumption/income (%)	5.9	6.0	..
Life expectancy at birth (years)	70	73	75
Total fertility rate (births per woman)	3.6	2.1	2.1
Adolescent fertility rate (births per 1,000 women 15–19)	..	7	5
Contraceptive prevalence (% of married women 15–49)	50	66	60
Births attended by skilled health staff (% of total)	69	90	95
Under-five mortality rate (per 1,000 live births)	51	30	16
Child malnutrition, underweight (% of under age 5)	8.5	3.5	3.3
Child immunization, measles (% of ages 12–23 mos.)	93	95	96
Primary completion rate, total (% of relevant age group)	80	88	91
Gross secondary enrollment, total (% of relevant age group)	44	76	93
Ratio of girls to boys in primary & secondary school (%)	83	98	100
HIV prevalence rate (% population of ages 15–49)	0.1	0.1	0.1
Environment			
Forests (1,000 sq. km)	6	8	10
Deforestation (avg. annual %, 1990–2000 and 2000–2010)		-2.7	-1.9
Freshwater use (% of internal resources)	73.3	67.9	67.9
Access to improved water source (% total pop.)	81	90	94
Access to improved sanitation facilities (% total pop.)	74	81	85
Energy use per capita (kilograms of oil equivalent)	607	764	913
Carbon dioxide emissions per capita (metric tons)	1.6	2.1	2.4
Electricity use per capita (kilowatt-hours)	638	991	1,350
Economy			
GDP ($ billions)	12.3	21.5	46.4
GDP growth (annual %)	7.9	4.7	-2.0
GDP implicit price deflator (annual % growth)	4.5	3.3	5.0
Value added in agriculture (% of GDP)	18	11	9
Value added in industry (% of GDP)	34	30	31
Value added in services (% of GDP)	49	58	60
Exports of goods and services (% of GDP)	44	40	49
Imports of goods and services (% of GDP)	51	43	56
Gross capital formation (% of GDP)	27	26	24
Central government revenue (% of GDP)	30.7	26.5	31.0
Central government cash surplus/deficit (% of GDP)	-3.2	-2.4	-3.7
States and markets			
Starting a business (days)	..	11	11
Stock market capitalization (% of GDP)	4.3	13.2	20.8
Military expenditures (% of GDP)	2.0	1.5	1.3
Mobile cellular subscriptions (per 100 people)	0.0	1.3	116.9
Individuals using the Internet (% of population)	0.0	2.8	39.1
Paved roads (% of total)	76.1	68.4	76.0
High-technology exports (% of manufactured exports)	2	3	6
Global links			
Merchandise trade (% of GDP)	74	67	90
Net barter terms of trade index (2000 = 100)	109	100	95
Total external debt stocks ($ billions)	7.7	11.4	22.3
Total debt service (% of exports)	27.0	21.9	10.7
Net migration (thousands)	-25.2	-55.6	-20.0
Remittances received ($ millions)	551	796	2,004
Foreign direct investment, net inflows ($ millions)	76	752	433
Net official development assistance received ($ millions)	393	222	657

Turkey

Europe & Central Asia		Upper middle income	
Population (millions)	73.6	Population growth (%)	1.2
Surface area (1,000 sq. km)	784	Population living below $1.25 a day (%)	<2
GNI, Atlas ($ billions)	766.6	GNI per capita, Atlas ($)	10,410
GNI, PPP ($ billions)	1,247.3	GNI per capita, PPP ($)	16,940

	1990	2000	2011
People			
Share of poorest 20% in nat'l consumption/income (%)	..	5.6	5.7
Life expectancy at birth (years)	63	69	74
Total fertility rate (births per woman)	3.0	2.4	2.1
Adolescent fertility rate (births per 1,000 women 15–19)	..	46	32
Contraceptive prevalence (% of married women 15–49)	63	71	73
Births attended by skilled health staff (% of total)	76	83	95
Under-five mortality rate (per 1,000 live births)	72	35	15
Child malnutrition, underweight (% of under age 5)	8.7	3.5	..
Child immunization, measles (% of ages 12–23 mos.)	78	87	97
Primary completion rate, total (% of relevant age group)	92	..	100
Gross secondary enrollment, total (% of relevant age group)	50	71	82
Ratio of girls to boys in primary & secondary school (%)	79	82	95
HIV prevalence rate (% population of ages 15–49)	0.1	0.1	0.1
Environment			
Forests (1,000 sq. km)	97	101	115
Deforestation (avg. annual %, 1990–2000 and 2000–2010)		-0.5	-1.1
Freshwater use (% of internal resources)	13.9	18.5	17.7
Access to improved water source (% total pop.)	85	93	100
Access to improved sanitation facilities (% total pop.)	84	87	90
Energy use per capita (kilograms of oil equivalent)	975	1,200	1,551
Carbon dioxide emissions per capita (metric tons)	2.7	3.4	3.9
Electricity use per capita (kilowatt-hours)	926	1,643	2,477
Economy			
GDP ($ billions)	151	267	775
GDP growth (annual %)	9.3	6.8	8.5
GDP implicit price deflator (annual % growth)	58.2	49.2	8.9
Value added in agriculture (% of GDP)	18	11	9
Value added in industry (% of GDP)	32	31	28
Value added in services (% of GDP)	50	57	63
Exports of goods and services (% of GDP)	13	20	24
Imports of goods and services (% of GDP)	18	23	33
Gross capital formation (% of GDP)	25	21	24
Central government revenue (% of GDP)	..	..	22.8
Central government cash surplus/deficit (% of GDP)	..	..	-1.3
States and markets			
Starting a business (days)	..	38	6
Stock market capitalization (% of GDP)	12.7	26.1	26.0
Military expenditures (% of GDP)	3.5	3.7	2.3
Mobile cellular subscriptions (per 100 people)	0.1	25.4	88.7
Individuals using the Internet (% of population)	0.0	3.8	42.1
Paved roads (% of total)	..	34.0	89.4
High-technology exports (% of manufactured exports)	1	5	2
Global links			
Merchandise trade (% of GDP)	23	31	48
Net barter terms of trade index (2000 = 100)	109	100	89
Total external debt stocks ($ billions)	49	117	307
Total debt service (% of exports)	33.8	38.9	30.2
Net migration (thousands)	-150	-150	-50
Remittances received ($ billions)	3.2	4.6	1.1
Foreign direct investment, net inflows ($ billions)	0.7	1.0	16.0
Net official development assistance received ($ millions)	1,304	327	839

Turkmenistan

Europe & Central Asia		Upper middle income	
Population (millions)	5.1	Population growth (%)	1.2
Surface area (1,000 sq. km)	488	Population living below $1.25 a day (%)	..
GNI, Atlas ($ billions)	24.5	GNI per capita, Atlas ($)	4,800
GNI, PPP ($ billions)	44.3	GNI per capita, PPP ($)	8,690

	1990	2000	2011
People			
Share of poorest 20% in nat'l consumption/income (%)	6.9	6.1	..
Life expectancy at birth (years)	63	64	65
Total fertility rate (births per woman)	4.3	2.8	2.4
Adolescent fertility rate (births per 1,000 women 15–19)	..	21	17
Contraceptive prevalence (% of married women 15–49)	..	62	48
Births attended by skilled health staff (% of total)	..	97	100
Under-five mortality rate (per 1,000 live births)	94	71	53
Child malnutrition, underweight (% of under age 5)	..	10.5	..
Child immunization, measles (% of ages 12–23 mos.)	76	96	99
Primary completion rate, total (% of relevant age group)	..	..	..
Gross secondary enrollment, total (% of relevant age group)	..	..	..
Ratio of girls to boys in primary & secondary school (%)	..	..	..
HIV prevalence rate (% population of ages 15–49)	..	..	..
Environment			
Forests (1,000 sq. km)	41	41	41
Deforestation (avg. annual %, 1990–2000 and 2000–2010)		0.0	0.0
Freshwater use (% of internal resources)	..	1,773.0	1,989.3
Access to improved water source (% total pop.)	..	83	..
Access to improved sanitation facilities (% total pop.)	98	98	98
Energy use per capita (kilograms of oil equivalent)	4,789	3,163	4,226
Carbon dioxide emissions per capita (metric tons)	7.2	7.9	9.7
Electricity use per capita (kilowatt-hours)	2,293	1,698	2,403
Economy			
GDP ($ billions)	3.2	2.9	28.1
GDP growth (annual %)	35.4	5.5	14.7
GDP implicit price deflator (annual % growth)	-20.9	23.5	10.5
Value added in agriculture (% of GDP)	32	24	15
Value added in industry (% of GDP)	30	44	48
Value added in services (% of GDP)	38	31	37
Exports of goods and services (% of GDP)	39	96	78
Imports of goods and services (% of GDP)	27	81	45
Gross capital formation (% of GDP)	40	35	54
Central government revenue (% of GDP)	..	..	..
Central government cash surplus/deficit (% of GDP)	..	..	..
States and markets			
Starting a business (days)	..	..	..
Stock market capitalization (% of GDP)	..	..	..
Military expenditures (% of GDP)	..	2.9	..
Mobile cellular subscriptions (per 100 people)	0.0	0.2	68.8
Individuals using the Internet (% of population)	0.0	0.1	5.0
Paved roads (% of total)	73.5	81.2	..
High-technology exports (% of manufactured exports)	..	5	..
Global links			
Merchandise trade (% of GDP)	..	148	73
Net barter terms of trade index (2000 = 100)	..	100	221
Total external debt stocks ($ millions)	47	2,609	445
Total debt service (% of exports)	..	..	..
Net migration (thousands)	-34.7	-50.0	-54.5
Remittances received ($ millions)	..	..	..
Foreign direct investment, net inflows ($ millions)	79	131	3,186
Net official development assistance received ($ millions)	6.6	35.3	38.4

Turks and Caicos Islands

High income

Population (thousands)	39	Population growth (%)	2.1
Surface area (sq. km)	950	Population living below $1.25 a day (%)	..
GNI, Atlas ($ millions)	..	GNI per capita, Atlas ($)	..
GNI, PPP ($ millions)	..	GNI per capita, PPP ($)	..

	1990	2000	2011
People			
Share of poorest 20% in nat'l consumption/income (%)	..	..	..
Life expectancy at birth (years)	..	..	..
Total fertility rate (births per woman)	..	..	..
Adolescent fertility rate (births per 1,000 women 15-19)	..	..	..
Contraceptive prevalence (% of married women 15-49)	..	..	..
Births attended by skilled health staff (% of total)	..	88	100
Under-five mortality rate (per 1,000 live births)	..	..	..
Child malnutrition, underweight (% of under age 5)	..	..	..
Child immunization, measles (% of ages 12-23 mos.)	..	..	..
Primary completion rate, total (% of relevant age group)	..	84	..
Gross secondary enrollment, total (% of relevant age group)	..	95	..
Ratio of girls to boys in primary & secondary school (%)	..	98	..
HIV prevalence rate (% population of ages 15-49)	..	..	..
Environment			
Forests (sq. km)	344	344	344
Deforestation (avg. annual %, 1990-2000 and 2000-2010)		0.0	0.0
Freshwater use (% of internal resources)	..	..	..
Access to improved water source (% total pop.)	100	100	100
Access to improved sanitation facilities (% total pop.)	97	97	..
Energy use per capita (kilograms of oil equivalent)	..	..	..
Carbon dioxide emissions per capita (metric tons)	..	0.8	4.3
Electricity use per capita (kilowatt-hours)	..	..	..
Economy			
GDP ($ millions)	..	..	..
GDP growth (annual %)	..	..	..
GDP implicit price deflator (annual % growth)	..	..	..
Value added in agriculture (% of GDP)	..	..	..
Value added in industry (% of GDP)	..	..	..
Value added in services (% of GDP)	..	..	..
Exports of goods and services (% of GDP)	..	..	..
Imports of goods and services (% of GDP)	..	..	..
Gross capital formation (% of GDP)	..	..	..
Central government revenue (% of GDP)	..	..	..
Central government cash surplus/deficit (% of GDP)	..	..	..
States and markets			
Starting a business (days)	..	..	..
Stock market capitalization (% of GDP)	..	..	..
Military expenditures (% of GDP)	..	..	..
Mobile cellular subscriptions (per 100 people)	..	..	..
Individuals using the Internet (% of population)	..	..	..
Paved roads (% of total)	..	..	..
High-technology exports (% of manufactured exports)	..	20	2
Global links			
Merchandise trade (% of GDP)	..	..	..
Net barter terms of trade index (2000 = 100)	..	100	73
Total external debt stocks ($ millions)	..	..	..
Total debt service (% of exports)	..	..	..
Net migration (thousands)	..	..	..
Remittances received ($ millions)	..	..	..
Foreign direct investment, net inflows ($ millions)	0.0	0.4	97.0
Net official development assistance received ($ millions)	11.6	6.7	..

Tuvalu

East Asia & Pacific		Upper middle income

Population (thousands)	10	Population growth (%)	0.2
Surface area (sq. km)	30	Population living below $1.25 a day (%)	..
GNI, Atlas ($ millions)	48.8	GNI per capita, Atlas ($)	4,950
GNI, PPP ($ millions)	..	GNI per capita, PPP ($)	..

	1990	2000	2011
People			
Share of poorest 20% in nat'l consumption/income (%)	..	..	..
Life expectancy at birth (years)	..	..	..
Total fertility rate (births per woman)	..	..	..
Adolescent fertility rate (births per 1,000 women 15–19)			
Contraceptive prevalence (% of married women 15–49)	39	32	31
Births attended by skilled health staff (% of total)	100	100	98
Under-five mortality rate (per 1,000 live births)	58	43	30
Child malnutrition, underweight (% of under age 5)	..	..	1.6
Child immunization, measles (% of ages 12–23 mos.)	95	81	98
Primary completion rate, total (% of relevant age group)	..	110	..
Gross secondary enrollment, total (% of relevant age group)	..	80	..
Ratio of girls to boys in primary & secondary school (%)	..	112	..
HIV prevalence rate (% population of ages 15–49)	..	..	..
Environment			
Forests (sq. km)	10.0	10.0	10.0
Deforestation (avg. annual %, 1990–2000 and 2000–2010)		0.0	0.0
Freshwater use (% of internal resources)	..	..	..
Access to improved water source (% total pop.)	90	94	98
Access to improved sanitation facilities (% total pop.)	80	83	85
Energy use per capita (kilograms of oil equivalent)	..	..	..
Carbon dioxide emissions per capita (metric tons)	..	..	..
Electricity use per capita (kilowatt-hours)	..	..	..
Economy			
GDP ($ millions)	8.8	13.7	35.8
GDP growth (annual %)	3.6	-1.0	1.2
GDP implicit price deflator (annual % growth)	2.6	12.8	-1.2
Value added in agriculture (% of GDP)	26	18	23
Value added in industry (% of GDP)	15	7	12
Value added in services (% of GDP)	60	75	65
Exports of goods and services (% of GDP)	..	..	..
Imports of goods and services (% of GDP)	..	..	..
Gross capital formation (% of GDP)	..	..	..
Central government revenue (% of GDP)	..	..	..
Central government cash surplus/deficit (% of GDP)	..	..	..
States and markets			
Starting a business (days)	..	..	..
Stock market capitalization (% of GDP)	..	..	..
Military expenditures (% of GDP)	..	..	..
Mobile cellular subscriptions (per 100 people)	0.0	0.0	21.6
Individuals using the Internet (% of population)	0.0	5.2	30.0
Paved roads (% of total)	..	..	..
High-technology exports (% of manufactured exports)	..	28	..
Global links			
Merchandise trade (% of GDP)	58	36	71
Net barter terms of trade index (2000 = 100)	..	..	..
Total external debt stocks ($ millions)	..	..	..
Total debt service (% of exports)	..	..	..
Net migration (thousands)	..	..	..
Remittances received ($ millions)	..	..	..
Foreign direct investment, net inflows ($ millions)	..	-0.9	1.8
Net official development assistance received ($ millions)	5.1	4.0	42.7

Uganda

Sub-Saharan Africa   **Low income**

Population (millions)	34.5	Population growth (%)	3.2
Surface area (1,000 sq. km)	242	Population living below $1.25 a day (%)	38.0
GNI, Atlas ($ billions)	17.5	GNI per capita, Atlas ($)	510
GNI, PPP ($ billions)	45.3	GNI per capita, PPP ($)	1,310

	1990	2000	2011
People			
Share of poorest 20% in nat'l consumption/income (%)	4.9	5.9	5.8
Life expectancy at birth (years)	47	46	54
Total fertility rate (births per woman)	7.1	6.9	6.1
Adolescent fertility rate (births per 1,000 women 15–19)	..	180	131
Contraceptive prevalence (% of married women 15–49)	5	23	30
Births attended by skilled health staff (% of total)	38	39	57
Under-five mortality rate (per 1,000 live births)	178	141	90
Child malnutrition, underweight (% of under age 5)	19.7	19.0	16.4
Child immunization, measles (% of ages 12–23 mos.)	52	57	75
Primary completion rate, total (% of relevant age group)	..	60	55
Gross secondary enrollment, total (% of relevant age group)	11	16	28
Ratio of girls to boys in primary & secondary school (%)	78	91	99
HIV prevalence rate (% population of ages 15–49)	13.4	7.2	7.2
Environment			
Forests (1,000 sq. km)	48	39	29
Deforestation (avg. annual %, 1990–2000 and 2000–2010)		2.0	2.6
Freshwater use (% of internal resources)	..	0.8	0.8
Access to improved water source (% total pop.)	43	58	72
Access to improved sanitation facilities (% total pop.)	27	30	34
Energy use per capita (kilograms of oil equivalent)	..	..	..
Carbon dioxide emissions per capita (metric tons)	0.05	0.06	0.11
Electricity use per capita (kilowatt-hours)	..	..	..
Economy			
GDP ($ billions)	4.3	6.2	16.8
GDP growth (annual %)	6.5	3.1	6.7
GDP implicit price deflator (annual % growth)	44.4	11.1	4.9
Value added in agriculture (% of GDP)	57	29	23
Value added in industry (% of GDP)	11	23	25
Value added in services (% of GDP)	32	48	51
Exports of goods and services (% of GDP)	7	11	24
Imports of goods and services (% of GDP)	19	22	35
Gross capital formation (% of GDP)	13	19	25
Central government revenue (% of GDP)	..	10.8	16.4
Central government cash surplus/deficit (% of GDP)	..	–1.9	–3.9
States and markets			
Starting a business (days)	..	34	33
Stock market capitalization (% of GDP)	..	0.6	46.0
Military expenditures (% of GDP)	3.3	2.5	1.6
Mobile cellular subscriptions (per 100 people)	0.0	0.5	48.4
Individuals using the Internet (% of population)	0.0	0.2	13.0
Paved roads (% of total)	..	23.0	..
High-technology exports (% of manufactured exports)	..	4	22
Global links			
Merchandise trade (% of GDP)	10	31	45
Net barter terms of trade index (2000 = 100)	146	100	120
Total external debt stocks ($ billions)	2.6	3.5	3.9
Total debt service (% of exports)	81.4	10.6	1.7
Net migration (thousands)	233	–46	–135
Remittances received ($ millions)	..	238	949
Foreign direct investment, net inflows ($ millions)	–6	161	797
Net official development assistance received ($ millions)	663	853	1,580

Ukraine

Europe & Central Asia   **Lower middle income**

Population (millions)	45.7	Population growth (%)	-0.4
Surface area (1,000 sq. km)	604	Population living below $1.25 a day (%)	<2
GNI, Atlas ($ billions)	142.9	GNI per capita, Atlas ($)	3,130
GNI, PPP ($ billions)	321.9	GNI per capita, PPP ($)	7,040

	1990	2000	2011
People			
Share of poorest 20% in nat'l consumption/income (%)	9.5	8.8	9.7
Life expectancy at birth (years)	70	68	71
Total fertility rate (births per woman)	1.8	1.1	1.5
Adolescent fertility rate (births per 1,000 women 15–19)	..	35	27
Contraceptive prevalence (% of married women 15–49)	..	72	67
Births attended by skilled health staff (% of total)	100	100	99
Under-five mortality rate (per 1,000 live births)	19	19	10
Child malnutrition, underweight (% of under age 5)	..	4.1	..
Child immunization, measles (% of ages 12–23 mos.)	90	99	67
Primary completion rate, total (% of relevant age group)	95	91	97
Gross secondary enrollment, total (% of relevant age group)	95	99	94
Ratio of girls to boys in primary & secondary school (%)	102	100	99
HIV prevalence rate (% population of ages 15–49)	0.1	0.8	0.8
Environment			
Forests (1,000 sq. km)	93	95	97
Deforestation (avg. annual %, 1990–2000 and 2000–2010)		-0.3	-0.2
Freshwater use (% of internal resources)	49.0	72.5	72.5
Access to improved water source (% total pop.)	..	97	98
Access to improved sanitation facilities (% total pop.)	..	95	94
Energy use per capita (kilograms of oil equivalent)	4,852	2,721	2,845
Carbon dioxide emissions per capita (metric tons)	12.3	6.5	5.9
Electricity use per capita (kilowatt-hours)	4,787	2,778	3,550
Economy			
GDP ($ billions)	81.5	31.3	165.2
GDP growth (annual %)	-6.3	5.9	5.2
GDP implicit price deflator (annual % growth)	16.3	23.1	15.6
Value added in agriculture (% of GDP)	26	17	10
Value added in industry (% of GDP)	45	36	32
Value added in services (% of GDP)	30	47	59
Exports of goods and services (% of GDP)	28	62	54
Imports of goods and services (% of GDP)	29	57	59
Gross capital formation (% of GDP)	27	20	21
Central government revenue (% of GDP)	..	26.8	35.9
Central government cash surplus/deficit (% of GDP)	..	-0.6	-2.3
States and markets			
Starting a business (days)	..	40	22
Stock market capitalization (% of GDP)	..	6.0	15.5
Military expenditures (% of GDP)	0.5	3.6	2.5
Mobile cellular subscriptions (per 100 people)	0.0	1.7	123.0
Individuals using the Internet (% of population)	0.0	0.7	30.6
Paved roads (% of total)	93.7	96.7	97.9
High-technology exports (% of manufactured exports)	..	5	4
Global links			
Merchandise trade (% of GDP)	..	91	91
Net barter terms of trade index (2000 = 100)	..	100	124
Total external debt stocks ($ billions)	0	14	134
Total debt service (% of exports)	..	19.0	30.8
Net migration (thousands)	2	-547	-40
Remittances received ($ millions)	..	33	7,822
Foreign direct investment, net inflows ($ millions)	200	595	7,207
Net official development assistance received ($ millions)	..	..	750

United Arab Emirates

Population (millions)	7.9	Population growth (%)	4.9
Surface area (1,000 sq. km)	84	Population living below $1.25 a day (%)	..
GNI, Atlas ($ billions)	321.7	GNI per capita, Atlas ($)	40,760
GNI, PPP ($ billions)	377.9	GNI per capita, PPP ($)	47,890

	1990	2000	2011
People			
Share of poorest 20% in nat'l consumption/income (%)	..	..	..
Life expectancy at birth (years)	72	75	77
Total fertility rate (births per woman)	4.4	2.6	1.7
Adolescent fertility rate (births per 1,000 women 15-19)	..	26	24
Contraceptive prevalence (% of married women 15-49)	..	..	..
Births attended by skilled health staff (% of total)	..	100	100
Under-five mortality rate (per 1,000 live births)	22	12	7
Child malnutrition, underweight (% of under age 5)	..	..	..
Child immunization, measles (% of ages 12-23 mos.)	80	94	94
Primary completion rate, total (% of relevant age group)	91	86	..
Gross secondary enrollment, total (% of relevant age group)	62	85	..
Ratio of girls to boys in primary & secondary school (%)	106	102	..
HIV prevalence rate (% population of ages 15-49)	..	..	..
Environment			
Forests (1,000 sq. km)	2.5	3.1	3.2
Deforestation (avg. annual %, 1990-2000 and 2000-2010)		-2.4	-0.2
Freshwater use (% of internal resources)	..	1,936.0	2,665.3
Access to improved water source (% total pop.)	100	100	100
Access to improved sanitation facilities (% total pop.)	97	97	98
Energy use per capita (kilograms of oil equivalent)	11,292	11,190	8,271
Carbon dioxide emissions per capita (metric tons)	28.8	37.1	22.6
Electricity use per capita (kilowatt-hours)	8,594	12,722	11,044
Economy			
GDP ($ billions)	51	104	360
GDP growth (annual %)	18.3	10.9	4.9
GDP implicit price deflator (annual % growth)	3.3	11.5	15.4
Value added in agriculture (% of GDP)	1	2	1
Value added in industry (% of GDP)	59	49	56
Value added in services (% of GDP)	40	49	44
Exports of goods and services (% of GDP)	..	49	78
Imports of goods and services (% of GDP)	..	41	69
Gross capital formation (% of GDP)	..	22	25
Central government revenue (% of GDP)	..	6.5	..
Central government cash surplus/deficit (% of GDP)	..	0.1	..
States and markets			
Starting a business (days)	..	19	8
Stock market capitalization (% of GDP)	..	5.5	26.0
Military expenditures (% of GDP)	..	6.3	5.4
Mobile cellular subscriptions (per 100 people)	1.9	47.1	148.6
Individuals using the Internet (% of population)	0.0	23.6	70.0
Paved roads (% of total)	94.2	100.0	..
High-technology exports (% of manufactured exports)	0	1	3
Global links			
Merchandise trade (% of GDP)	69	81	136
Net barter terms of trade index (2000 = 100)	..	100	178
Total external debt stocks ($ millions)	..	..	..
Total debt service (% of exports)	..	..	..
Net migration (thousands)	260	469	3,077
Remittances received ($ millions)	..	..	..
Foreign direct investment, net inflows ($ millions)	-116	-506	7,679
Net official development assistance received ($ millions)	3.5	..	..

United Kingdom

High income

Population (millions)	62.7	Population growth (%)	0.8
Surface area (1,000 sq. km)	244	Population living below $1.25 a day (%)	..
GNI, Atlas ($ billions)	2,370.4	GNI per capita, Atlas ($)	37,780
GNI, PPP ($ billions)	2,255.9	GNI per capita, PPP ($)	35,950

	1990	2000	2011
People			
Share of poorest 20% in nat'l consumption/income (%)	..	6.1	..
Life expectancy at birth (years)	76	78	81
Total fertility rate (births per woman)	1.8	1.6	2.0
Adolescent fertility rate (births per 1,000 women 15–19)	..	29	30
Contraceptive prevalence (% of married women 15–49)	70	76	84
Births attended by skilled health staff (% of total)	..	99	..
Under-five mortality rate (per 1,000 live births)	9	7	5
Child malnutrition, underweight (% of under age 5)	..	..	..
Child immunization, measles (% of ages 12–23 mos.)	87	88	90
Primary completion rate, total (% of relevant age group)	..	..	..
Gross secondary enrollment, total (% of relevant age group)	84	102	105
Ratio of girls to boys in primary & secondary school (%)	102	101	100
HIV prevalence rate (% population of ages 15–49)	0.1	0.1	0.3
Environment			
Forests (1,000 sq. km)	26	28	29
Deforestation (avg. annual %, 1990–2000 and 2000–2010)		-0.7	-0.3
Freshwater use (% of internal resources)	8.3	10.8	9.0
Access to improved water source (% total pop.)	100	100	100
Access to improved sanitation facilities (% total pop.)	100	100	100
Energy use per capita (kilograms of oil equivalent)	3,597	3,785	3,012
Carbon dioxide emissions per capita (metric tons)	10.0	9.2	7.7
Electricity use per capita (kilowatt-hours)	5,357	6,115	5,733
Economy			
GDP ($ billions)	1,013	1,476	2,445
GDP growth (annual %)	0.8	4.2	0.8
GDP implicit price deflator (annual % growth)	7.7	0.7	2.6
Value added in agriculture (% of GDP)	2	1	1
Value added in industry (% of GDP)	34	27	22
Value added in services (% of GDP)	64	72	78
Exports of goods and services (% of GDP)	24	28	32
Imports of goods and services (% of GDP)	26	30	34
Gross capital formation (% of GDP)	20	18	15
Central government revenue (% of GDP)	..	37.1	36.8
Central government cash surplus/deficit (% of GDP)	..	3.9	-7.7
States and markets			
Starting a business (days)	..	13	13
Stock market capitalization (% of GDP)	83.8	174.6	118.7
Military expenditures (% of GDP)	3.8	2.4	2.6
Mobile cellular subscriptions (per 100 people)	1.9	73.8	130.8
Individuals using the Internet (% of population)	0.1	26.8	82.0
Paved roads (% of total)	100.0	100.0	100.0
High-technology exports (% of manufactured exports)	24	32	21
Global links			
Merchandise trade (% of GDP)	40	43	45
Net barter terms of trade index (2000 = 100)	..	100	101
Total external debt stocks ($ millions)	..	..	..
Total debt service (% of exports)	..	..	..
Net migration (thousands)	99	429	1,020
Remittances received ($ billions)	2.1	3.6	1.8
Foreign direct investment, net inflows ($ billions)	34	122	36
Net official development assistance received ($ millions)	..	..	..

United States

Population (millions)	311.6	Population growth (%)		0.7
Surface area (1,000 sq. km)	9,832	Population living below $1.25 a day (%)		..
GNI, Atlas ($ billions)	15,148.2	GNI per capita, Atlas ($)		48,620
GNI, PPP ($ billions)	15,211.3	GNI per capita, PPP ($)		48,820

	1990	2000	2011
People			
Share of poorest 20% in nat'l consumption/income (%)	..	5.4	..
Life expectancy at birth (years)	75	77	79
Total fertility rate (births per woman)	2.1	2.1	1.9
Adolescent fertility rate (births per 1,000 women 15-19)	..	46	30
Contraceptive prevalence (% of married women 15-49)	71	73	79
Births attended by skilled health staff (% of total)	99	99	..
Under-five mortality rate (per 1,000 live births)	11	9	8
Child malnutrition, underweight (% of under age 5)	..	1.1	..
Child immunization, measles (% of ages 12-23 mos.)	90	91	90
Primary completion rate, total (% of relevant age group)	..	99	104
Gross secondary enrollment, total (% of relevant age group)	91	93	96
Ratio of girls to boys in primary & secondary school (%)	100	100	100
HIV prevalence rate (% population of ages 15-49)	0.5	0.6	0.7
Environment			
Forests (1,000 sq. km)	2,963	3,002	3,044
Deforestation (avg. annual %, 1990-2000 and 2000-2010)		-0.1	-0.1
Freshwater use (% of internal resources)	16.4	16.8	17.0
Access to improved water source (% total pop.)	99	99	99
Access to improved sanitation facilities (% total pop.)	100	100	100
Energy use per capita (kilograms of oil equivalent)	7,672	8,057	7,069
Carbon dioxide emissions per capita (metric tons)	19.5	20.2	17.3
Electricity use per capita (kilowatt-hours)	11,713	13,671	13,394
Economy			
GDP ($ billions)	5,751	9,899	14,991
GDP growth (annual %)	1.9	4.2	1.7
GDP implicit price deflator (annual % growth)	3.8	2.2	2.2
Value added in agriculture (% of GDP)	2	1	1
Value added in industry (% of GDP)	28	23	20
Value added in services (% of GDP)	70	75	79
Exports of goods and services (% of GDP)	10	11	14
Imports of goods and services (% of GDP)	11	15	18
Gross capital formation (% of GDP)	18	21	15
Central government revenue (% of GDP)	..	20.1	17.0
Central government cash surplus/deficit (% of GDP)	..	0.5	-9.3
States and markets			
Starting a business (days)	..	6	6
Stock market capitalization (% of GDP)	53.2	152.6	104.3
Military expenditures (% of GDP)	5.3	3.0	4.7
Mobile cellular subscriptions (per 100 people)	2.1	38.8	92.7
Individuals using the Internet (% of population)	0.8	43.1	77.9
Paved roads (% of total)	..	66.2	100.0
High-technology exports (% of manufactured exports)	33	34	18
Global links			
Merchandise trade (% of GDP)	16	21	25
Net barter terms of trade index (2000 = 100)	103	100	95
Total external debt stocks ($ millions)	..	..	..
Total debt service (% of exports)	..	..	..
Net migration (thousands)	3.8	8.5	5.0
Remittances received ($ billions)	1.2	4.4	5.8
Foreign direct investment, net inflows ($ billions)	48	321	258
Net official development assistance received ($ millions)	..	..	..

Uruguay

Latin America & Caribbean		Upper middle income	
Population (millions)	3.4	Population growth (%)	0.4
Surface area (1,000 sq. km)	176	Population living below $1.25 a day (%)	<2
GNI, Atlas ($ billions)	40.0	GNI per capita, Atlas ($)	11,860
GNI, PPP ($ billions)	49.3	GNI per capita, PPP ($)	14,640

	1990	2000	2011
People			
Share of poorest 20% in nat'l consumption/income (%)	5.3	4.7	4.9
Life expectancy at birth (years)	72	75	76
Total fertility rate (births per woman)	2.5	2.2	2.0
Adolescent fertility rate (births per 1,000 women 15–19)	..	65	59
Contraceptive prevalence (% of married women 15–49)	..	77	..
Births attended by skilled health staff (% of total)	..	100	100
Under-five mortality rate (per 1,000 live births)	23	17	10
Child malnutrition, underweight (% of under age 5)	..	5.4	..
Child immunization, measles (% of ages 12–23 mos.)	97	89	95
Primary completion rate, total (% of relevant age group)	95	97	104
Gross secondary enrollment, total (% of relevant age group)	81	98	90
Ratio of girls to boys in primary & secondary school (%)	..	105	104
HIV prevalence rate (% population of ages 15–49)	0.1	0.6	0.6
Environment			
Forests (1,000 sq. km)	9	14	18
Deforestation (avg. annual %, 1990–2000 and 2000–2010)		-4.4	-2.1
Freshwater use (% of internal resources)	..	6.2	6.2
Access to improved water source (% total pop.)	96	98	100
Access to improved sanitation facilities (% total pop.)	94	96	100
Energy use per capita (kilograms of oil equivalent)	724	937	1,241
Carbon dioxide emissions per capita (metric tons)	1.3	1.6	2.4
Electricity use per capita (kilowatt-hours)	1,245	2,043	2,763
Economy			
GDP ($ billions)	9.3	22.8	46.7
GDP growth (annual %)	0.3	-1.9	5.7
GDP implicit price deflator (annual % growth)	106.8	3.5	8.0
Value added in agriculture (% of GDP)	9	7	10
Value added in industry (% of GDP)	35	25	25
Value added in services (% of GDP)	56	69	65
Exports of goods and services (% of GDP)	24	17	27
Imports of goods and services (% of GDP)	18	20	27
Gross capital formation (% of GDP)	12	14	19
Central government revenue (% of GDP)	23.8	24.7	30.8
Central government cash surplus/deficit (% of GDP)	0.5	-3.0	-0.6
States and markets			
Starting a business (days)	..	45	7
Stock market capitalization (% of GDP)	1.7	0.7	0.4
Military expenditures (% of GDP)	3.5	2.5	1.9
Mobile cellular subscriptions (per 100 people)	0.0	12.4	140.8
Individuals using the Internet (% of population)	0.0	10.5	51.4
Paved roads (% of total)	..	10.0	..
High-technology exports (% of manufactured exports)	3	2	6
Global links			
Merchandise trade (% of GDP)	33	25	40
Net barter terms of trade index (2000 = 100)	116	100	101
Total external debt stocks ($ billions)	4.4	8.5	14.3
Total debt service (% of exports)	40.9	27.3	11.1
Net migration (thousands)	-30.0	-26.0	-50.0
Remittances received ($ millions)	..	0	102
Foreign direct investment, net inflows ($ millions)	42	269	2,177
Net official development assistance received ($ millions)	52.4	17.4	16.1

Uzbekistan

Europe & Central Asia		Lower middle income	

		Population growth (%)	2.7
Population (millions)	29.3	Population growth (%)	2.7
Surface area (1,000 sq. km)	447	Population living below $1.25 a day (%)	..
GNI, Atlas ($ billions)	44.2	GNI per capita, Atlas ($)	1,510
GNI, PPP ($ billions)	100.3	GNI per capita, PPP ($)	3,420

	1990	2000	2011
People			
Share of poorest 20% in nat'l consumption/income (%)	10.6	7.8	..
Life expectancy at birth (years)	67	67	68
Total fertility rate (births per woman)	4.1	2.6	2.5
Adolescent fertility rate (births per 1,000 women 15–19)	..	25	13
Contraceptive prevalence (% of married women 15–49)	..	67	65
Births attended by skilled health staff (% of total)	..	96	100
Under-five mortality rate (per 1,000 live births)	75	61	49
Child malnutrition, underweight (% of under age 5)	..	7.1	4.4
Child immunization, measles (% of ages 12–23 mos.)	84	99	99
Primary completion rate, total (% of relevant age group)		95	93
Gross secondary enrollment, total (% of relevant age group)	101	88	106
Ratio of girls to boys in primary & secondary school (%)	..	98	98
HIV prevalence rate (% population of ages 15–49)	..	..	..
Environment			
Forests (1,000 sq. km)	30	32	33
Deforestation (avg. annual %, 1990–2000 and 2000–2010)		-0.5	-0.2
Freshwater use (% of internal resources)	..	370.7	342.7
Access to improved water source (% total pop.)	90	89	87
Access to improved sanitation facilities (% total pop.)	84	91	100
Energy use per capita (kilograms of oil equivalent)	2,261	2,058	1,533
Carbon dioxide emissions per capita (metric tons)	5.3	4.9	4.2
Electricity use per capita (kilowatt-hours)	2,383	1,780	1,648
Economy			
GDP ($ billions)	13.4	13.8	45.4
GDP growth (annual %)	1.6	3.8	8.3
GDP implicit price deflator (annual % growth)	4.0	47.3	15.1
Value added in agriculture (% of GDP)	33	34	19
Value added in industry (% of GDP)	33	23	36
Value added in services (% of GDP)	34	43	45
Exports of goods and services (% of GDP)	29	25	32
Imports of goods and services (% of GDP)	48	22	27
Gross capital formation (% of GDP)	32	16	23
Central government revenue (% of GDP)	..	..	..
Central government cash surplus/deficit (% of GDP)	..	..	..
States and markets			
Starting a business (days)	..	29	12
Stock market capitalization (% of GDP)	..	0.2	..
Military expenditures (% of GDP)	..	1.2	..
Mobile cellular subscriptions (per 100 people)	0.0	0.2	91.6
Individuals using the Internet (% of population)	0.0	0.5	30.2
Paved roads (% of total)	79.0	87.3	..
High-technology exports (% of manufactured exports)	..	..	..
Global links			
Merchandise trade (% of GDP)	..	40	51
Net barter terms of trade index (2000 = 100)	..	100	178
Total external debt stocks ($ billions)	0.0	5.0	8.4
Total debt service (% of exports)	..	..	..
Net migration (thousands)	-451	-400	-518
Remittances received ($ millions)	..	..	..
Foreign direct investment, net inflows ($ millions)	9	75	1,403
Net official development assistance received ($ millions)	2	186	216

Vanuatu

East Asia & Pacific		Lower middle income	
Population (thousands)	246	Population growth (%)	2.5
Surface area (1,000 sq. km)	12	Population living below $1.25 a day (%)	..
GNI, Atlas ($ millions)	669.6	GNI per capita, Atlas ($)	2,730
GNI, PPP ($ millions)	1,064.3	GNI per capita, PPP ($)	4,330

	1990	2000	2011
People			
Share of poorest 20% in nat'l consumption/income (%)	..	..	..
Life expectancy at birth (years)	63	68	71
Total fertility rate (births per woman)	4.9	4.5	3.8
Adolescent fertility rate (births per 1,000 women 15–19)	..	60	51
Contraceptive prevalence (% of married women 15–49)	15	28	38
Births attended by skilled health staff (% of total)	..	88	74
Under-five mortality rate (per 1,000 live births)	39	23	13
Child malnutrition, underweight (% of under age 5)	..	..	11.7
Child immunization, measles (% of ages 12–23 mos.)	66	61	52
Primary completion rate, total (% of relevant age group)	84	92	83
Gross secondary enrollment, total (% of relevant age group)	18	35	55
Ratio of girls to boys in primary & secondary school (%)	93	101	97
HIV prevalence rate (% population of ages 15–49)	..	..	..
Environment			
Forests (1,000 sq. km)	4.4	4.4	4.4
Deforestation (avg. annual %, 1990–2000 and 2000–2010)		0.0	0.0
Freshwater use (% of internal resources)	..	..	..
Access to improved water source (% total pop.)	62	76	90
Access to improved sanitation facilities (% total pop.)	35	41	57
Energy use per capita (kilograms of oil equivalent)	159	..	..
Carbon dioxide emissions per capita (metric tons)	0.5	0.4	0.5
Electricity use per capita (kilowatt-hours)	..	..	..
Economy			
GDP ($ millions)	158	272	760
GDP growth (annual %)	11.7	5.9	1.4
GDP implicit price deflator (annual % growth)	-1.0	2.2	1.9
Value added in agriculture (% of GDP)	21	23	20
Value added in industry (% of GDP)	14	11	10
Value added in services (% of GDP)	65	66	70
Exports of goods and services (% of GDP)	47	39	49
Imports of goods and services (% of GDP)	73	48	52
Gross capital formation (% of GDP)	33	20	..
Central government revenue (% of GDP)	26.1	19.4	..
Central government cash surplus/deficit (% of GDP)	-7.8	-0.7	..
States and markets			
Starting a business (days)	..	39	35
Stock market capitalization (% of GDP)	..	..	..
Military expenditures (% of GDP)	..	..	..
Mobile cellular subscriptions (per 100 people)	0.0	0.2	55.8
Individuals using the Internet (% of population)	0.0	2.1	8.0
Paved roads (% of total)	21.6	23.9	..
High-technology exports (% of manufactured exports)	20	0	..
Global links			
Merchandise trade (% of GDP)	73	42	46
Net barter terms of trade index (2000 = 100)	..	100	92
Total external debt stocks ($ millions)	38	96	202
Total debt service (% of exports)	2.3	1.6	1.6
Net migration (thousands)	-2.5	-7.1	..
Remittances received ($ millions)	8.2	34.7	21.8
Foreign direct investment, net inflows ($ millions)	13.1	20.3	58.1
Net official development assistance received ($ millions)	49.5	45.8	92.1

Venezuela, RB

Latin America & Caribbean		Upper middle income	
Population (millions)	29.3	Population growth (%)	1.5
Surface area (1,000 sq. km)	912	Population living below $1.25 a day (%)	6.6
GNI, Atlas ($ billions)	346.1	GNI per capita, Atlas ($)	11,820
GNI, PPP ($ billions)	363.9	GNI per capita, PPP ($)	12,430

	1990	2000	2011
People			
Share of poorest 20% in nat'l consumption/income (%)	4.5	4.0	4.3
Life expectancy at birth (years)	71	73	74
Total fertility rate (births per woman)	3.4	2.8	2.5
Adolescent fertility rate (births per 1,000 women 15-19)	..	93	88
Contraceptive prevalence (% of married women 15-49)	58	70	..
Births attended by skilled health staff (% of total)	..	94	..
Under-five mortality rate (per 1,000 live births)	31	22	15
Child malnutrition, underweight (% of under age 5)	6.7	3.9	3.7
Child immunization, measles (% of ages 12-23 mos.)	61	84	86
Primary completion rate, total (% of relevant age group)	79	83	95
Gross secondary enrollment, total (% of relevant age group)	56	60	83
Ratio of girls to boys in primary & secondary school (%)	105	105	102
HIV prevalence rate (% population of ages 15-49)	0.2	0.4	0.6
Environment			
Forests (1,000 sq. km)	520	492	460
Deforestation (avg. annual %, 1990-2000 and 2000-2010)		0.6	0.6
Freshwater use (% of internal resources)	..	1.3	1.3
Access to improved water source (% total pop.)	90	92	..
Access to improved sanitation facilities (% total pop.)	82	89	..
Energy use per capita (kilograms of oil equivalent)	2,216	2,335	2,669
Carbon dioxide emissions per capita (metric tons)	6.2	6.3	6.5
Electricity use per capita (kilowatt-hours)	2,463	2,655	3,287
Economy			
GDP ($ billions)	47	117	316
GDP growth (annual %)	6.5	3.7	4.2
GDP implicit price deflator (annual % growth)	41.7	29.5	28.1
Value added in agriculture (% of GDP)	5	4	6
Value added in industry (% of GDP)	61	50	52
Value added in services (% of GDP)	34	46	42
Exports of goods and services (% of GDP)	39	30	30
Imports of goods and services (% of GDP)	20	18	20
Gross capital formation (% of GDP)	10	24	23
Central government revenue (% of GDP)	24.5	21.2	..
Central government cash surplus/deficit (% of GDP)	3.0	-1.2	..
States and markets			
Starting a business (days)	..	141	144
Stock market capitalization (% of GDP)	17.8	6.9	1.6
Military expenditures (% of GDP)	1.9	1.5	0.8
Mobile cellular subscriptions (per 100 people)	0.0	22.4	97.8
Individuals using the Internet (% of population)	0.0	3.4	40.2
Paved roads (% of total)	35.6	33.6	..
High-technology exports (% of manufactured exports)	4	3	2
Global links			
Merchandise trade (% of GDP)	53	42	44
Net barter terms of trade index (2000 = 100)	90	100	259
Total external debt stocks ($ billions)	33.2	42.8	67.9
Total debt service (% of exports)	23.3	16.9	6.4
Net migration (thousands)	75.0	40.0	40.0
Remittances received ($ millions)	1	17	138
Foreign direct investment, net inflows ($ billions)	0.5	4.7	5.2
Net official development assistance received ($ millions)	76.4	76.1	45.3

Vietnam

East Asia & Pacific   **Lower middle income**

Population (millions)	87.8	Population growth (%)	1.0
Surface area (1,000 sq. km)	331	Population living below $1.25 a day (%)	16.9
GNI, Atlas ($ billions)	111.1	GNI per capita, Atlas ($)	1,270
GNI, PPP ($ billions)	285.5	GNI per capita, PPP ($)	3,250

	1990	2000	2011
People			
Share of poorest 20% in nat'l consumption/income (%)	7.8	7.5	7.4
Life expectancy at birth (years)	65	72	75
Total fertility rate (births per woman)	3.6	2.0	1.8
Adolescent fertility rate (births per 1,000 women 15–19)	..	26	24
Contraceptive prevalence (% of married women 15–49)	53	74	78
Births attended by skilled health staff (% of total)	..	70	93
Under-five mortality rate (per 1,000 live births)	50	34	22
Child malnutrition, underweight (% of under age 5)	40.7	30.1	20.2
Child immunization, measles (% of ages 12–23 mos.)	88	97	96
Primary completion rate, total (% of relevant age group)	..	98	104
Gross secondary enrollment, total (% of relevant age group)	36	64	77
Ratio of girls to boys in primary & secondary school (%)	..	93	102
HIV prevalence rate (% population of ages 15–49)	0.1	0.2	0.5
Environment			
Forests (1,000 sq. km)	94	117	139
Deforestation (avg. annual %, 1990–2000 and 2000–2010)		-2.3	-1.6
Freshwater use (% of internal resources)	..	12.6	22.8
Access to improved water source (% total pop.)	57	77	95
Access to improved sanitation facilities (% total pop.)	37	56	76
Energy use per capita (kilograms of oil equivalent)	271	370	681
Carbon dioxide emissions per capita (metric tons)	0.3	0.7	1.7
Electricity use per capita (kilowatt-hours)	98	295	1,035
Economy			
GDP ($ billions)	6.5	31.2	123.6
GDP growth (annual %)	5.1	6.8	5.9
GDP implicit price deflator (annual % growth)	42.1	3.4	20.9
Value added in agriculture (% of GDP)	39	25	22
Value added in industry (% of GDP)	23	37	41
Value added in services (% of GDP)	39	39	37
Exports of goods and services (% of GDP)	36	55	87
Imports of goods and services (% of GDP)	45	57	91
Gross capital formation (% of GDP)	13	30	35
Central government revenue (% of GDP)	..	..	..
Central government cash surplus/deficit (% of GDP)	..	..	..
States and markets			
Starting a business (days)	..	59	34
Stock market capitalization (% of GDP)	..	0.4	14.8
Military expenditures (% of GDP)	7.9	2.1	2.2
Mobile cellular subscriptions (per 100 people)	0.0	1.0	143.4
Individuals using the Internet (% of population)	0.0	0.3	35.1
Paved roads (% of total)	23.5	43.9	47.6
High-technology exports (% of manufactured exports)	..	11	9
Global links			
Merchandise trade (% of GDP)	80	97	165
Net barter terms of trade index (2000 = 100)	..	100	100
Total external debt stocks ($ billions)	23.3	12.9	57.8
Total debt service (% of exports)	..	7.5	3.2
Net migration (thousands)	-332	-287	-431
Remittances received ($ billions)	..	1.3	8.6
Foreign direct investment, net inflows ($ billions)	0.2	1.3	7.4
Net official development assistance received ($ billions)	0.2	1.7	3.5

Virgin Islands (U.S.)

High income

Population (thousands)	110	Population growth (%)	-0.1
Surface area (sq. km)	350	Population living below $1.25 a day (%)	..
GNI, Atlas ($ billions)	..	GNI per capita, Atlas ($)	..
GNI, PPP ($ millions)	..	GNI per capita, PPP ($)	..

	1990	2000	2011
People			
Share of poorest 20% in nat'l consumption/income (%)	..	..	..
Life expectancy at birth (years)	75	78	79
Total fertility rate (births per woman)	3.1	2.1	1.8
Adolescent fertility rate (births per 1,000 women 15-19)	..	43	23
Contraceptive prevalence (% of married women 15-49)	..	78	..
Births attended by skilled health staff (% of total)	..	98	..
Under-five mortality rate (per 1,000 live births)	..	..	..
Child malnutrition, underweight (% of under age 5)	..	..	..
Child immunization, measles (% of ages 12-23 mos.)	..	..	..
Primary completion rate, total (% of relevant age group)	..	..	..
Gross secondary enrollment, total (% of relevant age group)	..	..	..
Ratio of girls to boys in primary & secondary school (%)	..	..	..
HIV prevalence rate (% population of ages 15-49)	..	..	..
Environment			
Forests (sq. km)	236	219	201
Deforestation (avg. annual %, 1990-2000 and 2000-2010)		0.7	0.8
Freshwater use (% of internal resources)	..	..	..
Access to improved water source (% total pop.)	..	..	..
Access to improved sanitation facilities (% total pop.)	..	..	..
Energy use per capita (kilograms of oil equivalent)	..	..	..
Carbon dioxide emissions per capita (metric tons)	..	..	..
Electricity use per capita (kilowatt-hours)	..	..	..
Economy			
GDP ($ millions)	1,565	..	..
GDP growth (annual %)	7.1	..	..
GDP implicit price deflator (annual % growth)	4.1	..	..
Value added in agriculture (% of GDP)	..	..	..
Value added in industry (% of GDP)	..	..	..
Value added in services (% of GDP)	..	..	..
Exports of goods and services (% of GDP)	..	..	..
Imports of goods and services (% of GDP)	..	..	..
Gross capital formation (% of GDP)	..	..	..
Central government revenue (% of GDP)	..	..	..
Central government cash surplus/deficit (% of GDP)	..	..	..
States and markets			
Starting a business (days)	..	..	..
Stock market capitalization (% of GDP)	..	..	..
Military expenditures (% of GDP)	..	..	..
Mobile cellular subscriptions (per 100 people)	0.0	32.3	..
Individuals using the Internet (% of population)	0.0	13.8	27.4
Paved roads (% of total)	..	..	..
High-technology exports (% of manufactured exports)	..	..	..
Global links			
Merchandise trade (% of GDP)	..	..	..
Net barter terms of trade index (2000 = 100)	..	..	..
Total external debt stocks ($ millions)	..	..	..
Total debt service (% of exports)	..	..	..
Net migration (thousands)	-11.5	-5.1	-3.6
Remittances received ($ millions)	..	..	..
Foreign direct investment, net inflows ($ millions)	..	..	..
Net official development assistance received ($ millions)	..	..	..

West Bank and Gaza

Middle East & North Africa		Lower middle income	
Population (millions)	3.9	Population growth (%)	3.0
Surface area (1,000 sq. km)	6.0	Population living below $1.25 a day (%)	<2
GNI, Atlas ($ billions)	..	GNI per capita, Atlas ($)	..
GNI, PPP ($ billions)	..	GNI per capita, PPP ($)	..

	1990	2000	2011
People			
Share of poorest 20% in nat'l consumption/income (%)	..	..	7.4
Life expectancy at birth (years)	68	71	73
Total fertility rate (births per woman)	6.5	5.4	4.4
Adolescent fertility rate (births per 1,000 women 15–19)	..	81	49
Contraceptive prevalence (% of married women 15–49)	..	51	50
Births attended by skilled health staff (% of total)	..	97	99
Under-five mortality rate (per 1,000 live births)	43	30	22
Child malnutrition, underweight (% of under age 5)	..	..	2.2
Child immunization, measles (% of ages 12–23 mos.)	..	..	..
Primary completion rate, total (% of relevant age group)	..	98	91
Gross secondary enrollment, total (% of relevant age group)	..	81	84
Ratio of girls to boys in primary & secondary school (%)	..	102	106
HIV prevalence rate (% population of ages 15–49)	..	..	..
Environment			
Forests (sq. km)	91	91	92
Deforestation (avg. annual %, 1990–2000 and 2000–2010)		0.0	-0.1
Freshwater use (% of internal resources)	..	34.4	51.5
Access to improved water source (% total pop.)	97	92	85
Access to improved sanitation facilities (% total pop.)	87	89	92
Energy use per capita (kilograms of oil equivalent)	..	..	..
Carbon dioxide emissions per capita (metric tons)	..	0.3	0.6
Electricity use per capita (kilowatt-hours)	..	..	..
Economy			
GDP ($ billions)	..	4.1	..
GDP growth (annual %)	..	-5.6	..
GDP implicit price deflator (annual % growth)	..	2.9	..
Value added in agriculture (% of GDP)	..	..	..
Value added in industry (% of GDP)	..	..	..
Value added in services (% of GDP)	..	..	..
Exports of goods and services (% of GDP)	..	16	..
Imports of goods and services (% of GDP)	..	71	..
Gross capital formation (% of GDP)	..	33	..
Central government revenue (% of GDP)	..	..	..
Central government cash surplus/deficit (% of GDP)	..	..	..
States and markets			
Starting a business (days)	..	106	48
Stock market capitalization (% of GDP)	..	18.6	..
Military expenditures (% of GDP)	..	..	..
Mobile cellular subscriptions (per 100 people)	0.0	0.2	45.8
Individuals using the Internet (% of population)	0.0	1.1	41.1
Paved roads (% of total)	..	100.0	100.0
High-technology exports (% of manufactured exports)	..	..	..
Global links			
Merchandise trade (% of GDP)	..	..	..
Net barter terms of trade index (2000 = 100)	..	..	..
Total external debt stocks ($ millions)	..	..	..
Total debt service (% of exports)	..	..	..
Net migration (thousands)	-39.4	70.0	-90.0
Remittances received ($ billions)	..	1.0	1.5
Foreign direct investment, net inflows ($ millions)	..	62	154
Net official development assistance received ($ millions)	179	685	2,444

Yemen, Rep.

Middle East & North Africa		Lower middle income	
Population (millions)	24.8	Population growth (%)	3.1
Surface area (1,000 sq. km)	528	Population living below $1.25 a day (%)	17.5
GNI, Atlas ($ billions)	26.4	GNI per capita, Atlas ($)	1,070
GNI, PPP ($ billions)	53.7	GNI per capita, PPP ($)	2,170

	1990	2000	2011
People			
Share of poorest 20% in nat'l consumption/income (%)	..	7.4	..
Life expectancy at birth (years)	56	60	65
Total fertility rate (births per woman)	8.7	6.5	5.1
Adolescent fertility rate (births per 1,000 women 15-19)	..	98	69
Contraceptive prevalence (% of married women 15-49)	10	23	28
Births attended by skilled health staff (% of total)	16	27	36
Under-five mortality rate (per 1,000 live births)	126	99	77
Child malnutrition, underweight (% of under age 5)	29.6	43.1	..
Child immunization, measles (% of ages 12-23 mos.)	69	71	71
Primary completion rate, total (% of relevant age group)	..	58	63
Gross secondary enrollment, total (% of relevant age group)	..	45	46
Ratio of girls to boys in primary & secondary school (%)	..	55	75
HIV prevalence rate (% population of ages 15-49)	0.1	0.1	0.2
Environment			
Forests (1,000 sq. km)	5.5	5.5	5.5
Deforestation (avg. annual %, 1990-2000 and 2000-2010)		0.0	0.0
Freshwater use (% of internal resources)	139.6	161.9	169.8
Access to improved water source (% total pop.)	67	60	55
Access to improved sanitation facilities (% total pop.)	24	39	53
Energy use per capita (kilograms of oil equivalent)	210	267	298
Carbon dioxide emissions per capita (metric tons)	0.8	0.8	1.0
Electricity use per capita (kilowatt-hours)	123	139	249
Economy			
GDP ($ billions)	5.6	9.6	33.8
GDP growth (annual %)	6.3	6.2	-10.5
GDP implicit price deflator (annual % growth)	12.0	23.3	18.3
Value added in agriculture (% of GDP)	24	14	8
Value added in industry (% of GDP)	34	46	29
Value added in services (% of GDP)	41	40	63
Exports of goods and services (% of GDP)	12	41	30
Imports of goods and services (% of GDP)	17	34	35
Gross capital formation (% of GDP)	12	19	12
Central government revenue (% of GDP)	16.2	23.4	..
Central government cash surplus/deficit (% of GDP)	-6.7	-2.3	..
States and markets			
Starting a business (days)	..	72	40
Stock market capitalization (% of GDP)	..	..	..
Military expenditures (% of GDP)	6.6	4.9	4.4
Mobile cellular subscriptions (per 100 people)	0.0	0.2	47.0
Individuals using the Internet (% of population)	0.0	0.1	14.9
Paved roads (% of total)	9.1	..	..
High-technology exports (% of manufactured exports)	..	0	0
Global links			
Merchandise trade (% of GDP)	40	66	60
Net barter terms of trade index (2000 = 100)	..	100	157
Total external debt stocks ($ billions)	6.4	5.2	6.4
Total debt service (% of exports)	11.1	5.9	2.8
Net migration (thousands)	-50	-100	-135
Remittances received ($ billions)	1.5	1.3	1.4
Foreign direct investment, net inflows ($ millions)	-131	6	-713
Net official development assistance received ($ millions)	450	311	476

Zambia

Sub-Saharan Africa **Lower middle income**

Population (millions)	13.5	Population growth (%)	4.2
Surface area (1,000 sq. km)	753	Population living below $1.25 a day (%)	68.5
GNI, Atlas ($ billions)	15.7	GNI per capita, Atlas ($)	1,160
GNI, PPP ($ billions)	20.1	GNI per capita, PPP ($)	1,490

	1990	2000	2011
People			
Share of poorest 20% in nat'l consumption/income (%)	3.0	6.2	3.6
Life expectancy at birth (years)	47	42	49
Total fertility rate (births per woman)	6.5	6.1	6.3
Adolescent fertility rate (births per 1,000 women 15–19)	..	153	140
Contraceptive prevalence (% of married women 15–49)	15	22	41
Births attended by skilled health staff (% of total)	51	47	47
Under-five mortality rate (per 1,000 live births)	193	154	83
Child malnutrition, underweight (% of under age 5)	21.2	19.6	14.9
Child immunization, measles (% of ages 12–23 mos.)	90	85	83
Primary completion rate, total (% of relevant age group)	..	63	103
Gross secondary enrollment, total (% of relevant age group)	21	..	..
Ratio of girls to boys in primary & secondary school (%)	87	..	..
HIV prevalence rate (% population of ages 15–49)	13.8	14.4	12.5
Environment			
Forests (1,000 sq. km)	528	511	493
Deforestation (avg. annual %, 1990–2000 and 2000–2010)		0.3	0.3
Freshwater use (% of internal resources)	2.2	2.2	2.2
Access to improved water source (% total pop.)	49	54	61
Access to improved sanitation facilities (% total pop.)	46	47	48
Energy use per capita (kilograms of oil equivalent)	687	612	628
Carbon dioxide emissions per capita (metric tons)	0.3	0.2	0.2
Electricity use per capita (kilowatt-hours)	779	610	623
Economy			
GDP ($ billions)	3.3	3.3	19.2
GDP growth (annual %)	-0.5	3.5	6.5
GDP implicit price deflator (annual % growth)	106.4	30.8	12.9
Value added in agriculture (% of GDP)	21	22	20
Value added in industry (% of GDP)	51	25	37
Value added in services (% of GDP)	28	53	43
Exports of goods and services (% of GDP)	36	26	46
Imports of goods and services (% of GDP)	37	40	37
Gross capital formation (% of GDP)	17	17	25
Central government revenue (% of GDP)	20.4	19.6	17.4
Central government cash surplus/deficit (% of GDP)	..	1.8	-1.5
States and markets			
Starting a business (days)	..	35	17
Stock market capitalization (% of GDP)	..	7.2	20.9
Military expenditures (% of GDP)	3.7	1.8	1.6
Mobile cellular subscriptions (per 100 people)	0.0	1.0	60.6
Individuals using the Internet (% of population)	0.0	0.2	11.5
Paved roads (% of total)	16.6	22.0	..
High-technology exports (% of manufactured exports)	2	0	25
Global links			
Merchandise trade (% of GDP)	77	55	84
Net barter terms of trade index (2000 = 100)	207	100	193
Total external debt stocks ($ billions)	6.9	5.8	4.4
Total debt service (% of exports)	14.7	21.2	2.1
Net migration (thousands)	28.6	83.5	-85.0
Remittances received ($ millions)	..	36.3	46.3
Foreign direct investment, net inflows ($ millions)	203	122	1,982
Net official development assistance received ($ millions)	475	795	1,073

Zimbabwe

Sub-Saharan Africa   **Low income**

Population (millions)	12.8	Population growth (%)	1.4
Surface area (1,000 sq. km)	391	Population living below $1.25 a day (%)	..
GNI, Atlas ($ billions)	8.4	GNI per capita, Atlas ($)	660
GNI, PPP ($ billions)	..	GNI per capita, PPP ($)	..

	1990	2000	2011
People			
Share of poorest 20% in nat'l consumption/income (%)	..	..	..
Life expectancy at birth (years)	61	45	51
Total fertility rate (births per woman)	5.2	3.9	3.2
Adolescent fertility rate (births per 1,000 women 15-19)	..	88	56
Contraceptive prevalence (% of married women 15-49)	43	54	59
Births attended by skilled health staff (% of total)	70	73	66
Under-five mortality rate (per 1,000 live births)	79	106	67
Child malnutrition, underweight (% of under age 5)	8.0	11.5	10.1
Child immunization, measles (% of ages 12-23 mos.)	87	75	92
Primary completion rate, total (% of relevant age group)	..	..	..
Gross secondary enrollment, total (% of relevant age group)	47	..	..
Ratio of girls to boys in primary & secondary school (%)	97	..	..
HIV prevalence rate (% population of ages 15-49)	13.6	26.2	14.9
Environment			
Forests (1,000 sq. km)	222	189	153
Deforestation (avg. annual %, 1990-2000 and 2000-2010)		1.6	1.9
Freshwater use (% of internal resources)	..	34.3	34.3
Access to improved water source (% total pop.)	79	80	80
Access to improved sanitation facilities (% total pop.)	41	40	40
Energy use per capita (kilograms of oil equivalent)	888	790	764
Carbon dioxide emissions per capita (metric tons)	1.5	1.1	0.7
Electricity use per capita (kilowatt-hours)	862	853	1,022
Economy			
GDP ($ billions)	8.8	6.7	9.7
GDP growth (annual %)	7.0	-3.1	9.4
GDP implicit price deflator (annual % growth)	-0.9	0.6	18.8
Value added in agriculture (% of GDP)	16	18	16
Value added in industry (% of GDP)	33	24	37
Value added in services (% of GDP)	50	57	47
Exports of goods and services (% of GDP)	23	38	49
Imports of goods and services (% of GDP)	23	36	88
Gross capital formation (% of GDP)	17	14	23
Central government revenue (% of GDP)	24.1	..	..
Central government cash surplus/deficit (% of GDP)	-2.6	..	..
States and markets			
Starting a business (days)	..	97	90
Stock market capitalization (% of GDP)	27.3	36.4	112.9
Military expenditures (% of GDP)	4.6	5.2	1.6
Mobile cellular subscriptions (per 100 people)	0.0	2.1	72.1
Individuals using the Internet (% of population)	0.0	0.4	15.7
Paved roads (% of total)	14.0	19.0	..
High-technology exports (% of manufactured exports)	1	2	1
Global links			
Merchandise trade (% of GDP)	41	57	82
Net barter terms of trade index (2000 = 100)	98	100	110
Total external debt stocks ($ billions)	3.3	3.8	6.3
Total debt service (% of exports)	23.1	..	..
Net migration (thousands)	121	-200	-900
Remittances received ($ millions)	0.8	..	..
Foreign direct investment, net inflows ($ millions)	-12	23	387
Net official development assistance received ($ millions)	334	176	718

Notes

a. Includes Taiwan, China.

b. Includes Hong Kong SAR, China.

c. Estimates differ from statistics of the government of China, which has published the following estimates for military expenditure: 1.2 percent of GDP in 2000 and 1.3 percent in 2011 (see National Bureau of Statistics of China, www.stats.gov.cn).

d. Refers to area free from ice.

e. Excludes Montenegro.

f. Excludes South Sudan.

g. Excludes South Sudan after July 9, 2011.

Glossary

Access to improved sanitation is the percentage of population with adequate access to excreta disposal facilities (private or shared, but not public) that can effectively prevent human, animal, and insect contact with excreta. Improved facilities range from simple but protected pit latrines to flush toilets with a sewerage connection. To be effective, facilities must be correctly constructed and properly maintained. (World Health Organization and United Nations Children's Fund)

Access to improved water source is the percentage of the population with reasonable access to an adequate amount of water from an improved source, such as piped water into a dwelling, plot, or yard; public tap or standpipe; tube-well or borehole; protected dug well or spring; or rainwater collection. Unimproved sources include an unprotected dug well or spring, cart with small tank or drum, bottled water, and tanker trucks. Reasonable access to an adequate amount means the availability of at least 20 liters a person a day from a source within 1 kilometer of the dwelling. (World Health Organization and United Nations Children's Fund)

Adolescent fertility is the number of births per 1,000 women ages 15–19. (United Nations Population Division)

Births attended by skilled health staff are the percentage of deliveries attended by personnel trained to give the necessary supervision, care, and advice to women during pregnancy, labor, and the postpartum period; to conduct deliveries on their own; and to care for newborns. (United Nations Children's Fund, ChildInfo, and ICF International)

Carbon dioxide emissions per capita are emissions stemming from the burning of fossil fuels and the manufacture of cement divided by midyear population. They include carbon dioxide produced during consumption of solid, liquid, and gas fuels and gas flaring. (Carbon Dioxide Information Analysis Center)

Central government cash surplus/deficit is revenue (including grants) minus expense, minus net acquisition of nonfinancial assets. Before 2005 nonfinancial assets were included under revenue and expenditure in gross terms. The concept of cash surplus or deficit is close to the earlier overall budget balance (still missing is lending minus repayments, which is brought into the balance sheet as a financing item under net acquisition of financial assets). (International Monetary Fund)

Central government revenue is cash receipts from taxes, social contributions, and other revenues such as fines, fees, rent, and income from property or sales. Grants are also considered revenue but are excluded here. (International Monetary Fund)

Child immunization, measles, is the percentage of children ages 12–23 months at the time of the survey who received a dose of measles vaccine by age 12 months or at any time before the interview date. A child is considered

Glossary

adequately immunized against measles after receiving one dose of the vaccine. (World Health Organization and United Nations Children's Fund)

Child malnutrition, underweight, is the percentage of children under age five whose weight for age is more than two standard deviations below median for the international reference population ages 0–59 months. The data conform to the new Child Growth Standards released by the World Health Organization in 2006. (World Health Organization)

Contraceptive prevalence is the percentage of women married or in-union ages 15–49 who are practicing, or whose sexual partners are practicing, any form of contraception. (United Nations Children's Fund and ICF International)

Deforestation is the permanent conversion of natural forest areas to other uses, including shifting cultivation, permanent agriculture, ranching, settlements, and infrastructure development. Deforested areas do not include areas logged but intended for regeneration or areas degraded by fuelwood gathering, acid precipitation, or forest fires. Negative numbers indicate an increase in forest area. (Food and Agriculture Organization)

Electricity use per capita is the production of power plants and combined heat and power plants less transmission, distribution, and transformation losses and own use by heat and power plants plus imports less exports divided by midyear population. (International Energy Agency)

Energy use per capita is the use of primary energy before transformation to other end-use fuels, which is equal to indigenous production plus imports and stock changes, minus exports and fuels supplied to ships and aircraft engaged in international transportation, divided by midyear population. (International Energy Agency)

Exports of goods and services are the value of all goods and other market services provided to the rest of the world, including the value of merchandise, freight, insurance, transport, travel, royalties, license fees, and other services. Compensation of employees, investment income (formerly called factor services), and transfer payments are excluded. (World Bank, Organisation for Economic Co-operation and Development, and United Nations)

Foreign direct investment, net inflows, are investments to acquire a lasting management interest in an enterprise operating in an economy other than that of the investor. They are the sum of inflows of equity capital, reinvestment of earnings, other long-term capital, and short-term capital as shown in the balance of payments. Net inflows refer to new investments made during the reporting period netted against disinvesments. (World Bank and International Monetary Fund)

Forests are land under natural or planted stands of trees, whether productive or not. (Food and Agriculture Organization)

Freshwater use is total freshwater withdrawals for domestic, industrial, and agricultural use, not counting evaporation losses from storage basins. Internal resources refer to internal renewable resources only (flows of rivers and groundwater from rainfall in the country). Withdrawals can exceed 100 percent of internal renewable resources because river flows from other countries are not included, because extraction from nonrenewable aquifers or desalination plants is considerable, or because there is significant water reuse. (Food and Agriculture Organization and World Resources Institute)

GDP is gross domestic product at purchaser prices. It is the sum of gross value added by all resident producers in the economy plus any product taxes and minus any subsidies not included in the value of the products. It is calculated without deductions for depreciation of fabricated assets or for depletion and degradation of natural resources. (World Bank, Organisation for Economic Co-operation and Development, and United Nations)

GDP growth is the one-year rate of growth in real gross domestic product. (World Bank and Organisation for Economic Co-operation and Development)

GDP implicit price deflator is the one-year rate of price change in the economy as a whole. (World Bank, Organisation for Economic Co-operation and Development, and United Nations)

GNI is gross national income. It is calculated as gross domestic product (GDP) plus net receipts of primary income (employee compensation and investment income) from abroad. GDP is the sum of value added by all resident producers plus any product taxes (less subsidies) not included in the valuation of output. (World Bank)

GNI per capita is gross national income (GNI) converted to U.S. dollars using the World Bank Atlas method divided by midyear population. GNI is the sum of value added by all resident producers plus any product taxes (less subsidies) not included in the valuation of output plus net receipts of primary income (compensation of employees and property income) from abroad. GNI, calculated in national currency, is usually converted to U.S. dollars at official exchange rates for comparisons across economies. The World Bank Atlas method is used to smooth fluctuations in prices and exchange rates. It averages the exchange rate for a given year and the two preceding years, adjusted for differences in rates of inflation between the country and the Euro area, Japan, the United Kingdom, and the United States. (World Bank)

GNI, PPP, is gross national income (GNI) converted to international dollars using purchasing power parities (PPP). An international dollar has the same purchasing power over GNI that a U.S. dollar has in the United States. (World Bank)

GNI per capita, PPP, is gross national income (GNI) converted to international dollars using purchasing power parities (PPP), divided by midyear population.

Glossary

An international dollar has the same purchasing power over GNI that a U.S. dollar has in the United States. (World Bank)

Gross capital formation is outlays on additions to the fixed assets of the economy plus net changes in the level of inventories. Fixed assets include land improvements (fences, ditches, drains, and so on); plant, machinery, and equipment purchase; and the construction of roads, railways, and the like, including schools, offices, hospitals, private residential dwellings, and commercial and industrial buildings. Inventories are stocks of goods held by firms to meet temporary or unexpected fluctuations in production or sales and work in progress. According to the 1993 System of National Accounts, net acquisitions of valuables are also considered capital formation. (World Bank, Organisation for Economic Co-operation and Development, and United Nations)

Gross secondary enrollment, total, is the ratio of total enrollment in secondary education, regardless of age, to the population of the age group that officially corresponds to secondary education. Secondary education completes the provision of basic education that begins at the primary level and aims at laying the foundations for lifelong learning and human development by offering more subject- or skill-oriented instruction using more specialized teachers. (United Nations Educational, Scientific and Cultural Organization Institute for Statistics)

High-technology exports are products with high research and development intensity, as in aerospace, computers, pharmaceuticals, scientific instruments and electrical machinery. (United Nations Statistics Division's Commodity Trade database)

HIV prevalence rate is the percentage of people ages 15–49 who are infected with HIV. (Joint United Nations Programme on HIV/AIDS and World Health Organization)

Imports of goods and services are the value of all goods and other market services received from the rest of the world, including the value of merchandise, freight, insurance, transport, travel, royalties, license fees and other services. Labor and property income (formerly called factor services) and transfer payments are excluded. (World Bank, Organisation for Economic Co-operation and Development, and United Nations)

Individuals using the Internet refers to the percentage of individuals who have used the Internet (from any location) in the last 12 months. Internet can be used via a computer, mobile phone, personal digital assistant, games machine, digital TV, etc. (International Telecommunication Union)

Life expectancy at birth is the number of years a newborn infant would live if prevailing patterns of mortality at the time of birth were to stay the same throughout life. (Eurostat, United Nations Population Division, and World Bank)

Glossary

Merchandise trade is the sum of merchandise exports and imports measured in current U.S. dollars as a percentage of GDP. (World Trade Organization and World Bank)

Military expenditures data from SIPRI are derived from the NATO definition, which includes all current and capital expenditures on the armed forces, including peacekeeping forces; defense ministries and other government agencies engaged in defense projects; paramilitary forces, if these are judged to be trained and equipped for military operations; and military space activities. Such expenditures include military and civil personnel, including retirement pensions of military personnel and social services for personnel; operation and maintenance; procurement; military research and development; and military aid (in the military expenditures of the donor country). Excluded are civil defense and current expenditures for previous military activities, such as for veterans' benefits, demobilization, conversion, and destruction of weapons. This definition cannot be applied for all countries, however, since that would require much more detailed information than is available about what is included in military budgets and off-budget military expenditure items. (For example, military budgets might or might not cover civil defense, reserves and auxiliary forces, police and paramilitary forces, dual-purpose forces such as military and civilian police, military grants in kind, pensions for military personnel, and social security contributions paid by one part of government to another.) (Stockholm International Peace Research Institute)

Mobile cellular subscriptions are subscriptions to a public mobile telephone service using cellular technology, which provide access to the public switched telephone network. Post-paid and prepaid subscriptions are included. (International Telecommunication Union)

Net barter terms of trade index is the ratio of the export unit value index to the corresponding import unit value index measured relative to the base year 2000. (United Nations Conference on Trade and Development and International Monetary Fund)

Net migration is the total number of immigrants less the total number of emigrants, including both citizens and noncitizens, during the period. Data are five-year estimates for 1985–90, 1995–2000, and 2005–10. (United Nations Population Division)

Net official development assistance received is official development assistance flows (net of repayment of principal) as defined by the Development Assistance Committee (DAC) that are made to countries and territories on the DAC list of aid recipients. (Organisation for Economic Co-operation and Development)

Paved roads are roads surfaced with crushed stone (macadam) and hydrocarbon binder or bituminized agents, with concrete, or with cobblestones, as a percentage of all the country's roads, measured in length. (International Road Federation)

Glossary

Population is the midyear estimate of all residents regardless of legal status citizenship, except for refugees not permanently settled in the country of asylum who are generally considered part of the population of their country of origin. (Eurostat, United Nations Population Division, and World Bank)

Population below $1.25 a day is the percentage of the population living on less than $1.25 a day at 2005 international prices. Data are the most recent estimate since 2000. Figures in italics are for years other than 2011. (World Bank)

Population growth is the exponential growth rate from the previous midyear population. (World Bank)

Primary completion rate, total, is the percentage of students completing the last year of primary school. It is calculated by dividing the total number of students in the last grade of primary school minus the number of repeaters in that grade by the total number of children of official completing age. Because of the change from the International Standard Classification of Education 1976 (ISCED76) to ISCED97, data for years before 1999 are not fully comparable with data for 1999 onward. (United Nations Educational, Scientific and Cultural Organization Institute for Statistics)

Ratio of girls to boys in primary and secondary school is the ratio of the female to male gross enrollment rate in primary and secondary school. (United Nations Educational, Scientific and Cultural Organization Institute for Statistics)

Remittances received refers to personal transfers and compensation of employees. They comprise current transfers in cash or kind received by resident households from nonresident households and wages and salaries earned by nonresident workers or resident workers employed by nonresident entities. (International Monetary Fund and World Bank)

Share of poorest 20% in national consumption or income is the share of total national income or consumption that accrues to the poorest quintile. (World Bank)

Starting a business is the number of calendar days needed to complete the procedures to legally operate a business. If a procedure can be expedited at additional cost, the fastest procedure, independent of cost, is chosen. Data listed for 2011 are for June 2012. (World Bank)

Stock market capitalization is the share price times the number of shares outstanding. (Standard and Poor's)

Surface area is a country's total area, including areas under inland bodies of water and some coastal waterways. (Food and Agriculture Organization)

Total debt service is the sum of principal repayments and interest actually paid on long-term debt (public and publicly guaranteed and private nonguaranteed);

interest paid on short-term debt; and repayments (repurchases and charges) to the International Monetary Fund, expressed as a percentage of exports of goods and services and primary income. Exports of goods and services and primary income are the total value of exports of goods and services, receipts of compensation of nonresident workers, and investment income from abroad. (World Bank and International Monetary Fund)

Total external debt stocks are debt owed to nonresident creditors and repayable in foreign currencies, goods, or services by public and private entities in the country. They are the sum of long-term external debt, short-term debt, and use of International Monetary Fund credit. Debt repayable in domestic currency is excluded. (World Bank)

Total fertility is the number of children that would be born to a woman if she were to live to the end of her childbearing years and bear children in accordance with current age-specific fertility rates. (Eurostat, United Nations Population Division, and World Bank)

Under-five mortality rate is the probability that a newborn baby will die before age five if subject to current age-specific mortality rates. (United Nations Children's Fund, World Health Organization, World Bank, and United Nations Population Division)

Value added in agriculture is the net output of agriculture (International Standard Industrial Classification divisions 1–5 including forestry and fishing) after totaling outputs and subtracting intermediate outputs. (World Bank, Organisation for Economic Co-operation and Development, and United Nations)

Value added in industry is the net output of industry (International Standard Industrial Classification divisions 10–45, which includes mining, manufacturing, construction, electricity, water, and gas) after totaling outputs and subtracting intermediate inputs. (World Bank, Organisation for Economic Co-operation and Development, and United Nations)

Value added in services is the net output of services (International Standard Industrial Classification divisions 50–99) after totaling outputs and subtracting intermediate inputs. This sector is derived as a residual and may not properly reflect the sum of services outputs, including banking and financial services. (World Bank, Organisation for Economic Co-operation and Development, and United Nations)